The
Other
Mexico

The Other Mexico

The North American Triangle Completed

John Warnock

BLACK ROSE BOOKS

Montréal/New York
London

Black Rose Books No.Y301
Hardcover ISBN: 1-551640-29-5
Paperback ISBN: 1-551640-28-7
Library of Congress No. 95-79352

Canadian Cataloguing in Publication Data

Warnock, John W., 1933-
The other Mexico: the North American triangle completed

ISBN: 1-551640-29-5 (bound). —
ISBN 1-551640-28-7 (pbk.)

1. Mexico—Economic conditions—1982- 2. Mexico—Politics and
government—1970-1988. 3. Mexico—Politics and
government—1988- . I. Title.

HC135.W37 1995   972.08'34   C95-900718-0

Cover photo by Elaine Brière

Mailing Address

BLACK ROSE BOOKS
C.P. 1258
Succ. Place du Parc
Montréal, Québec
H2W 2R3 Canada

BLACK ROSE BOOKS
340 Nagel Drive
Cheektowaga, New York
14225 USA

A publication of the Institute of Policy Alternatives of Montréal (IPAM)

Printed in Canada

CONTENTS

ACKNOWLEDGMENTS

The research and writing of this book has been greatly aided by many friends and colleagues who have encouraged me through conversations and discussions over the past few years. Many have provided me with materials and contacts. In particular, I would like to thank those associated with Common Frontiers, the Canadian Centre for Policy Alternatives, and the Action Canada Network. I have received a great deal of information about Mexico from two U.S. organizations: the Institute for Agriculture and Trade Policy in Minneapolis and Mobilization on Development, Trade, Labor and the Environment in Washington. I am particularly indebted to Equipo Pueblo, The Other Mexico, Alianza Civica and Red Mexicana de Acción Frente al Libre Commerció in Mexico City. I would like to specially thank Ángel Sánchez for introducing me to the real Mexico.

The book would not have been possible without the support I received from the staff at the University of Regina Library, and in particular the Interlibrary Loan section. I would also like to thank the staff at the other libraries that I used: the University of British Columbia, the University of Washington, and the University of California at San Diego. The Saskatchewan Council for International Co-operation kindly allowed me to use their computer and the Internet to keep regular contact with Mexico. I also received ongoing support and help in kind from my colleagues at *Briarpatch Magazine*. My research trips to Mexico would not have been possible without the nonfiction award I received from the Canada Council.

Special thanks must go to the friends who took the time to carefully read my manuscript and make comments: Pedro Luis Sánchez, Luisa Mendoza and Barry Barlow. Kathy Prendergast provided me with editorial help. Of course, I am completely responsible for the text as it now appears.

Finally, I would like to thank the people at Black Rose Books: Dimitri Roussopoulos, Linda Barton, Natalie Klym, and Frances Slingerman.

John W. Warnock
Regina, Saskatchewan
May 31, 1995

THE NEOLIBERAL REVOLUTION

Most people know that the economy has not really recovered since the economic recession of the early 1980s, and that their job situation is much less secure. Families now need two incomes in order to maintain a middle-class lifestyle. They worry because the social programs they have counted on are being cut.

Everywhere, employers insist that wages and benefits must be cut in order to meet international competition. In spite of the fact that gross domestic product continues to increase, governments say they no longer have the ability to create jobs nor provide universal social programs. Following Margaret Thatcher, business leaders and politicians insist that "there is no alternative" to what is commonly called "globalization."

The Western industrialized world experienced a long period of steady economic growth from 1940 to the early 1970s. From the onset of the world economic recession of 1974, there has been a gradual decline in the rate of economic growth. For example, the average rate of growth of all members of the Organization for Economic Co-operation and Development (OECD) between 1966 and 1973 was 4.5 percent. For the period between 1986 and 1993, it was only 2.4 percent.

At the same time, there was a steady increase in the rate of unemployment. For the OECD as a whole, the average rate of unemployment between 1972 and 1981 was 4.8 percent. Between 1986 and 1993, it averaged 7.3 percent. Because the industrialized countries account for about 80 percent of the world's production, trade and investment, the economic decline impacted adversely on many Third World countries.[1]

The industrialized countries have reacted in different ways to the onset of the economic crisis. The Western European countries have moved towards a common market with common tariffs. They are trying to protect their high standard of living and comprehensive social security system.

The state socialist regimes in the former Soviet Union and eastern Europe have collapsed, replaced by authoritarian regimes reintroducing capitalism. Since the changes began in 1989, the economies of these countries have stagnated, unemployment and underemployment has skyrocketed, and the average standard of living has dropped dramatically. Western Europe has moved to dominate this newly created Third World area.

Africa has been hard-hit by the economic crisis in the industrialized West. Per capita income has continued to fall in most countries. The debt problem has impoverished governments. And with the end of the cold war, the industrialized countries have basically lost interest in the continent.

Japan has continued to dominate east Asia, but in the 1990s, the Asian power began to experience its first real economic crisis since the end of World War II. In general, the Asian countries which followed a policy of strong state involvement in economic development have done better during this period: Japan, South Korea, Taiwan, China and India.

There have been three world economic recessions since the end of world war II, bottoming in 1974, 1981 and 1992. In each case the following recovery has shown less dynamic growth in general and a higher level of permanent unemployment.

The impact on Latin America has been dramatic. Between 1972 and 1981 the real growth in gross domestic product per capita rose annually by 2.8 percent. But between 1982 and 1991, it fell on average 0.6 percent per year. The end result was that in 1991, the per capita gross domestic product for Latin America was less than in 1981.[2]

A central concern in Latin America is the failure of the economies to create jobs. In 1993, the World Employment Program (PREALC) of the International Labour Organization (ILO) reported that the only job sector growing in Latin America was the informal economy. The share of employment provided by private companies declined from 44 percent in 1980 to only 31 percent by 1992. They noted that since 1980 eight out of every ten new jobs were in the informal sector.[3]

The United Nations Development Program points out that despite the relative decline in growth in the industrialized countries, the gap between the rich and the poor continues to widen. In 1960, the ratio between the richest and poorest 20 percent of the world's population was 30 to 1. By 1980, it had increased to 45 to 1; by 1989, it had risen to 59 to 1.

Between 1960 and 1989, the countries with the richest 20 percent of the world's population increased their share of the world's total gross domestic production from 70.2 percent to 82.7 percent. The countries with the poorest 20 percent of the population saw their share drop from 2.3 percent to 1.4 percent.[4]

Economic stagnation has served to justify a move to free trade. Tariffs were significantly reduced during the Kennedy (1964-67) and Tokyo (1973-79) rounds of negotiations to modify the General Agreement on Tariffs and Trade (GATT). Tariffs were reduced an average of 35 percent during the Tokyo round. Further reductions were achieved during the Uruguay round, which concluded in December 1993. The GATT has now been re-placed by the World Trade Organization (WTO), which has considerably stronger power to enforce free trade.

Over this period, Japan and the East Asian small countries began ex-panding manufactured exports to North America and Europe. The indus-trialized countries reacted by using non-tariff barriers (NTBs) to try to protect their domestic market from cheap imports: anti-dumping duties, countervailing duties to offset perceived export subsidies, quotas on im-ports, voluntary export agreements, and state support for business develop-ment. The United States has been very vigorous in the use of NTBs, and a 1993 World Bank report concluded that about 25 percent of all imports were subjected to NTB restrictions, which actually brought U.S. tariffs up from the nominal 6 percent to a more realistic 23 percent.[5]

The general economic crisis formally began with the world recession of 1973. Corporate profits, which peaked in the mid-1960s, began to steadily de-cline. The largest corporations responded by going international — shifting production to those areas where costs were lowest while demanding the right to sell in any world market. They strongly supported the Uruguay Round of negotiations on the GATT, the Canada-U.S. Free Trade Agreement (CUSTA) and the North American Free Trade Agreement (NAFTA). They see the free market and free trade as answers to falling profit rates and stagnant national economic growth.[6]

Neoliberalism and Latin America

By the end of World War II most of the countries in Latin America had adopted the model of import substitution industrialization (ISI). The pol-icy of providing protection for domestic industry was designed to boost in-dustrial development and create jobs for the surplus labour which was in the rural areas. The policy was also seen as a response to the lack of foreign exchange. Luxury imports could be limited. Controlling trade would help overcome the fact that the international terms of trade ran against coun-tries that exported primary products and imported manufactured goods. Furthermore, it was known that all the advanced First World countries be-gan industrialization behind policies of high tariffs and controls on exports and imports.[7] However, the ISI policy ran out of steam around the same time as the first big increase in the price of oil in 1973 and the 1974 world recession.

By the 1970s, the ISI approach to development was widely criticized in Latin America. It did not create enough jobs. Unemployment and underemployment were steadily increasing. The majority of people in agriculture were neglected. The unequal distribution of income, wealth and status was worsening. The ISI strategy had created an aristocracy of labour, the minority who were in trade unions, but left most workers impoverished. It was too dependent on importing First World technology, which was not appropriate to countries with high levels of unemployment and underemployment. Government became indebted as they borrowed heavily from abroad. And they could not control inflation.

The ISI model could not produce a more equitable social and economic system given the class structure of Latin American countries. They were all dominated by a small group of the very rich. This capitalist class was quick to invest abroad; they were not dynamic entrepreneurs; they successfully avoided paying taxes; and they had the backing of the military and the U.S. government who saw even social democracy as a threat to U.S. interests in the area.

The economic crisis of the 1970s produced the wave of military dictatorships in Latin America. They introduced the "stabilization program" dictated by the international lenders and the International Monetary Fund (IMF). The primary policy goals were to reduce inflation and resolve the balance of payments problems.

But the stabilization efforts of the 1970s were not adequate to deal with hyperinflation and the growing debt crisis. The 1970s brought high international interest rates, and service payments on foreign debts could not be managed.

With the debt crisis of the 1980s, all countries in Latin America (except Cuba) adopted structural adjustment programs. They were imposed upon them by the IMF, the World Bank and the U.S. government. This policy package became known as the "Washington Consensus."

The core of the new policy was the same everywhere. Government fiscal spending was to be cut. Subsidies to the poor and farmers were the first to go. The tax system was "reformed," with cuts to corporate taxes and a reduction in the rate of income tax on those in the higher income brackets. Value added taxes were introduced and expanded.

In the finance area, interest rates were to be left to the market. Governments were encouraged to devalue their currencies and to allow the exchange rate to move towards the free market.

Trade liberation was pushed by the elimination of export and import licensing, quotas on imports, and the reduction of tariffs. Controls on foreign investment were lifted.

Privatization of state-owned enterprises was introduced. Governments were pushed to remove regulations which constrained the ability of corporations to increase their profits. And legislation was introduced to protect the property rights of foreign firms.

This was the formal policy package. But one of the real goals was to reduce the cost of labour. As in the industrialized countries, trade union rights and the ability to organize unions were subject to new attacks. By the mid-1980s, profit levels were recovering. For the majority of the population the Washington Consensus brought a drop in the standard of living. Real incomes fell everywhere throughout Latin America.

Many observers have concluded that these policies could only be implemented by military dictatorships or authoritarian regimes supported by the military and the police. The military dictatorships in Brazil, Chile, Argentina, and Uruguay began programs in the 1970s. Throughout the region, authoritarian regimes were notable for crushing trade unions and repressing the political left.

The end result for Latin America was the abandonment of the ISI approach to economic development and the adoption of the neoliberal model of export orientated industrialization (EOI).

Restricted Democracy

Our political leaders regularly remind us that the 1980s saw the triumph of democracy over dictatorship. Throughout Latin America, the military left office, turning the government over to the new regimes that were elected to office. As Lucrecia Lozano notes, in all these cases the dictators survived because of the strong support of the U.S. government. The U.S. "national-security doctrine" saw these unbelievably repressive regimes as bulwarks against the spread of communism. In the Western hemisphere, the enemy is still Cuba.[8]

In most of the cases in Latin America, the "redemocratization" took the form of pacts negotiated with the military regimes. The military voluntarily left office because they were unable to deal with the economic crisis. The pact allowed the military to keep substantial power, guaranteed the military its budget, and granted the officer class immunity from prosecution for the murders, crimes and human rights violations that characterized their regimes.

James Petras and Morris Morely argue that this change was a move towards only formal democracy: these new democracies are in reality hostages to the military. Furthermore, the newly elected governments all adopted neoliberal policies. When there is popular disapproval of such policies, they do not hesitate to use the military to maintain order.[9]

The new democratically-elected regimes are notable for their corruption. As Petras and Morley note, "Everywhere political theft of public property has reached monumental levels." Aside from outright corruption, privatization has allowed high government officials and their friends to appropriate state-owned enterprises at fire sale prices.

Lozano argues that in Latin America the popular concept of democracy is that of social democratization, the elimination of inequalities and mass participation in the governing process. This is clearly not happening under the neoliberal regimes elected in the 1980s. Petras and Morley agree. In all of the civilian governments there is "the almost total absence of populist policies and redistributive politics." Regardless of who puts these governments in office, the policies remain the same.

Carlos Vilas also emphasizes this point. While differing only in details, the governments that emerged from electoral processes are all implementing adjustment policies which follow a common model. These policies have a "proven ineffectiveness" in resolving the problems they try to confront. And they have had "a disastrous impact on the conditions of life of those with the lowest income and the fewest resources."[10]

Franz Hinkelammert argues that the new neoliberal economic regimes need the repressive state. The police state has replaced the social state. The previous populist states attempted to gain popular consensus for their policies. The neoliberal state is "clearly a classist civil society in which only the bourgeoisie has a voice and is taken into account."[11]

In many Latin American countries the state has taken over the private debts owned to foreign interests and is now attempting to pay them off through taxes on the poor. As Hinkelammert notes, the neoliberal state relies heavily on sales taxes, customs fees, departure fees and all types of state transactions. "Taxes are almost nonexistent for those in high income brackets." Tax evasion by those in the upper income brackets is the rule, not the exception. This reflects the weakness of the Latin American neoliberal state. Thus, he argues, "the state can only defend the existing order with the presence of the army."

The failure of the social democratic alternative is also notable. Throughout Latin America the parties of the Second International have embraced the neoliberal agenda. Carlos Andres Perez was elected president of Venezuela on a progressive nationalist platform and then proceeded to implement the IMF's austerity program. Michael Manley won the 1989 election in Jamaica while vigorously criticizing the neoliberal policies of Edward Seaga. Once in office, he embraced the same policies.

In Argentina Carlos Menem campaigned as a Peronist, supporting populist and nationalist policies. In office, he followed IMF neoliberal policies. The same can be said of the coalition government in Chile, headed by Patricio Alwyn of the Christian Democrats. The Socialist Party of Salvador Allende now supports the neoliberal agenda.

Other examples include the government of Jaime Paz Zamora in Bolivia, Rodrigo Borja in Ecuador and Vinicio Cerezo in Guatemala. All embraced neoliberal policies after being elected. Alberto Fujimora got elected as a populist opposed to neoliberal policies and once in office, imposed one of the most repressive IMF programs adopted anywhere.[12]

But as Vilas has stressed, none of these regimes have been able to guarantee the majority of the people in Latin America what they desperately want: stable access to food, employment, health, and education. In this hemisphere, the established order of capitalism, whether guided by a military dictatorship or an elected democracy, has been unable to create conditions for meeting such a basic need.[13]

Implementing Neoliberalism

Political economists often refer to the change from managed capitalism to free market capitalism as a "regime change." Wallace Clement argues that regimes are defined as "structures of power combining capital, labour, the state, and popular forces, bound together by hegemonic ideologies and practices." The regime is never stable as there is a constant struggle for power. The core struggle is over which social groups will define the system, either "sustaining the existing hegemony, or building an alternative one." The hegemony here is "the power to specify what is widely considered as normal, right, just and proper, thus setting the regime's standards of expectation."[14]

Why did Mexico change from ISI to neoliberalism? What were the major factors in propelling this change? Obviously, there was the influence of the international economic crisis and the pressure by the Washington institutions. But equally important was the push for the free trade option by Mexico's industries who had matured under the protection of ISI and had now become more internationally orientated.[15]

Corporate agriculture, emphasizing exports to the United States, also pushed for the change. The organization representing small and medium-sized business (CANACINTRA) had the most to lose. These enterprises developed under protectionism and would be most vulnerable to increased imports. Their opposition was muted by the government's commitment to general economic reforms and to the control of inflation. Popular support for the Institutional Revolutionary Party (PRI) went up after 1989, when President Carlos Salinas began to bring inflation under control. As has been demonstrated elsewhere in Latin America, the poor have been willing to give electoral support to right-wing governments who effectively control inflation.

One of the other key factors was the development of an alliance between the political elite and big business. The alliance was formalized by the wage and price control agreement of 1987.

Finally, there was the role of the technocratic elite. John Williamson of the Institute for International Economics notes that neoliberalism is often implemented by technocrats. In the Third World they are usually trained as economists in the industrialized countries. In Mexico most of the key people in the political elite during this period had advanced degrees earned in the elite universities in the United States. It was here that they obtained their ideological commitment to neoliberalism.

A technocrat, according to John Williamson, is an experienced applied economist who has "the skill of a successful politician, able to persuade others to adopt the policies that he or she has judged to be called for."[16]

Implementing a radical change in economic policy is not easy. Williamson notes that the technocratic team "must also command the instruments of concentrated executive authority." This is needed to "bypass vested interests."

Miguel Ángel Centeno agrees: "the new revolutions of the market appear to require the very same organizational qualities as the Leninist state." Because the changes provoke conflict and opposition, "only those with the appropriate amount of power will be able to accomplish the required tasks."[17]

In this respect, the Mexican one-party state has advantages over a pluralistic political system. The opposition has been fragmented and is ineffective. Still, Centeno argues, there were three crucial tasks at hand: maintaining political stability, generating political and economic support, and creating legitimacy for the new economic reforms.

This was made possible by developments within the Mexican state, Centeno notes. There was the centralization of power within the state apparatus in the financial planning area. There was a political elite with specialized training. And there was "the hegemony of a single, exclusive policy paradigm," the neoliberal model.

Political stability was maintained by the power of the one-party state. Dissent by labour, the peasants and the poor was controlled. The political left was effectively attacked. And public debate on alternative policies was simply foreclosed. Ideological control was maintained through control of the mass media. The new alliance with big business guaranteed financial support for the PRI.

But in the end, would the new neoliberal order be able to deliver the goods? It was not enough to guarantee high levels of profits for the large corporations, tax exemption for the rich, and the right of capitalists to invest in the United States or Switzerland. Would neoliberalism eventually benefit most of the population? How long would the general population be willing to accept declining real incomes and longer hours of work?

State force is not enough to guarantee social control. Mexico is no longer a militarist state. Hegemonic regimes must provide improved standards of living if they are to survive. President Salinas managed to skilfully manage the system right until the end. But compromises made to win the 1994 presidential election eventually led to the devaluation of the peso and the collapse of the economy. Today, the vast majority of Mexican feel betrayed.

In the past the PRI obtained its legitimacy by guaranteeing economic and social improvement to organized labour and the more politically active peasant sector. The Keynesian state was expanding social services and aid to the poor. But with the neoliberal changes, and the alliance with big business, the PRI lost its traditional legitimacy.

The collapse of the Soviet states and the move back to formal democracy in Latin America brought additional problems for the Mexican rulers. There was a new popular demand for democratic reform. But Carlos Salinas increased the centralization of power in the hands of the president. There was growing anger and cynicism over blatant electoral fraud, a call for debate on major issues, and a demand for the end of the "Stalinist press." There was anger over the abuse of human rights by the police and the military. And there was resentment over the extravagance of the wealthy elite who run the country.

The legitimacy of the regime came crashing down with the assassinations and the drug trafficking scandals of 1993 and 1994. This book is one account of the Mexican experiment.

Notes

1. Organization for Economic Co-operation and Development. *Monthly Economic Indicators*. Paris: OECD, December 1994.
2. United Nations. *World Economic Survey*. New York: United Nations, 1993.

3. "More Jobs, but How Good?" *Latin American Weekly Report*, October 28, 1993, p. 498.

4. United Nations Development Program. *Human Development Report, 1992*. New York: Oxford University Press, 1992.

5. World Bank. *World Development Report*. Washington: World Bank, 1993.

6. For a discussion of the general economic crisis, see Joyce Kolko, *Restructuring the World Economy*. New York: Pantheon Books, 1988; Bennett Harrison and Barry Bluestone, *The Great U-Turn*. New York: Basic Books, 1988; Richard Peet, ed. *International Capitalism and Industrial Restructuring*. Boston: Allen & Unwin, 1987; and John W. Warnock, *Free Trade and the New Right Agenda*. Vancouver: New Star Books, 1988.

7. For a discussion of import substitution industrialization and its problems, see Eliana Cardoso and Ann Helwege. *Latin America's Economy*. Cambridge: MIT Press, 1992.

8. Lucrecia Lozano, "Adjustment and Democracy in Latin America," *Social Justice*, Vol. 19, Winter 1992, pp. 48-58.

9. James Petras and Morris Morley, "Latin America: Poverty of Democracy and Democracy of Poverty," *Economic and Political Weekly*, Vol. 29, July 27, 1991, PE103-111.

10. Carlos M. Vilas, "Latin American Populism: A Structural Approach," *Science & Society*, Vol. 56, Winter 1992-93, pp. 389-420.

11. Franz J. Hinkelammert, "Our Project for the New Society in Latin America," *Social Justice*, Vol. 19, Winter 1992, pp. 9-24.

12. Tomás A. Vasconi y Elina Peraza Martell, "La Socialdemocracia y la America Latina," *Casa de las Americas*, Vol. 31, July-August 1990, pp. 14-26.

13. Carlos M. Vilas, "Latin America: Socialist Perspectives in Times of Cholera," *Social Justice*, Vol. 19, Winter 1992, pp. 74-83.

14. Wallace Clement, "Exploring the Limits of Social Democracy: Regime Change in Sweden," *Studies in Political Economy*, No. 44, Summer 1994, pp. 95-121.

15. The factors influencing the policy change are discussed by Manuel Pastor and Carol Wise, "The Origins and Sustainability of Mexico's Free Trade Policy," *International Organization*, Vol. 48, Summer 1994, pp. 459-489.

16. John Williamson, "In Search of a Manual for Technopols," in John Williamson, ed. *The Political Economy of Policy Reform*. Washington: Institute for International Economics, January 1994, pp. 11-28.

17. Miguel Ángel Centeno, *Democracy within Reason; Technocratic Revolution in Mexico*. University Park: The Pennsylvania State University Press, 1994, pp. 21-41.

Chapter I

THE POLITICAL CULTURE: DOMINATION AND REBELLION

When Hernán Cortés and his small army landed on the Gulf Coast of what is now Mexico in 1519, they found an advanced civilization. Mesoamerica is described as the area from the Panuco, Lerma and Sinaloa rivers in northern Mexico to the Nicoya Peninsula in Costa Rica. The population of this area was around twenty-five million. At that time, France had a population of around twenty million, and the United Kingdom and Spain around six million each.

When the Europeans arrived, most of the indigenous peoples in North America were at a hunting and gathering stage of economic development, although some of them had evolved to horticultural societies. But this was not the case in Mesoamerica. city-state societies had developed, based on highly productive irrigated agriculture. It is estimated that the Mayan city of Tikal reached 100,000 around 600 A.D. Teotihuacán, the religious centre northeast of Mexico City, had a population of over 100,000 during its peak around 300 A.D. And when Cortés arrived, Tenochtitlán had a population of over 80,000 and there were one million people living in the Basin of Mexico. Tenochtitlán, described by Cortés as "the most beautiful city in the world," was twice the size of Seville, Spain's largest city.

The Mesoamerican civilizations were highly developed. Their agricultural system far surpassed anything that the Spanish had ever seen. They marvelled at the Mesoamerican architectural and engineering achievements. Their science, astronomy and medicine were ahead of Europe. The arts were highly developed. The Aztecs had a system of universal education, not to be known in Europe until the twentieth century.

The state societies in Mesoamerica were similar to those elsewhere in the world. They had a highly stratified class system, with rulers chosen from noble families, a priestly class, scribes and other government workers, a professional military, an imperial bureaucracy, artisans, and at the bottom a large class of peasants and slaves.

Aztec society was militarist and imperialist. They subjugated other Mesoamerican civilizations and imposed tribute on them. When Cortés arrived, the Aztec imperial system was extracting one-third of all the product of 370 subjugated towns.

Like many agricultural state societies, the Aztecs worshipped the sun god, known in Mesoamerica as Huitzilopochtli. Their religious mythology held that the sun and earth had been destroyed and recreated four times, and that the destruction of the fifth sun would be the final end. Every morning Coatlicue, the mother goddess of earth and fertility, gave birth to Huitzilopochtli, who would kill his sister the moon goddess Coyolxauhqui and her brothers, the stars. In the evening Huitzilopochtli would enter the underworld until the earth mother once again gave birth to him.

The Aztecs believed that Huitzilopochtli, who was also the god of war, needed to be fed human blood to survive this ordeal in the underworld. Human sacrifice was necessary to be certain that the sun would rise in the morning. Thus imperial military expeditions were also necessary to acquire humans for sacrifice. There are disputes over the extent of this practice.

Like all known state societies, those in Mesoamerica were also patriarchal. Men clearly were in command, and there was a very clear sexual division of labour. Boys from the nobility were trained in religion, astronomy, philosophy, history, poetry, rhetoric and oratory and other skills needed for public life. Common boys were prepared for life as workers, agriculturalists and warriors.

The women of the elite classes were trained for motherhood and household chores like cooking, sewing, and embroidering. They were excluded from public life. The women of the poor classes performed household chores, raised the children, laboured in the fields, wove cloth, made pottery and produced food and goods for the marketplace.

As Frederick Peterson points out, in Aztec society, women were expected to be quiet, listen and not talk. Girls who were bold were severely punished. They were not allowed to talk at meals and were required to sit for long periods of time in silence. Girls were always shut in behind high walls and were forbidden to address boys. Whenever they went out they were accompanied by chaperons who closely watched them. Most of them left school to be married. Girls were taught the value of modesty, courtesy and conformity.

In Aztec society, polygamy existed for the noble class. Men in the hereditary royal families had many wives and demanded virginity. Nezahualpilli of Texcoco had many wives and concubines and 144 children. Montezuma II had two formal wives but a great many concubines, mainly daughters of nobles.

For ordinary people, monogamous marriage was the rule. Marriages were arranged by families for economic purposes. They were not consecrated until the wife had produced a child. The wife who produced no children was sent home to her family. Male father rights were protected by a strict moral code against adultery, which was punished by death. Homosexuals were hanged.

The Spaniards brought with them the Roman Catholic faith, the latifundia from the Romans, and machismo from the Moors. Women were kept apart from men and completely excluded from public life. Under the influence of the church, women were idealized both for motherhood and their beauty. They were to be loyal to their fathers and husbands.

The Moors occupied Spain for around 700 years. They were driven out by the Christian crusade, which culminated in 1492. The Spaniards brought the ideology of the *Reconquista* to the new world: the purge of Moslems and Jews and independent thinking, religious fanaticism, intolerance, absolute monarchy, patronage, the hierarchical class society, patriarchy, and the doctrine of *limpieza de sangre* (racial purity).[1]

The Conquest

Hernán Cortés and his 550 Spanish soldiers left Cuba to find gold and silver in Mesoamerica. There was the goal of Christianizing the heathens, but this was clearly secondary to the object of plunder. They stopped first in Yucatan, where Cortés found a Spanish priest, Geronimo de Aguilar, who was fluent in Mayan. Cortés landed at Potonchan in Tabasco, conquered the town, and accepted 20 young women as a gift. One of these was Malintzin, the daughter of an Aztec chieftain who had been sold into slavery to the Maya. The Spaniards called her Malinche or Marina. She became Cortés' mistress, counsellor, and interpreter. Her knowledge of the Aztec empire and its ways was crucial to Cortés' victory. Today she is known as Mexico's Quisling.

The Spaniards abducted indigenous women for their sexual use. True to the Roman Catholic church, they did not marry these women. But their offspring became the *mestizo* race. Cortés and his followers also branded indigenous girls and women as slaves and put them up for sale.

The Spaniards could not have defeated the Aztec empire without the assistance of their indigenous allies. Cortés formed alliances with the chiefs of Cempoala and then the Tlaxcalans and Texocans, all of which were subjugated by and paying tribute to the Aztecs. Marching inland from what is today Veracruz, Cortés met the representatives of Montezuma at Cholula, the great Mesoamerican religious and market centre.

According to the Spanish, Malinche discovered a plot by Montezuma's agents to kill the invaders. Cortés responded with the massacre of 4,000 unarmed Cholulans, including women and children. The Aztecs record an unprovoked massacre of the Cholulans.

From this time on, the indigenous people referred to the Spaniards as the *popolucas*, or barbarians. But with this display of military force and contempt for human life, Cortés gained the support of other subjugated peoples. In November 1519, they marched into the city of Tenochtitlán.

Montezuma hesitated to launch an all-out attack on Cortés because he believed that he was the white god Quetzalcóatl returning as had been predicted in Mesoamerican mythology. The legendary Toltec leader Quetzalcóatl was pictured as having long blond hair, a beard, and blue eyes.

The Aztecs faced another threat. A Spanish expedition commanded by Panfilo de Narvaez landed at Veracruz and brought smallpox — unknown in the Americas — which destroyed whole communities and brought famine when crops could not be planted or harvested.

For almost two years, Cortés manoeuvred to defeat the Aztecs. He was aided by an army of about 80,000 from his Mesoamerican allies. Montezuma II was stoned to death by his people for subservience to the Spanish invaders. His successor Cuitlahuac died from smallpox. Cuauhtémoc led the Aztecs during Cortés's final assault on Tenotchtitlán, which fell in August 1521. Cortés tortured Cuauhtémoc, trying to get him to reveal Aztec treasures, but he refused to talk. Later he hanged him. Today, he is a symbol of Mexican resistance to imperialism.[2]

Colonialism

The defeated Aztecs were immediately enslaved by the Spaniards. They were put to work throughout the empire tearing down Mesoamerican religious temples and replacing them with Roman Catholic churches and government buildings. Catholic missionaries came to convert the masses to what they believed to be the only true religion. The conversion of the Mexicans to Roman Catholicism was aided by the myth of the appearance of a dark-skinned image of the Virgin Mary at the great temple at Tepeyac, the shrine to Coatlicue, the Aztec goddess of the earth, fertility and creation. According to this myth, on December 12, 1531 the Virgin of Guadalupe urged the Church of Rome to convert the indigenous peoples to this version of Christianity.

The Spanish carried out a military campaign against the other indigenous peoples of Mesoamerica. Beltran Nuño de Guzmán marched west of what was now Mexico City into Michoacán, burning villages, murdering, and enslaving the inhabitants. In one well-remembered case, he dragged the Tarascan chief behind a horse and then burned him alive. From Michoacán, he took his terror and savagery north to Sonora.

Most important was the war against the Mayans, who bravely resisted the new imperialism. In 1546, the Spanish celebrated a major victory. Those who refused to accept the Spanish peace were slaughtered. Another 500,000 were sold into peonage. Those who survived continued to resist, moving to the higher country of El Peten. They were not finally conquered until 1697.

The Spanish and the Roman Catholic church set out to systematically destroy the indigenous culture. The books and codices through which the indigenous priests had recorded local history, science, astronomy, and the arts, were destroyed by Roman Catholic priests. Juan de Zumárraga, the first Archbishop of Mexico, reported that his monks had destroyed 500 temples and 20,000 religious idols. In 1562, Bishop Diego de Landa ordered a mass burning of Mayan manuscripts in the city of Mani. Today, only three Mayan codices remain, thirteen Mixtec, nine Aztec and a few others. The indigenous history of Mesoamerica was destroyed.

In the Yucatan, conversion of the indigenous peoples was aided by torture, under the direction of Bishop de Landa. (In 1992, the Roman Catholic church and other official organizations celebrated the 500th anniversary of Christopher Columbus's arrival in the Americas. The Mexican government under Carlos Salinas officially proclaimed this "The Encounter Between Two Cultures.")

The Roman Catholic church was not simply concerned with saving the souls of Indians. By the time of the war for independence in 1810, it owned one-half of all the productive land in the country and had numerous business enterprises. The church leaders were known as the "bankers of Mexico."

The Spanish greed for gold and silver led to the expansion of mining in Mexico. Important silver mines were opened in Compostela, Zacatecas, Guanajuato, Taxco, Pachuca, and elsewhere. They relied on Indian forced labour. Textile mills and small industry developed.

The Spanish transformed Mexican agriculture. Wheat farming and cotton production were introduced. Sugar plantations were established, and commercial production of cacao and tobacco was developed. Stock-raising followed the introduction of horses, cattle, and sheep. The indigenous peoples were removed from their most productive land which was given to Spaniards.[3]

The Caste Society

The key to early Spanish rule was the *encomienda* system, established in 1503. The Spanish needed not only land but labour. In Mesoamerica, the large indigenous population provided this labour. Titles were given to specific stretches of land and at the same time, to a specified number of Indians who were put under the "trust" of the *encomendero*. The owner of the land was given control over the labour of the Indians on his land. They would work on his land, or they could be sold to other landowners. The Indian was tied to the land in a situation which was a combination of serf and slave. The *encomenderos* also had complete control over Indian women, to use as concubines or to sell into slavery. Cortés, for example, was given an *encomienda* of 23,000 Indians.

However, the imperial government feared that this system would lead to the reestablishment of feudalism. A new policy was established in 1550, the *repartimiento*. All Indian males were required to perform forty-five days of labour per year. Local Spanish authorities would send them off to work in the mines, textile mills or on plantations.

But the *hacienda* became the dominant system of agricultural production during the rapid drop in indigenous population and the resulting shortage of labour. The colonists purchased large tracts of lands, commercially farmed only a small percentage of the land, and raised horses and cattle. The landowner lived in a huge house surrounded by a high wall. Behind the wall was the Roman Catholic chapel, the owner's store, and the jail.

Indian and *mestizo* families were invited to move onto the land, occupy a house, and receive a small portion of land on which to grow food for consumption. In return, the *hacendado* controlled his labour and paid him in goods from the store. The labourer was known as a peon. He could not leave the *hacienda* until his debts were all paid, which rarely occurred. The system guaranteed the landowner labour and gave the peon a small bit of security, but at a high price.

The *hacienda* was more than an economic system. It was a system of rural power. If the peon was obedient and submissive, he would receive small favours from the owner. If he was rebellious or expressed his anger, he would be tied to the whipping post and flogged.

The Spanish introduced a rigid class society. At the top were the *peninsulares*, men of the peninsula who had come to Mexico to rule. They were the colonial ruling class, occupying all important state and church positions.

Below them were the *criollos*, who were pure blood Spanish but who had been born in Mexico. They held less important offices and were the local business and landlord class. No matter how rich they were, they were relegated to a second class status. In the Spanish caste system they nevertheless held a position of high status due to their white skin. By 1800, there were an estimated one million whites in Mexico, of which around 70,000 were *peninsulares*.

At the time of the defeat of the Aztecs, there were close to 2,500 Spaniards in Mexico, of which only six were women. Over the next few decades, few European women came to Mexico. The rape and seizure of indigenous non-white women, characteristic of the military conquest of Mexico, resulted in the mixed-blood *mestizo* race. In the sixteenth and seventeenth centuries, the term *mestizo* was close to the term "bastard." These children often went unrecognized by their fathers and lived with their mothers. They were denied their birthright and the right to own land. By 1800, they comprised about 25 percent of the Mexican population.

At the bottom of the caste system was the indigenous population. They had been devastated by the introduction of new diseases for which they had no natural resistance: smallpox, typhoid fever, measles, malaria and yellow fever. By 1625, the indigenous population of Mesoamerica had fallen from twenty-five million to around one million. They were converted to Christianity, and for the most part, survived at a subsistence level in communal villages or as peons on *haciendas*.

In 1537, the Pope declared that the indigenous peoples of Mexico were human beings and were not to be slaughtered, but converted to Christianity. Formal slavery for Indians was abolished in 1542 and was replaced by blacks from Africa, who were still considered "natural slaves" by the church. By 1650, there were around 120,000 African slaves in New Spain.

Rámon Eduardo Ruiz notes that the Spanish created a "pigmentocracy." Status in colonial New Spain was based on a combination of wealth, skin colour and ancestry. Whiteness was the key to social status, but class was also important. Wealthy *mestizos* or mulattos were "passable" into high society if they had money. The social objective was to marry a person with a lighter skin.

The political culture was also highly patriarchal. Men owned and controlled all wealth and property. Women in upper and middle class society were to be wives only and were not to work outside the home. But this was not the case for poor women, who were expected to work to help support the family.

For three hundred years, the Spanish ruled Mexico through an authoritarian colonial system. Even the local *criollos* were denied any real influence on policy. Mexico developed within the international system of colonial mercantile capitalism with an emphasis on exporting primary products for the mother country and importing manufactured Spanish goods. But the weakness of industry in Spain permitted the development of local manufacturing for the local market. Only the rich could afford Spanish goods.[4]

Independence

As in all white settler colonies, conflict arose between the interests of the colonizers and the representatives of the imperial centre. In Mexico, the *criollos* resented the quick high profits going to Spain, the prestige of ruling, and the fact that they were denied the good jobs. Socially, they were discriminated against, in spite of their wealth. But they were not liberals. They were an economic ruling class, and they lorded over the vast majority who were poor. Politically, their primary concern was that Napoleon had occupied Spain, deposed Ferdinand VII, and placed his brother Joseph on the throne.

The rebellion against Spanish rule in Mexico was led by Father Miguel Hidalgo, a parish priest in Dolores, Guanajuato. He had absorbed the political philosophy of the French Revolution. But he belonged to a liberal group which strongly believed in the rights of property. He defied the church by openly fathering two daughters. On September 16, 1810 he distributed arms to the workers and peasants, summoned a crowd, and asked the Mexicans if they were ready to fight to recover their lands which had been stolen by the Spanish.

As the army of mainly Indians marched, it grew to 60,000, captured towns and pillaged them. At the city of Guanajuato, they were joined by miners, captured the city, killed almost all the Spaniards, and looted their businesses and residences. It was not only a war for independence, it was class war. The rebel army overran other towns and cities. But Hidalgo stopped short of Mexico City, which he could have taken. No one knows exactly why. Instead, he retreated toward Guadalajara, where he was welcomed as a liberator. But as his army began to desert him, they were ambushed by Spanish soldiers, and Hidalgo was captured and executed.

The leadership of the rebellion was assumed by Father José María Morelos, a *mestizo* of African ancestry, also from Michoacán. In September 1813, he convened a congress at Chilpancingo, Guerrero which declared Mexico's independence and drafted a constitution which promised universal suffrage, abolished slavery and all caste systems, prohibited torture, and proposed an income tax. However, as the Spanish forces were replenished, the rebel army shrunk with each defeat, and Morelos was also captured and executed. Between 1815 and 1820, the rebel army was reduced to guerrilla warfare.

The *criollos* in New Spain were very concerned with political developments in Spain. In 1814, Ferdinand VII had been restored to the throne, but in 1820, liberals revolted, the liberal Constitution of 1812 was restored, and a parliament was convened. The *criollos,* fearing the rise of liberalism, sought a way to seize power while maintaining autocratic rule.

Mexican independence was engineered by Augustín de Iturbide, a wealthy *criollo* who had fought with the Spanish against Hidalgo and Morelos. With a small army he joined forces with Vincente Guerrero. He announced his *Plan de Iguala* which would guarantee the power of the Roman Catholic church, independence with a Mexican monarch, and equal political rights for those born in Mexico. On September 27, 1821, Iturbide marched into Mexico City and was welcomed and supported by Spanish royalists. Independence was, in effect, a coup by the rich.[5]

Generals and Liberals

From independence in 1821, to the outbreak of the domestic revolution in 1910, Mexico was ruled by a series of *caudillos* who gained office by coup d'etat. Iturbide tried to establish himself as emperor in 1821, but he was ousted by General Antonio López de Santa Anna, a *criollo* with inherited wealth who dominated Mexican politics between 1822 and 1855.

During this period, some of Mexico's long-standing political traditions were established: whites ruled over non-whites, and rich over poor; the president became all-powerful in the political system; the legislative and judicial branches of government were under the control and domination of the president; and what is known in Mexico as *personalismo* was firmly established.

Mexico developed as a federal state, but the central government clearly dominated. The military played a central role in the political process — not only as an instrument of state repression, but also directly in the governing process. Every president had to deal with military revolts.

Elections were used to try to give legitimacy to presidential regimes. From the very beginning, political leaders regularly resorted to gross electoral fraud. Santa Anna developed another of Mexico's traditions: each new president and his circle of friends would become rich while holding office.

The church was openly involved in the political process, always supporting the rich over the poor, and opposing democracy and liberal reforms. In the rural areas, the church worked closely with the large land-owners to support conservative politics.

General Santa Anna went into exile after the war with the United States in 1847 led to the loss of what is now Texas, California, New Mexico, Arizona, Nevada, Utah and part of Colorado. The final concession for Mexico was the sale of the Mesilla Valley, now part of Arizona and New Mexico.

The period of Mexican history between 1855 and 1876 is called *La Reforma* — the liberal period dominated by Benito Juárez — which began with the revolt of guerrilla bands in the south in 1854, led by Juan Alvarez, an Indian *caudillo*. The liberal reformers were largely middle-class *mestizos*.

In March 1854, the liberals revealed their *Plan de Ayutla*, a manifesto designed to gain the support of moderates who opposed the Santa Anna dictatorship. In 1855, their armies entered Mexico City without resistance. Alvarez became president and Juárez his Minister of Justice.

The central issue for the liberals was the power of the Roman Catholic church. The liberals strongly believed in individual ownership of land and, having removed the authority of church courts, ordered the church to sell off all its commercial land. However, this policy proved to be ill-conceived. The church held about one-half of all the valuable land in Mexico, and it was sold to rich landowners. The Indians lost title to their historic, communal lands while the peasants were merely transferred from ecclesiastical to secular landlords. The church accumulated capital and became further established as the "banker of Mexico."

The liberal Constitution of 1857 stressed the federal nature of Mexico but then gave most of the government powers to a one-chamber legislature, the congress. The liberal government, weak and under attack from the rich, collapsed in 1858, and the conservative forces, backed by the church and the army, launched a civil war.

Named president by what remained of the congress, Benito Juárez mobilized the masses to defend the constitution. Juárez was a full-blooded Zapotec Indian, a lawyer for the poor, and a liberal activist who had been arrested and jailed by Santa Anna. He was a moderate liberal, a very religious man, and supported free trade. In 1959, as president, he issued new reform laws which confiscated church property without compensation, curtailed monasteries, nationalized the cemeteries, and introduced civil marriage. The civil war continued, but with support from the poor majority, Juárez and the liberal forces triumphed in December 1860.

But the country was economically vulnerable, and taxes brought no revenues. Little was acquired from the sale of church properties, although

the wealth of the church was estimated to be 20 percent of the nation's total. In July 1861, President Juárez was forced to suspend payments on the
foreign debt. The governments of Spain, France and England retaliated by
sending warships to the harbour of Veracruz. They supported the military
intervention of the French, who tried to turn Mexico into a French colony
under a monarchy headed by Archduke Maximillian of Austria. The foreign intervention had the support of Mexican conservatives.

But liberals, anti-imperialists and the masses rallied behind Juárez and
slowly began to win military victories against the French. Juárez's forces defeated Maximillian at Querétaro in 1867, where the Austrian invader was
shot. In his final term as president, Juárez became another *caudillo*, pushing
for expanded powers for the presidency. The great liberal manipulated elections, intimidated the congress, and imposed political candidates in the
states. He died in office in 1872, however, the lasting impact of his national
leadership was the curtailment of the powers of the church, the end of monarchy, the discrediting of the political conservatives, and the dream of free
elections.[6]

Porfiriato

From 1876 to the outbreak of the revolution in 1910, Mexico was
dominated by Porfirio Díaz. He was a *mestizo* from Oaxaca with Mixtec roots
and a political ally of Juárez. Like Juárez, he was from a poor family. He
rose through the ranks of the liberal movement primarily as a military
leader. He objected when Juárez cut the size of the army in 1867, ran
against him for president in 1871, and led an unsuccessful military revolt
against him when he was president. In 1876, he built his political and military base in Brownsville, Texas with U.S. support and then led an army into
Mexico City, staged an election, and declared himself president.

Díaz is considered the real father of the Mexican system of *pan o palo*:
those who follow orders eat bread; those who resist are subject to the club.
Through an expanded patronage system Díaz established his loyal followers
in political office. Those who objected faced state repression or murder.
The police were well-paid and loyal. In the country, he created the infamous *rurales*, roving quasi-police who terrorized disgruntled peasants. The
press was controlled, bribes were paid, and those who dared to criticize the
government were beaten and sometimes shot. Workers who tried to organize trade unions or to go on strike faced the repression of the police, the
military and the *rurales*. The regime found that shooting was the easiest way
to break a strike.

Díaz perfected the Mexican system of central political control over local officials. The president appointed all governors, congressmen, and even
many mayors. The appointments were followed by sham elections.

The inner circle of political allies enriched themselves while in office.
Díaz came more to identify with the rich criollos and the *Científicos* — technocratic advisers. He also kept the army on his side by currying favour with
the generals. Many loyal generals were appointed governors of states while
the army itself remained a conscript army of the poor.

Over the years, Díaz built a strong alliance with the large landowners,
and the *hacienda* system grew in importance. By 1900, one percent of the
population held 97 percent of the fertile land. Holdings of over 300,000
acres were not unusual. For example, the *hacienda* of Don Luis Terrazas in
Chihuahua was eight times the size of the famous King Ranch in Texas, and
William Randolph Hearst, the U.S. publisher, had a ranch of eight million
acres. In contrast, around 82 percent of the rural population was landless.

Under the dictatorship of Díaz, the Mexican economy recovered. The
key was foreign, and particularly American, investment. As Ramón Eduardo
Ruiz points out, by 1911, American investment in Mexico exceeded one billion pesos, "twice that of Mexicans and greater than the value of property
held by Mexicans and Europeans together."

U.S., French, and English interests financed and controlled the railroads. In 1884, Díaz changed the mining legislation and abolished the
Spanish tradition which reserved subsoil right to the country as a whole.
French, German, and American mining interests moved into Mexico. The
most influential were the Guggenheim mining companies and the copper
empire of Colonial William Greene. American and British investors came
to control the Mexican petroleum industry.

By 1910, 80 percent of the banking system was owned and controlled
by foreign interests. Foreign ownership of land greatly increased and by
1910, Americans owned over 100 million acres, around 22 percent of Mexico's land surface, including some of the best agricultural, mining and tim-
ber lands. John Mason Hart notes that foreign agricultural businesses
controlled fourteen of the sixteen largest agribusiness operations in Mexico. Foreign interests owned much of the industrial agricultural operations
in sugar, cotton, and sisal hemp.

Mexican industry concentrated on the domestic market; the textile,
steel, paper, cement, brewery, glass, tobacco, sugar, and food processing
industries grew steadily. But this model resulted in uneven development.
Technology and machinery were imported, but because these industries
were capital intensive, few Mexicans were employed. When Mexican

manufacturers found that they could not compete with better quality imports, they demanded and received government subsidies, exemption from taxation, and protections. Domestic monopolies were the inevitable outcome.

This period of development is commonly referred to as the *Porfiriato*, and it is seen as one basic model. It is characterized by authoritarian government, state repression of labour and *campesinos*, close government collaboration with big business, reliance on foreign investment and technology, and close political ties with the U.S. government.[7]

The Revolution

The Mexican revolution began in 1910, when Porfirio Díaz announced that he was going to seek reelection and named Ramón Corral, who had murdered and enslaved the Yaqui Indians of Sonora, to be his vice president.

The opposition was launched by the liberal section of the capitalist class who wanted constitutional reform and an end to military rule. They were led by Francisco Madero, a wealthy Mexican land owner who had extensive interests in banking, mining and manufacturing. Madero was based in the north of Mexico, where he had the open support of American interests. Why had the Americans changed sides? The primary reason seemed to be that Díaz had rebuked Standard Oil and was giving British oil interests preferential treatment.

From his headquarters in Brownsville, Texas, Madero and his supporters published their *Plan de San Luis Potosí*, demanding effective elections, no reelection of presidents, and that Díaz leave office. In May 1911, an angry demonstration in Mexico City demanded that Díaz resign. Despite military support, Díaz signed his resignation and went into exile.

Madero was elected president in October 1911, but the wealthy liberal reformer was not prepared to meet the social and economic demands of the majority. His army burned the villages in Morelos, however, they were not able to stop the agrarian reformers led by Emiliano Zapata. There were local military revolts in the northeast, Chihuahua and Juárez. In February 1913, Mexico City was devastated by military conflict. The U.S. ambassador secretly negotiated a settlement, which included the resignation of the Madero government. General Victoriano Huerta assumed power, and Madero and his vice president, Pino Suárez, were murdered.

General Huerta's coup d'etat was welcomed by Mexico's conservative forces. He had established his reputation by killing rebellious Indians and by ruthless repression of the Zapatista agrarians. After taking power, he imprisoned 110 members of the congress and had himself declared president by those who remained.

Forces of the popular opposition, however, were only mobilized by the coup, and in southern Mexico, the agrarian reformers under Zapata began an all-out attack on the large *haciendas* and distributed land to the peasants. In Chihuahua and Durango, Pancho Villa built an army of the poor and began attacking large *haciendas*.

As the rebel armies began moving towards the capital, Alvaro Obregón, a middle-class ranchero in Sonora, mobilized an army; in Coahuila the large landowner, Venustiano Carranza, did the same. Fearing the rebellion by the landless peasants, Carranza blocked Villa's advance on Mexico City, and encouraged Obregón. The then new American president, Woodrow Wilson, openly sided with Carranza and while at the same time opposed the Huerta dictatorship after Huerta strengthened his links with the British government and British oil interests. The U.S. responded by seizing Veracruz, thereby cutting off Huerta's much needed revenues from customs duties.

In the south, Zapata and the rural forces battled the murderous federal forces, defeating them in March 1914. The rich and powerful grew fearful when a People's Court sentenced the officers to death by firing squad. In July 1914, the armies of Carranza and Obregón marched into Mexico City and Huerta fled into exile.

In the meantime, the class war in the countryside continued. By the end of 1914, the armies of Villa and Zapata held about two-thirds of the country. Carranza, the land baron, was determined to block the demands for land reform. The Aguascalientes convention in November 1914, failed to resolve the class conflicts between the revolutionary leaders. Carranza and Obregón fled to Veracruz, still held by the U.S. military, while the armies of Villa and Zapata occupied Mexico City. But the *agraristas* could not agree on how to run the government. Zapata and his supporters went back south to their farms, Villa returned to the north, and provisional president Eulalio Gutiérrez was left in Mexico City to try to run the government.

From Veracruz, Carranza launched a political attack against the radicals. He decreed land reforms, and announced the legalization of trade unions, support for organizing, and a minimum wage for all workers — even farm workers — along with promises for political and legal reforms. At the same time, General Obregón launched a military attack on Villa's forces.

The key to the outcome of the conflict was Carranza'a alliance with organized labour. In return for a host of promises, the trade unions formed six Red Battalions which fought with Carranza against Villa. In the crucial battle between Obregón and Villa at Celaya, 9,000 of the 20,000 soldiers were from the Red Battalions revealing that the hoped-for alliance between peasants and workers was smashed.

The U.S. government, understanding that Carranza and Obregón were much more conservative than Villa and Zapata, granted diplomatic recognition to Carranza, sent him economic and military aid, and enforced an embargo on any aid to Villa.

Having defeated Villa, Carranza no longer needed labour support. He disbanded the Red Battalions and labour militants in the House of the World's Workers were arrested. When a general strike was called in protest, Carranza jailed the trade union leaders and used death threats to break the strike.

Carranza then sent General Pablo Gonzáles and the federal troops to fight against Zapata, but by this time, most *haciendas* in Morelos had been taken by the popular forces and the land distributed to the peasants, fulfilling the cry of the *agraristas*, "Land to the Tiller." Under Gonzáles, the federal forces began a scorched earth campaign. Peasants and their families were massacred and prisoners were sent to forced labour in the Yucatan. Nonetheless, the peasants pulled together and drove the federal armies back to Mexico City. An estimated two million Mexicans had died in the civil war. The economy lay in ruins.

The liberal reformers, fearing that all would be lost, forced Carranza to call a constitutional convention in December 1916. Delegates loyal to Villa and Zapata were not permitted. The result was the Constitution of 1917.

The constitution promised land reform, a new charter for labour, and guaranteed the rights of private property. Article 27 allowed the national state to dictate to private property holders in the name of national sovereignty and the public interest. It also declared that all natural resources, and in particular subsoil rights to minerals, belonged to the people as a whole. The central state would be the great arbitrator in economic disputes. And it entrenched the liberal demand for a strict separation between church and state.[8]

Revolutionary Millionaires

The period between 1920 and 1934 is usually called the period of reconstruction. Some historians refer to it as the period of rule by the "revolutionary millionaires." The political system was dominated by Generals

Obregón and Calles. Jean Meyer describes their rule as "enlightened despotism," where the state knew what had to be done, needed full powers, and required Mexicans to obey.

Venustiano Carranza assumed the office of president in May 1917, after a special election. He had no alternative but to accept the Constitution of 1917, but he made it clear to everyone that he was not going to enforce it. He opposed land reform and supported the expansion of large agricultural estates with repressive labour practices. He informed foreign investors he would not enforce the principles of national ownership of resources. He used the army to break strikes and arrested strike leaders for treason. He sent General Pablo Gonzáles on a campaign against Zapata in Morelos. Crops and villages were burned and they executed thousands of civilians for supporting the Zapatistas. Carrancistas arranged the murder of Zapata.

In 1920, there was a military and political struggle to see who would be the next president. General Gonzáles announced his candidacy and mobilized his army. Carranza named Ignacio Bonillas as his candidate and set his army on the march. General Obregón mobilized and began a march on Mexico City. General Plutarco Elías Calles revolted in Sonora. In the end, Obregón marched into the capital, Carranza fled and was murdered, and Obregón staged an election for the presidency.

Obregón had become a very large landowner and had virtually captured the national market for chick-peas. He got support from the U.S. government by promising not to enforce the constitutional guarantes on oil and mineral rights. He built his support as had Díaz, through the patronage of public office, i.e., he tried to buy off the generals by increasing their number and looking the other way as they filled their pockets.

He formed an alliance with Luis Morones, head of the Regional Confederation of Mexican Workers (CROM), using him to crush the more radical trade unions. The special relationship with the president allowed Morones to extract tribute from employers and build his membership.

Obregón also built an alliance with the Agrarian Leagues and the National Agrarian Party (PNA), led by Antonio Díaz Soto y Gama, a close associate of Zapata. But when it came to land reform, he did very little. Only three million acres were distributed, to 624 villages. Land for the tiller remained a dream.

In 1923, Obregón announced that he was backing General Calles to succeed him in the 1924 election. Although Calles came from a wealthy family in Sonora, Catholic leaders, the *hacendados,* and many generals opposed the choice. There was an armed rebellion which lasted a few months, but with military aid from Washington, Obregón was able to suppress it. Calles was elected president and dominated Mexico for the next ten years.

Calles set, as one of his primary tasks, the taming of the generals. The army had 14,000 officers and took 40 percent of the national budget. Presidents Carranza and Obregón had also given them high government positions. Calles supported the peasants and workers, to build a political base against the army. He established a professional officer class and improved the living conditions of the *peons* forced into the army.

Still, there was no great change. Election campaigns began, but the outcome was decided by military force and fraud. In the 1927 election the generals revolted, and Calles used armed force to crush them. The leaders of the revolt were shot.

In the 1929 election, the generals rebelled again. Calles called on the professional army, and the workers and peasants came to his defence; the generals were crushed and there were more firing squads.

The second item on the agenda of the "enlightened despots" was the curtailment of the power of the Roman Catholic church. The church hierarchy had backed the dictatorships of Díaz and Huerta. They opposed the revolution, opposed public education, and backed the large landowners. The hierarchy also strongly opposed the Constitution of 1917. Their message to the poor was that they must suffer in this life, and the reward for their loyalty would be the Kingdom of Heaven.

Obregón began a mass literacy program for the 80 percent of Mexicans who could not read or write and established a public school system. The church resisted, but Calles carried on the program.

In 1926, the church openly challenged the constitution. Calles responded by ordering foreign priests out of the country and closing the religious schools, monasteries and convents. The church responded by striking: the priests were ordered not to conduct religious ceremonies.

Between 1926 and 1929, the Catholic Action mobilized a military organization against the government, the Cristero War. When the army crushed the organized rebellion, the conservatives resorted to guerrilla warfare. They burned schools and killed and mutilated teachers. Murder was widespread on both sides. After three years of turmoil, a compromise was reached, negotiated by U.S. ambassador Dwight Morrow. Even so, most states passed laws limiting the number of priests. The church eventually ordered its followers to abandon violence and condemned guerrilla attacks.

The other major issue in the 1920s was land reform. The government moved to redistribute what agricultural land was still owned by the church. But it could do nothing in northern Mexico, where the powerful *hacendados* were in firm control. The U.S. government put great pressure on Obregón not to act against U.S. ownership of land, which was substantial. In return for military support, he pledged to take no action on the issue of American land ownership.

In southern Mexico, peasants were not peons on *haciendas* but lived in free villages. They continued to demand the return of their lands which had been seized by *hacendados* and corporate farms. Many joined the Cristero War for a different reason: the federal government was not carrying out promised land reform. Very little land distribution was made during the 1920s.

The question of presidential succession again arose. The Constitution of 1917 had been amended to provide a six year term for the president with no reelection. But this did not prevent Calles from continuing to dominate Mexican politics. In the 1928 election, Obregón, backed by Calles (known as *jefe maximo*), ran again for president. He was opposed by General Francisco Serrano and General Arnulfo Gómez. When the newcomers became convinced the election would be rigged, they staged a military revolt, and were defeated, captured, and executed. Obregón won over his two dead opponents.

However, the day after the election, Obregón was assassinated by a supporter of the Cristero War. Calles named Portes Gil to be president, the first of three puppet presidents. In 1929, Calles formed the Party of the Mexican Revolution (PNR) to try to end the domination of Mexican politics by generals. But he continued the Mexican tradition of grossly rigging elections.

The period of Mexican rule by Calles is referred to as *Maximato*, signifying long rule by a dominant president. In the latter part of his regime, social reform was abandoned. Land reform was virtually halted. The rural education program was cut back drastically. Calles stopped supporting CROM and unionization dropped off.

During the 1930's Depression, exports dropped, particularly petroleum, mineral, and agricultural products. National income fell and unemployment rose. Farm workers were expelled from the United States to return home in poverty. The hardest hit were the majority of Mexicans who lived in the rural areas, had no land, and relied on large landowners for waged work.

Economic liberalism was dropped in 1932 and Alberto Pani introduced the Keynesian policies of the activist state. As strikes and radical political activity increased, Calles launched a war on the small Communist Party, deporting its leaders to a penal colony. The Gold Shirts appeared to fight communists and Jews. But the people at the top of the political system grew richer than ever before. The era ended when Calles named General Lázaro Cárdenas to be the candidate of the PNR, in the 1934 presidential election.[9]

The Cárdenas Revolution

By the time Cárdenas became president, the Mexican political culture was well established. Capitalism was entrenched, and what socialist movement existed, was very weak. There was tremendous disparity in wealth, income and status between the inner circle who ruled the country and the great majority of peasants and workers. There was a strong caste system, with the white descendants of the Spanish colonizers having power at the top. The majority, who were *mestizos,* came to dominate political office and could become rich through business activities.

In the rural areas, where the majority lived, political and economic life was dominated by wealthy, powerful *hacendados,* who had their own White Guards to protect their interests against the majority of landless *mestizos* and Indians. Wages for those in the urban proletariat were very low, at a subsistence level. In this situation, the military and the police were necessary to control the poor majority. These state institutions have a long history of human rights abuse, disappearance, torture and repression.

Mexico was a federal system, with state and local bosses (*caciques*) having substantial power. At the federal level, the system of government was completely dominated by the president. Patronage was essential for the operation of the system.

In contrast to other Latin American countries, the liberal reform movement had succeeded in curtailing the power of the Roman Catholic church. Its control over the mass of the population was limited to its ideological influence.

Lázaro Cárdenas was the most important Mexican president. A poor *mestizo* with Tarascan Indian background, he grew up in the small town of Jiquilpan, Michoacán. He fought in the armies of Carranza and Obregón and had been a progressive and honest governor of Michoacán. He did not forget his past.

Cárdenas took office in the middle of the Depression, a time of high unemployment and considerable poverty and hunger in the rural areas. The average annual income of small farmers was about $45 per year and there were 650 strikes in 1935. There were even strikes by agricultural workers, whose wages averaged around 10 cents a day. Landless peasants began seizing land. The Mexican volcano was beginning to rumble.

When the landlords sent the White Guards to attack the peasants, Cárdenas responded by forming the peasants' leagues and ordered the army to give rifles to a new peasant militia. He distributed 18.4 million hectares to one million peasants. Foreign-owned land was the first to be seized and redistributed.

As the conservative forces mobilized against the government, Cárdenas created a workers' militia in Mexico City. He forced officers and office holders to pledge support to him or leave. He broke with the forces behind Calles. The revolt by General Saturnino Cedillo was crushed and he was shot. Cárdenas won popular support by living modestly, in glaring contrast to past presidents, and by keeping his office open to the common people. In a complete break with the past, he spent most of his time outside Mexico City, meeting with the people on the local level.

Trade union organizing was encouraged and when the oil companies refused to grant a pay increase to their unionized workers, Cárdenas nationalized the foreign owned companies. Since the turn of the century, the oil companies had invested around $100 million in Mexico but had reaped profits estimated at $5 billion. The people rallied behind the president. He was the first president to enforce the Constitution of 1917.

Cárdenas' most enduring accomplishment was the restructuring of the revolutionary party, renamed the Party of the Mexican Revolution (PRM). In 1936, he backed the formation of the Confederation of Mexican Workers (CTM) as the central labour organization in Mexico. With close to one million members, it dwarfed the CROM and the General Confederation of Workers (CGT), sponsored by the Communist Party. It was formally affiliated with the reorganized Mexican Revolutionary Party (PRM).

The power of the CTM was limited by the formation of the Federation of Unions in the Service of the State (FSTSE), who were independently affiliated with the PRM. In addition, Cárdenas decreed that the CTM could not organize peasants. They would be organized and affiliated to the PRM via the National Confederation of Peasants (CNC).

Cárdenas also created the Nation Confederation of Popular Organizations (CNOP), and had it affiliate with the PMR. This sector included white collar workers, professionals, civic and business organizations, youth, and women's organizations. Within the party, this became the most influential sector.

Cárdenas was not a socialist; he was a capitalist reformer. He built the power of the peasants, workers and the middle class to oppose the dominant power of the "bankers alliance," the wealthy, foreign capital, the rural oligarchs, the church, and the military. The state and the PMR were to moderate conflicts between the classes and regions in the general public interest. The corporatist state was to provide stability which would permit economic growth and increased well being for all classes.[10]

The One-Party State

Under the Mexican system of government, the president is all-powerful. He is elected for a six-year term and under the constitution cannot be reelected. Under President Carlos Salinas, there were twenty-two cabinet positions appointed by the president. The president also has direct responsibility for the government of the Federal District. The most powerful cabinet position is *Gobernacion*, which is roughly equivalent to the traditional ministry of the interior. Presidents usually are chosen from those who hold important cabinet positions.

The legislative branch of the federal government has a Chamber of Deputies and a Senate. Their composition was changed in 1993. The Chamber of Deputies has 500 members, 300 elected by constituency and another 200 from a list, according to proportional representation. No one party may now have more than 63 percent of the seats. The Senate was expanded to include four from each state and the Federal District; three senators are allocated to the majority, and the fourth seat is allocated to the strongest minority party. The Chamber is elected every three years, and members cannot run for reelection. The Senators serve for six years, one half are elected every three years, and they cannot seek reelection. The prohibition on reelection prohibits the development of any power base in the legislature.

The Supreme Court is appointed by the President; the court then appoints all the local and district judges.

Mexico is a federal system, loosely based on the American model, but highly centralized. Around 85 percent of all government revenues go to the central government. The states are left with about 12 percent and the municipalities around 3 percent. Municipalities get 80 percent of their funding from the federal and state governments.

In Mexico, there is no separation between the state and the Institutional Revolutionary Party (PRI). It is commonly referred to as the "state party." It has ruled virtually unopposed since 1929. But in the Mexican case, the state dominates the party.

The President totally controls the PRI. He names the next candidate for president, who then goes through the ratification process of a national election. This is called the *dedazo*, or "the fingering." The president names the candidates of the PRI for all state governors, senators and deputies. He can also order governors to resign — for whatever reason he chooses.

The president completely dominates the legislative branch. He prepares the budget, which is ratified. He introduces legislation, which is then passed. Since the PRI was formed, the legislature has never refused to pass a law requested by the president, and has never passed a law opposed by the president. It is a rubber stamp for the president.

For example, Alan Riding points out that between 1917 and 1984 the Congress amended the constitution on 369 occasions, "to suit the whims of a succession of presidents." President Carlos Salinas de Gortari (1988-94) amended the constitution many times, including very important articles, changing principles that were the heart of the revolution. President Ernesto Zedillo quickly amended the constitution to suit the demands of foreign investors and the U.S. government during the monetary crisis in early 1995.

The Supreme Court is also a political institution, filled with appointees loyal to the PRI. Since the PRI was formed, the Supreme Court has never declared unconstitutional any action by the president or any piece of legislation.

The mass media in Mexico is totally dominated by the state and the PRI. All the major newspapers are controlled by the PRI, and the system of patronage and bribery guarantees that the news is favourable. The radio stations are controlled by the PRI and business interests loyal to the PRI. Television is by far the most important media in Mexico, and it is dominated by Televisa, owned by Emilio Azcárraga, who has strong loyalties to the PRI and the free market economy. Mexicans often describe their media as "Stalinist television."

The president, as head of the PRI, has the power to appoint leaders of the organizations formally affiliated — the trade unions, the peasant organizations and the popular groups.

Patronage is the heart of the one-party system. Working for the government is the primary route for personal advancement. Stephen Morris estimates that eighteen thousand elective and twenty-five thousand appointive positions change hands every six years. Other estimates are that forty-five thousand jobs at the top change with each president. Payments are made to the party. Jobs are even sold by the party. There is nothing like a civil service as it is known in North America.

Personal relationships are most important. One quickly finds that there is a significant gap between the law and how it is applied. For example, since the 1970s, governments and state-owned enterprises are required by law to have competitive bidding for contracts. This is widely considered a joke. PRI supporters and their businesses get the contracts. It is impossible to get a license to do business without making a payment to an office holder or the PRI. High-level inspectors expect a "surcharge" that is often 10 percent of the value of the contract.

Bribery has been widely reported in the area of tax collection. Tax evasion by businesses, the rich, and those working in the informal economy are the order of the day. Stephen Morris quotes the Salinas government, in 1989, claiming that "70% of companies do not pay their taxes." Bribery and corruption have been notorious since the increase in the importance of the export of illegal drugs to the United States. The system is so deeply entrenched that many Mexicans doubt that it can be changed.

The Mexican system of co-optation of dissent takes place both through the state and the official organizations affiliated with the PRI. The state and party system are hierarchical and authoritarian. Discipline is imposed from the top down. The men at the top of the party also hold key positions with the state. But the party does operate at the local level, to mobilize support for the government, to hear complaints, and to fix problems. On the local level it is there to constantly remind the people that there is no alternative, and that if they want something done, it has to be done through the PRI. Those who try to go around the PRI are punished.

The result of the formal political system and total domination by the PRI is that the Mexican president has enormous political power. Some call the Mexican system a dictatorship. It has been classified by political scientists as a "corporate state," similar to the Italian government under Mussolini or the Spanish government under General Franco. The key is state control of the trade unions. Regardless, Mexico is the oldest one-party state in the world.

The Mexican writer, Octavio Paz, has called Mexico a "benevolent monarchy." Because of the power of the president, he is almost immune to criticism. Professor Martin Needler suggests that "democratic elements can safely be ascribed to facade and authoritarian ones to reality." The democratic image projected by the president and his supporters is "more palatable for public consumption, while the country's rulers are not eager to have their power limited or restrained."

In Canada and the United States, supporters of the North American Free Trade Agreement (NAFTA) claimed that President Carlos Salinas was "modernizing" the Mexican political system, moving towards a truly democratic political system. Yet, inside Mexico, people argued that the opposite was true. Since the 1988 presidential election, where the people rose up and voted heavily for two candidates who opposed the ruling PRI, Salinas increased the centralization of power in the hands of the president and used an iron hand to repress the opposition.

This is not to say that the Mexican one-party state cannot be altered. It is clear that the political system has changed over the years, and is evolving. The church has been stripped of much of its power. The military, so dominant prior to World War II, has far less power today. In the 1980s, the centre-right National Action Party (PAN) increased its popular support. In 1989, the new centre-left Party of the Democratic Revolution (PRD) was formed. While the PRD has faced electoral fraud and state repression, they are determined to bring real political democracy to Mexico.

Beginning in the 1980s, there has been a proliferation of popular organizations outside the structure of the PRI, demanding political change and social justice. It is clear to anyone who spends any time in Mexico that a growing percentage of the population wants the country to move towards a truly democratic system.[11]

Notes

1. Frederick Peterson, *Ancient Mexico*. New York: Capricorn Books, 1962; Eric Wolf, *Sons of the Shaking Earth*. Chicago: University of Chicago Press, 1970; Demetrio Sodi M., *The Great Cultures of Mesoamerica*. Mexico, D.F.: Panorama Editorial, 1991; Silvia Garza Tarazone, *La Mujer Mesoamericana*. Mexico, D.F.: Editorial Planeta Mexicana, 1991; Michael C. Meyer and William L. Sherman, *The Course of Mexican History*. New York: Oxford University Press, 1979, pp. 3-94; Hubert Herring, *A History of Latin America*. New York: Alfred A. Knopf, 1961, pp. 24-57; Ronald Wright, *Stolen Continents*. Toronto: Penguin Books, 1993, pp. 15-63; and Ramón Eduardo Ruiz, *Triumphs and Tragedy*. New York: W. W. Norton Co, 1992, pp. 15-37.

2. Wolf, *op. cit.*, pp. 152-175; Herring, *op. cit.*, pp. 127-134; Meyer and Sherman, *op. cit.*, pp. 95-129; Ruiz, *op. cit.*, pp. 38-53; and Wright, *op. cit.*, pp. 15-48.

3. Wolf, *op. cit.*, pp. 152-255; Wright, *op.cit.*, pp. 143-176; Maria Sten, *The Codices of Mexico*. Mexico, D.F.: Panorama Editorial, 1990; Michael D. Coe, *The Maya*. London: Thomas and Hudson, 1980; William T. Sanders and Barbara J. Price, *Mesoamerica; The Evolution of a Civilization*. New York: Random House, 1968; Victor Von Hagen, *The World of the Maya*. New York: Mentor Books, 1960; and Muriel Porter Weaver, *The Aztecs, Maya and their Predecessors*. New York: Academic Press, 1981.

4. Herring, *op. cit.*, 117-217; Meyer and Sherman, *op. cit.*, pp. 95-263; Ruiz, *op. cit.*, pp. 54-132; Eduardo Galeano, *Open Veins in Latin America*. New York: Monthly Review Books, 1973; and Eric R. Wolf, *Europe and the People Without History*. Berkeley: University of California Press, 1982.

5. Herring, *op. cit*, pp. 243-259; Ruiz, *op. cit.*, pp. 144-185; and Meyer and Sherman, *op. cit.*, pp. 264-297.

6. Herring, *op. cit.*, pp. 304-335; Meyer and Sherman, op cit., pp. 373-479; and Ruiz, *op. cit.*, pp. 185-268.

7. Ruiz, *op. cit.*, pp. 269-313; John Mason Hart, *Revolutionary Mexico*. Berkeley: University of California Press, 1987, pp. 1-186; and Leslie Bethell, *Mexico Since Independence*. Cambridge: Cambridge University Press, 1991.

8. Hart, *op. cit.*, pp. 237-369; Ruiz, *op. cit.*, pp. 314-338; Herring, *op. cit.*, pp. 354-362; Meyer and Sherman, *op. cit.*, pp. 511-566; and John Womack Jr., "The Mexican Revolution, 1910-1920," in Bethell, *op. cit.*, pp. 125-200.

9. Herring, *op. cit.*, pp. 363-375; Hart. *op. cit.*, pp. 348-279; Meyer and Sherman, *op. cit.*, pp. 523-595; Ruiz, *op. cit.*, pp. 339-385; and John Meyer, "Revolution and Reconstruction in the 1920s," in Bethell, *op. cit.*, pp. 201-240.

10. Herring, *op. cit.*, pp. 376-383; Ruiz, *op. cit.*, pp. 386-409; Meyer and Sherman, *op. cit.*, pp. 596-623; Allan Knight, "The Rise and Fall of Cárdenismo, 1930-1946," in Bethell, *op. cit., pp. 241-320; L. Vincent Padgett*, The Mexican Political System. Boston: Houghton-Mifflin, 1976, pp. 62-117; and Judith Hellman, *Mexico in Crisis*. New York: Holmes and Meier, 1988, pp. 33-58.

11. Padgett, *op. cit.*, pp. 62-117; Alan Riding, *Distant Neighbours*. New York: Vintage Books, 1984, pp. 66-93; Tom Barry, ed. *Mexico: A Country Guide*. Albuquerque: Inter-Hemispheric Education Resource Center, 1992, pp. 12-23; Martin D. Needler, *Mexican Politics: The Containment of Conflict*. New York: Praeger, 1990; and Stephen D. Morris, *Corruption and Politics in Contemporary Mexico*. Tuscaloosa: University of Alabama Press, 1991.

Chapter 2

THE ECONOMIC CHALLENGE

Like most former colonies, Mexico has had a very difficult time developing a national economy which provides employment for its population and a rising standard of living. It has always been part of the capitalist world, and there has never been a time when support for a socialist option was very strong. Thus Mexican development has ranged between two poles within the capitalist system, the open free market economy and state-directed development.

In Mexico, one approach to development is commonly called *Porfiriato*, after the administration of General Porfirio Díaz, who ruled Mexico between 1876 and 1911. Díaz governed Mexico with an iron hand, repressing strikes and the political left with the police and military, controlling the peasants through the *rurales*, the paramilitary state police, and supporting death squads. The present system of *personalismo* was really established during the *Porfiriato*.

The Mexican economy was developed by encouraging foreign investment, commercialization of agriculture, and emphasis on expanding trade with the United States. One of the results of this system of development was the entrenchment of gross inequalities in income, wealth, political influence, and status. The indigenous population, stripped of their land, fell to the level of absolute poverty.

Mexican economic development followed the Latin American pattern established after the wars for independence between 1810 and 1825. While formal colonialism ended, the economies followed the mercantile colonial pattern: the export of agricultural products and minerals, and the importation of manufactured goods.

Why did the colonial pattern of economic development persist? First, there was the widespread adoption of the ideology of free trade as advocated by local liberals and the imperial powers. Secondly, the Latin American ruling classes were tied to the mercantile order — they included agricultural and livestock exporters, local owners of mines, and the heads of merchant and financial houses. They captured state power as liberal reformers.

Today many Mexicans note the similarities in policies and state practices between *Porfiriato* and the neoliberal regimes of Miguel de la Madrid and Carlos Salinas de Gortari.[1]

The Dependency School

The second approach to Mexican development has been known as import substitution industrialization (ISI). This theory was primarily developed and promoted by the United Nations Economic Commission for Latin America (CEPAL) under the leadership of Raúl Prebisch. James M. Cypher has described this as a "semi-independent and humanistically Keynesian path to capitalist development."[2]

In the post World War II period the world capitalist economy expanded considerably. Within this system there was an international division of labour, roughly between the industrialized countries (the centre) and the less developed countries (the periphery). Prebisch noted that for Latin American nations, the foreign demand was for primary agricultural products and minerals, and this demand directed the development of their economies. The Latin American economies reacted to foreign market demands rather than concentrating on the demands of their own internal economies. In contrast, in their own development process, the highly industrialized countries all had a primary focus on developing their domestic market.

There were several characteristics of the Latin American economies that promoted this structure of development. To begin with, there was a shortage of capital, which led to an overdependence on extraction of natural products for export and importing direct foreign investment. Secondly, the structure of this trade created chronic balance of payments problems. Because the price and demand for natural products lagged behind that of manufactured goods, exports from the periphery did not provide enough revenue to pay for imports. The third problem had to do with the adoption of new technologies. In the industrialized countries, workers who were displaced by technology in primary sectors of the economy (farming, forestry, mining) were absorbed in secondary industry and the waged service sector. This was much less the case in Latin America, which had chronic unemployment and underemployment.

The Prebisch school of economic development also concluded that foreign direct investment caused many problems. With their imported technology and marketing skills, the transnational corporations (TNCs) blocked the development of local manufacturing. They imported intermediate and capital goods, which caused a shortage of foreign exchange, and managed to avoid paying taxes while getting government subsidies. The TNCs contributed to income inequality by developing enclaves of privileged workers, stimulated the market for foreign goods which had to be im-

ported, and employed inappropriate capital-intensive technology in countries which were experiencing high unemployment. Finally, the transnational corporations developed sophisticated systems of intracorporate trade
and transfer pricing which enabled them to avoid taxes and to take capital
out of the country.

The dominant liberal economic view is that countries best develop by
a system of free markets, free trade, the importation of foreign technology, and increased foreign investment. At the core of this theory of economic development is the notion of international comparative advantage:
countries produce those goods for which they are best suited. For the dependency school of economics based in Latin America, the free market
free trade theory seemed to be another ideological defence of the status
quo.

The dependency school pointed out that all of the industrialized First
World countries developed behind high tariffs with controls on imports
and state subsidies for private enterprise. For example, Great Britain
adopted free trade only after it was the dominant manufacturer of textiles
and steel. All the continental European countries developed behind high
tariffs. The United States introduced high tariffs right after independence
and raised them even higher during their rapid period of industrialization
following the Civil War. "Late development" in Japan and the Soviet Union
also took place behind high tariffs, accompanied by strict control of imports and exports, a virtual prohibition on foreign investment, and active
state promotion of development. Why shouldn't the underdeveloped countries in the periphery adopt a similar strategy?

Import Substitution Industrialization

Most of the Latin American countries began adopting an import substitution strategy during the 1930s. The Depression limited their exports
and their revenues, and they had no alternative but to begin producing
their own goods. Protectionism was also supported as a way to defend jobs.
But when World War II began this changed; economies began to boom, demand increased but imports were in short supply.[3]

During the 1940s, the Mexican government adopted the general import substitution policies widely in place in Latin America. Mexican businesses and industries were protected from foreign competition by high
tariffs, the prohibition of imports of many luxury goods, quotas on the imports of other goods, and a licensing system for imports. Imports which
were used to further economic development were given priority.

One of the key programs in the ISI development strategy is the control of foreign exchange and the flow of capital in and out of the country. For example, during World War II the Canadian government prohibited the export of capital and controlled capital flight by requiring permits. This was an essential part of mobilizing and directing the national economic development plan. However, Mexico did not adopt this policy. From the 1970s on, capital flight became a serious economic and political problem.

In 1941, the Mexican government passed the Law of Manufacturing Industries, which provided tax exemptions during their first five years of operation. Duties paid on imported machinery and materials used in production were rebated. The banking system remained private, but it received direction from the government. Lending was channelled to industrial development and commercial agriculture. Nacional Financiera, Sociedad Nacional de Credito (NAFINSA) was transformed into a state development bank.

Petróleos De México (PEMEX) was the most important state-owned enterprise. The expansion of the petroleum industry stimulated the private sector, which helped support it. In turn, low energy prices acted as a subsidy to industry.

Agriculture was expanded through a government-financed irrigation program. This expansion was also enabled by the use of high-yielding varieties of wheat and rice. Emphasis was placed on growing agricultural products for export, and in particular, fruit, tomatoes and strawberries for the U.S. market. The government supported the production of feed grains and legumes to feed cattle for export to the United States.

Foreign investment also increased during this period. While there existed state controls designed to preserve majority Mexican ownership, there were many ways to get around these restrictions. Business and industry benefitted from very low taxes on high personal incomes, interest earned from investment, and corporate profits. Low interest rates were maintained to stimulate investment.

Not too long ago, economists, politicians, and representatives of international organizations proclaimed the period of ISI development Mexico's "economic miracle." Between 1950 and 1974, Mexico's real growth (discounted for inflation) averaged a phenomenal 6.4 percent per year. The inflation rate over this period was only 3.1 percent. Real economic growth was twice the rate of increase in the population. The exchange rate was stable, standing at 12.5 Mexican pesos to the U.S. dollar.

The industrial sector grew very rapidly. In 1950, it accounted for 21.5 percent of gross domestic product; by 1970, it had reached 30.1 percent.

Between 1960 and 1980, the manufacturing sector grew an average 7.6 percent per year.

There was a shift from the country to the city. The percentage of people living in cities rose from 43.2 percent in 1950 to 60.4 percent in 1970. The labour force and employment also grew. The service sector expanded by well over 6 percent per year between 1960 and 1980. The dynamic economic growth provided new jobs and higher wages, and Mexico began developing a middle class. By 1980, for example, manufacturing workers in Mexico were earning about one-third the income of their American counterparts.

Capital was flowing into Mexico, and it was mainly foreign direct investment in productive enterprises. It was not speculative capital, and there was no problem with capital flight. While ISI industrialization is commonly associated with strong state involvement in the economy, this was not the case in Mexico. Public sector spending was limited, only accounting for around 2.5 percent of gross domestic product.[4]

It is common to mark a change in the Mexican economy with the first oil shock of 1973. President Luis Echeverría Alvarez (1970-76) attempted to raise personal and corporate taxes and introduce luxury and capital gains taxes. In a major confrontation with big business the president backed down. The government's budget deficit rose, and Echeverría made up the difference by rapidly increased government borrowing from abroad.

The other major change that happened after 1973 was the increase in the inflation rate. During the period from the end of World War II to 1972, the inflation rate averaged only 3.2 percent. Between 1973 and 1976 it averaged 16.7 percent and between 1977 and 1981 it averaged 23.8 percent.

A world recession began in 1974, the first since the end of World War II. The Echeverría administration sought to deal with the declining domestic market by shifting emphasis to production for export. In 1975, they offered a 75 percent subsidy on imported machinery and equipment that was to be used in industries manufacturing for export. Manufactured exports rose on average 35.3 percent per annum between 1970 and 1976.

With the drop in private investment, Echeverría expanded the role of the government in the economy, creating an additional 800 state-owned enterprises. This move was strongly opposed by big business. When he attempted to tax the rich, Mexican capitalists began taking their money out of the country. Borrowing abroad had increased the foreign debt to $19.6 billion by 1976. The annual balance of payments deficit on trade in goods and services rose to $3.2 billion. Rumours of devaluation encouraged more capital flight.

The financial crisis came near the end of 1976. Rather than openly de-value the peso, Echeverría decided to let it float on the international money market. It fell immediately by 50 percent. The International Mone-tary Fund intervened, and the Mexican government was forced to adopt a tough austerity program. As a result, there was a recession in 1976-77. But even in that relatively bad year, economic growth was 4 percent.

The crisis of 1976 marked the end of the ISI period. Between 1976 and the world economic crisis of 1981-82, the Mexican government tied its de-velopment strategy to increasing exports, particular petroleum products.[5]

The Failures of Import Substitution Industrialization

There were some major problems with import substitution industriali-zation in the Mexican context. As Judith Hellman and Edur Velasco Ar-regui have stressed, it was a "trickle-down" approach in a society which was dominated by a small, wealthy upper class and a privileged political elite. The benefits of economic growth were concentrated in the hands of the economic elite; they were to invest, and the workers at the bottom would benefit.[6]

In the period between the end of World War II and 1973, wages for workers rose slowly and did not keep pace with inflation. In contrast, prof-its rose dramatically. The gap between the rich and the poor greatly in-creased. As Hellman notes, in 1958 the income of the richest 5 percent of Mexicans was twenty-two times that of the poorest 10 percent. By 1980, the income of the top 5 percent was fifty times greater than that of the 10 per-cent at the bottom.

Taxation policy greatly benefited the rich and the corporations. Taxes on the rich were the lowest in Latin America and among the lowest in the world. The unwillingness of the government to tax the rich revealed who had power in Mexico.

Under the Mexican system of ISI, protection favoured those industries making end products, particularly in the consumer goods area. These com-panies preferred to import intermediate goods used in the production process. Backward linkages to new domestic manufacturers did not fully de-velop. The result was a serious balance of payments problem. As Velasco Ar-regui points out, by 1981 for every one dollar of manufactured goods exported Mexico spent six dollars to import intermediate and capital goods. When the government attempted to promote investment in the in-termediate and capital goods area, foreign transnational corporations moved in and secured dominant positions.

The Mexican ISI strategy also hurt basic agriculture. Assistance went to commercial agriculture and large estates. The vast majority of farmers who raised maize and beans were left out, and their economic status declined. Mexico began to depend heavily on imports of basic grains from the United States. While the percentage of people living in rural areas declined, the absolute number increased. Most of these people fell below the official poverty line.[7]

While many jobs were created, importing Western technology and joint ventures with foreign firms led to capital-intensive industrialization. Thus the rise in jobs did not keep up with the rise in population and the urbanization of the labour force. Low-income, non-waged jobs in the informal economy increased.

Those workers who were fortunate enough to be working for a state-owned enterprise or a large private industry benefitted from the existence of trade unions. In Mexico, unionized workers not only had higher wages, they also had fringe benefits and social security protection that nonunionized workers did not have. Thus, the minority of workers who were unionized became an elite sector of the Mexican working class, with middle-class economic status. There was an increasing gap in the standard of living between organized workers and those who were not.

The success of the ISI approach to development depended on the domestic capitalist class. James M. Cypher describes the Mexican capitalist class at this time as still fundamentally a merchant capitalist class. They were concentrated in trade, banking and finance, mining, and landed estates. This class of capitalist is characterized by the "rentier ethos." It is primarily concerned with raising the price, rather than entrepreneurship or improving its product. In Mexico, the dominant capitalists were commonly referred to as the "bankers' alliance," indicating the reality of conglomerate alliances, based in family groups. They were more than willing to concentrate their investment in government bonds with high interest rates rather than in more risky capital ventures.

In the 1970s, much of the risk investment in Mexico was carried out by the state. There is nothing inherently wrong with using state enterprises for economic development. Japan, South Korea and Taiwan have used this approach with dynamic results. But Mexico has a different political culture. Given the one party political system with its tradition of patronage and nepotism, it was inevitable that these industries would be less efficient than they might have been. Their primary goal was not to maximize profit but to fulfill other social goals.

In the end, ISI came to a halt in Mexico because of the gross inequalities in income and wealth. The vast majority of Mexicans simply did not have enough income to buy most consumer goods. The need was there, but the "effective demand" of the domestic market was greatly limited.[8]

PEMEX and the PRI

Petroleum was first discovered near Tampico in 1901. It was developed primarily by British and American corporations. Following the Mexican Revolution, the Constitution of 1917 proclaimed that all subsoil mineral rights belonged to the Mexican people. The U.S. government intervened directly to support the oil companies in their political disputes with the Mexican government.

The issue came to a head during the Presidency of Lázaro Cárdenas. In 1935 he supported the formation of the Mexican Oil Workers Union (STPRM) and backed them in their attempt to get a contract with the oil companies. The union took their grievance to the Federal Board of Conciliation and Arbitration, which found that profits were very high and that the wages and salaries the companies were paying were the lowest in the world. The board ordered a 27 percent increase in wages, and when the companies refused to follow the directive, Cárdenas nationalized them, and Petróleos De México (PEMEX) was born. This was one of the most popular government actions in the history of Mexico; March 18, the day of the takeover, is celebrated as a national holiday.

The STPRM was originally a militant union with radicals in leadership positions. When they went on strike in 1940, President Cárdenas used the army to crush it. In 1949, President Miguel Alémán also used the military to break another strike. Thugs were used to bring the leadership under the control of the PRI.

There was no clear policy direction for PEMEX. In 1954, President Adolfo Ruiz-Cortinez declared that PEMEX was to provide a social service to Mexicans, low priced petroleum products to help stimulate the economy. But with prices fixed well below world prices, PEMEX could not earn enough profits to conduct needed exploration.

PEMEX was closely linked to the state party. PRI politicians demanded that their friends be hired. Contracts were granted to friends of the government without bids. Gasoline stations were granted as a part of PRI patronage.

The PRI government linked the STPRM closely to the party and the state. Beginning in 1946, the union received a rakeoff of 2 percent of the value of all PEMEX contracts. Union bureaucrats were put on the boards of private firms which had contracts with PEMEX. PEMEX even paid for all the expenses of the union leadership. In 1959, STPRM began to openly sell jobs with PEMEX, with company approval. In an arrangement with the company, "ghost workers" (known in Mexico as "aviators") were regularly paid salaries although they did no work. The union also received 5 percent of the salary of PEMEX employees. PEMEX became the most important institution in the PRI patronage system.

In the 1950s, Joaquín Hernández Galacia became the leader of the STPRM. "La Quina" (The Boss) modernized the system of patronage and corruption. He establish a string of businesses owned by the union: farms, cattle ranches, factories, grocery stores, movie theatres, bars, and night clubs. Its own companies were guaranteed 50 percent of PEMEX's subcontracting business. La Quina established a dual system for work: PEMEX employees with permanent jobs, and casual employees who were totally dependent on the union hall for work. La Quina used the casual workers as his private army to intimidate opponents and control union meetings.

The STPRM was part of the Confederation of Mexican Workers (CTM) which was officially linked to the ruling PRI. STPRM officials also served the PRI as Senators, members of the Chamber of Deputies, state governors, and municipal officials.

La Quina was ruthless in dealing with his opponents. Thugs were widely used. Heriberto Kehoe, who became general secretary of the union in 1976, tried to break part of the union away from La Quina's control; he was assassinated in 1977. Kehoe's successor, Oscar Torres Pancardo, was assassinated in 1983.

While the STPRM developed into the most corrupt union in Mexico, its employees were the country's highest paid blue collar workers. PEMEX created a tremendous number of jobs. In the 1970s, it contributed over one-third of the state revenues, and petroleum was by far the most important export.[9]

The Oil Boom

In May 1972, PEMEX revealed that it had discovered a new field of oil near Villahermosa, Tabasco, on the Gulf of Mexico. There had been so little investment in the industry that in 1973, at the time of the first OPEC oil price increase, Mexico was importing 100,000 barrels of oil a day from Venezuela. Between 1972 and 1977, oil exploration increased, and Mexico's proven oil reserves rose to 72 billion barrels, ranking Mexico fifth in the world.[10]

President Echeverría played down the new oil discoveries. He feared U.S. domination of the industry and increasing ties and dependence on the U.S. economy. Oil was a very touchy nationalist political issue. He did not want Mexico to go the way of Venezuela and become totally dependent on oil as an export. This approach changed when President José López Portillo took office in 1976.

López Portillo appointed a friend of his, Jorge Díaz Serrano, as director general of PEMEX. He was a wealthy oil contractor with extensive investments in the United States and Mexico. He had even been a business partner with George Bush. With a new group of technocrats he tried to put PEMEX on a more businesslike basis. While the official policy of the new government was to extract only 1.1 million barrels of oil per day, Díaz Serrano believed that this resource should be developed and exported as quickly as possible.

In 1979, López Portillo launched his Industrial Development Plan to diversify industry, decentralize its development, and to foster exports. New ports were to be built. A range of incentives were given to industries, particularly those which developed outside Mexico City and Guadalajara. Additional tax breaks were given to corporations. Portillo's "alliance for profits" declared that his priority was friendship with business rather than social reform. Unlike Echeverría, he was unwilling to try to tax corporations or the rich, and he borrowed heavily abroad.

But the strategy did not work. Trade with the United States became more important than ever before, and was the primary source of investment in the oil industry, and the primary market for oil and natural gas. In 1976, petroleum products accounted for 16 percent of exports; by 1981, 75 percent. Oil production steadily rose to four million barrels per day by 1982.

Between 1978 and 1981, economic growth rose to 8.5 percent annually. Alan Riding, then a correspondent in Mexico City, notes that "the mood of euphoria in the country was fed by the 1979 oil price hike, which doubled PEMEX's export earnings and stimulated further exploration."[11]

There was a dramatic expansion of business contracts with PEMEX. The American firm, Brown and Root, became the favourite company for exploration. As Judith Teichman notes in her study of the period, the Monterrey group of Mexican businessmen, most hostile to Echeverría's populist program, benefitted greatly during the López Portillo administration. Patronage expanded.[12] Riding argues that the "massive corruption at all levels of the monopoly" cost the country billions of dollars in lost revenues. Businessmen and politicians established large bank accounts and real estate investments abroad.[13] But who cared? It was black gold. No manufacturing was required, just extract and sell. A one-time bonanza of riches.

However, by 1978, manufactured exports began to drop. There was a crisis in agriculture and even food exports began to drop. The oil boom had resulted in an overvalued peso which hurt traditional exports. The growing balance of payments deficit was offset by additional foreign borrowing.

Even the oil industry faced a balance of payments problem. PEMEX imported machinery, equipment and technology to develop the oil industry. PEMEX borrowed heavily; its debt rose to $22 billion by 1982. As Riding recalls, "foreign bankers would literally line up outside Díaz Serrano's office for an opportunity to lend money."

Within Mexico, there was opposition to the petrolization strategy. Nongovernment economists stressed that the petroleum and petrochemical industries were very capital intensive. A great deal of investment is required to create a single job. By channelling investment into this sector, the government was neglecting Mexico's more labour intensive sectors. Despite the massive investment, relatively few jobs were being created and unemployment and underemployment were rising.

The president changed Article 27 of the constitution to give PEMEX rights over all of the nation's land. Peasants found PEMEX taking their land, destroying it with their equipment, and polluting it. They organized demonstrations, blockades and occupations. The president responded with the army.

The petroleum industry, while Mexican-owned, was creating the familiar enclave zones of development associated with transnational corporations. Wages and salaries were much higher than in the country as a whole, and those who found jobs had a relatively high standard of living. In contrast, social conditions for those living in Tabasco near the oil enclaves were deplorable.

In June 1979, a well in the Gulf of Campeche blew out of control and began dumping 30,000 barrels of oil a day into the Gulf of Mexico. This went on for over nine months. Oil drifted as far as Texas. The environmental disaster was blamed on shoddy work by the drilling contractor, Sedco International, an American firm, and inadequate PEMEX supervision. Environmentalists and nationalists vigorously objected to PEMEX's policy of burning natural gas at oil drilling sites. The political left denounced petrolization as an unjust economic strategy which promoted inequality.

The Debt Crisis

The economic crisis that hit Mexico was not just the result of poor government planning. Owners of capital throughout the world were worrying about high inflation rates and low profits. The Organization for European Economic Co-operation and Development (OECD) sponsored a study headed by Paul McCracken, which was released in 1977. It advocated high interest rates, restraint on spending by governments, cuts in social programs, and a deliberate increase in the levels of unemployment. What was needed was "the democratic disciplinary state" to fight inflation and raise profits. The problem, as the authors saw it, was that the ordinary people had expectations which were too high.

In September 1979, the World Bank and the International Monetary Fund met at Belgrade, Yugoslavia. Paul Volcker, chairman of the U.S. Federal Reserve Bank, was instructed to undertake a tight money policy to avoid a run on the U.S. dollar. On October 6, 1979, the bank began to raise interest rates. Throughout the world, interest rates steadily rose to peak, in 1981, at almost 20 percent. Mexico's interest payments on the foreign debt rose proportionally.

The new policy direction was reinforced by the election of Margaret Thatcher in Great Britain and Ronald Reagan in the United States. They advocated a right-wing monetarist approach to inflation. By 1980, the high interest rate policies of Western governments had succeeded in provoking the deepest recession the world had seen in half a century. The industrialized countries responded by cutting back on their purchases from the Third World.[14]

By the spring of 1981, the world recession had resulted in a glut of oil on the international market. PEMEX announced new prices for oil which undercut the floor set by OPEC. Prices continued to fall. Oil revenues dropped. The Mexican government continued to borrow abroad to cover the shortfall, which was $6 billion in 1981. In 1982, they agreed to a sale to the U.S. Strategic Reserve that had prices as low as $25 a barrel, down from $38 in 1981. In August 1982, the Mexican government announced that it could not make its debt payments and declared a moratorium.

By 1982, Mexico's debt had risen to $82 billion, around 60 percent of the gross domestic product. In August, Minister of Finance Jesús Silva Herzog flew to Washington to meet with the U.S. government. He was there to beg for relief. Paul Volcker, chairman of the Federal Reserve Board, helped him secure around $6.5 billion in emergency funds. The Bank for International Settlements (BIS) in Switzerland began to intervene to try to protect the investments of its members, the central banks.

The International Monetary Fund (IMF) sent a delegation to Mexico City to discuss the request from the government for $3.9 billion in additional credits. Mexico rescheduled $19.7 billion worth of loans, but on tough terms, 1.75 percent above the world prime rate, the London Inter Bank Offered Rate (LIBOR).

Judith Teichman points out that, during the López Portillo administration big business had profited handsomely. They received extensive government subsidies and had paid little in the way of taxes. Corporate concentration increased while the banks made profits, and the rich moved their money out of the country.

The peso declined by 75 percent in 1982, and economic growth came to a halt. Plants shut down and unemployment rose. The rate of inflation rose to 100 percent per year. President López Portillo was forced to do something.

On September 1, 1982, the president suspended foreign exchange operations for the first time in history. Strict foreign exchange controls were announced. All foreign currency accounts were frozen, and the private banks were nationalized. The president blamed the economic crisis on the rich who had taken their capital out of the country, aided by the banks. "We cannot stand with our arms crossed while they tear out our entrails," he proclaimed.

As John Dillon notes, the U.S. banks were relieved by the nationalization. The private Mexican banks might have gone bankrupt. And with the state now owning the banks, it was much more likely that the foreign investors would collect their debts.[15]

At the height of the crisis, President López Portillo declared "I will defend the peso like a dog." When he left office he built a huge mansion on a hill in Cuajimalpa, a northwest district of Mexico City. Mexicans refer to it as "the hill of the dog."

The Structural Adjustment Program

Mexico was forced to pay a heavy price for the temporary bailout. The IMF imposed a structural adjustment program, as demanded by the international bankers. Its objective was to change the direction of the Mexican economy from import substitution industrialization, with its emphasis on developing the internal market, to export promotion for both manufacturing and agriculture. Increasing exports would allow Mexico to increase foreign exchange which would then be used to pay down the foreign debt, with interest.

The Mexican government was forced to abandon the constitutional rule which prohibited foreign corporations from owning more than 49 percent of a Mexican operation. They agreed to begin a process of privatizing state-owned corporations, join the General Agreements on Tariffs and Trade (GATT), reduce tariffs, and eliminate import quotas and licenses. The government agreed to promote foreign investment in export industries, and they agreed to debt equity swaps, where bank debt was to be traded for foreign-owned equity in productive enterprises.

The IMF and the international banks also instructed the Mexican government to cut government spending, particularly on state enterprises and social programs. The Mexican government agreed to implement wage controls, beginning with freezing the minimum wage. Prices for government goods and services would be raised. A high interest rate policy was implemented. Price increases were announced for basic foods like tortillas and bread, previously subsidized as part of an anti-poverty program.

President Miguel de la Madrid (1982-1988) announced a plan for his six year administration. The first two years would be a period of economic austerity, then there would be two years of financial and economic stabilization, and then he promised two years of economic growth.

But de la Madrid was hesitant to abandon the state-directed policies of the post World War II period. He did not follow IMF orders to immediately remove import controls and subsidies; they were phased out gradually.

Still, the impact on the mass of Mexican people was dramatic. The standard of living fell, and people were angry. In 1983, the PRI suffered a series of electoral defeats, as the people turned to the National Action Party (PAN) in desperation. In response, the PRI once again resorted to electoral fraud and political repression.[16]

The Mexican economy continued to contract. Exports to the United States declined. Revenues from oil exports continued to fall. Interest rates remained high, resulting in high foreign debt payments. The de la Madrid administration was shaken by the 1985 earthquake in Mexico City, its inability to function in the crisis, and the rise of political opposition, particularly at the local level.

A key point for the de la Madrid administration came with the negotiations with the IMF in 1986. A new agreement was reached, which included a $1.9 billion loan from the World Bank. Export orientated development became the central policy of the government.

Trade liberalization accelerated. In 1986, the government joined the GATT. New legislation promoted the *maquiladora* free trade zones along the U.S. border. Foreign investment was encouraged by the promise of low wages, deregulation, and low taxes. Government incentives were given to companies in the export business.

Inflation rose to 150 percent in 1987, and this stifled investment. The de la Madrid administration established the Pact of Solidarity (PECE), which was signed by business organizations and the PRI-dominated organizations representing labour and peasants. It allowed the government to set wages and try to control prices. The government continued with its policies of privatization, deregulation, and reduction of tariffs.[17]

Political opposition to the government's policies increased as the standard of living of the large majority of Mexicans fell steadily and unemployment continued to rise. Within the PRI the Movement of Democratic Renovation (or Democratic Current) was created, calling for a return to a state-directed economic policy, internal democracy, and an end to electoral fraud. At the party's convention in March 1987, this dissident group was defeated and then expelled.

The stage was set for the "second earthquake," the presidential election of July 1988.

Salinas Takes Office

Miguel de la Madrid chose Carlos Salinas de Gortari to be his successor as president. Salinas had been the Minister of Budget and Planning in his cabinet and had been the author of the new policy of economic liberalism.

Salinas was opposed for president by Cuauhtémoc Cárdenas, the leader of the Democratic Current, and the son of Lázaro Cárdenas, Mexico's most popular president. Cárdenas formed a centre-left coalition (the National Democratic Front or FDN) with a number of small parties. The National Action Party (PAN) also selected a popular candidate for president, Manuel Clouthier.

The campaign was a popular uprising against the one-party state and the government's approach to the economic crisis. Huge political rallies were held for Cárdenas. The PRI was able to retain control of the federal government only through a massive electoral fraud.

When Carlos Salinas assumed the office of president on December 1, 1988, he had to deal with the economic crisis and the fact that he had no legitimacy. Public opinion polls showed that 90 percent of Mexicans believed that he was in office because of fraud. He also had to restore the confidence of foreign investors.

Salinas acted quickly to demonstrate that he was in firm control. He launched a military attack on La Quina, head of the petroleum workers union, arrested him and some of his cohorts, and named a successor to head the union. La Quina had refused to endorse the PRI candidate for president, and oilworkers had voted heavily for Cárdenas.

Salinas also appointed tough PRI stalwarts to key government jobs, people like Fernando Gutiérrez Barrios and Miguel Nazar Haro, who were widely known to be abusers of human rights. This was seen as a warning to the political opposition. The military and police were used to crush strikes. The PRD was controlled through more sophisticated electoral fraud. And Salinas formed an alliance with the PAN in order to get his economic policies through the legislature with minimal opposition.

The *Wall Street Journal* noted on September 25, 1989, that the use of the military rather than negotiations with unions and political opponents "drew cheers from the sacadolares," those who had taken their capital out of the country. The president had to restore business confidence.[18]

The new president also had to deal with the debt problem. In 1989, Mexico was expected to pay $10 billion in interest and $5 billion in principal. U.S. Secretary of the Treasury, Nicholas Brady, put forth a plan to renegotiate the debt of all the Third World debtor countries, provided they opened their doors to foreign investment. In April 1989, the Salinas administration began negotiating with the foreign bankers. They also signed a "letter of intent" with the IMF promising carry out further liberal economic reforms.

The negotiations with the foreign bankers carried on into 1990. Some banks accepted a 35 percent reduction in value of their loans to Mexico. Others agreed to lower their interest rates. Few offered additional loans. But the Brady Plan agreement seemed to give the Salinas administration international credibility, and the crisis was used by the Mexican elite to argue that the country had no alternative but to adopt the liberal export-orientated development model.[19]

Carlos Salinas had always advocated economic liberalization. As president he carried on with the policies he had started while in the de la Madrid administration. In May 1989, all regulations on foreign investment were repealed. Petrochemical companies were reclassified as secondary manufacturing to escape the constitutional requirement that the oil industry be nationally owned and controlled. The pact for wage and price controls (PECE) was renewed.

In April 1990 Salinas announced that the banks would be reprivatized. They were sold to groups of powerful Mexican capitalists. Tariffs were cut to rates below those demanded by the IMF. In 1991, the constitution was changed to permit private and even foreign ownership of *ejido* lands, communal farm lands controlled by the indigenous population.

Tax reforms were designed to increase profits and investment. The tax on business income was reduced from 42 percent in 1988 to 35 percent in 1991. The nominal taxes on those in the upper income bracket were reduced from 60.5 percent to 35 percent. Additional revenue would be raised by expanding the value added (or goods and services) tax, first set at 15 percent and then reduced to 10 percent. A new 2 percent corporate asset tax was introduced to raise taxes from small and middle-sized companies.

Deregulation was introduced in the areas of transportation, communication, petrochemicals and fisheries. In the financial sector, Salinas abolished controls on interest rates and maturities for banks in March 1989. Interest rate subsidies to Mexican development banks were reduced.

Privatization of state-owned enterprises was pushed. In 1982, there were 1,155; by 1993 the number had fallen to around 200. The large, important state corporations were bought by the rich family conglomerates and foreign investors. Many of the smaller companies were just shut down.

The standard structural adjustment packages called for drastic cuts in government expenditures. Salinas agreed. Government involvement in supporting the incomes of small farmers through the National Basic Food Company (CONASUPO) ended, and the subsidies for food for low income families were also cut.

Cuts in government spending transformed the budget deficit from 12.5 percent in 1988 to a surplus of 0.7 pcecent and a balanced budget in 1994. State expenditures for nonfinancial matters fell from 45 percent of GDP in 1982 to 25 percent in 1991.

Interest rates were maintained at very high levels to attract foreign capital and to stem the rate of inflation. All Mexicans seemed to agree that the most important achievement of the Salinas administration was the reduction in the rate of inflation. It fell from 180 percent in 1988 to only seven percent in 1994.[20]

In March 1990, it was learned that the Salinas government had asked the United States for a North American Free Trade Agreement (NAFTA). This proposal was designed to tie Mexico's economy to the United States, entrench the new policies of economic liberalism, and to encourage Mexican capitalists to reinvest in Mexico.

The Salinas development strategy emphasized Mexico's international comparative advantage, as the liberal economists like to put it. What is that advantage? Low wages, low costs of production, and cheap energy.

Many stress the role that the IMF and the international banks had in transforming Mexico's development strategy. But within Mexico they had their allies in the technocratic elite in the PRI.

Within the PRI there are *camarillas* or family political cliques which wield great power. These are the patron-client centres of power that are so characteristic of the Mexican political system. Ideologically, they have links to the two streams in the PRI: the Cárdenas tendency, which supports populist, nationalist policies and the dominant faction, associated with President Miguel Aléman (1946-1952). The latter group has been dominant since the defeat of Miguel Henriquez Guzmán in the election of 1952. Its ties are to the big capitalists.[21]

Carlos Salinas had ties to the Aléman clique through Antonio Ortiz Mena, his uncle, who was Treasury Minister between 1958 and 1970. But his opening to power was his membership in the de la Madrid *camarilla*.

All Mexico's political leaders have had close ties with political leaders of the past, extensive family connections, and career loyalties. But education is also very important. Within Mexico, the shift to liberal economics has led to a decline in the status of the Autonomous National University of Mexico (UNAM), which has a Marxist, political economy and nationalist tradition. Instead, the private institutions teaching economic liberalism have increased in prestige: The College of Mexico, Autonomous Technological Institute of Mexico City, and the Technological Institute of Higher Studies in Monterrey.

In recent years, many of the technocratic elite in the PRI have received their higher education in the United States. They have chosen the high prestige private American universities for the wealthy, which teach liberal economics. The most popular have been Harvard, Yale, MIT, Stanford and the University of Chicago.

President Miguel de la Madrid was educated in economics at Harvard University. Carlos Salinas has a doctorate in economics and public administration from Harvard. Ernesto Zedillo has a doctorate in economics from Yale. Among the key figures in the Salinas cabinet and inner circle, Yale's graduate program in economics dominated. This trend is symbolic of Mexico's shift from being part of the Latin American community to economic integration with the United States.

The political and economic establishment in North America, as well as the international lending organizations, have all exuberantly praised the past two Mexican administrations for rejecting state-directed development and adopting neoliberal policies. They have been enthusiastic in their promotion of the North American Free Trade Agreement. No longer is there any mention of the "Mexican miracle" of import substitution industrialization.

Within Mexico, the business organizations which at one time were quite hostile to the PRI became its strongest supporters. However, the liberal economic reforms have been hard on the majority of the population. Their standard of living has dropped, their working hours have increased and their daily lives have become much more difficult. While Mexicans were pleased with the drop in the rate of inflation, their support for the other programs, even NAFTA, has been less enthusiastic.

Notes

1. See Alan Riding, *Distant Neighbors*. New York: Vintage Books, 1989, pp. 22-41; Donald Hodges and Ross Gandy, *Mexico 1910-1982: Reform or Revolution?* London: Zed Press, 1983, pp. 5-27; Herbert Herring, *A History of Latin America*. New York: Alfred A. Knopf, 1961, pp. 338-353; and Ramón Eduardo Ruiz, *Triumphs and Tragedy*. New York: W. W. Norton, 1992, pp. 410-466.

2. For a discussion of the dependency school see James M. Cypher, *State and Capital in Mexico*. Boulder: Westview Press, pp. 5-39; Judith A. Teichman, *Policymaking in Mexico: From Boom to Crisis*. Boston: Allen and Unwin, 1988; Eliana Cardosa and Ann Helwege, *Latin America's Economy*. Cambridge, Mass.: MIT Press, 1992, pp. 55-72; Miguel Sandoval Lara and Francisco Arroyo García, "The Mexican Economy at the End of the Century," *CEPAL Review*, No. 42, December 1990, pp. 195-205; and John W. Warnock, *The Politics of Hunger*. Toronto: Methuen, 1987, pp. 59-79.

3. See Celso Furtado, *Economic Development of Latin America*. Cambridge: Cambridge University Press, 1970, and Andre Gunder Frank, *Capitalism and Underdevelopment in Latin America*. New York: Monthly Review, 1969.

4. See Jorge Eduardo Navarrete, "Mexico's Stabilization Policy," *CEPAL Review*, No. 41, August 1990, pp. 31-44; Teichman, *op. cit.*, pp. 23-43; Cypher, *op. cit.*, pp. 5-15; and Diana Alarcon and Terry McKinley, "Beyond Import Substitution," *Latin American Perspectives*, Vol. 19, Spring 1992, pp. 72-87.

5. Nora Lustig, "Equity and Growth in Mexico," in Simon Teitel, ed., *Towards a New Economic Development Strategy for Latin America*. Washington: Inter-American Development Bank, 1992, pp. 219-258.

6. Judith Adler Hellman, *Mexico in Crisis*. New York: Holmes and Meier, 1988, pp. 59-102; Cardosa and Helweg, *op. cit.*, pp.l 84-99; and Edur Velasco Arregui, "Industrial Restructuring in Mexico During the 1980s," in Ricardo Grinspun and Maxwell A. Cameron, eds., *The Political Economy of North American Free Trade*. Montreal: McGill-Queens University Press, 1993, pp. 163-175.

7. See David Barkin, *Distorted Development; Mexico in the World Economy*. Boulder: Westview Press, 1990, pp. 11-40.

8. See also Sylvia Maxwell, *Governing Capital*. Ithaca: Cornell University Press, 1990, pp. 165-192; and Robert E. Looney, "Mechanisms of Mexican Economic Growth," *Journal of Social, Political and Economic Studies*, Vol. 12, Spring 1987, pp. 77-94.

9. Dan La Botz, *Mask of Democracy*. Boston: South End Press, 102-113.

10. For a good overview of this period see Teichman, *op. cit.*

11. Riding, *op. cit.*, p. 166.

12. Teichman, *op. cit.*, pp. 69-74.

13. Riding, *op. cit.*, pp. 168-169.

14. John W. Warnock, *Free Trade and the New Right Agenda*. Vancouver: New Star Books, 1988, pp. 27-40; and Joyce Kolko, *Restructuring the World Economy*. New York: Pantheon Books, pp. 17-54.

15. John Dillon et al, *Debt Bondage of Self Reliance*. Toronto: GATT-Fly, 1985, pp. 31-40; and Manuel Pastor Jr. and Gary A. Dymski, "Debt Crisis and Class Conflict in Latin America," *Capital and Class*, No. 43, Spring 1991, pp. 203-231.

16. See Teichman, *op. cit.*, pp. 111-126; Hellman, *op.cit.*, pp. 218-230; and David Barkin, *Distorted Development*. Boulder: Westview Press, 1990, pp. 99-111.

17. Clement Ruiz Duran, "Mexico: The Transfer Problem, Profits and Welfare," in David Felix, ed. *Debt and Transfiguration*. London: M.E. Sharpe, 1990, pp. 171-196.

18. Matt Moffett, "Mexico's Capital Flight Still Rakes Economy Despite the Brady Plan," *Wall Street Journal*, September 25, 1989, pp. A-1, 10.

19. Eliot Kalter and Hoe Ee Khor, "Mexico's Experience with Adjustment," *Finance and Development*, Vol. 27, September 1990, pp. 22-25; Mohamed A. El-Erian, "Mexico's Commercial Bank Financing Package," *Finance and Development*, Vol. 27, September 1990, pp. 26-27.

20. For the structural adjustment program of Salinas, see Judith Teichman, "The Mexican State and the Political Implications of Economic Restructuring," *Latin American Prespectives*, Vol. 19, Spring 1992, pp. 88-104; Alejandro Alvarez Bejar and Gabriel Mendoza Pichardo, *Mexico 1988-1991: Un Ajuste Economico Exitoso?* Mexico City: Universidad Nacional Autonoma de México, 1991; Nora Lustig, *Mexico: The Remaking of an Economy*. Washington: The Brookings Institution, 1992; and Inter-American Development Bank, *Economic and Social Progress in Latin America*. Washington: IADB, 1992, pp. 130-136.

21. For an analysis of the Salinas *camarillas*, see Roderic A. Camp, "Camarillas in Mexican Politics: The Case of the Salinas Cabinet," *Mexican Studies/Extudios Mexicanos*, Vol. 6, Winter 1990, pp. 85-107; and Miguel Ángel Centeno, *Democracy within Reason; Technocratic Revolution in Mexico*. University Park: The Pennsylvania State University, 1994, pp. 157-171.

Chapter 3

MAQUILA MEXICO

The rapid industrialization of Mexico under the policy of import substitution mainly benefitted the larger industrial cities in central Mexico. The oil boom brought economic change to the states on the Gulf of Mexico while the northern states bordering the U.S. were left out of this development.

A programme to stimulate their development was created in the early 1960s by President López Mateos, but nothing much came of this. Further stimulus came in 1964, when the U.S. government cancelled the *bracero* program which gave Mexicans permits to travel to the United States to do farm work.

At about the same time, a Mexican government delegation headed by Octaviano Campos-Salas, Minister of Industry and Commerce, visited the Far East, where they saw the development of the export processing zones which were attracting U.S. investment for assembly manufacturing.

In 1962, the U.S. government had passed sections 806 and 807 of the U.S. customs code which facilitated overseas manufacturing by American firms. American manufacturers could export partly fabricated products to low-wage countries for labour-intensive assembly. Then they were to reimport the product for final manufacturing in the United States. Customs duties would be added only to the value added in the foreign country.

In Mexico the term *maquiladora* is used to describe these in-bond processing plants under U.S. trade law. The Spanish term *maquila* means the portion of the farmer's corn the miller keeps for grinding the corn.

In 1965, changes were made in Mexican and American laws to permit the establishment of the Border Industrial Program (BIP). Originally, there was to be a zone for such manufacturing within 20 kilometres of the border, however, in reality, the BIP created an enormous free trade zone all along the Mexican border. The regulations allowed foreign and Mexican manufacturers to import raw materials, parts, components, machinery, tooling equipment, and everything else needed for the transformation or processing, assembly and finishing of products to be entirely exported.

The advantage that the Mexican government promoted was access to inexpensive labour located close to the United States. The Export Processing Zones in less developed countries normally offered corporations exemption from local taxation, freedom from any foreign currency exchange regulations, unrestricted repatriation of profits, and exemption from any financial reporting requirements. In many of the zones, the governments even built the factories and leased them at subsidized rates to the corporations. Other government subsidies included infrastructure support, training workers, and low public utilities rates. The Mexican government offered many of these incentives in the BIP.[1]

In his study on Mexico in the global economy, Harley Shaiken notes that in the 1980s, the electronic industry identified other significantly lower costs of production in the Mexican border zones. Electricity rates were only about 33 percent of U.S. rates, water 60 percent, natural gas 65 percent. Construction costs were between 33 and 50 percent, and land and building leasing costs were 50 to 80 percent of U.S. rates. Another unofficial benefit was the absence of Mexican government enforcement of environmental and health and safety regulations.[2]

The Mexican government hoped that U.S. plants would locate in Mexico rather than in Asia. The government representatives from the U.S. states hoped for "twin plant" development in U.S. cities located near the Mexican border.

Both the Mexican and American governments hoped that the development of the BIP would provide needed employment in Mexico and reduce the number of Mexicans illegally entering the United States every year. The Mexican government hoped that the BIP would attract the large American corporations that would bring new technology and train Mexican workers. The same hope is being expressed for the North American Free Trade Agreement (NAFTA).

Offshore Manufacturing

The move towards offshore manufacturing began in the 1960s as a reaction to the decline in profits in manufacturing in the advanced industrialized countries. For example, *The Economist* recorded that the rate of return on capital in the European Economic Community had fallen from 14 percent in 1960 to below 5 percent in 1975, and then fell further to only 4 percent in 1980. Bennett Harrison and Barry Bluestone report that the rate of return for U.S. corporations peaked in 1965 at 9.8 percent, declined to 4.5 percent in 1974, rose to 6 percent in 1977, and then fell to 4.5 percent in 1980. Manufacturing abroad where labour costs were lower was seen by companies as one method of restoring profitability.[3]

In her study of the *maquila* industries in Mexico, Patricia Wilson stresses the key role of lower labour costs. Export processing zones (EPZs) were developed first in Hong Kong and Puerto Rico, then expanded in South Korea, Taiwan, Singapore, Malaysia and the Philippines in the 1960s.[4]

The first industries which moved to the EPZs were textiles, garment, shoe, and toy production. They utilized very low-wage women workers. The next major industry to move overseas was the electronics industry. It also utilized primarily women workers. U.S. corporations believed this strategy was necessary in order to compete with Japanese production, which had ready access to women workers in Southeast Asia, and European production, which had access to cheap migrant labour from North Africa and the Middle East.

Similar assembly operations lagged in the Western hemisphere. EPZs were developed in the late 1960s in Haiti, which claimed to have the lowest wages in the Caribbean. In the 1980s, the strategy of developing EPZs spread to the Dominican Republic, Barbados, Jamaica, Trinidad and Tobago, and the Central American republics.

Wilson argues that the lack of development of assembly operations in Latin America was primarily due to the economic strategy of import substitution. Trade unions had developed in these countries and they had significant influence on government policy. There was strong political opposition to a development strategy which stressed very low wages for manufacturing for an export market.

In addition to low labour costs, the key to success of the EPZ is a docile work force. Wilson claims that the manufacturing-for-export policy was most successful in Hong Kong, Taiwan, Singapore and South Korea because these governments "maintained an authoritarian control over the labour force."

The British colonial government maintained Hong Kong as a free market zone where there was no minimum wage and strict regulations on trade unions. The trade unions that did exist were company unions controlled by the Kuomintang Party. Labour legislation banned general unions, sympathy strikes, and political strikes. Public policies subsidized the private cost of labour through training programs, social assistance payments and subsidized housing.

In Singapore, the government "routed Communist influence in the labour movement and established a single officially recognized (and controlled) union." In 1968, the one-party state passed laws which took away labour rights that had been established when Singapore was a British colony.

Taiwan was a right-wing military dictatorship which operated under martial law between 1947 and 1986. They followed the Japanese model of state capitalism but established many EPZs. Trade unions were outlawed and the police and military were regularly used to repress labour demands.

South Korea was also dominated by the military. With the support of the U.S. government, authoritarian governments crushed the political left and trade unions. The military and police were regularly used to deal with labour problems. The development of EPZs came after the military coup in 1961.

The latest entry into the field of manufacturing for export is the People's Republic of China. While the Communist Party continues to direct and control overall economic development strategy, it is simultaneously introducing free market pricing and private industry. In 1993, China had the lowest wages in manufacturing in east Asia, averaging only 24 cents per hour. The dictatorship also controls trade unions and prohibits strikes. In the toy industry, for example, women typically work a 14-hour day, often seven days a week, and are paid around $21 per month.[5]

The development of the border industrialization program in Mexico was hindered by the fact that in 1970, wages were more than double those of the Asian countries mentioned above. For the manufacturing-for-export policy to succeed it was necessary for the Mexican government to bring down labour costs. This was accomplished during the 1980s through a policy of devaluation of the Mexican peso, rapid inflation, government controls on wage increases, and political repression of the trade union movement.[6]

Expanding *Maquiladoras*

The period after 1965 showed a slow growth in the *maquiladora* program. By 1971, only 205 plants had been established employing only 20,000 people. In an effort to encourage more investment, the Mexican government limited taxation on the *maquila* operations to the value added in manufacturing so that by 1974, the number of plants had risen to 455, employing 76,000 people.

The economic recession in the United States in 1973-74 impacted heavily on the *Maquila* plants. Many were shut down, investment dropped, and workers lost their jobs. Business blamed the government of Luis Echeverría for new regulations which tried to improve labour standards for *maquila* workers. The president's populist pronouncements seemed to encourage labour militancy in the border zone.

The official unions tied to the Confederation of Mexican Workers (CTM) began to lose control of their workers, resulting in demands for higher wages. The industry began to expand again after 1977, when the López Portillo government granted additional incentives to investors and the U.S. economy rebounded.

General government policy towards the *maquila* industry changed after the debt crisis of 1982, the intervention of the International Monetary Fund and the foreign banks, and the election of Miguel de la Madrid as president. The import substitution industrialization policy was abandoned, and the government became committed to a manufacturing-for-export policy.

In August 1983, a new government decreed that 20 percent of *maquila* production should be directed to the domestic market. The de la Madrid administration placed top priority on accumulating foreign exchange in order to pay for debt charges, thus, the new administration also encouraged capital-intensive investment which employed relatively few workers but earned foreign exchange.[7]

Since the economic crisis of 1982, PRI administrations have emphasized the reduction of Mexico's real wages to develop international competitiveness. When López Portillo left office in 1982, he devalued the peso. Leslie Sklair points out that this had the effect of reducing the minimum wage in the *maquila* zones from a historic high of $1.53 per hour to $.76 per hour. During President de la Madrid's term of office (1982-1988) real wages fell another 40 percent because of further devaluations, wage controls and rapid inflation. Carlos Salinas renewed wage controls in 1989 and launched a vigorous campaign against trade unions and strikes.[8]

The Salinas administration introduced the Foreign Investment Regulation of May 1989, designed to encourage foreign investment in areas outside the border zone. The Maquiladora Decree of December 1989 removed more regulations and permitted the plants to sell up to 50 percent of their output in Mexico. New zones were to be developed in the interior of Mexico, supposedly to make it easier for Mexican firms to supply the foreign investors. The *maquiladoras* became a central focus of economic development strategy.

The key to the success of the *maquila* strategy has been the reduction of Mexican wages. In the 1970s, labour costs averaged 18 percent of total operating costs in the *maquila* plants. By 1990, they had dropped to about 12 percent, and were now considerably less than they were in East Asia. A study by el Colegio de la Frontera Norte for 1990 reported that average wage in the Mexican *maquila* plants was $1.20 per hour, which compared favourably to $2.50 per hour in South Korea and $3.00 per hour in Taiwan. In the industries that hire mainly women workers, like textiles and electronics, Mexican wages were competitive with wages in the Philippines, Malaysia and Indonesia. By 1992, there were 2,000 *maquila* plants in Mexico employing around 500,000 people.[9]

A recent study of Japanese *maquiladoras* concluded that "the first and foremost factor" driving investment was labour costs. Production workers in the 66 plants surveyed were paid on average $50 per week or between $1.10 and $1.25 per hour. Fringe benefits were "relatively small," and included food coupons, transportation subsidies, parties, subsidized cafeterias, and paid vacations. Managers were paid between $1,500 and $3,000 per month, "approximately half that in the United States."[10]

Alejandro Alvarez, an economist at the National Autonomous University of Mexico, records that in real terms Mexican wages in general fell from $2.96 per hour in 1980, to $1.37 in 1987. "In 1990, the daily average wage was 30,000 pesos (the equivalent of three national minimum wages) or $9.50 per day (based on an average work week of forty-seven hours), more or less what is paid per hour in comparable manufacturing industry in the United States." Thus, Alvarez argues, the "artificial cheapening of labour costs" due to government policies has provided a significant subsidy to American, Japanese and other corporations manufacturing in Mexico. For 1990, it has been calculated that "American industry saved $25,000 per employed worker." Subsidized labour worked out to "a total of $10 billion, a little more than the Mexican external debt service in the same year."[11]

Studies of the *maquila* industries show structural changes over the years. In 1979, the most important industries by numbers of plants and employees were electronics, apparel, furniture, transport equipment, toys and leather. In that year 77 percent of the employees in *maquila* plants were women. In recent years, there has been a notable shift. Electronics remains the most important single industry, but its share of workers has fallen from 59 percent to just over 40 percent. The most rapidly growing sector is the automotive industry; the number of plants has tripled since 1979, and today, around one-quarter of all workers are employed in this sector. There has also been a steady rise in the percentage of men working in the *maquila* industries.

The overall growth of the *maquila* industry, however, has fallen off in recent years. The number of plants increased by 24.1 percent in 1988, but only by 6.9 percent in 1994. Many believe that NAFTA will undermine the advantages that the BIP had. That remains to be seen.[12]

Women Workers

Throughout the world, women supply cheap labour for manufacturing, particularly for enterprises located in free trade zones. Fiona Wilson has argued that studies of working women in Mexico play down or ignore the impact of gender roles. She stresses that "women's entry into waged work has had to conform with existing moral codes in order to be considered socially acceptable." In particular, it was necessary to be assured that when women worked outside the home "the protection of a woman's honour constituted an integral part of an employment contract." Employment in small-scale industries — extensions of household production — guaranteed this social control. But was this true of working in larger manufacturing plants?[13]

In the period of economic stabilization and the move towards the more competitive free market, there has been a downward push on wages. Women have been seen as a cheap, hard working and less rebellious labour force. The Interamerican Development Bank has reported that over the 1980s, women's wages declined more sharply than men's wages.

Companies introduced homework, contracted out to women for considerably less than the minimum wage. With the dramatic rise of the unregulated informal economy, there has also been an increase in home-based workshops which are commonly clandestine or concealed. As Wilson points out, in Mexico, the state's role has traditionally ended at the door of the household, deemed to be the man's private space while government regulation and taxation applies only to what is done in the public sphere.

Work is also divided on a hierarchical basis, according to social prestige, power, influence and income. Wilson argues that historically, women workers have been portrayed as "secondary" workers, having "less valuable skills and more appropriately engaged in domestic forms of work and organization."

The terms "sweated labour" or "downgraded labour" have been used to identify disadvantaged workers, those who are especially vulnerable to exploitation. These have traditionally been the employers' family members, women and children, immigrants, and ethnically distinct groups. Downgraded labour takes place most often in service or domestic relations of production. But even when working in formal jobs, downgraded workers are often considered unsuitable for organized labour. They are deemed not to be "true workers," and they are often excluded from protective legislation and enforcement.

A great deal of research has been done on women workers in the *maquiladora* factories of the Border Industrial Program. Much of the research is done within the context of the international restructuring of capitalist production, with transnational corporations seeking cheaper labour, wherever it can be found. The Mexican BIP has been widely compared to the Asian free trade zones, as both of them have relied primarily on employing young women workers at very low wages in unregulated enterprises.

Early studies of Mexico done by June Nash and Mariá Fernández-Kelly concentrated on the degree of exploitation of women workers. Generally, they followed the studies done by Esther Boserup, who argued that when Western capitalism spread into Third World countries, the status of women in those areas fell. Boserup claimed that work in industry does not liberate women from traditionally patriarchal social controls; rather, women become more oppressed since they must work full-time outside the house and also perform all the traditional domestic chores. Nash and Fernandez-Kelly reported that this was true of *maquila* workers, and concluded that as wage workers these women became even more dependent on men.

The exploitation of women in the *maquila* industries is possible because of the Mexican patriarchal culture. The subordination of women permits the superexploitation of their labour.[14] In the Mexican *maquila* zones, as in other free trade zones, women make up around 75 percent of the labour force. They are paid the minimum wage, which in the early 1990s was on average $4 per day. The Mexican government has exempted these firms from most worker-protection requirements. As Susan Tiano points out, state labour standards are virtually nonexistent. Workers deemed to be "inefficient" can be dismissed without severance pay. Workers are hired on a "temporary" basis for up to six months and then dismissed, to be rehired again, in order not to have to pay higher wages or provide fringe benefits. Where trade unions exist in the *maquila* industries, their primary role is to discipline workers.

Management in the *maquila* zones takes the position that women do not need to be paid higher wages because it is presumed that women's wages are secondary in their families. Managers also argue that women have "innate" work capacities which make them preferred workers for certain industries, like electronics, clothing and food.[15]

Ruth Pearson points out that the sectors of manufacturing which predominantly employ women workers are those in which labour costs are the largest component of manufacturing costs. In the sectors where labour costs are a lower percentage of total costs, like the transport industry and electrical machinery, men are employed.[16]

All the studies have found that women work in the *maquila* industries because they need the income to support the households where they live, as daughters, wives and mothers. Many have migrated to the border zone area to find work.

In the workplace, the relations of production are based on gender roles. Gay Young argues that "male manager and female operators reproduce at work the traditional patterns of male domination. The factory resembles a family for young women workers — with 'big brother' and 'father' as compelling images of patriarchy in the plant." Women report that they constantly face sexual harassment and even rape by male supervisors.[17]

The CTM trade unions that exist in the border zones are completely male dominated. Devon Peña reports in her survey of *maquila* workers in Ciudad Juárez that the majority of women preferred independent unions or informal plant coalitions to the male-dominated CTM unions. These unions not only support management; they also enforce patriarchal controls.[18]

Susan Tiano reports that the corporations sponsor beauty pageants, makeup demonstrations, cooking classes and sex education seminars to "reinforce workers' traditional notions of femininity." Male managers try to monitor the personal lives of women workers. Special gifts and favours are given employees. It is standard procedure to check women employees for contagious diseases and pregnancy.[19]

Pearson reports that women's physical appearance is an important factor in employment. Women are often rejected for employment because of appearance — they are deemed to be "ugly workers." In one study, the plant owners admitted that they preferred "prettier women." They justified this by saying that "the *feas* [ugly ones] caused a lot of problems and were always jealous."

Wilson notes that government and political leaders have not objected to the exploitation of women workers in the free trade zones. This silence is symptomatic of the attitude these patriarchal societies have toward young women as industrial workers.

What we see here is another example of downgraded labour. Employment in "formal" industries becomes "informalized" once women become the bulk of the labour force. This change is due to the way gender roles interact with class roles.

Wilson concludes that "when women are employed in registered factory work, aspects associated with 'informality' are introduced in the terms and conditions of employment." The result is that "women's entry into waged work has not brought emancipation in the same way that, historically, it hastened the end of different forms of servitude for men."

Nevertheless, studies show that women actively seek *maquila* employment because they desperately need the income. Tiano's study found that many *maquila* workers preferred waged work to full-time domestic responsibilities. Independently earned income gives women greater bargaining power within the household. The rapid turnover of women *maquila* workers was found to be due to their belief that their wages were too low. They could cross the border into the United States and earn $4 per hour.[20] But having an independent income has not resulted in a social revolution for women in Mexico. Rarely do they earn enough income to provide a sense of security. As bad as working conditions are in the *maquila* factories, women still migrate to the zones seeking employment. It is better than other options.

Zenith Moves to Mexico

In 1969, Zenith Corporation established a plant in the maquiladora zone at Matamoros, in the state of Tamaulipas, across the border from Brownsville, Texas. It came to assemble television tuners, but soon became the largest single employer in the Border Industrial Program.

In 1978, Zenith established a *maquila* plant to produce television components at Reynosa, up the Rio Grande river from Matamoros. It was twinned with a plant in the McAllen, Texas Foreign Trade Zone. By 1988, it operated eighteen plants in Mexico and employed 22,000 people. It now manufactures most of its televisions in Mexico. Mexico has become the largest single exporter of television sets to the United States.

Harley Shaiken conducted a study of Zenith's operations in Mexico in 1988. Management personnel told him Zenith chose Mexico because it was close to the North American market, gave U.S. management more control over the operations, made it easier to use U.S. parts, the quality of work was the highest in the company, and the productivity of Mexican plants was 20 percent higher than U.S. plants. The level of automation is the same as in plants in the United States.[21]

The company reported that it was easier to work in Mexico than in the United States. "There are less restrictions, there are less negotiating points that one has to field as the by-product of doing the job there." The one problem was high turnover, due to the drawing power of the U.S. border.

One engineering manager told Shaiken that he was surprised that they hadn't closed down all the U.S. plants and completely moved to Mexico. The quality of work in plants in Mexico was very high. "Why pay $10 an hour when you can pay ninety cents?"

The CTM union has a presence in the *maquila* plants in the state of Tamaulipas. One manager told Shaiken that the leadership of the CTM union "played a key role in controlling the work force for the company." The industrial relations manager told him that the union had "almost no impact on the company's operations on the shop floor."

The most serious strike in the Reynosa *maquiladora* was at the Zenith plant in 1983. At the time, Zenith employed 7,000 workers in this plant, the largest in the BIP, and paid them $3.40 per day. The workers, hard-hit by the devaluation of the peso and the loss of real income, asked for an emergency pay raise. There was also concern over the differences in wages paid in different Zenith plants in the border zone. The leadership of the CTM union did not respond to the workers' demands, so the workers instituted a wildcat strike. Leaders of the unofficial strike were jailed and workers were beaten, threatened and intimidated.

Daniel López, leader of the dissident workers, was released from jail and headed a reform slate which challenged CTM control of the union. They won an overwhelming victory, and for the first time women were elected to the union local's executive.

Following normal practice, the CTM declared the election null and void. A second election was called, and the results were the same. This time, the CTM leaders, working with Zenith management, forced the elected leaders to resign. Four of them staged a hunger strike in the central square of Reynosa until they were hauled away by the police. Strike leaders were dismissed from their jobs and put on a blacklist which was circulated to other *maquila* firms. Company and CTM intimidation broke the resistance over time.

During the strike, business leaders, newspapers and political representatives of the city claimed that union militancy would drive the plants to other border zone locations. The defeat of the workers certainly encouraged Zenith, which expanded its operation in Reynosa to 9,000 workers by 1987. But as management told Harley Shaiken, the strike convinced the company that "it would be dangerous to put everything in one city or under the control of one union."

In 1984, Zenith also established a high-tech plant in Chihuahua City. It was announced that the city was chosen because of its highly skilled work force and government-subsidized training programs. It also closed one of its plants in Chicago and moved it to the *maquila* zone in Ciudad Juárez. Its factory in Evansville, Indiana, which employed 1,400 workers at between $6 and $7 per hour was also shut down and replaced by a *maquila* plant. The labour savings were reported at around $300 million per year. Production at the plant in El Paso has also been cut and work shifted to Mexico.

Zenith has used its plants in Mexico as a powerful bargaining tool in negotiations with its workers in the United States. Sklair reports that in 1987, Zenith convinced its workers in Springfield, Missouri to accept a 8.1 percent pay cut and a wage freeze through 1989. In return, Zenith promised to keep its Springfield plant open another five years. At this time, Zenith had 22,000 employees in Mexico and only 12,000 in the United States.[22]

Processing Food

The 1989 presidential Decree on Maquiladoras was designed to expand the development of operations into the central part of Mexico. One of the goals of the Salinas administration was to increase food exports from Mexico to the United States. An example of this type of *maquila* plant is the Green Giant operation at Irapuato, Guanajuato.

Green Giant is a unit of Pillsbury Company of Minneapolis, which is now a subsidiary of Grand Metropolitan PLC of London, which also owns Haagen Dazs and Burger King. The plant in Irapuato employs 1,200 people on a three-shift operation, all year long. It processes broccoli and cauliflower for the U.S. and Canadian markets and plans to open a mushroom growing and processing facility. Because its product is exported, it can qualify as a *maquila* plant. Other transnational food corporations operating in Irapuato include Del Monte, Campbell's, Birdseye, Simplot Foods and Basic American Foods. Strawberries and tomatoes are also major crops grown in the area for export to North America.

In 1990, Del Monte announced that it was planning to lay off 1,300 workers in plants across the United States. One plant that was closed in 1991 was the frozen food plant in Watsonville, California, whose production was shifted to Irapuato. It employed 400 people, most of whom were Mexican women who had emigrated to the United States to find work. The California workers' average pay was $7.56 per hour. The Teamsters Union, which represented the workers in Watsonville, estimates that the company saved $6 million a year in wages by moving to Mexico.

These plants are attracted to this area of Mexico because of the availability of low-priced farm products. They contract with local farmers. The fruits and vegetables are harvested primarily by women and children who are employed on a piecework basis and normally do not earn the minimum wage.

The other advantage for these companies is abundant, cheap labour for the processing plants. Employees are mainly women, and most of them start work at age twelve. In 1992, women who cut cauliflower and broccoli earned, on average, $6.70 per day, or $.84. per hour. But many workers earned considerably less. For example, a male fork lift operator earned only $5.20 per day; other women workers earned only about $5.30 per day. The company regularly lays off its workers so it can claim that they are temporary, seasonal workers, who earn lower wages. Many of the workers who earned only $5.30 per day had worked there since the plant opened in 1983.

Under Mexican law, employees can participate in productivity bonuses. At Green Giant in 1992, this brought the workers on average $17 a month extra. Federal labour law also provides for profit sharing, which is paid at the end of the year. In 1991, Green Giant paid an average of about $70 per worker in profit sharing. Workers complain that under the *maquila* system, foreign corporations do not have to report on export profits and thus avoid paying profit shares. At the local Del Monte plant, whose main product is processed tomatoes for the Mexican market, profit sharing in 1991 paid workers up to $700 extra.

In 1989 Grand Metropolitan took over Pillsbury after a bitter fight. It cost the London conglomerate $5.8 billion. Corporate headquarters in London asked Green Giant to increase its profit rate above the traditional 15 percent level. Gary Klingl, president of Green Giant, admitted in May 1991 that part of that profit strategy was the cheap labour incentive of moving to Mexico.[23]

The Automotive Industry

The automotive industry is the most dynamic industry in Mexico. It developed during the period of import substitution industrialization, behind protective tariffs and quotas on imports. Manufacturers developed plants around Mexico City to serve the Mexican market. These manufacturers included the American Big Three (Ford, GM and Chrysler), plus Volkswagen and Nissan. The workers were represented by official trade unions, affiliated with the CTM.

In the 1960s and 1970s, worker militancy increased, and in five of the seven plants, workers threw out the local CTM union leadership, gained democratic control over their contracts and waged successful strikes, which resulted in the formation of the independent auto workers' unions.

Companies reacted by building new plants in the northern states near the U.S. border for which they received significant government subsidies. They carefully selected employees to weed out possible union activists and signed "protection contracts" with CTM unions. Wages were substantially lower in the new plants and eventually, the workers at their older plants near Mexico City were pressured to sign concession contracts lowering wages to the levels of the new plants. Some Mexico City plants were closed. With the active support of the PRI government, management gradually forced the democratic unions out of the Mexico City plants and restored the old CTM unions.[24]

In 1992, however, Volkswagen management tore up the existing contract, locked out 14,000 workers at Puebla, and fired 300 trade union activists. With the support of the Salinas administration, they imposed a new contract and union leadership on the workers. The average wage at Volkswagen at this time was only $1.87 per hour.[25]

Before Magna International of Ontario began building its new auto parts plant at Puebla in 1992, it signed a "protection contract" with the Revolutionary Confederation of Workers and Peasants (CROC), which is also an "official" trade union federation affiliated with the governing PRI. Unskilled workers earn $1.30 per hour and skilled workers up to $2.63 per hour. Magna pays its Ontario workers on average $20 per hour.[26]

Business Week reports that in 1992 the average pay for Mexican auto workers was between $1.25 and $2.50 per hour. In the border areas, the pay is even lower. For example, in the summer of 1993 the Chrysler plant at Monterrey was paying an average of $1.20 per hour.[27]

Lower labour costs are not the only threat to Canadian and American automotive workers. The automotive industry in Mexico is adopting the Japanese form of production. The shift is to enterprise trade unions, with each plant having its own union. Industrial unionism as we know it in North America is under attack. The CTM unions have bought into this change in return for obtaining a captive dues-paying membership.

All the new automotive plants in Mexico have established the Japanese system of team production. Workers are assigned to a few broad classifications, which gives management great flexibility in control over the plant floor. There are promotional steps in each classification, with differential wages, and promotion is on the basis of merit. There are no seniority rights, nor do union contracts have grievance procedures.

Harley Shaiken's detailed study of the establishment of the Ford plant at Hermosillo, Senora is most revealing. This highly automated plant produces 165,000 Ford Tracers and Escorts for the U.S. market. In 1989 this plant produced the highest quality Ford vehicles in North America. In that year the plant required only twenty-four hours of labour per car for stamping and assembly. Total labour compensation costs were around $2 per hour compared to $30 at their main plant in Detroit.[28]

At the Hermosillo plant there are no skilled trades, there are minimal perks, and subcontracting is extensive. The Japanese team system is in place. It puts a high priority on *kaizen,* or improvement in worker productivity. The team system of operation facilitates the implementation of speed-up on the assembly line as well as plant rationalization which eliminates workers.

The most serious problem in Mexico is surplus labour and the lack of jobs. Thus, the automobile industry has its pick when hiring from an enormous reserve army of labour, hiring young workers with no union experience. When Ford opened its plant at Hermosillo in 1987, the average age of the workers was 22.9 years. The workers were also highly educated: 10 percent had attended technical school, 31.5 percent had attended university and another 50 percent were high school graduates.

Shaiken reports that Ford managers from the United States were very impressed with the team approach to production and wanted to see it introduced into North American plants. He quotes managers at the Hermosillo plant: "The CTM union is here, but it's almost as if they're not here. They've been a positive factor. There really is no union-management confrontation." *Business Week* quotes one Big Three executive in Mexico City: "We'd put a lot more plants in Mexico if it weren't for the United Auto Workers."

Kevin Middlebrook's study of the automotive industry in Mexico stresses the key role of the CTM in making the system work. The official unions have helped defeat the more democratic and militant trade unions. They work with management to enforce the contract, and they help to weed out dissident workers. CTM contracts include an "exclusion clause" that requires the employer to fire any worker who has been expelled from his union. It is not unusual for the CTM to collude with management to fire an entire elected union local leadership. As Middlebrook concludes, because of its links to the ruling state party, the CTM has little incentive to negotiate effectively for its members. "Many CTM leaders have been more intent on controlling workers for political purposes than on developing an institutionalized presence in the workplace." This does not mean that there is fascist-style peace in the workplace. Workers continue to strike, even when their chances of winning are virtually nil.

There is a high turnover rate in the automotive industry as well. Employees work eight or nine hours a day, six days a week. The speed of the assembly line is fast and work is hard. Wages are very low compared to auto workers in the industrialized countries. The standard of living for Mexican autoworkers is also very low compared to their counterparts in the industrialized countries. The workers know it, for many of them have been sent abroad for training.[29]

The Balance Sheet

How successful has the *maquila* strategy been? In 1992, Mexico's exports totalled $46.2 billion dollars. Exports from the *maquiladora* program totalled $18.7 billion, or 40.5 percent of the total. These exports were second only to petroleum products in earning foreign exchange. Imports in 1992 totalled $62 billion, of which the *maquiladoras* accounted for $13.9 billion, or 22.4 percent of the total. However, Mexicans who work in the border zones flock to the United States to buy consumer goods, which they claim are better and cheaper than in Mexico.

At the end of 1993, there were 2,195 *maquila* plants which employed 541,000 people. Many argue that these jobs would not have existed without the special program. Furthermore, the large foreign corporations are training Mexican workers and providing management positions for graduates of Mexican colleges and universities.

The *maquila* program is not limited to foreign corporations. In 1990, 43 percent of the capital invested in *maquiladora* businesses was Mexican and only 33 percent was from the United States.[30]

The Salinas government has hoped that the *maquila* strategy would result in a transfer of new technology to Mexico. Harley Shaiken's study has shown that in the automotive, electronic and computer areas the new plants are employing new state of the art technologies. But does this mean that the technology is being transferred to Mexico? Economists point to the very low spending on research, development, science and technology in Mexico, particularly by the private sector. So far there is no sign yet of a secondary takeoff in manufacturing due to the acquisition of knowledge, as has occurred in South Korea, Taiwan, Hong Kong and Singapore.

On the other hand, the in-bond assembly program has remained an enclave development in Mexico. Mexican firms provide less than 2 percent of the inputs into *maquila* manufacturing. As Alejandro Alvarez argues, "this means that effective integration with the rest of the economy is nonexistent." The Salinas administration is hoping that NAFTA will solve this problem.

While the *maquila* program has created 500,000 jobs, far more than that have been lost as Mexico has reduced its tariffs and eliminated other protections. The consequent invasion of consumer goods from Asia has forced the shutdown of many Mexican companies.

The *maquila* program has also done little to solve the unemployment and underemployment problem in Mexico. Every year, 1.1 million Mexicans enter the labour force. Furthermore, the *maquila* program has brought capital-intensive investment. The "surface mounting technologies" associated with assembly operations have automated jobs which used to be manual.

In 1990, 87 percent of the *maquila* plants were located in the border zones close to the United States. In that same year, 75 percent of the employment was concentrated in four states: Chihuahua, Baja California, Tamaulipas and Sonora. This has created an enormous environmental problem. The area is torrid semi-desert, and there is a very serious shortage of water. Toxic contamination is widespread. With no taxes on the corporations, management staff living in the United States, and workers surviving on bare survival wages, there has been no tax base for local governments. Infrastructure facilities lag far behind local needs and workers are forced to live in shantytowns.

The introduction of the BIP had a dramatic impact on the cities of Matamoros, Reynosa and Camargo-Río Bravo, in the state of Tamaulipas, which borders on Texas. Population increased by 64 percent between 1970 and 1990. More than 40 percent of the housing units in the three cities did not have sewer facilities. Unemployment and underemployment (mainly part-time work) was around 20 percent in 1990. An estimated 51 percent of the people in the region were living below the poverty line. While the wages in the *maquila* plants were low by U.S. standards, they were among the highest in Tamaulipas.[31]

Unemployed and desperate Mexicans flock to the border zone and are willing to take any kind of job. But working conditions in these plants are often horrendous. Health and safety regulations have been virtually nonexistent in Mexico, and where they do exist, they are not enforced.

Wages in the *maquiladoras* have declined in real terms over the years. U.S. and Mexican government figures show that the average real wage for *maquila* workers peaked in 1981 at an equivalent of $2.60 per hour, declined to around $1.05 in 1986, and then rose steadily to around $1.65 in 1992. The increase is mainly attributed to new investment in the automotive industry, which hires men at higher wages.[32]

Guillermo Sander and Francisco Mendoza conducted a study of wages and fringe benefits in the *maquiladoras*. Labour costs dropped dramatically after the onset of the debt crisis in 1982 but began to rise again in 1988 and 1989. In 1989, the wages of a blue collar worker in a *maquila* factory in Juárez provided only around 27 percent of the minimum subsistence requirements for the standard basket of products and services considered the absolute minimum. A *maquila* worker in Chihuahua needed to earn four times the minimum wage to purchase the same package of goods and services.[33]

The promoters of the *maquila* program in Nogales brag that "the cost of labour here is cheaper than almost any place in the world." Jorge Carrillo points out that discontent is not just due to low wages and poor working conditions, there is also "the unstable level of unionization in the industry, the continued erosion of social benefits for workers, and great volatility in the level of employment."[34]

The level of unionization varies greatly. But the unions are all affiliated with the organizations linked to the governing party, the PRI: the Mexican Confederation of Workers (CTM), the Confederation of Revolutionary Workers and Farmers (CROC), or the Confederation of Mexican Revolutionary Workers (CROM). The primary role of these unions is to provide "social peace."

In Tamaulipas, the official CTM unions have a stronghold; in 1989, 85 percent of the *maquila* workers were in trade unions. Workers there have the highest wages on average in the *maquiladoras*. But these are CTM unions, and there is no workers democracy. As Carrillo points out, these unions "do not tolerate internal union dissent, the proliferation of independent labour organizations, or significant numbers of individual worker demands."

In contrast, in Baja California, only 5 percent of the *maquila* workers were organized in 1989. The plants that were unionized signed "protection contracts," which made them as weak as company unions, known as "white unions" in Mexico.

Workers do not seek representation by the CTM unions. These unions are corrupt, antidemocratic and work closely with management to control worker dissention. Contracts are negotiated and accepted without consulting workers. Even in workplaces where women are the vast majority, the CTM unions are completely controlled by men. Women workers complain constantly of sexual harassment, assault and discrimination from the company management and from their union leaders.

One of the obvious effects of the border *maquila* program is to increase illegal migration of Mexicans to the United States. The population of the Mexican border cities has increased dramatically with the *maquiladoras* and consequently, the border zone has provided a point of entry for Mexicans sneaking into the United States.

The study by el Colegio de la Frontera Norte for 1990 argued that this emigration was inevitable given the low wages and poor working and living conditions in the *maquila* factories. Wages in the *maquiladoras* averaged only

$1.20 per hour that year. Mexicans who crossed the border could earn at least $4.50 per hour, and the living conditions were much better. It is expected that the approval of NAFTA will stimulate more emigration to the United States.[35]

Notes

1. Bennett Harrison and Barry Bluestone, *The Great U-Turn; Corporate Restructuring and the Polarizing of America*. New York: Basic Books, 1988, pp. 7-11; Leslie Sklair, *Assembling for Development*. Center for U.S. Mexican Studies, University of California, San Diego, 1993, pp. 24-42; Jorge Carrillo, "The Evolution of the Maquiladora Industry," in Kevin J. Middlebrook, ed., *Workers and the State in Mexico*. Center for U.S.-Mexican Studies, University of California, San Diego, 1991, pp. 213-241; Alejandro Alvarez, "Mexico: Maquila Country." Solidarity Not Competition Conference, Toronto, Ontario, May 4, 1991, 9 pp.; and David Ehrenthal and Joseph Newman, "Explaining Mexico's Maquila Boom," *SAIS Review*, Winter-Spring 1988, pp. 189-211.
2. Harley Shaiken, *Mexico in the Global Economy*. Center for U.S.-Mexican Studies, University of California, San Diego, 1990, pp. 92-99.
3. *The Economist*, February 8, 1986; Harrison and Bluestone, *op. cit.*, pp. 7-8.
4. Patricia A. Wilson, *Exports and Local Development; Mexico's New Maquiladora Industry*. Austin: University of Texas Press, 1992, pp. 7-49.
5. Richard Smith, "The Chinese Road to Capitalism," *New Left Review*, No. 199, May-June 1993, pp. 55-99; Martin Wolf, "The Sleeping Giant Awakes," *The Financial Post*, July 3, 1993, p. 43.
6. See also Gregory K. Schoepfle and Jorge F. Perez-López, "Export Assembly Operations in Mexico and the Caribbean," *Journal of Inter-American Studies and World Affairs*, Vol. 31, Winter 1989, pp. 131-161.
7. See Sklair, *op. cit*, pp. 167-180; Alvarez, *op. cit.*; Carrillo, *op. cit.*; and "The Mexican-American Border," *The Economist*, Vol. 325, December 12, 1992, pp. 21-25.
8. Sklair, *op. cit.*, p. 66.
9. Yazmín Venegas Peralta, "Para los Trabajadores Jóvenes, más Atractivo Salir Hacia EU Que Ingresar a las Maquiladores," *El Financiero*, January 6, 1992, p. 12.
10. .Martin Kenney and Richard Florida, "Japanese Maquiladoras: Production Organization and Global Commodity Chains," *World Development*, Vol. 22, No. 1, 1994, pp. 27-44.
11. Alvarez, *op. cit.*
12. Tom Buckley, "Maquiladora Productivity Rose in '93," *The News*, March 22, 1994, p. 27; John M. Nagel, "More for the Money," *El Financiero International*, January 16, 1995, p. 10.
13. Fiona Wilson, "Workshops as Domestic Domains," *World Development*, Vol. 21, January 1993, pp. 67-80.
14. June Nash and Mariá Fernández-Kelly. *Women, Men and the International Division of Labor*. Albany: State University of New York Press, 1983; and Ester Boserup, *Women's Role in Economic Development*. New York: St. Martin's Press, 1970.
15. Susan Tiano, "Maquiladoras in Mexicali: Integration or Exploitation?" in Vicki L. Ruiz and Susan Tiano, eds., *Women on the U.S.-Mexican Border*. Boston: Allen & Unwin, 1987, pp. 77-101.

16. Ruth Pearson, "Male Bias and Women's Work in Mexico's Border Industries," in Diane Elson, ed., *Male Bias in the Development Process*. Manchester: Manchester University Press, 1991, pp. 133-163.

17. Gay Young, "Women, Development and Human Rights: Issues in Integrated Transnational Production," *Journal of Applied Behavioural Science*, Vol. 20, No. 4, 1984, pp. 383-401.

18. Devon Peña, "Tortuosid: Shop Floor Struggles of Female Maquiladora Workers," in Ruiz and Tiano, *op. cit.*, pp. 129-154.

19. Susan Tiano, "Women's Work and Unemployment in Northern Mexico," in Ruiz and Tiano, *op. cit.*, pp. 17-39.

20. *Ibid.*

21. Shaiken, *op. cit.*, pp. 98-105.

22. Sklair, *op. cit.*, pp. 120-135; Maxine Durand, "Maquila Madness in Mexico," *International Viewpoint*, No. 196, December 10, 1990, pp. 24-26.

23. Jim Carlton, "Not-so Jolly Green Giant Casts a Long Shadow," *The Globe and Mail*, September 24, 1992, C-5; Tony Kennedy, "Ho Ho Ho Giant Recast as Ogre," *The Globe and Mail*, May 14, 1991, B-8; and Rebeca Hernández Marín, "El Bajio Granero ... de EU," *Epoca*, No. 91, March 1, 1993, pp. 20-23.

24. See Kevin Middlebrook, "The Politics of Industrial Restructuring," *Comparative Politics*, Vol. 23, April 1991, pp. 275-298; and Dan La Botz, *Mask of Democracy*. Montréal: Black Rose Books, 1992, pp. 148-160.

25. "Mending the People's Car," *Economist*, Vol. 324, August 22, 1992, pp. 31-32; and Mary McGinn, "VW Threatens to Run Away from Mexico," *Labor Notes*, No. 162, September 1992, pp. 4, 14.

26. Drew Fagan, "Magna Makes It in Mexico," *The Globe and Mail*, March 18, 1993, pp. B-1.

27. "Detroit South," *Business Week*, March 16, 1992, pp. 98-103.

28. Shaiken, *op. cit.*, pp. 21-85.

29. See also "The Mexican Worker," *Business Week*, April 19, 1993, pp. 84-92; and Luz Mariá de la Mora-Sánchez and José Ángel Canela-Cacho, "The Mexican Automotive Industry under NAFTA," *Policy Options*, Vol. 15, January-February 1994, pp. 35-39.

30. Sergio Miranda Gonzáles, "El Sector Maquilador Cobra Importancia en el Comercio Exterior," *Excelsior*, March 8, 1993, F-1; Javier Palacios Neri, "En el Umbral de una Nueva Industria Maquiladora de Exportación," *El Financiero*, January 7, 1993, 31-A; Miguel Marón Manzur, "Tendencias Recientes de la Industria Maquiladora," *El Financiero*, April 1, 1993, 31-A; and Tricia A. Berg, "El Dilema de las Maquiladoras," *Excelsior*, March 20, 1992, 4-A.

31. Dianne C. Betts and Daniel J. Slottje, *Crisis on the Río Grande*. Boulder: Westview Press, 1994, pp. 18-25.

32. Harry Browne and Beth Sims, *Runaway America*. Albuquerque: Resource Center Press, 1993, pp. 19-24.

33. Guillermo Sander and Francisco Mendoza, "Compensation Overview," *Twin Plant News*, May 1990, pp. 34-37.

34. Carrillo, op. cit.

35. Venegas Peralta, *op. cit.*

Chapter 4

CORPORATE POWER

The transformation of Mexico into a neoliberal regime required a major break with the past. The peasants would have to give up their demand for land reform and the workers would have to accept significant reductions in wages and benefits. The nationalism which sought independence from the United States would have to be defeated and the political left contained. Furthermore, Mexico's historic links with Spanish Latin America would need to be replaced by close ties with the United States. All in all, this task required a strong, authoritarian administration whose first task would be to convince the corporate elite that the revolutionary party had changed and was now firmly on their side.

The modern Mexican state had emerged under the leadership of President Lázaro Cárdenas (1934-1940). A mixed economy of private and public enterprise was initiated. Cárdenas saw the state playing a positive role in society, as a controlling or guiding force; as he argued in his inaugural address, "The state alone embodies the general interest, and for this reason only the state has a vision of the whole. The state must continually broaden, increase and deepen interventions."[1]

The Cárdenas state was a nationalist and populist state. This was reflected in his view of the revolutionary party, now known as the Institutional Revolutionary Party (PRI). It was to be a coalition of popular interests. Big business was not invited to be a part of the revolutionary party because Cárdenas believed that it already had too much control over the state. A populist party was necessary to provide a balance to this concentration of economic and political power.

In 1917, legislation required all chambers of commerce to affiliate with the National Confederation of Chambers of Commerce (CONANACO). Industries were required to join the Confederation of Industrial Chambers (CONCAMIN). An important subgroup of the latter organization was the National Chamber of Consumer Goods Industries (CANACINTRA), which represents small and medium sized businesses. These business organizations have been important pressure groups influencing government policy. Legally, they are consultative organizations of the government.

In 1929 the Mexican Confederation of Employers (COPARMEX) was formed as an explicitly antisocialist business organization to oppose the populist PRI. Its slogan was "not class struggle but class collaboration."[2]

The "bankers' alliance," a conservative alliance of domestic capitalist, foreign capital, the large landowners, and the church, completely dominated Mexico from the period of President Miguel Alémán (1946-1952) through to 1970. The alliance prospered during this period of dynamic growth behind the protection and subsidies of the import substitution strategy of development.

Small and medium-sized businesses benefitted from the focus on the development of the national economy. Thus the move to the liberal regime was generally opposed by CANACINTRA, the National Confederation of Small Business (CNPP) and the National Confederation of Chambers of Small Business (CNCPC).[3]

In the 1970s, the Mexican state came to own or control some central sectors of the economy, like the railroads, the airlines, electrical power, and the petroleum industry. But, as Mexican political scientist Pablo González Casanova has pointed out, the public sector accounted for less than 10 percent of the gross domestic product.[4] This is even less than in Canada.

While big business organizations were outside the governing party, this hardly meant that they were excluded from the decision making process. They had enormous influence on government policy. There were two important factors which enhanced the power of big capital. First, taxes on large corporations and the rich were very low and the state did not make any serious effort to collect them. Second, there were no foreign exchange controls; the rich were free to transfer their capital out of the country at will.[5]

Confronting the PRI

The power of big business was demonstrated during the presidency of Luis Echeverría Alvarez (1970-76). When he was chosen to be the PRI candidate he had the reputation of being a traditional PRI loyalist and a hard liner against the political left. Once in office he launched an attack on government corruption and announced a policy of "shared development." This was an attempt to revive the old populist Cárdenas coalition.

Echeverría proclaimed an attack on Mexico's gross social inequality. More government funds were to go to education, health and public housing. The work week was to be cut from forty-eight to forty hours. Echeverría promised more land reform, told big business that government loans had to be repaid, and in the nationalist tradition, he demanded that the laws and regulations on foreign investment actually be enforced. He pursued a foreign policy of greater independence from the United States.

But what really shocked the bankers' alliance was his proposal to pay for this program through a new taxation system. Previous governments had imposed very low tax burdens on business. For example, in 1960, Mexico had one of the lowest income taxes in the world; revenues from this source amounted to only 2.41 percent of gross domestic product. In 1981, Mexico had one of the lowest tax collection rates of any country with similar per capita income.[6]

It was impossible to have a progressive income tax because it could be moved from one category to another to dodge high rates, and it was very easy to deduct personal expenses. There was no obligation to reveal wealth in property. Thus, the income tax fell mainly on wage earners.

The other main problem with tax collection was the collusion between the rich and the bureaucrats supposedly collecting the taxes. The rationale for such a tax policy was one we all know: the rich were supposed to promote investment.

Without any system of foreign exchange controls, wealthy Mexicans had acquired homes and bank accounts in the United States. With the long border and no regulation, it was easy to hide cash. Politicians had bank accounts and property abroad, and even middle-class Mexicans tried to acquire bank accounts in the United States. Echeverría proposed to increase the tax rate on the corporations and those in the upper income brackets, and to end the anonymity of wealth. He added a fixed tax on income from government bonds and private securities. Real estate taxes were raised, and a luxury tax was imposed on some consumption items, like restaurants, night clubs and hotels.

All the business organizations opposed the tax increases, seeing them as the first step towards foreign exchange controls. They felt the president was attempting to cut back on their liberty and that he posed a threat to the security of their property.

The result was a capital strike. The rich began to take their money out of the country, and they withdrew their funds from domestic investment. The national rate of growth fell from 7.1 percent to 4.5 percent.

Politically, big business responded in 1975 by forming the Co-ordinating Council of Businessmen (CCE), a united front against Echeverría's policies. Of all the important business organizations, only CANACINTRA, representing small and medium sized businesses, did not join. When the government proceeded with land redistribution in Durango and Sinaloa, the CCE called on its members to shut their plants and lock out workers in support of large landowners. Many did so. The landowners themselves had already begun a production strike, and they also obtained court injunctions which halted the land redistribution. Capital showed its power.

The taxation reforms that Echeverría adopted did not produce additional revenue. The rich continued to avoid paying. The government bureaucracy, long accustomed to accepting bribes, refused to press for collection. The attempts to implement legislation to control foreign investment were blocked by the bureaucracy. As David Barkin stresses, because of this obstruction the treasury "depended for its income on taxing a very narrow base: middle-class consumption, foreign trade, and salaried wage earners." Historically, the Mexican government "has systematically been unable to impose substantial taxes on profits because of powerful opposition from the capitalists."[7]

Confronted by the capital strike, Echeverría responded by expanding the role of the state in production. Between 1970 and 1976 the number of state enterprises rose from eighty-four to 845. Government spending went from 23.6 percent to 36.6 percent of gross domestic product, and when the rich refused to pay taxes, the government borrowed abroad. The foreign debt rose from $4.5 billion to $19.6 billion. The balance of payments deficit in the current account quadrupled as capital flowed outward and exports dropped off.[8]

The result was the first major debt crisis in 1976. The International Monetary Fund imposed its first structural adjustment program on Mexico, and the peso was devalued for the first time. The crisis revealed who had real power.

Capital Flight

The Echeverría presidency demonstrated the inability of a government to successfully manage the economy as long as the rich and powerful are able to remove capital from the country.

No one knows how much capital the rich have taken out of Mexico. But there have been some good estimates: in 1986, Morgan Guaranty estimated that between 1976 and 1985 $53 billion had left. During this period Mexico's foreign debt went up by $75 billion. By 1987, Mexican assets abroad were estimated at $87 billion.[9] Manuel Pastor, using World Bank data, estimates that between 1973 and 1987, $60.1 billion left Mexico. During that period the foreign debt increased by $95.4 billion.[10]

Rudiger Dornbusch argues that the $60 billion number "is, in all likelihood, a substantial underestimate of assets owned by Mexicans abroad." If

one were to include the interest earned by this investment it would total between \$80 and \$100 billion. This would be roughly equal to the external
debt.[11]

Capital flight from Mexico occurs because there are no foreign exchange controls. Money is just transferred between banks, or one can just
take a briefcase full of cash across the border.

David Barkin points out that, for Mexico, much of the capital flight
does not show up in balance-of-payments statistics. For Mexicans, the trans-
fers often take the form of underinvoicing exports, overinvoicing imports,
the undeclared export or import of goods and services (commonly known
as smuggling), and the use of "transfer pricing" by international firms. The
drug trade has also been a very important form of smuggling.[12]

In 1989, the *Wall Street Journal* ran a front page story on how American
banks and investment firms work hard to get Mexicans to invest in the
United States. Citibank, for example, had \$7.7 billion in outstanding cred-
its in Latin America but had \$20 billion in deposits made by Latin Ameri-
cans. Mexicans are very large investors in real estate in southern California.
As soon as the IMF or the World Bank make a loan to Mexico, agents from
American brokers like Merrill Lynch would flood into Mexico to get companies and individuals to put that money into U.S. accounts.[13]

Mainstream economists argue that owners of capital have the right to
invest anywhere they want, without government controls. The International
Monetary Fund always includes this right of property in the structural adjustment programs which it imposes on Third World countries. They have
insisted on this in the Mexican case.

People take their capital out of a country if they think rates of return
will be higher elsewhere or their investment is more secure. But capital
flight has hurt Mexico badly. Much of the capital that has left came directly
from foreign loans which are being paid back at a tremendous cost to Mexicans who are not capitalists. Capital flight limits domestic economic growth,
has made income distribution worse, eliminates a potential base for needed
tax revenues, restricts government spending, and reduces the availability of
foreign exchange. One of the uniform results of capital flight has been
strong inflationary pressure. As they say throughout Latin America, the rich
grabbed the money lent by the international bankers. The poor are left to
pay off the debt through the expansion of value added taxes.

Manuel Pastor's study of capital flight in Latin America points out that
those countries which have had government foreign exchange controls have
done much better than those like Mexico, which have not had them.
In those countries with controls (Brazil, Chile, Colombia, and Peru), capi-

tal flight amounted to only 6 percent of foreign debt. In those countries with no foreign exchange controls (Argentina, Mexico, Uruguay, and Venezuela), capital flight amounted to 54.2 percent of foreign debt.[14]

The absence of foreign exchange controls is a powerful political weapon in the hands of big capital. Advocates of the free market stress that the threat of capital flight imposes a needed discipline on policymakers. These economists, and the IMF, agree that wealthy individuals should have a virtual veto over government policy. This is, of course, economic blackmail. If an elected government promises to do something to aid workers, peasants or the poor, the rich threaten to pull their money out of the country. Instead of democracy, what we have in this situation is rule by a privileged economic elite.

Business Backs the National Action Party

There are many business organizations in Mexico, with diverse interests, and they never line up unanimously on one side of an issue. Francisco Valdés Ugalde divides them into two broad categories, the "moderates" and the "radicals." The moderates are mainly the industrialists and financiers from central Mexico, and historically they have benefitted from a close relationship with the PRI. The radicals are identified with business centres farther from Mexico City and have dominated organizations like COPARMEX and CONCANACO. These businesses have had less influence with the PRI and have generally opposed the expansion of the state into economic activity.[15]

The opposition of much of big business to the PRI government continued through the presidency of José López Portillo (1976-1982). The government concluded that the expansion of the oil industry was the best hope for economic development. Oil accounted for only 17.6 percent of all exports in 1976 but rose to 74.4 percent in 1981. By 1981, PEMEX provided 25 percent of all tax revenues. Between 1978 and 1981, Mexico's annual growth rates rose to 8.5 percent. The expansion of the oil industry was financed by borrowing from foreign banks. The bubble burst with the collapse of oil prices in 1981 and the onset of the world recession.[16]

But Mexicans with money continued to invest abroad, particularly in real estate in the United States. In Texas alone, between 1975 and 1981, Mexicans invested $8 billion in real estate and had $16.4 billion in cash deposits in banks. There was nothing illegal about this. President López Portillo acquired a great deal of wealth while in office and invested it abroad. It had become a Mexican tradition.[17]

By the summer of 1982, Mexico's foreign debt had risen to $80 billion and the government could not make the payments to the banks. The value of the peso fell by 76 percent and the economy came to a halt. The country was bankrupt, and the IMF had to intervene.

President López Portillo introduced an emergency program. All foreign currency accounts in Mexican banks were frozen, banks were nationalized, foreign currency exchange operations were closed, and government controls on foreign exchange were introduced for the first time in history. This drastic action was an attempt to halt capital flight.[18]

The nationalization of the banks brought strong opposition from CONCANACO and COPARMEX. But unity was absent; even the Business Co-ordinating Council (CCE) was unable to present a united position in opposition. Valdés argues that this was due to previous years of harmonious relations with the PRI, the petroleum boom from which many benefited, and "the political advantage enjoyed by the business class during the preceding 'good years'." In addition, the opposition received no support from the U.S. government which took the position that the nationalization had protected the banks from impending insolvency.[19]

The moderate business groups began to reestablish links with the new PRI government headed by Miguel de la Madrid. The free-market radicals formed a new organization called Mexico in Freedom and shifted their political support to the opposition National Action Party (PAN).

In the northern states, many businessmen backed the PAN, which called for less government involvement in the economy and an end to electoral fraud. In a number of elections in the first half of the 1980s, the PRI was forced to use extensive electoral fraud and state power to hold on to office. The CCE, the most powerful of Mexico's business groups, backed the opposition to the PRI. In 1986, Manuel J. Clouthier, a prominent business leader, ran for governor of the state of Sinaloa for the PAN and then became the PAN candidate for the presidential election in 1988.

Yemile Mizrahi studied the role of entrepreneurs in the recent elections in the state of Chihuahua. In 1983, the PAN won control of most of the cities in the state in a relatively clean election. But in 1986 the PRI used massive fraud to win the state-wide elections. He found that businessmen were frustrated, exhausted, worried about their own affairs, and had lost hope. Many dropped out of electoral politics.[20]

In Chihuahua, support for the PAN was primarily from small and medium-sized businessmen. Big business gave its support to the PRI. Mizrahi concludes that "large entrepreneurs have greater economic and personal links with the government." In 1992, these businessmen were incorporated into the PRI through the Financial Campaign Committees (CFCs).

The small businessmen supported the PAN's call for democracy and the end of fraud and corruption. Mizrahi found that these businessmen felt that "the large entrepreneurs have benefitted disproportionately from the government," and that they felt "politically marginalized." In contrast, big business believed that "their interests are better served by a more authoritarian regime that allows the executive to distribute government favours and concessions with a high degree of discretion." Thus, the demands by the PAN for the rule of law "represents a threat to those entrepreneurs who benefit from their privileged access to government officials."

Beginning in 1982, President de la Madrid began moving in the direction of the neoliberal model of development. The structural adjustment program of the IMF required the usual austerity measures, and business was also pushing in this direction. But capital flight continued. In 1981 bank deposits held abroad were 13 percent of domestic deposits; by 1985 they had risen to 43 percent. Between 1982 and 1985 private sector investment in Mexico contracted by 19.4 percent. The president had no alternative but to make peace with the capitalists.[21]

Business pressure on the government peaked in 1985. The president then announced that Mexico would join the General Agreement on Tariffs and Trade (GATT). The import substitution model for development was officially abandoned for export orientated industrialization.

The final major demand by business was for wage controls. In November 1987, President de la Madrid implemented the Economic Solidarity Pact (PECE) which froze wages and controlled some prices. Future wage increases were now under centralized government control.

The influence that big business had with the PRI could be seen in the selection of the new president. Carlos Salinas de Gortari had been in charge of economic planning and was responsible for the harsh cuts in government spending under structural adjustment. He was strongly opposed by Fidel Velázquez and the Confederation of Mexican Workers (CTM). The peasants did not support him, nor did the urban poor. Miguel Ángel Centeno reports that "from various interviews with PRI bureaucrats it appears that there was little real support for Salinas among the rank and file that managed the political machinery." The reformist Democratic Current was strongly opposed to Salinas.

In May 1987, Jorge de la Vega, head of the PRI, met with a group of businessmen who insisted that the next president must continue the policies of neoliberalism. In June 1987, Augustín Legorreta, the head of CCE, made it known that their organization backed Salinas. Centeno reports that when Salinas was selected the private sector "was ecstatic."[22]

Economic Concentration

In Mexico, it is commonly said that 300 families run the country. Business interests in Mexico are concentrated in regional conglomerates, known as *grupos*. They are patriarchal, family organizations. The main groups are 60 to 100 years old, and they represent inherited wealth.[23]

Monopoly power developed under the policies of protectionism and the national laws which hindered foreign ownership. Big business also benefitted from low taxation, a result of its close ties to the state party. All the major *grupos* have had links with one or more of the private banks. The result is that wealth in Mexico is primarily family owned, in contrast to the United States or Canada.

For example, in 1993 there were 200 Mexican firms which traded stock on the stock exchange, the Bolsa Mexicana de Valores. Some of the family owned conglomerates trade a percentage of their stock, but normally not more than 20 percent. Around 70 percent of the stock on the exchange is represented by eight companies: Banamex — Accival, Cementos Mexicanos, Grupo Carso, Grupo Cifra, Fomento Económico Mexicano, Grupo Financiero Bancomer, ICA and Teléfonos de Mexico.[24]

The Mexican economy, in general, is highly monopolized. In 1990, 2,500 firms, representing only 2.2 percent of all businesses, accounted for 52 percent of all employees and 66 percent of all production. In the industrial sector, five or fewer firms have more than 50 percent of sales in most of the sectors. For example, Cemex controls 60 percent of the cement market, engineering giant ICA controls 50 percent of the heavy construction industry, Vitro controls 90 percent of the flat glass market, Televisa's four channels have 95 percent of the viewers, and now-privatized Telmex has virtual monopoly status in telecommunications.[25]

Carlos Morera, an economist at the National Autonomous University of Mexico (UNAM), has been studying the concentration of the economy for many years. He argues that 150 families, who control 72 large conglomerate businesses and nineteen investment houses, control about 25 percent of the gross domestic product. The privatization of the state-owned enterprises and banks has greatly increased the private concentration of capital in Mexico. In the era of neoliberalism and NAFTA, these major groups are all forming joint ventures with major American corporations. But they are strong enough to insist on majority Mexican control.[26]

In 1991, a survey by *Expansion*, Mexico's most important business magazine, concluded that the ten largest conglomerates accounted for 56 percent of total sales, mobilized 61 percent of total assets, and represented 53.7 percent of employment.[27]

Janet M. Tanski, an economist at New Mexico State University, conducted a survey of studies done on economic concentration in Mexico. They all show steadily increasing concentration of power. In 1988, 1.5 percent of all manufacturing firms accounted for 71.4 percent of all value added in production, 34.3 percent of all employees, and paid wages which were three times as high as those of small manufacturers. The concentration in each manufacturing sector was much higher than in the United States, with the four largest firms having on average 70.8 percent of sales in each category.

The dominant family groups steadily increased their share of sales during the 1970s and 1980s. Even during the "lost decade" of the 1980s, they increased their wealth. A study by the Centre for Information and National Studies (CIEN) in 1989 found that between 1982 and 1988 the net profits of the seventy-two largest companies in Mexico increased by 1,634 percent. During this period small companies faced low productivity, low profits, obsolete equipment, low capacity utilization, lack of credit, and low labour productivity.[28]

Valdés argues that economic concentration in Mexico will not help solve one of its most pressing problems, lack of real jobs. The large corporations tend to be capital intensive, hiring relatively fewer people. In Canada, the top 500 corporations employ 18.5 percent of the labour force, compared to 10.4 percent in the United States, and only 2.8 percent in Mexico.[29]

The concentration of economic power has been greatly enhanced by the privatization of state-owned enterprises and the banks. The de la Madrid administration sold 743 companies and the Salinas administration sold another 415. Some of these were just shut down. The sales brought the government $22.1 billion. Between June 1991 and July 1992, a total of eighteen of the nationalized banks were sold to private groups for $12.4 billion.

José Luis Calva, an economist at UNAM, notes that "the privatization process was the simple transfer of revenues from the public sector to the private one. Instead of breaking up the public monopolies, the monopolies were passed on to private owners because free competition was not established." The Mexican public has failed to see much improvement in the performance of the privatized firms, particularly Teléfonos de Mexico (Telmex). [30]

Privatization has not resulted in more efficient operation of these companies, although the new owners have eliminated 400,000 jobs in the process. Claudia Fernández of *El Financiero International* reports that the privatized companies in financial difficulty in 1994 "represent 80 percent of the assets sold to the private sector." The common problem with these companies is "maladministration by their private owners."

David Barkin, an economist at the Metropolitan Autonomous University in Mexico City, points out that both *Forbes* and *Business Week* criticized the privatization process. "The privatization of Mexico's government holdings was systematically channelled to President Salinas' 'cronies' in a cynical abuse of the process in which it is rumoured that the President himself is a major participant enjoying enormous wealth as a result of his private holdings."[31]

A study by the Institute for Economic Investigations of UNAM in 1994 reported that after the privatizations, 50 percent of the country's assets were held by the top five business conglomerates.[32]

The largest Mexican business organization is the Business Co-ordinating Council (CCE), an umbrella group of business organizations. But within this group power is concentrated in the hands of three organizations: the Mexican Council of Businessmen (CMHN), the Mexican Association of Insurance Institutions (AMIS) and the Mexican Association of Brokerage Houses (AMCB). They have 42 percent of the votes in the CCE although they account for only 121 of more than 900,000 individual members.[33]

Politically, the most influential business organization today is the Mexican Council of Businessmen (CMHN). This closely knit group represents thirty-seven of the richest and most powerful men in Mexico. They control seventy companies which account for about 22 percent of the Mexican gross domestic product.

In 1982, President Miguel de la Madrid invited the CMHN to meet regularly with him for breakfast at the presidential mansion. These regular meetings were continued by President Carlos Salinas, and these businessmen were his closest advisers. When Salinas travelled to the United States and Canada in April 1991, to promote the North American Free Trade Agreement, he brought along eleven businessmen, eight of whom were from the CMHN.[34]

The special relationship between big business interests and the political leadership of the PRI is completely open. Carlos Salinas made no attempt to hide it.

Financing the PRI

On February 23, 1993, in the upper class Polanco district of Mexico City, there was a special dinner held at the home of Antonio Ortiz Mena, prominent businessman, former head of the Inter-American Development Bank, and Carlos Salinas' uncle. Present were key officials of the ruling Institutional Revolutionary Party (PRI): Genaro Borrego, president of the National Executive Committee and Miguel Alémán, Secretary of Finance. But the key person at the dinner was Carlos Salinas de Gortari, President of Mexico.

The invited guests were thirty very wealthy Mexican businessmen. This was not a social gathering. According to the official version, Borrego told the guests that he would like each of them to contribute $25 million to the PRI to help finance the 1994 Presidential election. The $750 million to be raised would be more than ten times the amount Bill Clinton raised during the 1992 U.S. presidential election.

The dinner meeting was soon reported in *El Economista* and *El Financiero*. The television networks and PRI-backed newspapers chose to ignore the story, but it was featured in two smaller newspapers, *Uno Mas Uno* and *La Jornada*.

In the Chamber of Deputies, representatives from the two major opposition parties, the conservative National Action Party, and the social democratic Party of the Democratic Revolution (PRD) attacked the meeting and the financing of the governing party by plutocrats. Negotiations with the PRI on proposed electoral reforms were scuttled.[35]

In his fourth state-of-the-nation speech on November 1, 1992, Salinas pledged that the PRI government would "advance on three fundamental aspects of political reform: first, to make transparent the source of party funding; second, to place ceilings on the cost of electoral campaigns; and third, to work on the communications media and the procedures which will guarantee advances in the impartiality of electoral processes."[36]

The dinner meeting came just before the PRI was holding its sixteenth party convention on March 4, celebrating sixty-four years in power. President Salinas defended the financing arrangement. He and others argued that the "independent financing" provided by the businessmen would help make the PRI less dependent on government sources for financing election campaigns.

The businessmen who attended the meeting were quite open about why they were strong supporters of President Salinas and the PRI. As the left-wing political weekly *Proceso* noted, almost all of them had benefitted greatly from the privatization of state-owned enterprises, and almost all of them had acquired major interests in one of the nationalized banks when they were privatized.

Representing large financial conglomerates, these businessmen had been strong supporters of the PRI government's move towards economic liberalization, and in particular NAFTA. As Gustavo Lomelin put it in *El Financiero*, "the alliance between the elite and the PRI is an attempt to guarantee the permanence of the neoliberal policies." Carlos Salinas and his business colleagues agree with Ronald Reagan: NAFTA is to be "the new economic constitution for North America."

Emilio Azcárraga, the head of the Televisa monopoly, and reportedly the richest man in Latin America, said he would have given $70 million to the PRI if he had been asked to do so. The policies of his close friend Carlos Salinas had been good for business in Mexico.

Ortiz Mena told reporters at a subsequent press conference that "the gain that businessmen get from supporting the PRI is the security of their investments." The goal of the neoliberal project in Mexico and elsewhere is to make it impossible for future governments to undertake either a Keynesian or socialist road to development.

Raymundo Riva Palacio of *El Financiero* noted that the meeting between Salinas and the plutocrats was not unusual. In the recent past there had been many other similar meetings. The consultation process was well known.

Alfredo Marquez of *El Economista* outlined the close ties that had been made between the PRI and big business since 1987. When the Commission to Finance and Strengthen the PRI was formed that year, twenty-five very rich businessmen were made members. Claudio X. González, president of Kimberly Clark and president of the powerful Co-ordinating Council of Businessmen (CCE), has been a very close adviser to President Salinas.

In the 1990 and 1991 state elections, big businessmen were represented on all the PRI state committees established to finance the campaigns. They were key to raising funds for the 1992 elections in the states of Chihuahua, Michoacán and Durango, where the PRI is reported to have spent $10 million. A few of these businessmen also hold elected office for the PRI. Denise Dresser reports that in the 1991 federal elections 17 percent of the PRI's candidates came from the business sector.[37]

Yet the political fallout from the meeting posed problems for President Salinas. The PRI announced that it was going to abandon this particular financing project. However, this did not mean that the PRI had admitted that they were doing something wrong; they simply established an alternative plan for raising funds from business for the 1994 presidential election.

Senator Carlos Sales Gutiérrez was put in charge of the new campaign. A new goal was set at $1 billion, to be raised before the Congress approved the campaign spending limits. Twenty businessmen were appointed to raise the funds; the majority had been at the famous February dinner. In June and July 1993, the fundraisers met with groups of businessmen who support the PRI. They asked each to give one million new pesos ($333,000). Some businessmen chose not to organize a group of donors; instead, each donated a minimum of $5 million. During the 1994 presidential campaign businessmen would also provide the PRI with planes, trucks, hotel rooms, publicity and personnel, free of charge.[38]

In July 1993, *Forbes* magazine noted that Mexico had thirteen billionaires, up from eight in 1992. Only the United States, Japan and Germany had more. Ten of the thirteen were known to have been at the famous February dinner: Emilio Azcárraga, Jeronimo Arango, Ángel Losada, Pablo Aramburuzabala, Lorenzo Zambrano, Carlos Slim, Bernardo Garza, Eugenio Garza, Adrián Sada, and Alberto Bailleres.[39] The party of the Mexican revolution had become the party of the Mexican bourgeoisie.

Notes

1. James M. Cypher, *State and Capital in Mexico.* Boulder: Westview Press, 1990, pp. 10-11.

2. Tom Barry, ed. *Mexico: A Country Guide.* Albuquerque: The Inter-Hemispheric Education Resource Center, 1992, p. 173.

3. Francisco Valdés Ugalde, "From Bank Nationalization to State Reform: Business and the New Mexican Order," in Maria Lorena Cook et al, eds., *The Politics of Economic Restructuring.* Center for U.S. Mexican Studies, University of California, San Diego, 1994, p. 221.

4. Cited in Judith Hellman, *Mexico in Crisis.* New York: Holmes & Meier, 1988, p. 50.

5. Sylvia Maxfield, *Governing Capital.* Ithaca: Cornell University Press, 1990, pp. 165-185; Rodiger Dornbusch, "Mexico's economy at the Crossroads," *Journal of International Affairs,* Vol. 43, Winter 1990, pp. 321-323; and Judith Teichman, *Policymaking in Mexico.* Boston: Allen & Unwin, 1988, p. 38.

6. Carlos Elizondo, "In Search of Revenue: Tax Reform in Mexico under the Administrations of Echeverría and Salinas," *Journal of Latin American Studies,* Vol. 26, February 1994, pp. 162-169.

7. David Barkin, *Distorted Development: Mexico in the World Economy.* Boulder: Westview Press, 1990, p. 91.

8. Teichman, *op. cit.,* pp. 45-56; Hellman, *op. cit.,* pp. 187-215.

9. Sunli Gulati, "Capital Flight: Causes, Consequences and Cures," *International Affairs,* Vol. 42, Fall 1988, pp. 165-166.

10. Manuel Pastor, Jr., "Capital Flight from Latin America," *World Development,* Vol. 18, No. 1, 1990, p. 3.

11. Dornbusch, *op. cit.,* pp. 321-322.

12. Barkin, *op. cit.,* pp. 57-75.

13. Matt Moffett, "Mexico's Capital Flight Still Racks Economy Despite Brady Plan," *Wall Street Journal,* September 25, 1989, A-1, A-10.

14. Pastor, *op. cit.*, pp. 11-12.

15. Valdes, *op. cit.*, pp. 220-229.

16. See Teichman, *op. cit.*

17. Hellman, *op. cit.*, p. 222.

18. See Barkin, *op. cit*, pp. 99-111; Teichman, *op. cit.*, pp. 111-126; and Hellman, *op. cit.*, pp. 217-228.

19. Valdés, *op. cit.*, *p. 222.*

20. Yemile Mizrahi, "Rebels Without a Cause? The Politics of Entrepreneurs in Chihuahua," *Journal of Latin American Studies*, Vol. 26, February 1994, pp. 137-158.

21. Maxfield, *op. cit.*, pp. 173-174.

22. Miguel Ángel Centeno, *Democracy within Reason*. University Park: The Pennsylvania State University Press, 1994, pp. 10-15.

23. Valdés, *op. cit.*, p. 228.

24. Augusta Vargas Medina, "Los Dineros de la Bolsa, en Pocas Manos," *Epoca*, March 8, 1993, pp. 42-43.

25. Marcos Chavez, "Los Advances de la Modernización," *El Financiero*, January 21, 1992, p. 4.

26. Josue Rodriquez, "Avanzan los Monopolios," *Motivos*, No. 35, March 23, 1992, pp. 8-11.

27. Valdés, *op. cit.*, *p. 233-234.*

28. Janet M. Tanski, "Capital Concentration, Mexican Conglomerates and the Proposed North American Free Trade Agreement," *Review of Radical Political Economics*, Vol. 25, December 1993, pp. 72-90.

29. Valdés, *op. cit.*, p. 234.

30. See Claudia Fernández, "Private Matters," *El Financiero International*, October 31, 1994, p. 8; and Claudia Fernández, "The Down Side," El Financiero International, November 7, 1994, p. 16.

31. John Summa, "Mexico's New Super-Billionaires," *Multinational Monitor*, Vol. 15, November 1994, pp. 24-26.

32. Wayne A. Cornelius, "Foreword," Cook et al, *op. cit.*, p. xiv.

33. Valdés, *op. cit.*, p. 228.

34. Matt Moffett, "Robert Hernández and the Nuevos Ricos," *Globe and Mail*, May 9, 1992, B-4; Madelaine Drohan, "Owners of Mexico throw Support behind Trilateral Deal," *Globe and Mail*, April 16, 1991, B-22.

35. See *El Economista*, March 2, 3 & 8, 1993; *La Jornada*, March 7, 1993; *El Financiero*, March 8, 1993; Jésus Ramírez Cuevas, "Privatiza," *Motivos*, No. 85, March 8, 1993, pp. 8-10; Rafael Rodríguez Casteñada, "Borrego, 29 Magnates y el Presedente de la República," *Proceso*, No. 853, March 8, 1993, pp. 6-9.

36. "Time for Serious Political Reform," *Latin America Weekly Report*, No. 44, November 12, 1992, p. 4.

37. Denise Dresser, "Embellishment, Empowerment, or Euthanasia of the PRI? Neoliberalism and Party Reform in Mexico," in Cook et al, *op. cit.*, pp. 139-140.

38. *El Financiero*, August 9, 1993, p. 1.

39. "The Millionaires," *Forbes*, July 5, 1993, pp. 76-77.

Chapter 5

CONTROLLING DISSENT

Structural adjustment policies and the new neoliberal approach to development were bound to foster opposition. While the very poor would benefit from the reduction in the rate of inflation, they would be hurt by the reduction in social spending and the cuts to food subsidy programs. The decline in real wages would be hard on workers and the emerging middle class. In addition, small business would be hurt by the move to trade liberalization. Peasants would suffer from the elimination of price supports and other government subsidy programs.

Many political and academic observers, looking at Latin America and east Asia, concluded that the implementation of neoliberalism required "authoritarian" governments, if not outright military dictatorships. How would it work in Mexico?

Mario Vargas Llosa called Mexico "the perfect dictatorship." It was a strongly authoritarian government which had been very successful in camouflaging reality. It was a one-party state, but it held regular elections and changed presidents, creating the illusion of a democratic country.

Mexico fit the model for the implementation of the neoliberal revolution. Power was centralized in the hands of the president, the mass of the population had very little influence on government policy, and there was cohesion of interests between the political and economic elite. Following the 1982 debt crisis, an ideological hegemony was established: import substitution industrialization or Keynesianism was ruled out as an option and totally ignored. Finally, there was outside support from the U.S. government, the international lending organizations, and foreign capital.[1]

There were other key factors which made implementation of neoliberalism relatively easy in Mexico. The poor and unemployed could flee to the United States, where in 1991, 13.5 million Mexicans already lived. There was no major political party on the left to become a rallying point for the opposition. The trade union movement was under the control of the president and the state party. The peasants were divided in their loyalties and ideological orientation. The mass media was completely under the control of the state party, the PRI.

The policy of neoliberalism would be implemented by the technocratic elite which had come to control the Mexican state. Most of these technocrats had been trained in U.S. universities where they had been socialized to neoliberalism. The political wing of the PRI had clearly been subordinated.

However, the 1988 election had demonstrated that there was considerable opposition to the neoliberal policies of President Miguel de la Madrid and his finance minister, Carlos Salinas. The new president had to undermine the support for Cuauhtémoc Cárdenas, keep control over the trade union movement, and renew ties with the peasants. The PRI would need to reestablish itself as the patronage arm of the state.

PRONOSOL and Concertación

Under the structural adjustment program imposed on Mexico after the 1982 debt crisis, spending on social programs had been drastically cut. In 1980, spending on education, health and welfare was the equivalent of 7.2 percent of Gross Domestic Product; by 1989, it had fallen to 6.0 percent. The International Monetary Fund, the World Bank and the U.S. government were all pressuring governments to abandon universal social programs and concentrate on smaller-scale programs which specifically targeted the most needy. The ideology of neoliberalism rejects the old Keynesian principles which held that social programs were citizenship rights.

The idea for the National Solidarity Program (PRONOSOL) was developed by Carlos Salinas while he was working on his doctorate at Harvard University. His concern was that spending on general social programs did not bring a political payoff for the party in office. The targeting of programs would allow the government to tie the money to groups of supporters, making them very aware of their dependence on the party in power.[2]

The first new program Salinas established after taking office was PRONOSOL, popularly known in Mexico as Solidarity. It was under the direct control of the president. In addition to its own budget, it had access to funds allocated to other departments.

The program targeted groups which had the potential for opposing the PRI. The Solidarity Funds for Production provided credit to 400,000 low income farmers. Over $20 million was provided through the Solidarity Funds for Indigenous Communities, which covered 18,000 local development projects for fifty indigenous groups. Cash and credit was provided under Women in Solidarity for setting up small businesses. It also provided university scholarships and distributed milk to children and food baskets to poor families.

Much of the spending went to infrastructure projects such as health clinics, the rehabilitation of schools, sports centres, drinking water and sewage improvements, installation of electricity, roads, and even low-income homes. Grants were given to municipalities to repair infrastructure.

This was not a program to eliminate poverty. As Denise Dresser points out, the total budget for 1990, divided among the seventeen million people said to live in "extreme poverty," would have provided each with only 15 cents.

Solidarity was a major public relations effort of the PRI. Propaganda regularly appeared on television and radio. President Salinas went on almost weekly "Solidarity tours," travelling around the country handing out money for projects, cutting ribbons, opening new buildings, all highlighted on the evening news. In a major tour before the 1991 federal election, Salinas handed out more land titles than had been distributed in the previous fourteen years.

The program did not necessarily target the most needy. Analysts have demonstrated the political nature of the program; it was used to try to undermine the opposition Party of the Democratic Revolution (PRD). Dresser reports that in 1991, Solidarity was operating in 171 out of the 173 municipalities controlled by the opposition parties. The tortilla program was directed mainly to the urban areas where the PRI suffered its heaviest losses in the 1988 presidential election. In 1992, the budget directed 12 percent of all spending to the relatively small state of Michoacán, the home base of Cuauhtémoc Cárdenas. The highly publicized gift from the state (the PRI) served to remind the poor that the PRD could not deliver similar programs if it were elected to local or state office. The president controlled all revenues.

Salinas followed the plan set forth in his dissertation. In order to receive the Solidarity grants, there had to be a local community structure in place. The government claims that there are now over 100,000 local Solidarity organizations, with an average of 120 members. Thus Solidarity committees and organizations came to be seen as a new PRI structure, or a parallel party system. Dresser notes that PRONOSOL regional co-ordinators figured prominently as PRI candidates for the Senate and Chamber of Deputies in the 1991 mid-term elections (and they won by larger margins than other *priístas*).

The foundation of the Mexican one-party state is the patron-client relationship between the state and social organizations. During the 1970s and 1980s, there was a growth of independent trade unions, peasant organizations and urban popular organizations which were outside the formal structure of the PRI. During the "lost decade" of the 1980s, these organizations became quite critical of the policies of Miguel de la Madrid and in the 1988 presidential election, they supported Cuauhtémoc Cárdenas. One of the main tasks facing Carlos Salinas was to bring these organizations back under the control of the state party.

In Mexico, this process is known as *concertacíon*. The state makes a settlement or agreement with an organization which is always accompanied with government funds or specific policy advantages. The Mexican political system has been based on clientelism, which recognizes that social and political organizations are subordinate to the state, and in return they receive material reward. The Solidarity program was ideally suited to promote this "divide, buy off, and conquer" strategy pursued by the Salinas administration.[4]

The Salinas administration was able to establish *concertacíon* agreements under Solidarity with a number of the large peasant groups that were independent of the PRI. This included the National Union of Regional Peasant Organizations (UNCORA), the Independent Federation of Agricultural Workers and Peasants (FIOAC), and the National "Plan de Ayala" Co-ordinating Committee (CNPA). These groups were the more militant of the peasant organizations. Not only was the government successful in co-opting them, the issue split all the peasant organizations and reduced their ability to provide a united front against the policies of the Salinas administration.[5]

The effectiveness of the policy of *concertacíon* can be seen in the strategy adopted by the Salinas administration in implementing one of its most controversial policies, changing Article 27 of the constitution. The Article guaranteed the rights of peasants to communal land owned by the state, the *ejido* lands.

President Salinas's rural development strategy called for the privatization of these lands. In general, peasants opposed this policy, but when the proposal was made by the administration, it was combined with government financial supports. As Jonathan Fox reports, all the major peasant organizations were split on the issue. Payments were made to organizations for the backlog of lands officially granted to *ejidos* but still controlled by large landowners. Those organizations who still opposed the policy changes were threatened with loss of government support programs.

Solidarity also became the major weapon in the strategy of breaking the ties of the urban popular movements with the PRD. Solidarity committees were created in the barrios where these organizations were strong. This strategy was successful. Many organizations, while loyal to the principles of democracy put forth by the PRD, were unwilling to give up the advantages that came from the agreements with the state. Many of those groups who wished to participate in the *concertación* process backed the formation of the Labour Party (PT), set up by the Salinas administration to divide the political left.[6]

Solidarity also targeted the indigenous peoples, concentrated in the southern states. They are mainly poor peasants, living on communal *ejido* lands. The opposition PRD was trying to win the support of indigenous and poor peasant organizations. The PRD took a strong stand against changes to Article 21 of the constitution.

The contributions of Solidarity to the official National Indigenous Institute (INI) increased the budget by eighteenfold in the first three years of the Salinas administration, enabling INI to provide economic development projects. These projects were delivered through the Regional Solidarity Funds, and were to be distributed through autonomous councils. There was resentment from local PRI organizations over their exclusion from the administration of the program, and the fact that the INI was working with independent peasant and indigenous organizations. Consequently, the INI was also pressured to mobilize support for the 1991 change in the constitution regarding *ejido* lands.[7]

Political Repression

While Mexican governments use co-optation to deal with political dissent, they also have a long history of political repression. Those who are detained by the police and the military regularly face torture, and if they are political threats to the government, they face the real possibility of death or disappearance. Those who are arrested and charged with an offence regularly face "paid witnesses," or professional liars, testifying against them.

Political repression is not limited to the military and the various police forces. Rich families, particularly large landowners in rural areas, have for generations employed private armies to repress rebellious peasants and indigenous peoples trying to keep what land they have left. In addition, the state has used elements in its official organizations as thugs to intimidate, brutalize and even kill political opponents.

In the area of human rights in general, Mexico has a record quite different from that of the United States and Canada. In his testimony before the U.S. House of Representatives on February 25, 1993, American businessman Christopher Whalen argued that Mexico was "an authoritarian state, where there is a government of men, not of laws." Whelan, who works extensively in Mexico and publishes *Mexico Report*, added, "It is as if there is no legal infrastructure. Everything is arranged by benefactors and contacts."[8]

In the area of human rights violations, impunity rules the day. When a case receives considerable publicity, and the government concludes that some action is required, those responsible may be removed from office. But they are rarely indicted for anything. Normally, they are just transferred to another part of the country where they carry on as before. Anyone who has spent any amount of time in Mexico knows that Mexicans want this system changed.

A few examples from the recent past will illustrate how determined the Mexican government can be when faced with serious political opposition.

1968 was a year of international student unrest and rebellion against authoritarian governments, even in Mexico City. Student political activities in July 1968 were met with extreme repression from the riot police. Schools were invaded, students attacked and beaten, tortured while in custody, and a number were killed. In response, the students proposed a general strike and formed a National Strike Committee.

The demands of the students were for an end to government abuse, release of political prisoners, abolition of the sedition acts, abolition of the special riot police, the end to military occupation of schools, and a full public inquiry into police and government repression.

This platform was combined with a general outrage that the Mexican government was spending hundreds of millions of dollars on preparation for the 1968 Olympics games while millions of Mexicans were living in extreme poverty.

Throughout July 1968, the student demonstrations built up to 500,000 activists, and they began to get support from the general public and organizations not linked to the PRI. On October 2, 6,000 students gathered for a local demonstration in Plaza of the Three Cultures in an area known as Tlatelolco. They were surrounded by 10,000 soldiers who opened fire on the crowd. No one knows exactly how many were killed, but most say around 500. Hundreds of others were wounded and 1,500 were arrested.

The government action worked: the general public was terrorized, the student movement was broken, and the National Strike Council told students to return to classes.[9]

When Carlos Salinas de Gortari named his first Cabinet, he appointed Fernando Gutiérrez Barrios to be Secretary of the Interior (Gobernacíon). The most powerful position in the federal cabinet, it is in charge of national elections and state security. Gutiérrez co-founded and served in the infamous Federal Security Directorate (DFS), a secret police organization, until 1970. It is widely reported that in 1968, he was directly in command of the forces that massacred the students at Tlatelolco.[10]

The early 1970s also saw notable examples of brutal political repression. On June 10, 1971, Corpus Christi Day, more than 10,000 students began a march to the Monument of the Revolution in the centre of Mexico City. The purpose of the demonstration was to call for the release of students held as political prisoners since the 1968 massacre. But it is also clear that the leaders wished to see a revival of the 1968 student movement.

The students were met this time by a private paramilitary organization known as the *halcones* (falcons). They had been recruited and financed by the northern capitalists at Monterrey who were strongly opposed to the populist reform policies of President Luis Echeverría. The *halcones* had been trained and equipped by the Department of the Federal District, which was under the control of right-wing elements of the PRI.

Around 1,000 *halcones* waited for the students, who were trapped in the area by special service and riot police. They attacked the students with pistols, machine guns, knives and cattle prods, after the police fired tear gas. The student demonstrators were rooted out and beaten, even when they were in churches and hospitals. Around fifty students were killed, another fifty "disappeared," and hundreds were wounded. The government claimed it was a clash between rival student political factions. Echeverría responded by releasing student prisoners and trying to co-opt their leaders into the government.[11]

In the 1960s and early 1970s, a number of guerrilla movements sprang up in Mexico, pushing the demands of landless peasants. In the state of Guerrero, there was the Nationalist Revolutionary Civic Association led by Genaro Vázquez Rojas and later the Party of the Poor under Lucio Cabañas Barrientos. There was other activity in the states of Chihuahua, Campeche, Tabasco, Veracruz, Oaxaca and Chiapas. Most of these guerrilla groups were led by university students and left-wing intellectuals. There was also the Armed Revolutionary Movement (MAR) which wanted to establish an urban revolutionary movement.

The man in charge of ending the guerrilla movements was Fernando Gutiérrez Barrios, the Deputy Minister of the Interior. He created the White Brigade under the DFS, to be run by Miguel Nazar Haro. At Military Camp Number One in Mexico City the brigade tortured, killed and "disappeared" hundreds of people suspected of being a threat to the government. Nazar Haro is reported to have personally participated in the torture of suspected guerrillas. Later, in the early 1980s, Nazar Haro was indicted for corruption and dismissed from office, reportedly because of his connections with the Guadalajara drug cartel.

Yet when Carlos Salinas became President, he appointed Nazar Haro to head a new Mexico City Police Intelligence Division. Salinas also appointed Javier García Paniagua as chief of police in Mexico City. García Paniagua had preceded Nazar Haro as head of the DFS and had also acquired a reputation as a protector of Mexico's big drug traffickers.

The Human Rights Movement

In Mexico, popular resistance to political repression grew following the 1985 earthquake. While searching through the rubble of the office of the Attorney General of Mexico City, rescuers found two cars containing the bodies of several Colombian prisoners and a lawyer. The bodies had been mutilated, and their hands were tied behind their backs. The person who was responsible for the tortures was not charged but, in fact, was appointed Minister of the Supreme Court a few months later.

Many Mexicans decided enough was enough. A number of independent human rights organizations were formed. Today there are 200 affiliated with a Mexican network, "All Rights for All." Two of the most prominent groups are the Mexican Commission for the Defence and Promotion of Human Rights, founded by Mariclaire Acosta, and the Eureka Committee for the Defence of Prisoners, the Persecuted, Disappeared Persons, and Political Exiles, founded by Rosario Ibarra de Piedra. The opposition PRD has also created a human rights commission to document the attacks on their activists and supporters.

Carlos Salinas faced a political crisis in the spring of 1990. On May 21, Norma Corona Sapien, a university professor who was president of the Sinaloa Human Rights Commission, was assassinated. The previous president of the commission, Jesús Michel Jacobo, had been gunned down in 1987 and no one had ever been arrested.

At the time of her assassination, Corona had been investigating the February 1990 murder of a Mexican lawyer and three Venezuelan university professors. Their tortured bodies were found in a shallow grave on March 11. After Corona began the investigation, she started to receive death threats, not unusual in Mexico. The Federal Judicial Police (PJF) had arrested the four victims and were the suspected murderers.

Sinaloa has been a major centre of illegal drug production and trafficking for the U.S. market. In this state, the drug traffickers have had a very close relationship to the local PRI and the police and military establishment. Miguel Ángel Félix Gallardo, known as the "El Padrino" of Mexican drug trafficking, was a close friend of the PRI governors, Leopoldo Sánchez Celis and Antonio Teledo Corro. Mexicans believe that Corona was killed because she was going to publicize the links.

In May the Inter-American Commission on Human Rights of the Organization of American States, issued a report supporting the allegations of the National Action Party (PAN) that there had been massive fraud in the local land state elections in Chihuahua and Durango in 1985 and 1986. They concluded that the state election codes were in violation of the American Convention on Human Rights which guarantees people the right to free elections.

Then, in early June, Americas Watch sent the president a copy of their first report on Mexico, *Human Rights in Mexico: A Policy of Impunity.*, to be released shortly. It recounted "an array of abuses that have become an institutional part of Mexican society: killing, torture and other mistreatment by the police during criminal investigation, disappearances, election-related political violence, violence related to land disputes, abuse directed against independent unions, and violations of freedom of the press." Adolfo Aguilar Zinser noted that this was "no different from that of any dictatorship."

The problem for Salinas was that all this bad publicity for Mexico was coming the very week he was to meet with George Bush to jointly announce the beginning of the negotiations to create the North American Free Trade Agreement (NAFTA). Publicity of Mexico's horrendous human rights record could contribute to opposition to NAFTA in the U.S. Congress.[13]

Salinas quickly announced the creation of the National Human Rights Commission (CNDH) just before flying off to Washington. Many Mexicans have argued that the primary purpose of the CNDH is to act as a public relations agency for the government. The legislation creating the commission prohibits it from investigating human rights cases where the judicial system is already involved, or any cases related to electoral or trade union activity, areas close to the heart of the PRI. Nevertheless, the commission's reports, while generally being ignored by the government, have contributed to the increase in awareness of human rights abuse in Mexico.

The extent of the use of political repression in Mexico can be illustrated by looking at several of the more recent cases.

Indigenous Peoples

In May 1990, Amnesty International visited the Triqui indigenous peoples who live on communal land in western Oaxaca. They have been under vicious attack by large landowners who have the support of local PRI authorities. These landlords wish to drive the Triqui people off their valuable agricultural land.

In 1981, the Triqui peoples formed the Movement for Triqui Unity and Struggle (MULT). Between February 1989 and the visit by Amnesty International, eighteen Triqui peasants had been killed, including a number of MULT leaders. Juan Manuel Hernández was shot by hired gunmen who worked for landlords. Aurelia Martínez Alvarez was tortured and shot in his house by soldiers from the military base at San Juan Copala. Paulino Martínez Delia and his nephew Bonifacio Merino Delia were both shot after they publicly denounced landlords for their attacks on the Triqui. Manuel Velazco Ortega was shot while working on his house by a group of men wearing police uniforms. Santiago Merino Hernández was shot by hired gunman and his house raided and burned down.

Miguel Ángel Velasco, A MULT leader, received death threats for his political activities. His ten-year-old son and a twelve-year-old friend were abducted by hired gunmen and were never seen again.

In all cases, friends and relatives reported the murders to the state authorities, but there were not even any superficial investigations. Many other Triqui have been arrested, detained and tortured.[14]

The indigenous peoples and peasants in the state of Chiapas have been under constant attack for many years. In February 1989, for example, eight peasants were killed in Pijijiapan when about fifty men — reported to be landowners and their hired gunmen — opened fire on peasants who had gathered to meet landowners and local agents of the public ministry to discuss land issues.

As in Oaxaca, the conflict is caused by local landlords who want to drive the indigenous people off their land. For example, in February 1990, peasants were evicted from their homes on the Las Alpes ranch by 500 federal judicial and public security police led by local landowners with their hired gunmen (*pistoleros*). In April 1990, 600 police, a local landowner, and his hired gunmen swept through the communities of Emiliano Zapata, Paso Achiote and Union y Progreso before dawn, forcibly evicting all families without even giving them time to take their possessions. People were beaten and arrested. In 1992, President Salinas sent 15,000 troops into Chiapas to support local authorities.

In Chiapas, the Catholic church has generally backed the indigenous peoples. The original inhabitants have never been given legal title to land they have occupied and farmed for thousands of years. In 1989, the local Bishop of San Cristóbal de las Casas, Samuel Ruiz García, created the Fray

Bartolomé de las Casas Human Rights Centre to document the repression. Peasants and indigenous peoples have been subjected to expulsion, torture, illegal detainment, and death. The conflict reached the press in Canada in 1991, when Joel Padron, a Roman Catholic priest, was arrested for giving support to the indigenous population. At the time, an estimated 6,000 people were being held in jail.

Human Rights organizations in Mexico claim that the José Patrocinio Gonzáles Garrido was one of the most brutal PRI governors in the history of Mexico. Those who dared to oppose the PRI faced jail sentences just for demonstrating and were often charged with subversion, sedition or terrorism.

But the vote was always delivered to the state party. In the 1988 presidential election, where the official results gave Carlos Salinas 50.5 percent of the vote cast, Gonzóles Garrido delivered Chiapas with an alleged 89.9 percent of the vote. Yet the peasants in this area were strong supporters of Cuauhtémoc Cárdenas, as were peasant organizations independent of the PRI-controlled National Confederation of Peasants (CNC).

How did President Salinas react to the international criticism of the rule of Patrocino Gonzáles? In January 1993, he appointed him Secretary of the Interior, which made him director of the infamous Federal Judicial Policy and head of the Federal Electoral Commission, which put him in charge of the 1994 presidential election.[15]

Political Opponents

President Carlos Salinas was determined to destroy the Party of the Democratic Revolution, which rejected the neoliberal model of development and refused to accept the official results of the 1988 election. Salinas stepped up the process of co-optation in areas where the PRD had electoral strength. But he also stepped up political repression against the party.

How significant is this repression? The Centro de Derechos Humanos Miguel Augustín Pro Juárez reports that cases involving political militants brought to them increased from 405 in 1991 to 547 in 1992. The human rights commission of the PRD claimed that 290 of their supporters and activists had been killed between 1988 and the end of 1994.

Mariclaire Acosta stated in 1991 that her organization (CMDPHD) felt that the human rights situation was going to get worse. "There is not the will to implement democracy in this country. On the contrary, each day the government is more openly authoritarian."

Michoacán, the home state of Cuauhtémoc Cárdenas, is a PRD strong-hold. We have seen that it was the focus of President Salinas's Solidarity program. At the same time, human rights abuses against local PRD activists have been high.

Shortly after the July 1992 election for governor, where electoral fraud was widely reported, four PRD supporters were ambushed and machine-gunned to death. Between July and October of that year, another five PRD activists were murdered.

In September 1992, Morelos Marx Madrigal Lachino was kidnapped by two armed men wearing PJF uniforms. He was released after three days of interrogation. His crime was being a representative of one of the inde-pendent citizens organizations that had observed the July election and re-ported massive fraud.

In that same month, eight municipal police officers in Tiquicheo, Michoacán were ambushed, four of them killed and the other four wounded. The municipality was controlled by the PRD, and two of the po-lice officers had been active members of the PRD.

Aguilla is a rural community of 15,000 in the Michoacán highlands. In this relatively impoverished state, marijuana and poppies have been the sav-ing grace for poor peasants. It has also been a target of the federal War on Drugs.

In December 1989, the people in this town rose up, threw the local PRI government out of office by a vote of three to one, and put in its place representatives of the newly formed PRD. The elected mayor was Solomon Mendoza Barajas, a local farmer.

But just before the election, the PJF arrived, carried out searches of many houses, and took dozens of locals off to prison. They sacked the house of the local PRD leader and machine gunned it. Raids continued regularly over the months. On May 5, the citizens decided to fight back, and in a shootout three federal agents and two campesinos were killed.

Hundreds of police arrived and 100 people were arrested, including women and children. One detainee died while in custody. PJF agents beat a six-year-old boy to death for refusing to tell where his father was. When Mayor Mendoza protested, he was detained in jail, beaten and tortured. Agents broke into his house, planted marijuana and cocaine evidence, and charged him with possession of illegal drugs.

The case was taken to the National Human Rights Commission. On November 28, 1990, the CNDH recommended that all charges be dropped and those detained released. On December 11, President Salinas ordered the federal Attorney General to comply with the recommendation.

Many Canadians first learned of human rights abuses in Mexico in 1993, when Dr. Mario Rojas Alba was given political refugee status. Dr. Rojas was a federal member of the Chamber of Deputies for the opposition PRD.

In January 1991, he was investigating the 1988 kidnapping, torture and murder of José Ramón García, a leader of the left-wing Revolutionary Workers Party (PRT). This is one of the most widely publicized human rights cases in Mexican history, and it was the first major test case under President Salinas.

Dr. Rojas visited three ex-policemen in a Cuernavaca prison who told him the names of the people responsible. They were members of the security forces of the state of Morelos, acting under the orders of Governor Antonio Rivas Palacio. The next, day Dr. Rojas was kidnapped, taken to a field, and slashed across the head with a machete. His life was saved when some peasants came by and his kidnappers fled.

With his lawyer, Dr. Rojas reported the facts of the García case and the attack to President Salinas's Attorney General, Morales Lechuga. The Salinas administration agreed to prosecute the policemen responsible if Dr. Rojas would agree not to involve the PRI governor. When he refused, his safety escort was lifted. Fearing for his life, he and his family fled to Canada. The killers were never prosecuted.[16]

Persecuting Women

Women have also been subject to attack when they have joined in the struggle against the system. The abuse they suffer is often sexual. In March 1989, eight women, some pregnant, were arrested and accused of crimes related to abortion. They were held incommunicado for almost twenty hours by members of the Intelligence Directorate in Tlaxcoaque, Mexico City. The women were threatened with death, stripped, kicked and beaten. Two days before their arrest the Salinas government had published a policy in the government's *Official Gazette* which stipulated that individuals held in police custody were not to be held incommunicado and that detainees should be treated "with the greatest respect and dignity."

The Anti-Narcotics Brigade of the Attorney General of the Republic was established by President Salinas, who appointed General Javier Coello Trejo as its head. In one of the most notorious human rights cases, nineteen young women were raped by the personal bodyguards of Coello Trejo in early 1989. He claimed that his men were framed as part of a smear campaign by drug traffickers.

The bodyguards were protected by Fausto Antonio Valverde, ex-director of Interpol, head of the Federal Judicial Police, and Coello Trejo's right-hand man. Salinas tried to protect him by transferring him to Washington, D.C., to head a new U.S.-Mexico drug enforcement program.

Because of the many charges of torture levelled against Coello Trejo, and a great deal of bad publicity coming just when he was beginning to promote NAFTA, President Salinas removed him from the PJF. But he was never prosecuted. Instead, Salinas named him Consumer Rights Prosecutor. As Mariclaire Acosta remarks, "This created a stir among business people who said 'Now we're going to get tortured if we raise prices!'"

Lucia Martínez of the Nationally Co-ordinated Urban Poor People's Movement reports that one of their leading neighbourhood activists, Cristina Rivera Vargas, was kidnapped, tortured and raped by the judicial police of Mexico City in February 1990.

There probably would not have been any action taken against the official rapists without the persistent work of the National Network Against Violence Against Women, a coalition of fifteen women's organizations. A few were prosecuted.

Neli Marquez of the Independent Coalition of Peasant Organizations argues that rape by the army and police agents is a general practice when a village is invaded. This happened in three villages in her home state of Chiapas in March 1989.

Amnesty International reports that women are stripped and threatened with rape while in police custody. Victims say that prison guards sexually abuse male and female prisoners. They report that in January 1990, three women detained in Oaxaca while marching to a demonstration alleged that they were sexually abused and forced to sign false confessions.

Women from the Union de Colonias Populares of Irapuato, Guanajuato reported that twenty-one women in their organization were kidnapped, beaten and held in detention in early 1990. Two pregnant women were beaten in the stomach, and one of them miscarried as a result. One who was released was put out in the street in her underwear. The men in the leadership of the UCOPI were warned to look after their women or they would be raped.

As Amnesty International concludes, "the victims of torture are not limited to specific sectors of the population," they include political activists, peasants, human rights activists, people suspected of being in the drug industry, and women and children.[17]

A Favourable Press

The mass media in Mexico has been controlled by the PRI through ownership, and economic and political pressure. Journalists will tell you that there is a system of "self-censorship," where they know what they can and cannot publish. For example, there is a long-standing tradition that the mass media will not directly criticize the president.

Journalists in Mexico who write articles critical of the PRI or their governments, or report on the corruption in the narcotics area, are asking for trouble. They are regularly subjected to death threats, attacks, beatings and assassination. PEN International documented the deaths of twenty-eight journalists between 1988 and 1992. The Mexican magazine *Comunicacíon* reported that between 1990 and 1993 there was an average of one attack on a journalist every five days.

The Mexican Committee to Protect Journalists says that sixty-eight journalists have been murdered since 1982, but others put the figure as high as 300. Mariclaire Acosta insists that Mexico has the highest number of murdered journalists of any country in Latin America. The International Press Institute notes that "Mexico has an annual Press Freedom Day, but there have been occasions when this has seemed like a bad joke."

In the fall of 1991, members of the Canadian Committee to Protect Journalists went to Mexico to discuss the situation with Mexican journalists. They reported that nineteen journalists had been murdered since 1988 and that at that rate more journalists would be killed during the regime of Carlos Salinas than any other president.

Mexican journalists reported that they were under greater pressure than ever before, because of the rise of the PRD as a serious opposition and the desire of President Salinas for good public relations while the North American Free Trade Agreement was under negotiation.

The journalists reported that they receive unidentified telephone threats to themselves and their families, unidentified people come into their office and suggest that they "tone down" their criticism or drop a story they are developing, and of course they are offered the *embute*, the usual bribe.

On June 10, 1990, Alfredo Cordova Solorzano, editor of the Tapachula, Chiapas daily *Uno Mas Uno* and a correspondent for *Excelsior* was shot in his home by three men. He had written several articles on the connection between powerful local families and the drug trade.

Jorge Enrique Toledo Coutino wrote an article in his newspaper, *El Dia*, complaining about the beating his father had received from the PJF.

He was persecuted, jailed, and his newspaper in Chiapas was shut down. After a great deal of public pressure, he was finally released one year later.

One highly publicized case involved Dr. Victor Manuel Oropeza, a journalist and left-wing political activist. He was a regular columnist for two local newspapers in Ciudad Jaurez, Chihuahua. He began to write a series of articles exposing the connections of the PJF to drug trafficking. He also wrote about Manuel Buendia, a journalist murdered in 1984 by the Federal Security Police.

On July 3, 1991, Oropeza's body was found. He had been tortured and murdered. The PJF took charge of the investigation and produced some alleged murderers. They had signed confessions after being tortured by the PJF. The case was so obviously false that the Attorney General's human rights officer, Maria Teresa Jardei Alonso, resigned in protest.

On February 2, 1993, Roberto Mancilla Herrera, who had been reporting on the serial murders of gay men in Chiapas, was found shot in his car.

Intimidation from the government and the PRI is not limited to regular journalists. In 1990, three well-known and respected Mexican academics, Adolfo Aguilar Zinzer, Lorenzo Meyer, and Jorge Castañeda all received death threats after publishing articles critical of Salinas's economic policies.[18]

Torture with Impunity

Torture is prohibited under the Mexican Constitution of 1917. Mexico has ratified international human rights treaties which prohibit torture and require governments to take action to prevent it. In 1990, the Salinas administration enacted the Federal Law to Prevent and Sanction Torture, which carries a prison sentence of between two to ten years. But all human rights organizations, whether Mexican or international, insist that torture is a regular practice in Mexico. In July 1990, the Campeche state Bar Association argued that 99 percent of criminal suspects detained in the state were tortured or ill treated.

In July 1991, the Tijuana-based Binational Human Rights Center identified fifty different torture techniques used by police after interviewing 158 persons who had been detained. They included electric shocks to genitals, burning through fingernails with red-hot metal clips and the use of the electric cattle prod. In recent years, because of increased publicity, the police have emphasized techniques that don't leave as many body marks. Most popular is *la bolsita*, putting a plastic bag over a person's head and fastening it airtight. The other popular technique is *Tehuacanazo*, forcible introduction of carbonated water into the victims nostrils. The carbonated water is usually laced with hot chili powder. *Submarino humedo* is also widely used, holding a person's head under water.

Why is torture so widely used? First, there is the Mexican legal tradition. Those who are accused of a crime in Mexico are normally convicted by their own confession, which is signed while in police custody. Judges normally accept these confessions as adequate evidence for conviction.

Then there is the issue of impunity. Amnesty International argues that "a principal factor why torture is widespread is the almost total impunity extended to torturers. Police officers implicated are rarely subject to an investigation and even less frequently prosecuted."

Americas Watch agrees. Rarely are human rights violators prosecuted. "It is far more typical for police officers who engage in serious abuses to be dismissed from duty or transferred to another area. Those arrested are often charged with lesser crimes than those actually committed." For example, rather than being charged with torture, they are charged with abuse of authority, which carries a much lighter sentence.

In June 1990, President Carlos Salinas stated that "my government intends to abolish impunity while at the same time assuring respect for human rights and making more efficient and honest the protection of public security and the imparting of justice." Yet human rights organizations agree with the Miguel Augustín Jesuit Human Rights Centre in Mexico City which argues that repression has increased during the Salinas administration.

On January 1, 1994, the poor peasants of Chiapas began their uprising against NAFTA and Salinas's agricultural policies. The president responded with an all-out military attack. Human rights organizations and the press responded quickly. Within a few days the world saw pictures of murdered peasants lying in the street, tortured, their hands tied behind their backs. President Salinas gave the military amnesty for its human rights abuses.

One year later, President Ernesto Zedillo ordered a military attack on the same Zapatista rebels. On February 8, 1995, unidentified federal police agents entered a house in Yanga, Vera Cruz which allegedly harboured supporters of the peasant rebels. Six people were taken to jail, beaten, and tortured. Rosa Hernández was blindfolded, chained, a wet sheet was put over her, and the police gave her electric shocks all over her body. In Chiapas, the military brutalized peasants suspected of supporting the Zapatistas, and destroyed their property; many were detained, tortured, and some have disappeared. One of President Zedillo's major promises was to transform the police and the judicial system.

Why is this repression continuing? Under the existing Mexican political system, repression is necessary as an instrument of social control of the opposition. When dissidents do not respond to the carrot of co-optation, patronage or corruption, they face an escalating level of the stick, from warnings, threats, loss of job, arrest, imprisonment and torture. Political assassination is the ultimate deterrent.

It may be that Carlos Salinas and his American-educated technocrats would have liked very much to eliminate human rights abuses. But the reality of the Mexican one-party state is that these technocrats at the top must rely on the PRI organization to carry out the elections that give a sense of legitimacy to the government in Mexico City. Torture and abuse are deeply entrenched in the local PRI system.

Mexicans are very cynical about promises and speeches by PRI officials, dismissing them as mere propaganda and empty rhetoric. Politicians are judged on what they do, not what they say. For example, while Carlos Salinas was promising to improve human rights, the president's Office for Social Communications was declaring some of his most prominent opponents "enemies of the president." These were mainly academics who dared to publicly oppose his policies. People on this list received death threats.[19]

Notes

1. For one view of this issue see Miguel Ángel Centeno, *Democracy Within Reason*. University Park: The Pennsylvania State University Press, 1994, 1-41.

2. Carlos Salinas de Gortari, *Political Participation, Public Investment, and System Support*. Ph.D dissertation, Harvard University, 1978.

3. See Denise Dresser, *Neopopulist Solutions to Neoliberal Problems* Center for U.S.-Mexican Studies, University of California, San Diego, 1991; and Wayne A. Cornelius et al, *Transforming State-Society Relations in Mexico*. Center for U.S-Mexican Studies, University of California, San Diego, 1994.

4. For a discussion of this see Jonathan Fox, "The Difficult Transition from Clientelism to Citizenship," *World Politics*, Vol. 46, January 1994, pp. 151-184.

5. See Dresser, *op. cit.*; Cornelius, *op. cit.*; and Jonathan Fox, "Political Change in Mexico's New Peasant Economy," in Maria Lorena Cook et al, *The Politics of Economic Restructuring*. Center for U.S.-Mexican Studies, University of California, San Diego, 1994, pp. 243-276.

6. See Paul Lawrence Haber, "The Art and Implications of Political Restructuring in Mexico: The Case of the Urban Popular Movements," in Cook et al, *op. cit.*, pp. 277-303.

7. Jonathan Fox, "The Difficult Transition from Clientelism to Citizenship," *op. cit.*

8. Carlos Puig, "En torno de TLC ocurre todo lo que al gobierno Mexicano la gustararia que no ocurriera," *Proceso*, No. 852, March 1, 1993, p. 23.

9. See Judith Hellman, *Mexico in Crisis*. New York: Holmes and Meier, 1986, pp. 173-186.

10. Mike Tangeman, "Mexico: Prospects for Change," *Democratic Left*, Vol. 19, March-April 1989, pp. 19-20.

11. Hellman, *op. cit.*, pp. 202-204.

12. Alan Riding, *Distant Neighbors*. New York: Vintage Books, 1989, pp. 102-103; Peter A. Lupsha, "Drug Lords and Narco-Corruption: The Players Change but the Game Continues," in Alfred W. McCoy and Allan A. Block, eds. *War On Drugs*. Boulder: Westview Press, 1992, pp. 180-181; Larry Rohter, "Former Mexican Soldier Describes Executions of Political Prisoners," *New York Times*, February 19, 1989, A-1; A-20; and Jonathan Marshall, "CIA Assets and the Rise of the Guadalajara Connection," in McCoy and Block, *op. cit.*, pp. 201-203.

13. Americas Watch, *Unceasing Abuses*. New York, September 1991, pp. 10-11; Amnesty International. *The Norma Corona Sapien Case*, August 13, 1990; Inter-Church Committee on Human Rights in Latin America, *Human Rights Abuses in Mexico*. Toronto, 1991; Ellen L. Lutz, "Human Rights in Mexico: Cause for Continuing Concern," *Current History*, Vol. 92, February 1993, pp. 79-81; Adolfo Aguilar Zinser, "Mexico: The Authoritarian Friend and Partner," *Peace and Democracy News*. Vol. 6, Winter 1992, p. 42.

14. Amnesty International, "Mexico: Report of the Human Rights Violations against Members of the Triqui Indigenous Group." Ottawa: Amnesty International, 1991; and Amnesty International, *Mexico: Torture with Impunity*. New York, September 1991, pp. 13-14.

15. Centro de Derechos Humanos Fray Bartolomé de las Casas, *Informe de Los Casos Mas Significativos de Violacion a Los Derechos Humanos en Chiapas*, March-June 1990. Justicia y Paz, Mexico City, June 1990; "Barefoot in Chiapas,": *Economist*, Vol. 322, January 11, 1992, p. 42; Linda Diebel, "Nowhere to Hide," *Toronto Star*, March 14, 1993, F-1; Americas Watch, 1991, *op. cit.*, p. 26.

16. Jesús Ramírez Cuevas, "Repression," *Motivos*, Vol. 2, March 1, 1993, pp. 20-23; Tim Wise, "Mexico's Hottest Industry," *Dollars & Sense*, February 1993, pp. 16-17; Lutz, *op. cit.*, p. 79; "NAFTA versus Human Rights," *Central America Update*, October 1992, pp. 60-61; Andrew Reding, "Drugs, Politics and Reform in Mexico," *Z Magazine*, Vol. 3, December 1990, pp. 87-93; Amnesty International 1991, *op. cit.*, pp. 11-12; Americas Watch 1991, *op. cit.*, p. 5; Linda Hossie, "A Free Trade in Human Rights?" *Globe and Mail*, March 20, 1993, D-3; John Ross, "The Bloody Trail of Carlos Salinas," *The Nation*, November 22, 1993, pp. 614-617.

17. Mariclaire Acosta, "The Democratization Process in Mexico: A Human Rights Issue," *Resist*, No. 232, January 1991, pp. 1-8; Tim Girvin, "Murder with Impunity," *Index on Censorship*, No. 19, November 1990, pp. 3-5; Elaine Burns, "Mexican Women Protest Official Rape," *Guardian*, March 21, 1990, p. 15; Americas Watch 1991, *op. cit.*, p. 12; and Amnesty International 1991, *op. cit.*, pp. 13, 26.

18. Louise Dennys, "Mexico's Record Badly Tarnished," *Globe and Mail*, April 7, 1993, A-21; Keler Leon, "Freedom to Kill the Press," *Toronto Star*, April 20, 1993, A-17; Ellen Saenger, "Danger in Mexico," *Bulletin*, Spring 1992, pp. 17-21; Oliver Ward, "Terror Muzzles Mexican Media," *Toronto Star*, January 27, 1992, A-11; Alberta Manguel, "Shooting the Messenger," *Globe and Mail*, November 30, 1991, D-3; "World Press Freedom Review: Mexico." *IPI Report*, December 1990, p. 21; and Americas Watch 1991, *op. cit.*, pp. 29-31.

19. Amnesty International 1991, *op. cit.*, pp. 25-27; Americas Watch 1991. *op. cit.*, pp. 9-10;
    "Torture Techniques Total 50," *Globe and Mail*, July 4, 1991, A-12; Wise, *op. cit.*, p. 17;
    Tom Barry, ed, *Mexico: A Country Guide*. Albuquerque: The Inter-Hemispheric Education
    Resource Center, 1992, pp. 61-70; Gervin, *op. cit.*, pp. 3-4; Elizabeth Kadetsky, "Rounding
    Up the Usual Suspects," *The Nation*, February 14, 1994, pp. 200-202; National Commis-
    sion for Democracy in Mexico, "Testimonies of Torture," February 10, 1994, p. 8.

Chapter 6

THE STRUGGLE FOR LABOUR RIGHTS

When Carlos Salinas took office on December 1, 1988 he was determined to demonstrate that he was in charge. He also wanted to show potential investors that the new administration was going to be hard on trade unions.

The manufacturing-for-export development strategy called for "the liberalization of the labour market." Throughout the world, this has included an attack on trade unions and the rights of workers. Minimum wages fell, workers' fringe benefits were cut back, and social programs that aided workers were slashed. In the industrialized world, unemployment insurance programs and pensions were under attack. The state openly intervened in strikes on the side of the owners.

In all countries, trade unions were on the defensive, trying to keep what they had gained in collective bargaining and together with other popular groups, mobilized to try to protect social programs. But as companies and governments shed jobs, membership declined, and it became increasingly difficult to organize new places of employment. Mexico was no different.

On January 10, 1989, Carlos Salinas ordered the police and military troops to attack the home of Joaquin "La Quina" Hernández Galicia, the leader of the powerful petroleum workers union (STPRM). A bazooka was used to blow down the door of his house. There was a shootout with La Quina's bodyguards, and La Quina and fifty other union leaders were arrested for "corruption and gangsterism." When the union went on strike against PEMEX in protest, Salinas sent in the army to take over the oil operations.

A week later, President Salinas named the new leader of the union, Sebastian Guzmán Cabrera. The high officials of STPRM agreed. So did the leadership of the Mexican Confederation of Labour (CTM). The union leaders organized a successful ratification vote by packing the union halls with PRI supporters.

La Quina was a powerful union leader. He was personally corrupt, but not more so than many other leaders of the "official" unions linked to the PRI. He had obtained for the regular petroleum workers wages which were among the highest in Mexico. His crime was that he opposed Salinas's plan for the piecemeal privatization of PEMEX, the state-owned oil monopoly. In the 1988 presidential election La Quina had told his members to vote

for Cuauhtémoc Cárdenas, the left-wing candidate for president who opposed privatization of PEMEX, and they had.

In addition, the union had filed charges of fraud against Mario Ramón
Geteta, formerly head of PEMEX, governor of the state of Mexico, and personal friend of Salinas.[1]

The press in North America emphasized these activities, arguing that
they showed that Salinas was committed to cleaning up corruption. But
no one in Mexico was fooled. The new leadership of the STPRM was loyal
to the PRI, and the nature of the union leadership did not change. That
the issue was not corruption, but loyalty to the president, was demonstrated in how Salinas dealt with the National Union of Educational workers (SNTE).

The SNTE is reported to be the biggest trade union in Latin America.
Since 1972, it was ruled by Carlos Jonguitud Barrios, who had seized power
in an armed attack on the union headquarters. A PRI loyalist, he served on
the National Executive Committee and was rewarded by being made governor and senator from his home state of San Luis Potosí.

Within the SNTE, Jonguitud formed the Revolutionary Vanguard, an
organization of loyalists who named him "president for life."

Like all major unions in Mexico, the members had no power to choose
their own leaders. In 1979-80 dissident members formed the National Co-
ordinating Organization of Education Workers (CNTE), a militant organization within the union. It mobilized around 300,000 members, or about
one-third of the teachers. Thousands were expelled from the SNTE for opposition to the leadership. Around 150 were murdered.

Tough and corrupt, Jonguitud was one of the most powerful union
bosses (*charros*) in Mexico. But he was a friend and supporter of Carlos Salinas, and he had used all his powers to support Salinas in the 1988 election.

In early 1989, teachers were earning about $150 per month, about
one-third what they were making in 1980. Salinas's Secretary of Education
offered them a 10 percent pay increase. About half of the teachers went on
an illegal strike, which included a march of 300,000 teachers on Mexico
City. The leadership of SNTE denounced the strike.

But the leadership of the union had been unable to deliver "social
peace" to the PRI. After conferring with Salinas, Jonguitud retired and
Elba Gordillo was selected to head the union. Gordillo was a member of
the Revolutionary Vanguard and loyal to Jonguitud and the PRI. The membership had no voice in this decision. In return, the Salinas administration
gave the teachers a 25 percent wage increase.[2]

Unions and the PRI

Canadians and Americans who attended meetings and other conferences with Mexicans in the early 1990s were often puzzled by the fact that the representatives from the major trade union confederations in Mexico supported NAFTA and the neoliberal policies advanced by President Carlos Salinas. As these unions are affiliated with the International Labour Organization (ILO) and the International Confederation of Free Trade Unions (ICFTU), representatives from unions affiliated with the Canadian Labour Congress (CLC) and the American Federation of Labour-Congress of Industrial Organization (AFL-CIO) must deal with these representatives as brothers and sisters.

However, the ILO and the ICFTU are both products of the Cold War. They have been preoccupied with the lack of independence for trade unions in countries dominated by communist parties. They have not looked at capitalist countries to see if their labour practices meet the fundamental ILO requirements: the right to free association, the right to collective bargaining and to strike, the right to employment and a living wage, the right to nondiscrimination and the right to a safe and healthy workplace. Mexican workers do not believe that they have any of these rights.

Mexican workers and trade unions participated in the 1910-17 revolution. The Red Battalions, formed by the House of World Labour in Mexico City, had backed Venustiano Carranza. But the new president had no intentions of allowing the development of an independent, militant trade union movement. When a general strike was called for in Mexico City in 1916, Carranza closed the house of labour, arrested the strike leaders, and began repressing the trade union movement.

The Constitution of 1917 gave workers rights which were the most progressive in the world at the time. The problem has always been the recognition and administration of these rights.[3]

The Mexican precedent was set in 1918, with the formation of the Regional Confederation of Mexican Workers (CROM). In 1919, the leadership in CROM signed a secret agreement with Alvaro Obregón. In return for support of Obregón in the 1920 presidential election, CROM received funding and privileged political support from the government. This arrangement continued, the confederation took a very pro-government position and in return received official support from Presidents Obregón (1920-1924) and Plutarco Elías Calles (1924-1928).

By 1925, CROM was the dominant confederation in Mexico and claimed to have two million members, around two-thirds of all organized workers. It came under the control of Luis Morones, who maintained close links with the American Federation of Labour craft unions in the United States. CROM set the pattern for trade union behaviour in Mexico: in return for official government support, it disciplined workers and blocked strikes.

The leadership in CROM became more dependent on funding from the state, and more corrupt. During the presidency of Calles, the CROM leaders signed another secret agreement, this time pledging to inform the administration of all strike plans and to support all government decisions and decrees. In return, CROM got more money and Morones was made Minister of Labour. Other union officials got high political appointments.

As part of the alliance with the state, CROM was mandated to battle the General Labour Confederation (CGT), the left wing union organization with strong elements of both communism and anarcho-syndicalism. CROM still exists today and has its strength in the textile industry.

In the 1920s, workers found that their strikes were declared illegal and that often the president sent in the military to suppress them. Morones, as Labour Minister and head of CROM, declared that no member union could go on strike without the support of the union confederation. Corruption was rampant. Morones brazenly displayed his own personal wealth. The CROM blackmailed employers, using the threat of calling strikes, and companies paid off. But unions began to break away from CROM.

In 1928, while campaigning for president, Alvaro Obregón was assassinated. Calles named an interim president, Emilio Portes Gil, who hated the CROM. He launched a concerted campaign against the confederation, and it began to collapse. Portes Gil established the Boards of Conciliation and Arbitration, and gave them the power to officially recognize trade unions and strikes. This was a period of labour militancy and popular opposition to the authoritarian leadership in CROM. The end result was that by the time Lázaro Cárdenas became president in 1934, the trade union movement was splintered and weak.

The Depression of the 1930s raised the spectre of left-wing revolution. For many in Mexico, President Cárdenas was too left-wing. While Governor of Michoacán, Cárdenas had faced the united opposition of the church, the Cristeros, and the large landowners. In response, he had formed the Michoacán Regional Confederation of Workers, and organizations of both peasants and workers, and armed them. Now as president, Cárdenas took the position that workers had the right to strike. In the summer of 1935, former president Calles began mobilizing to try to overthrow Cárdenas.

The trade union movement, fearing a fascist coup, united behind the Cárdenas government. In February 1936, President Cárdenas personally confronted the Monterrey capitalists over the lockout of workers at the Vidriera glass works. He threatened nationalization, and they backed down. Cárdenas won labour support, and the result was the formation of the Confederation of Mexican Workers (CTM). In the beginning, the CTM had a class-struggle orientation. Vincente Lombardo Toledano, a CTM founder, was general secretary between 1936 and 1941. Its original motto, "For a Society without Classes," was later changed to "Social Peace."[4]

In 1938 Cárdenas reorganized the Party of the Mexican Revolution (PRM). The CTM and CROM became part of the "labour sector" of the ruling party. With strong support from the state party, the CTM grew and became the dominant labour federation in Mexico.

The president also created the Federation of Unions of Workers in the Service of the State (FSTSE). The SNTE is affiliated with FSTSE. Under Mexican law its members are prohibited from joining other trade union federations. State employees in Mexico do not have the right to strike. Under the president's plan, white collar workers were to be separated from blue collar workers.

Lázaro Cárdenas was a populist nationalist. He wanted to create a corporatist state which involved co-operation between all sectors of the society. He was afraid that a coalition between a strong trade union movement and peasants would create the base for a more radical left-wing party, one that could dominate Mexican politics.

In addition to splitting the trade unions, Cárdenas created the National Peasant Confederation (CNC), which was then officially linked to the revolutionary party. Cárdenas then decreed that workers and peasants could not belong to the same organizations.

Within the trade union movement in Mexico there have always been many political factions. The two major factions in the 1940s were identified with Lombardo Toledano, who was associated with the Communist Party, and Fidel Valázquez, who was on the political right.

In 1941, Valázquez became general secretary of the CTM. Following the Cold War strategy developed in Washington in 1947, the right wing, under Valázquez, expelled Toledano and the communists from the CTM. The left-wing and militant sectors of the trade union movement broke with the CTM and formed the Unitary Workers' Confederation (CUT). They led mass demonstrations against antistrike legislation introduced by President Miguel Aléman (1946-52).[5]

Aléman mounted an anticommunist attack on the militant opposition trade unions and the CUT. Between October 1948 and June 1951, known leftists and union militants were expelled from the three most important CTM affiliates: railroad, mining-metalworking, and petroleum workers' unions. The left was defeated in the trade union movement, and Valázquez became the authoritarian leader of the CTM. At age ninety-four, he still heads this confederation.

In 1952, President Alémanfacilitated the formation of the Confederation of Revolutionary Workers and Peasants (CROC). Alémanrepresented the right-wing, pro-business arm of the PRI. His goal was to undermine the strength of the CTM. Both the CTM and CROC were ideologically and political loyal to the PRI, but they would compete for government favours and the membership of union locals. Today CROC mainly represents small unions. Its largest affiliate, the Union of Garment Workers and Allied Trades (STCSRM), represents only 30 percent of the workers in the textile industry.

Over the years other smaller union organizations have been formed, but all have been basically loyal to the PRI. In 1966, the PRI organized the Congress of Labour (CT), a confederation of all the "official" unions and confederations who are formally linked to the PRI. The CTM dominates the CT.[6]

There are also "white unions" in Mexico, what North Americans call company unions. Those in the large industries are affiliated with the National Federation of Autonomous Union Associations (FNASA). The company unions in smaller plants are affiliated with the National Federation of Independent Unions (FNSI). These company unions are widespread in the Monterrey industrial area. In the state of Nuevo Leon, "white unions" comprise two-thirds of the organized workers.

Today the only truly independent trade union federation is the Authentic Labour Front (FAT), formed in 1960. Originally, it was a Roman Catholic confederation like the Confederation of National Unions (CSN) in Québec. Today, it fights for democratic labour rights and opposes government-trade union collusion. Its membership is small because the Mexican state and the "official" unions do everything in their power to deny it new union registrations.[7]

Corporatism

Since 1918, the main Mexican trade unions and their federations have been closely linked to the state and its political party. In Mexico this political system is often referred to as *corporativismo*, the corporate state. There is

Mexican Labour Congress Membership
(Affiliated with the PRI)

Organization	Percentage
CTM	30
National Confederations:	
CROC	7
CROM	3
Four others	2
FSTSE	34
National Industrial Unions	15
Independent Organizations	9
Total	100

Source: Durand Ponte, 1991, Table 4.1.
NOTE: In 1992 the estimated trade union membership was four million.

close co-operation between capital and labour. Many in Mexico compare it to the state-labour situation that existed in Mussolini's Italy. But others do not believe that this analogy is accurate, for while the PRI is closely linked to big business, it is not an openly fascist party. Thus the term "official" is given to the unions which are affiliated with the PRI, indicating that they are under state control.

The ruling PRI often appoints union leaders. The key precedent was established in 1948, when President Miguel Aléman used the police and the military to remove the radical leaders of the railway worker's union (STFRM) and named the new secretary general, Jesús Díaz de Leon. A dictatorial ruler of this union, he was known as *El Charro* for his fancy cowboy clothes. Since then all dictatorial and corrupt leaders of trade unions have been known as *charros*.

The leadership of the CTM regularly gives support to controversial presidential policies. For example, in 1968 the official unions strongly supported the government when it was widely criticized for the massacre of unarmed students at Tlatelolco. They supported the brutal suppression of the

left-wing guerrilla bands in the 1970s. In 1977, they originally opposed political reforms, including the legalization of left-wing political parties; but
they eventually agreed to the proposals.

In 1987, Fidel Velázquez called for the expulsion of the Democratic
Current from the PRI, including its most famous leader, Cuauhtémoc
Cárdenas. As Victor Manuel Durand Ponte argues, "rather than supporting
proposals for internal PRI democratization, the CTM again revealed that
the traditional labour leadership's greatest fear is the democratization of
the political system and of Mexican society more generally."[8]

The official trade union leadership supported the Economic Solidarity
Pacts (PECE), which froze wages and resulted in a steady decline in workers' real incomes. They supported the privatization of state-owned enterprise, even though this resulted in the loss of 400,000 union jobs, and they
have supported the basic neoliberal economic agenda, including joining
the General Agreement on Tariffs and Trade (GATT) and NAFTA.

On a practical level, the leadership of the CTM has worked to discour-
age strikes and to crush militant movements within their member unions.
Working together with the PRI, they have fought the development of an independent trade union movement.

During election campaigns the official unions turn out their members
for the demonstrations, get out the vote for the PRI, and harass the political opposition. The annual May Day rally in Mexico City is confined to official unions and is a display of labour support for the PRI government.

The leadership of the official unions benefit greatly from their ties to
the state. The PRI governments regularly use the police and the military to
crush dissident unions. The CTM and the PRI use their power on the
Boards of Conciliation and Arbitration to stop strikes, to declare others illegal, and to frustrate the collective bargaining process.

For example, in the famous railway strikes of 1958-59, organized by
rank and file members, the government refused to accept the new democratically-elected union leaders and eventually charged union secretary
general, Demetrio Vallejo, and other union leaders, with subversion and sedition. Several received eleven-year jail sentences.

Representatives from official unions sit on many government boards.
They are also granted a share of PRI positions in the Senate, the Chamber
of Deputies, and state legislatures.

The dues collected from the rank and file members are relatively low
because wages are low. But the union leadership completely controls how
the money is used. The official unions also get various donations and contracts from the PRI and the government, and they benefit from payoffs

from employers. The leadership of the official unions become wealthy while holding office, many becoming millionaires.[9]

As Ilaá Bizberg has argued, the control of the major trade unions has been essential to the development of the one-party state and industrialization in Mexico. Workers' salaries were kept low during the initial period of industrialization. In most countries, opposition to neoliberalism has been led by the organized working class, but not in Mexico. Most importantly, PRI control of the major trade unions has prevented the development of a serious opposition party on the left, either Marxist or social democratic.[10]

During the period of industrialization (1950-76) the organized workers in Mexico were able to make considerable gains in wages and fringe benefits. Labour's share of the gross domestic product rose from 25 percent in 1950 to 36 percent in 1976. The current economic crisis has served as an excuse for a general attack on labour. Labour's share of GDP had dropped to below 25 percent by the middle of Carlos Salinas's sexenio.[11]

Organized workers in Mexico have always received wages higher than those without unions. Members of trade unions originally received benefits that other workers did not get. The Mexican Institute of Social Security (IMSS) was created in 1943. It provided pensions, medical care and family planning services to unionized workers and their dependents. The IMSS now provides services to all regular, full time salaried workers. The Security and Social Services Institute for Government Workers (ISSSTE) provides similar services for members of FSTSE.

In return for supporting the government in the 1968 massacre, the Echeverría administration created the Workers' Housing Institute (IN-FONAVIT) to help finance housing for union members. The National Fund for Workers Consumption (FONACOT) provided cheap loans to organized workers to help them buy household goods. In 1977, President José López Portillo created the Workers Bank (BO) to provide banking services.[12]

Especially important to the official unions is their role on the Federal Conciliation and Arbitration Boards. Unions which are not officially recognized by the state are denied benefits of the federal labour code. The representatives of the official unions and the PRI on these boards regularly deny recognition to independent unions.

The contracts of official unions contain exclusion clauses recognizing the union as the sole bargaining agent; all workers are required to join the union. These contracts also include a clause that requires the employer to fire any employee who loses his union membership. The leadership of the official unions and the company management regularly use these clauses to dismiss dissident workers and anyone trying to change the union leadership.

Strikes are controlled by the Arbitration and Conciliation boards. To have a legal strike, unions must pass a myriad of tests contained in the 700-page Federal Labour Law. No union can ever meet all the requirements. This gives the boards the arbitrary power to approve or block any strike. The official unions use this power to punish dissident workers and union locals.

If the board rules a strike is "illegal," the employer can dismiss the workers at will. The board can also declare a strike to be "nonexistent" if they deem it will "threaten the balance between the rights of labour and those of capital." When such a declaration is made, workers must return to their jobs within forty-eight hours.[13]

State Repression

Despite the control of official trade unions by the state party, there has been a long history of labour struggle in Mexico. The higher wages and the social wage were not simply granted to workers to buy their loyalty; they were the end result of political and collective bargaining action.

The shift to neoliberalism was not welcomed by the organized working class. At the time of the 1982 debt crisis, the Congress of Labour and the CTM both strongly opposed the structural adjustment program. The CTM advanced a Keynesian-based alternative economic program. It called for progressive taxation, restrictions on capital flight, and using petroleum profits for national development. The program was viewed as an attempt to revive the Cárdenas alternative of "revolutionary nationalism."

With Miguel de la Madrid in office, the CTM faced the reality of the alliance between the leadership of the PRI and the business community in early 1983. They responded by forming an alliance with the independent trade unions and the political left. A co-ordinated strike program was developed. However, the government split the labour movement by negotiating special agreements with the other confederations, CROC, CROM and FSTSE.[14]

Mexican workers also have a long history of struggling for democratic rights and independent trade unions. In the 1970s, and into the early 1980s, there was a grass roots movement which was strong in the automobile, steel, metalworking, mining, electrical, and nuclear industries, as well as in the universities. The conflicts were with the official unions and the government. As the demand for democracy increased, the official unions and the government responded with violence.[15]

The strategy for Mexican economic development pursued by Presidents de la Madrid and Salinas is the classic IMF-World Bank model emphasizing production for export and the attraction of foreign investment. Central to this strategy is the necessity of low wages. During the 1980s, real wages in Mexico fell by 65 percent, primarily because of rapid inflation.

But the PRI government has also relied on wage and price control agreements with organized labour. The Salinas government renewed the Pact for Stability and Economic Growth (PECE) in December 1988, to run through 1994. Under this program, real wages have been consistently falling. For example, in 1991 the inflation rate was down to 18.8 percent but the average increase in wages and salaries under the Pact was only 4.3 percent. The leadership of the PRI unions agreed to this process.[16]

The neoliberal policies of the Presidents de la Madrid and Salinas inevitably led to clashes with workers. The presidents stepped up the use of the police and the military in disputes with organized labour.[17]

Police and state violence were used to break the 1982 strike at Acer-Mex and the 1985 strike at Aceros de Chihuahua. Union activists were assassinated during both strikes. The attempt by the democratic Mexican Electricians Union (SME) to get a wage increase in 1987 led to a strike, which the Federal Conciliation and Arbitration Board ruled was illegal. The de la Madrid government then sent in the military and the police to ensure that there was no disruption in the delivery of electrical power.

Between 1976 and 1987, the Telephone Workers Union went on strike five times against TELMEX, and in each case World War II legislation was invoked and the military, the police and private police were used to break the strikes. In December 1990, TELMEX was privatized, and the union was reduced to fighting to limit job losses.

The privatization of Fundidora steel in Monterrey in 1986 was achieved through the occupation by the Mexican army. The National Miner and Metal Workers Union (STMMRM) accepted the eventual closing of the plant.

The state-owned fish processing industry was privatized by the de la Madrid government, and the militant Tepepan Refrigeration Workers Union was virtually abolished.

In 1983, the militant nuclear industry workers (SUTIN) went on strike for higher wages. Management refused to negotiate, and the Federal Board of Conciliation and Arbitration upheld this decision. Government reorganization of the industry eliminated the union.

In 1987, the de la Madrid government privatized Aero México and laid off thousands of workers. The unions went on strike in protest and faced the Mexican army and police at all workplaces. The Federal Board of Conciliation and Arbitration declared the strike illegal, the union was broken, and 90 percent of the workers lost their jobs. Several union activists and lawyers were arrested on phoney charges.

Workers at the Tornel Rubber Company wanted something done about hazardous working conditions. They found President Salinas was just as tough as de la Madrid. When their CTM union refused to do anything, they petitioned for an independent union. The Federal Board of Conciliation and Arbitration declared in 1989 that they were to remain with the CTM. The dissident workers were attacked by CTM thugs with police support, the company fired the workers, and replacement workers were hired.

President Salinas decided to privatize the Cananea Copper Mine, the largest in Latin America. In 1989, the average wage in the mine was only $33 per week. The mine was occupied by 5,000 Mexican soldiers. With the co-operation of the leadership of the National Mine and Metal Workers Union (STMMRM), the mines were privatized, 700 workers were fired, and the union local was broken.

When the workers at Modelo Brewery in Mexico City tried to elect their own leaders in early 1990, the Salinas government and the leaders of the CTM combined to crush them. When they went on strike, the Federal Board of Conciliation and Arbitration ruled the strike illegal and 5200 workers were fired. Riot police attacked the workers camped outside their workplace. In the end, the CTM won and half the workers were not hired back.

On May 31, 1992, the Mexican army and federal security police occupied the port of Veracruz in order to smash the unions that opposed the privatization of the port authority. Three companies, with strong links to top officials of the PRI, bought the state assets. In July, workers were re-hired, but union activists did not get jobs.[18]

In July 1992, 14,000 workers at the Puebla Volkswagen plant went on strike to protest the agreement negotiated by their CTM union leaders. The company went to the Federal Board of Conciliation and Arbitration which allowed them to tear up the existing contract, shut the plant and fire the workers. It reopened shortly thereafter, hundreds of union militants were not rehired, and the workers were forced to take a cut in pay. President Salinas said he intervened directly because the VW workers were opposed to the introduction of the team concept of production, which was important to his program of Mexican industrial restructuring.[19]

The Ford strike at the Cuautitlán plant near Mexico City is a good example of the Salinas labour strategy. In 1987, the Company shut its plant, laid off its 5,000 workers, and declared the contract void. A new contract was signed with CTM leaders which cut wages by 50 percent, and eliminated seniority. When the plant reopened, only 3,800 workers were hired back. When the union local tried to choose its own leaders, it was confronted by the company, the police and the CTM. On January 8, 1990, CTM thugs attacked the workers in the plant. They even fired on them, killing one and wounding nine others. Ford workers occupied the plant. At the request of Ford of Mexico, the Salinas government used the police to remove the workers.

This case received a lot of media attention. Ford workers in the United States and Canada formed a solidarity alliance with the Mexican Ford workers. Due to all the public pressure, Ford in Mexico was forced to have a certification vote. While the vote was in progress, 2,000 heavily armed police surrounded the plant. There was no secret ballot. Workers were asked "Do you want the Confederation [CTM] to represent you?" Each response was recorded on television.

The vote went 1,328 for the CTM and 1,112 for the new union. Those who voted against the CTM were dismissed from their jobs. To get their jobs back, workers were forced to sign a statement declaring that when they voted for the new union they did so "due to confusion or lack of reflection." Now they agreed to "fully accept union discipline."[20]

Despite the Mexican Revolution, the constitution and a very progressive labour code, the trade union movement in Mexico has been relatively weak. No one knows exactly how many workers are in trade unions. The confederations greatly exaggerate their membership figures, and there is no official government count. One of the most detailed independent studies, made in the late 1970s, concluded that only around 16 percent of the economically active population was unionized. Another estimate, done by Manuel Camacho in 1978, estimated that there were five million union members out of a labour force of 18.8 million. That would put the figure at 27 percent.[21]

The trade union movement has been hurt badly by the policies and repression of the de la Madrid and Salinas administrations. A great many jobs have been lost through privatization and cut backs in public spending. The PRI-dominated boards of Conciliation and Arbitration have been very tough on unions and organizing efforts. In 1992, the Mexican press estimated that union membership had dropped to around four million.[22]

The policy of the de la Madrid and Salinas administrations has been to keep Mexican wages as low as possible. This policy has been supported by business interests, international bankers, and the World Bank and the International Monetary Fund.

However, this policy can only be self defeating. Real wages are falling, inequality is increasing, unemployment is rising, and 30 percent of the economically active population is now working in the informal economy. The new plants being built in Mexico use the latest in technology and hire relatively few workers. While 1.1 million new workers enter the job market each year in Mexico, the free market economy of de la Madrid and Salinas created only 360,000 jobs per year. The polarization of Mexican society is getting worse. The new policy is unlikely to produce the economic and political stability sought by its supporters.

Trinational Solidarity

During the period from 1990 through 1993, popular organizations in Canada, the United States and Mexico formed coalitions to oppose NAFTA. They worked together in trinational meetings developing solidarity and trust. The three organizations also developed an alternative proposal for North American trade and development.

The position of independent trade unions in Mexico was put forth by the Mexican Action Network on Free Trade (RMALC) and endorsed by their counterparts in the United States and Canada. To begin with, there was strong opposition to the low wage strategy followed by the PRI governments. The objective of any agreement, it was argued, should be to bring the wages and standards of work in Mexico up to the highest levels that exist in Canada and the United States.[23]

The first challenge was seen to be protecting human rights for workers in Mexico and Mexicans working in the United States. RMALC asked the Mexican government to "ratify the American Convention on Human Rights of the Organization of American States and accept the authority of the Interamerican Human Rights Court regarding the issue of human rights." They also requested that the three countries "establish effective mechanisms for the defence of human rights, similar to those in force in the European Community." Governments should ratify and accept the United Nations Covenant in favour of the Protection of Migrant Workers' and Their Families' Rights. These proposals were rejected by the governments of all three countries.

RMALC also called for the three governments to commit themselves to the covenants of the International Labour Organization on trade union freedoms, collective bargaining rights, democratic rights, the right to strike, an end to child labour, and equal rights and pay for women.

Representatives of the three coalitions called for the creation of a

North American Trade Commission, which would include "broad, plural and democratic participation." A Regional Labour Commission, democratically selected and elected, should be created to promote wage recovery programs and improved labour working conditions.

Of equal concern was the state of safety and health in the workplace. The laws and regulations in Mexico are weak and enforcement is rare. For example, the Salinas government insisted that there were no cases of occupational cancer in Mexico, but the country manufactures asbestos, vinyl chloride, chromates, and petrochemical products, all of which are known to cause cancer.[24]

The three coalitions also argued that "the violation of labour rights should be conceived as an unfair trade practice, and for that reason subject to trade sanctions without affecting each country's sovereignty." All of these proposals were rejected by the three governments.

When NAFTA was finally approved, it contained "side deals" demanded by the U.S. Congress covering labour and environmental issues. They were denounced by labour and environmental groups in all three countries as completely inadequate. The three governments only committed themselves to enforcing their existing legislation. No new standards were created, and no supranational enforcement body was created.

In September 1993, *El Financiero* reported that of the 700,000 companies in Mexico, only 20 percent met the safety and hygiene requirements required by NAFTA. Those not in compliance could be fined under the accord. José Antonio Legaspi, director of medicine and safety at the Ministry of Work and Social Security (STPS), reported that aside from not complying with standards in the workplace, many companies hire minors and pay wages which are below the minimum wage.

The ministry's survey found that contrary to widespread belief that the large companies have better safety conditions, medical services, and inspection practices, the large Mexican companies have the highest rate of accidents. Those with fewer than five employees had the lowest rate.[25]

The ratification of NAFTA has served to stimulate international solidarity efforts among workers and their allies in the three countries. In the United States the Coalition for Justice in the Maquiladoras has concentrated on environmental contamination by U.S. transnational corporations. The Border Committee of Workers aids women workers in the maquiladora industries. There is also the North American Worker to Worker Network, based in North Carolina, which serves as an international information clearing house.

Individual trade unions in the United States and Canada are forging links with their counterparts in Mexico. One of the first was the Ford Democratic Movement where Ford workers in the United States and Canada gave support to the struggle by the Ford workers in Cuautitlán.[26]

The Trinational Mujer a Mujer is based in Mexico City, San Antonio, and Toronto and gives support to unorganized women workers, particularly garment workers. The Maquila Women Workers' Network has also been formed; it has concentrated on the use of toxic chemicals in maquiladora assembly plants.

In Canada, Solidarity Works, an organization of labour unions and individual activists, has formed the Maquila Organizing Project with the Authentic Labour Front (FAT), the Mexican independent trade union confederation. They are giving support to FAT's effort to organize women in the textile and garment plants in the Maquiladora zone at Parras, in northern Coahuila.

One of the most publicized cases of trade union solidarity centred on the General Electric motor plant in the maquiladora zone at Juárez, Chihuahua. This plant opened in 1989, when GE shut down their plant at Decatur, Illinois. At the U.S. plant, GE paid workers an average of $13.50 per hour, more than twice the daily wages of the plant set up in Juárez.

In 1992, the FAT signed a Strategic Organizing Alliance with United Electrical Workers of America. UE gave them financial and other assistance in trying to organize the Mexican plant.

American workers visiting the site discovered that GE was using chemicals banned in the United States, did not pay workers properly for overtime, did not give light work to pregnant workers, provided inadequate protective equipment, made no effort to see if workers had been adversely affected by being exposed to toxic chemicals, and did not comply with Mexican regulations on health and safety.

When GE learned that the unions were trying to organize the plant they began to fire and lay off workers suspected of organizing activity. They did what they could to obstruct the organizing drive, including violating Mexican law.

On February 4, 1994, the UE, with the full support of FAT, filed the first complaint under the NAFTA side agreement on labour with the U.S. Department of Labor. They were joined by the Teamsters, who filed a complaint against Honeywell. The Teamsters had signed a similar Strategic Organizing Alliance with FAT, and Honeywell had also fired workers.

In the GE case, the FAT was able to get an unprecedented secret ballot vote for union representation. That vote was held on August 21, 1994, and the union lost. GE had violated Mexican law during the organizing drive by threatening to fire workers, threatening to close the plant, and promising to raise wages if the union was defeated.

Despite this setback, Benedicto Martínez of the FAT commented that the vote was important because "the achievement of a secret ballot election marks a major advance for Mexican workers." The campaign was also a major advance in worker-to-worker co-operation.

It is clear that fundamental trade union rights do not exist in Mexico. Efforts to organize and represent workers have been hindered by the alliance between the one-party state and the official unions. Workers have also experienced extensive repression by the state. But workers in the United States and Canada are experiencing similar difficulties as they try to confront the power of corporations in the new neoliberal world. International solidarity efforts may provide only small victories but they do give encouragement and provide hope.

Notes

1. See Dan La Botz, *Mask of Democracy; Labor Suppression in Mexico Today.* Montréal: Black Rose Books, 1992, pp. 101-113.

2. See Maria Lorena Cook, "Organizing Opposition in the Teachers' Movement in Oaxaca," in Joe Foweraker and Ann L. Craig, eds. *Popular Movements and Political Change in Mexico.* Boulder: Lynne Rienner Publishers, 1990, pp. 199-212.

3. Ramón Eduardo Ruiz, *Triumphs and Tragedy.* New York: W. W. Norton & Co., 1992, pp. 359-362; La Botz, *op. cit.*; pp. 61-65; and Kevin J. Middlebrook, "State-Labor Relations in Mexico: The Changing Economic and Political Context," in Kevin J. Middlebrook, ed., *Unions, Workers, and the State in Mexico.* Center for U.S.-Mexican Studies, University of California, San Diego, 1991, pp. 1-15;

4. Donald Hodges and Ross Gandy, *Mexico 1910-1982; Reform or Revolution?* London: Zed Press, 1983; and L. Vincent Padgett, *The Mexican Political System.* Boston: Houghton Mifflin Co., 1976, pp. 118-147.

5. Barry Carr, "Labor and the Political Left in Mexico," in Middlebrook, *op. cit.,* pp. 121-152.

6. Victor Manuel Durand Ponte, "The Confederation of Mexican Workers, the Labor Congress, and the Crisis of Mexico's Social Pact," in Middlebrook, *op. cit.,* pp. 85-104.

7. George W. Grayson, "The Labor Movement," in George W. Grayson, ed. *Prospects for Democracy in Mexico.* London: Transaction Publishers, 1990, pp. 123-145.

8. Durand Ponte, *op. cit.,* p. 102.

9. Grayson, *op. cit.*

10. Ilán Bizberg, "Modernization and Corporatism in Government-Labour Relations," in Neil Harvey, ed., *Mexico: Dilemmas of Transition.* London: Institute of Latin American Studies, 1993, pp. 299-317.

11. David Barkin, "Building Trinational Labor Solidarity in an Era of Free Trade," *New Solutions*, Vol. 3, Summer 1993, pp. 3-9.

12. Bizberg, *op. cit.*, pp. 303-304; and Grayson, *op. cit.*, pp. 132-137.

13. J. Fernando Franco, "Labor Law and Labour Movement in Mexico," in Middlebrook, *op. cit.*, pp. 105-120; and Enrique de la Garza Toledo, "Independent Trade Unions in Mexico: Past Developments and Future Perspectives," in Middlebrook, *op. cit.*, pp. 153-183; and La Botz, *op. cit.*, pp. 39-60.

14. Durand Ponte, *op. cit.*

15. Garza Toledo, *op. cit.*

16. Alejandro Alvarez, " Economic Crisis and the Labor Movement in Mexico," in Middlebrook, *op. cit*, pp. 26-55; and Alejandro Alvarez and Gabriel Mendoza, "Mexico: Neo-Liberal Disaster Zone," in Jim Sinclair, ed. *Crossing the Line*. Vancouver: New Star Books, 1992, pp. 26-37.

17. The histories of state repression are taken from La Botz, *op. cit.*; Alvarez, *op. cit.*; and Garza Toledo, *op. cit.*

18. "Mexican Port Unions Smashed," *The Pacific Tribune*, September 28, 1992, p. 7.

19. "Union Unrest Soars on Eve of NAFTA," *Latin American Weekly Report*, August 13, 1992, pp. 4-5; "Mending the People's Car," *Economist*, Vol. 324, August 22, 1992, pp. 31-32; and Mary McGinn, "VW Threatens to Run Away from Mexico," *Labor Notes*, No. 162, September 1992, pp. 4, 14.

20. Dianne Feeley, "Ford Battles Mexican Workers," *Against the Current*, Vol. 5, August 1990, pp. 15-17.

21. Middlebrook, *op. cit.*, p. 9.

22. Alejandro Toledo Patiño, "The Crisis of Mexican Unionism," *Against the Current*, Vol. 9, August 1991, pp. 32-34; and Matt Witt, "Mexican Labour: The Old, the New and the Democratic," *Multinational Monitor*, Vol. 12, February 1991, pp. 30-34.

23. See selected papers from Mexican Action Network on Free Trade (RMALC), Common Frontiers (Toronto) and the Citizens Trade Campaign (Washington), Trinational Conference, Washington, D.C., March 25-27, 1993.

24. See Pharis J. Harvey, "Labour Rights in Mexico." Testimony before the U.S. House of Representatives, Ways and Means Committee, February 20, 1991; and Ray Marshall, "Trade-Linked Labour Standards," in La Botz, *op. cit.*, pp. 39-60.

25. "Safety in the Workplace: Mexico's Achilles Heel," *Trade News Bulletin*, Vol. 2, October 7, 1993, pp. 2-3.

26. Robin Alexander and Peter Gilmore, "The Emergence of Cross-Border Labor Solidarity," *NACLA Report on the Americas*, Vol. 28, August 1994, pp. 42-48; and Bob Jeffcott, "Cross-Border Comrades," *Briarpatch Magazine*, Vol. 23, October 1994, pp. 33-35.

Chapter 7

DEMONSTRATION ELECTIONS

The Institutional Revolutionary Party (PRI) has dominated the Mexican political system for sixty-six years. In the presidential elections from 1929 through 1982 the PRI received, on average, 89 percent of the votes cast. At least those are the official figures.

The only challenge from the left came in the 1952 presidential election. Miguel Henríquez Guzmán, a wealthy retired general, formed the Federation of Peoples' Parties and tried to revive the Cárdenista alliance of the rural and urban poor. According to the official results, he received only 16 percent of the vote.

The PRI was also challenged by the National Action Party (PAN), a conservative pro-Roman Catholic party formed in 1939. Ideologically, it supported the rights of private property and the individual. It was captured by bankers, industrialists, owners of large farms, and the well-off middle class and posed no real challenge to the broad electoral base of the PRI.

There have been minor Marxist and socialist parties on the left. After 1946, the Communist Party was banned, but at no time has any opposition party offered any serious challenge to the PRI. The system of patronage, co-optation, and repression, have proved to be adequate. Those who were frustrated by the system opted out; abstentionism rose to include between 40 and 50 percent of eligible voters.[1]

The PRI began a process of political liberalization in 1963. Embarrassed by the fact that there were only members of the dominant party in the Chamber of Deputies, President Adolfo López Mateos (1958-1964) introduced a system of proportional representation. The 1963 electoral law reform guaranteed opposition parties seats in the Chamber of Deputies, the lower house of the federal legislature, if they obtained 2.5 percent of the national vote. But the legal parties could not muster that many votes.

The one-party state was also embarrassed during the 1976 presidential election when only two small parties nominated a candidate for president. These formal elections were necessary to provide a sense of legitimacy to the system. As a result, the new president, José López Portillo, enacted a new electoral law in 1977; parties could gain representation in the Chamber of Deputies if they obtained 1.5 percent of the popular vote nationally or registered 65,000 members. The size of the Chamber of Deputies was increased to 400. Of these, 300 were to be elected by constituency, but 100 were to be allocated to the minor parties according to their proportion of the total vote. It was hoped that this would guarantee at least a token opposition in the legislature. The opposition parties were also guaranteed some public financing for elections, representation on electoral boards, and free radio and televsion time.[2]

But the law had a clause which guaranteed that no opposition party could grow too strong; if it did, it would lose 50 percent of its PR seats. As Wayne Cornelius has noted, there is a widespread perception that the PRI will do "whatever is necessary" to prevent the emergence of a competitive, liberal democratic system, "whatever the cost in terms of its own legitimacy."[3]

The PRI was able to co-opt some of the parties that emerged under the new electoral system. The Authentic Party of the Mexican Revolution (PARM) did not get 1.2 percent of the vote in the 1982 election but was reestablished by the PRI as an ally on the electoral commissions. The Popular Socialist Party (PPS), which had developed behind Vincente Lombardo Toledano as a left labour party, moved to the right and began to regularly support the PRI. The Party of the Cárdenas Front for National Reconstruction (PFCRN) grew out of the Workers' Socialist Party (PST), identified with Herberto Castillo, but it also drifted to the right and became dependent on PRI support. These parties receive financial aid from the PRI and today, their primary function is to try to divide the left opposition. They are often referred to as the "satellite parties."

In Mexico, electoral commissions which supervise the elections and issue the official vote tallies have been under the complete domination of the PRI. These commissions take votes away from the major opposition parties and allocate them to the small parties allied to the PRI.

The liberalization reflected in the reforms to the electoral system should not be confused with a commitment to democracy. The initial reforms came after the student massacre of 1968 and the guerrilla groups of the early 1970s. Political observers viewed them as an attempt to bring the political opposition into the formal electoral and parliamentary process where they could be more easily controlled.[4]

Thus the main goal of liberalizing the electoral system was an attempt to preserve PRI domination and to confer some legitimacy on the one-party regime. Allowing more parties to exist in the legislature, and the opposition to win a few elections, helps in Washington but does nothing to change the basic authoritarianism.[5]

During the presidency of Miguel de la Madrid (1982-1988), opposition to the PRI grew at the municipal level and in some of the northern states. De la Madrid at first introduced a new policy of encouraging free elections at the municipal level. The PAN won some local elections, including those in seven major cities. Cornelius argues that the PRI was confident that they would win in any case, but local PRI officials objected strenuously to allowing the PAN to win.

The turning point seemed to come with the July 1983 municipal elections, in which PAN produced large victories in important cities like Chihuahua and Durango. From that date on the PRI returned to electoral fraud and using military and police intervention to try to block real opposition.

In municipal elections in the northern state of Coahuila in December 1984, the PRI-dominated electoral commission declared the state party the winner over the PAN. Angry PAN supporters, convinced there was extensive fraud, burned two city halls. The police opened fire on the demonstrating crowds, killing two people and wounding thirty-five more. President de la Madrid sent in the army to restore order in the two cities.

The mid-term elections in 1985 revealed the determination of the PRI to re-establish its complete domination in the electoral area. The de la Madrid administration predicted that the PRI would win an overwhelming victory. With only partial results tabulated, the PRI announced that it had won all 300 contests for the Chamber of Deputies. They also declared that they had won all seven gubernatorial contests.[6]

The PAN was particularly strong in the state of Sonora, which borders on Arizona. Yet the PRI claimed to have won the contest for governor by a vote of three to one, all the seats in the state legislature, and control of all municipalities. The PAN was stunned.

How did the PRI do it? They used all the usual tricks. The electoral commission inflated the voters' list by millions of "phantom" voters, thousands of PAN voters had their names cut from the list, and ballot boxes were stuffed. Furthermore, the de la Madrid administration rolled out the armed forces, sending more than 20,000 soldiers to Sonora.

The president had hoped that clean elections would boost the legitimacy of his administration, but the foreign press was out in force: the strategy failed.

To this day, the PRI still uses the old tried and true techniques for winning elections whenever necessary. There is the *carrousel*, the busses which transport PRI voters from one polling station to another on election day. There is *tacos* voting, where members of the unions affiliated with the PRI

through the Mexican Workers Confederation (CTM) are given ten to fifteen pre-marked ballots, which they do not separate but put in the box
folded together. There are the election-day breakfasts, where the PRI puts
on a big feast and then takes the people en masse to the voting station.
Representatives from the opposition parties are denied access to the polling stations, particularly when the votes are being counted. The ballot
boxes are *embarazada*, pregnant with PRI ballots before voting begins. Ballot
boxes are stolen and ballots disappear. Journalists and observers are har-
assed and beaten by PRI thugs.[7]

Why did the president return to the "bare knuckle tactics" of the past?
Some observers say the shift reflected the split in the PRI between the technocrats in Mexico City and the local bosses who were determined to stay in
office no matter what the cost. There is another explanation; it was, as Cornelius writes, "an attempt to convey an image of firm control at a time
when the government needed to sustain its austerity program and implement some highly controversial economic restructuring policies."[8]

The 1988 Election

The first real challenge to the PRI came in the presidential election in
1988. First, the National Action Party (PAN) nominated Manuel Clouthier,
a popular businessman who had been previously associated with the PRI.
Then, on October 4, 1987, there was the *destape*, or unveiling. Miguel de la
Madrid named Carlos Salinas de Gortari to be his successor. In Mexico, this
is known as the *dedazo*, when the outgoing president "fingers" the next
president.

For the left-wing Democratic Current in the PRI, the selection of Salinas was the last straw; they withdrew from the party. Cuauhtémoc Cárdenas,
son of popular president Lázaro Cárdenas and former PRI governor Xicoténcatl of Michoacán, was nominated by the PARM for President. The
PPS and the PFCRN also broke with the PRI and endorsed Cárdenas. He
was also endorsed by the Mexican Socialist Party (PMS). With the small Social Democratic Party, the Green Party and others, they formed the National Democratic Front (FDN). They were joined by urban, student,
labour, feminist, environmental and Amerindian organizations. As Andrew
Reding remarked, the FDN was "Mexico's rainbow coalition."[9]

Thus the 1988 presidential election was the first national election
where there was any significant challenge to the traditional one-party system. There was a dramatic outpouring of mass support for Cárdenas, re-

flected in huge political rallies. The PRI was forced to use all its manipulative and repressive weapons to stay in office.

In December 1986, President de la Madrid changed the composition of the Federal Electoral Commission (CFE) to reflect party representation on a proportional basis. This gave the PRI a 19 to 12 advantage which they used to control all decisions.

The CFE closed registration six months before the election to exclude youth and those who had been abstaining. Both groups favoured Cárdenas by a wide margin, according to public opinion polls. When the PMS withdrew its candidate from the campaign and backed the FDN, the CFE refused to re-print the ballots.

The PRI used its majority on the CFE to systematically exclude the opposition parties from every aspect of the election. They completely controlled the voters' lists. Numerous people who did not exist were included. The PRI eliminated hundreds of thousands of known opponents. PAN supporters found they could not get their voting credentials.

Intimidation increased. Two of Cárdenas' key aides, who were working to set up an independent network for monitoring the voting results, were assassinated in Mexico City. The right-wing paramilitary group, *Antorcha Campesina*, linked to the PRI, intimidated voters in rural areas. In many areas where the PRI had little opposition they "won" 99 percent of the vote. Some voting districts reported more votes than there were people.[10]

On July 6, 1988, people turned out in huge numbers to vote. There was a popular uprising against the de la Madrid administration, the economic austerity program, and the authoritarian practices of the one-party state. By 7 p.m. on election night, government authorities realized that Salinas had lost. The election results were being sent by local PRI officials to the CFE by computer, protected by a secret code.

In a series of reports, *El Financiero* documented the electoral fraud. The election returns were very slow. One of the PAN representatives at the CFE noted that the technicians were using a different entry code than that supplied to the opposition parties. He entered the code and discovered that the opposition parties were being given altered results. The screen showed that the opposition had a three to one lead in one district in Tamaulipas.

However, when the PAN representative tried to print the screen, the employees at the CFE, patronage appointees of the PRI, shut down the entire computer system. At this point, 59 percent of the votes had been counted. Although the election results were delayed for over a week, Salinas immediately announced that he had been elected and was congratulated by U.S. President Ronald Reagan.

The official results released were dramatically different from those seen by the PAN representative. Enough votes were manufactured to give Salinas a very slim majority victory. These results were confirmed by the PRI-controlled Congress in September 1988.[11]

Despite the mass turnout for the campaign and the election, the CFE reported that voter turnout had been the lowest ever for a presidential election. In districts where FDN support was obviously strong, the turnout was reported to be low. Where the PRI was in control, everyone voted.

One example will illustrate the scope of the fraud. Poll watchers from the two opposition parties were able to tabulate 80.5 percent of the votes cast in the state of Guerrero on the basis of copies they made of official tally sheets at the local polling stations. These results produced 359,369 votes for Cárdenas and 90,796 for Salinas. When the official vote count was released by the CFE, Salinas was credited with 309,202 votes and Cárdenas with 182,874.[12]

In Mexico, gross electoral fraud is widely recognized as normal. Public opinion polls after the election reported that 90 percent of the population believed that Salinas was not elected legally. The PRI had survived the second earthquake.[13]

Reestablishing Authority

The public relations damage resulting from the rigged election continued for months. In the Chamber of Deputies the opposition parties protested vehemently, particularly when they were called on in September to confirm the official results of the election. Equally disastrous was the swearing in of the new president on December 1, 1988.

Fearing an ugly event in front of the world's press, the PRI negotiated an agreement with the opposition parties. In return for a promise not to disrupt the ceremony, the opposition parties were each given ten minutes for a public statement, to be carried on national television.

The opposition parties used their time to denounce the PRI and the fraudulent electoral process. When Carlos Salinas entered the Chamber, all the members from the parties of the FDN walked out. The members from the PAN all held up large placards denouncing the PRI.

The damage was contained somewhat, thanks to the PRI's control of the press. Television crews carefully excluded any coverage of the demonstrations, including a huge protest rally and march by supporters of the FDN through Mexico City.

President Salinas moved quickly to demonstrate his authority as the

Table 7.1
1988 Mexican Presidential Election Results

Candidate	Early Returns (59%)	Late Returns (41%)	Official Results
Cardenas (FDN)	4,554,599 (40.4%)	1,402,389 (16.8%)	5,956,988 (30.3%)
Salinas (PRI)	4,116,365 (36.5%)	5,524,964 (66.0%)	9,641,329 (49.1%)
Clouthier (PAN)	2,227,283 (19.8%)	1,039,876 (12.4%)	3,267,159 (16.6%)
Total	11,272,283	8,368.332	19,640,722

SOURCE: *El Financiero,* August 5, 1988.
NOTE: The totals for several minor candidates have been dropped.

new president. The key economic portfolios in the cabinet were filled with young technocrats committed to neoliberalism. Foreign investors were pleased. The political positions were dominated by hard-line PRI politicians. Manuel Bartlett, who presided over the "cybernetic fraud" of the CFE computers, was made Minister of Education. Mexico City, which had voted overwhelmingly for Cárdenas, was given notorious human rights abusers to head police operations.

As Mariclaire Acosta points out, like all new presidents Salinas declared a war against corruption. Joaquín Hernández Galacia (La Quina) of the petroleum workers was jailed. Augustín Legorreta, a high official with Operadora de Bolsa, the major brokerage house, was charged with fraud. Miguel Ángel Félix Gallardo, Mexico's best-known drug lord, was arrested. A few corrupt policemen were also arrested.[14]

During the election campaign Salinas had promised that "those who are against my party will have to attend to the consequences." Cuauhtémoc Cárdenas and his supporters would bear the brunt of this pledge.

The arrests were generally popular. By the end of 1989, Salinas had established majority support in all the public opinion polls. As Andrew Reding argues, the sacrifice of a few public figures was required to save the one-party system as a whole.[15]

The PRI faced the largest opposition ever in the Chamber of Deputies. There were 260 members of the governing party, 138 from the parties which made up the FDN, and 101 from the PAN. The president did not have enough votes for the 60 percent majority needed to amend the constitution.

However, the president had many resources at his command. Salinas was able to offer the satellite parties funds to return to the fold. When the new Party of the Democratic Revolution (PRD) was formed in May 1989, only the Mexican Socialist Party (PSM) joined. The others returned to the fold, and soon began running candidates against the PRD.[16]

Salinas's second move was to neutralize the opposition of the PAN. Because business leaders of the PAN were very supportive of the neoliberal economic agenda which Salinas was promoting, he was able to forge an alliance with the leadership of the PAN. In return for support in the legislature, Salinas agreed to let up in the political attack on the PAN.

President Salinas's strategy was reflected in two elections which were held on July 2, 1989, in Baja California and Michoacán.

Support for the PRI had been declining in Baja California, while support for the PAN was increasing. In the 1988 presidential election, Cárdenas and the FDN finished first with 36.8 percent of the votes; 36.7 percent voted for the PRI and 31 percent for the PAN.

In January 1989, President Salinas forced PRI governor Xicoténcatle Leyva Mortera to resign, and named an interim replacement. At the same time, he announced a $600 million public works program. In March, he named Margarita Ortega to be the PRI candidate for governor. Other major spending programs were announced prior to the election. It was PRI politics as usual.

The PPS and the PFCRN, now back in the fold, nominated their own candidate for governor. The newly-formed PRD nominated a radical woman, Martha Maldonado.

The PAN nominated Ernesto Ruffo, the popular mayor of Ensenada and well-known businessman, as its candidate. Wary of the PRI, they took no chances. This time, they mobilized an army of poll watchers. Their well-organized team tabulated returns and announced the results on July 3: 52 percent for Ruffo and only 41 percent for Ortega. This put President Salinas on the spot. Rather than undermine the alliance with the PAN, he accepted the voters' decision, the PAN's victory.[17]

The July 2, 1989 election for the state legislature in Michoacán provides a direct contrast. In the 1988 presidential election, the official returns showed that Cárdenas had carried the state three-to-one over Salinas.

Shortly after taking office in December 1988, President Salinas removed Martínez Villicana, the PRI governor of Michoacán, who was much disliked. A public works program worth $800 million was announced in January 1989.

Supporters of Cárdenas in Michoacán held open primaries to nominate candidates for the election for the state legislature. At the time, the PRD had not yet been formed. The PPS did not participate. The PFCRN put up its own slate of candidates, as did the PARM.

The PRI-controlled electoral commission claimed that the PRI won fourteen seats and the PRD only four. The PRD produced copies of voting results from the polls which indicated that they had won fourteen of the seats. The results tabulated by the independent observers from the Democratic Assembly for Effective Suffrage (ADESE) gave the PRD fifteen seats.

How could the results have been so different from 1988? The PRI engaged in all the fraudulent tricks in the book. First, there was a low turnout, only around 28 percent of eligible voters. In addition, around 100,000 votes for the PRD candidates had been annulled! The PRI, despite all the vote manipulation, received only 194,000 official votes. The votes allocated to the satellite parties denied the PRD a majority of those reported.[18]

The Mid-Term Election

The key election for the PRI was the federal election of August 18, 1991. All the members of the Chamber of Deputies and half of the Senate would be elected. The 1988 election had given the opposition parties 45 percent of the seats in the lower house and four Senate seats. Salinas wanted the PRI to have 60 percent of the seats in the Chamber of Deputies so that he could amend the constitution at will. He also needed a big victory to restore his legitimacy.

The PRI introduced "reforms" to the federal electoral law in 1990. The most important reform was the creation of a new voters' list, with every registered voter having an identification card with a photograph, fingerprint, and signature. The opposition parties hoped that this would help cut down multiple voting.

On the other hand, electoral coalitions, similar to that used by the FDN of 1988, were banned. There was also a "governability" clause which established that if any party won a plurality of the 300 district seats and received 35 percent of the vote, it would automatically get a voting majority of

representatives in the Chamber of Deputies. This would enable the PRI to
have control without having to bargain with its small client parties.

The legislation also created a new Federal Electoral Institute (IFE),
which was to be chaired by the Minister of the Interior (*Gobernacion*). Its
composition gave a comfortable majority to the PRI, guaranteeing them
complete control of the election process. In addition, the reform created a
Federal Electoral Tribunal (TFE) with the power to arbitrate electoral disputes. The magistrates were to be appointed by the president; of the 384
appointed, 90 percent were members of the PRI.

A new electoral list was created. According to the official 1990 census,
forty-six million Mexicans were eligible to vote, but only thirty-nine million
appeared on the electoral list. Voters disappeared in the PRD strongholds.
The census report itself caused a great deal of controversy in Mexico. Areas
of the country which voted heavily for the PRD in 1988 did not show any increase in population over the 1980 census; areas where the PRI held its
strength grew remarkably.[19]

When it came to distributing the voter identification cards, the government produced only thirty-six million. On August 5, the government publicly burned three million voter identification cards which they said could
not be delivered. Political observers generally agreed that around ten million potential voters were disenfranchised.

The Independent Democratic Assembly for Effective Voting Rights
(ADESE) charged, in its report of August 20, that there were "six million
people who were not registered to vote, 11 million who registered but
were never given their voter registration card, plus seven million Mexicans who work in the United States and are denied their right to vote [in
Mexico]."[20]

The landslide victory for the PRI was welcomed by the U. S. government, the international financial agencies, and foreign investors. The election had demonstrated that President Salinas and his economic reforms
were supported by a strong majority.

Undoubtedly, there was more support for the PRI than in 1988. The
President was successfully tackling inflation, economic growth was returning, and there was increased spending on Solidarity and the new pro-PRI
organizations. The left was split again, and the PRD had not demonstrated
any ability to win state and local elections.

Jorge Alcocer, a well-known political commentator, stressed that under
Salinas the PRI had worked hard to mobilize the local party machines.
They had more funds, and they turned out the vote. In this most important
election, the PRI organizations had resorted to all the prehistoric practices

that traditionally gave them every office. The PRI leadership had targeted for special attention the areas where Cárdenas had done well in 1988.[21]

The PRI had always received a much higher percentage of votes in the rural areas. In 1988, for example, the official figures gave Salinas 34 percent of the vote in the urban areas and 77 percent in the rural areas. For opposition parties and independent organizations, observation of election day events is much more difficult and dangerous in rural areas. In the 1991 election, rural voters supposedly gave 77 percent support for the PRI.[22]

John Gledhill, writing about Michoacán, notes that "it is possible for people to harbour profound antagonisms towards the existing order without acting to challenge it simply because of fear of repression or resignation to the practical impossibility of change." Intimidation by local PRI loyalists, particularly strong in rural areas, increases because the PRD does offer the possibility of change.[23]

However, the official totals from the August 1991 election were hard to believe. The vote for the PRI supposedly increased from 9.2 million in 1988 to 14.1 million in 1991. Voter participation supposedly increased from eighteen million (50 percent) in 1988 to 23.5 million (70 percent) in 1991. Mid-term voting had always produced a lower turnout than for presidential elections. Guadalupe Pacheo Méndez has shown that the abstention rate in elections had been steadily rising in mid-term elections since 1961, and had reached 56.6 percent in the 1985 election. If we are to believe the official election results, this was dramatically reversed in 1991. But there was no evidence of popular enthusiasm for the election, as there was in 1988.[24]

The official results gave the PRI 290 of the 300 electoral districts and 20 percent of the 200 seats distributed by proportional representation. Federally, the official vote total was 65 percent for the PRI, 18 percent for the PAN, and only 8 percent for the PRD. The PRI was given thirty-one of thirty-two Senate seats and all six governorships. In the Chamber of Deputies, the system gave twenty-three seats to the PRI ally, the PFCRN, and only forty-one seats to the PRD!

In Mexico City, where a quarter of the population lives and where even the official figures showed that Salinas was defeated by 2 to 1 in 1988, the PRI claimed to have won in all forty electoral districts. In Michoacán the PRI insisted it had won all thirteen seats for the Chamber of Deputies. In the states of Chihuahua and Nuevo Leon, strongholds of the PAN, the PRI claimed victory.

Throughout Mexico, the public believed that it was fraud as usual. The National Accord for Democracy (ACUDE) monitors elections in Mexico; it has members from all political parties and is committed to free elections. The ACUDE conducted a thorough analysis of the vote in Mexico City and the states of Guanajuato and San Luis Potosí and concluded that "free suffrage and respect of the constitutional right to vote has once again not been respected."

The Mexican Institute for Political Studies found that "The electoral results are on principle suspicious because they are mounted in enormous, profound and flagrant contradictions." They concluded that as many as seven to nine million votes were "inflated." In 60 percent of the polling booths it would have been impossible to record as many votes as were alleged to have been cast. In Mexico, this is referred to as *turbo* voting. For example, during the July 7, 1991 state election in Nuevo Leon, ACUDE calculated that *turbo* voting, in voter booths where the PRI was given over 90 percent of the votes cast, inflated the vote total by 350,000.

In August 1991, concurrent elections for governor were held in Guanajuato and San Luis Potosí. When the official results were released they showed landslide victories for the PRI. There were mass demonstrations and protests in the two states over the fraud. Even *The New York Times* and *The Wall Street Journal*, both strong supporters of President Salinas, questioned the extent of the victory claimed by the PRI.

The PAN launched formal protests of electoral results in 158 of the 300 electoral districts. The PRD formally protested in forty-nine. Political scientist Javier Garrido, writing in *La Jornada*, concluded that "on August 18 the government put forward the most vast, complete, and sophisticated electoral fraud in the electoral history of Mexico."[25]

Andrew Reding, of the Mexico Project of the World Policy Institute, argued that political reform in Mexico does not work "because it is not intended to work." Corruption is necessary to enforce presidential authority. "Torture is indispensable to the maintenance of a healthy respect for arbitrary rule." The "simulation of reform" serves as a cover to the existing regime and also provides an opportunity to imprison political adversaries.[26]

Adolfo Aguilar Zinser, a professor of economics at the National Autonomous University, pointed to the reality of the Mexican political system. "The more competitive an election is in Mexico, the greater abstentionism will be. Because in a contested election, the stakes for the PRI become much clearer, its intimidation and manipulation tactics become more pronounced, and as a result for the population at large, the costs of voting for the opposition become higher."[27]

Denise Dresser, an American political scientist who observed the November 1990 election in the state of Mexico, adds that "electoral fraud has a double impact. It not only brings about a certain electoral result — it also acts as a vaccine against participation."[28]

Concentrating on Michoacán

Michoacán is a relatively poor agricultural state to the west of Mexico City. It has a long historic tradition of support for revolutionary change. It was the birthplace and political training ground of Lázaro Cárdenas, the most popular Mexican president, who held office from 1934-1940. He represented the progressive and anti-imperialist wing of the PRI. Cuauhtémoc Cárdenas, now head of the PRD, is his son. While a member of the PRI, Cuauhtémoc Cárdenas was governor of Michoacán (1980-1986).

In 1988, the Federal Election Commission (CFE) reported that in Michoacán the vote was 382,787 for Cárdenas and 127,870 for Salinas, a massive vote against the PRI. The controversy here was over the total votes cast, with the CFE insisting that only 38 percent of eligible voters went to the polls.

Municipal elections were held in Michoacán in December 1989. By this time the PRD was getting organized as a party and had more representatives watching polling stations. Based on samples of election night returns, the PRD celebrated, believing that they had won in fifty-nine of the 113 municipalities, including the capital Morelia and the larger towns. Again, the electoral commission produced different totals, denying the PRD control of a majority of the municipalities.

Following the precedent established by the PAN in several of the northern states, PRD supporters occupied civic buildings in sixty-nine municipalities. They were prepared to take office by civil disobedience.

Carlos Salinas responded in the same way as his predecessor. In April 1990, he sent in the military who forcibly removed PRD supporters from the buildings. Many were arrested, beaten, tortured while in custody, and imprisoned. A few were killed and others disappeared. The PRI did concede the PRD control of fity-two municipalities. Mexican observers believe that this concession was granted because of criticism from the United States during the sensitive negotiations on the North American Free Trade Agreement (NAFTA).

One of the results of this confrontation was that the PRI agreed to a new election in Uruapan, the second largest city in the state. The PRI was determined to win this municipality. The election turned out to be the first test case for the new cybernetic fraud. A new voters' list was created by the Federal Electoral Commission. Those who operate the central computer system are referred to as "the political alchemists."

A report by ACUDE described how the new system worked. In consultation with local PRI party agents, federal electoral officials identified known PRD supporters. Their names were stricken from the list of registered voters. In Uruapan, the names of 18,000 local citizens were removed from the list. Then 14,500 names were added to the list, mostly fictitious persons. Many names appeared more than once. This practice allowed the commission to inflate the vote totals for the PRI. In addition, thousands of voter identification cards "disappeared." Cybernetic fraud produced a PRI majority.[29]

In the August 1991 federal election, the new Federal Electoral Institute (IFE) gave the PRI all thirteen of the Michoacán seats in the Chamber of Deputies. Few Mexicans believed these results.

One of the Mexican responses to electoral fraud has been extensive participation in extra-parliamentary political action; this includes long marches to Mexico city, demonstrations, hunger strikes, camp-ins, and the occupation of civic buildings.

This activity is carried out in the face of considerable government repression, from threats and job loss to violence by the police, the military, and the private armies (*guardias blancas*) which often act like death squads. Political activists who oppose the PRI face the possibility of being killed or disappearing.

It was in this context that the PRI and the PRD faced off for the July 1992 election for governor of Michoacán. President Salinas was determined to defeat the PRD in their key stronghold.[30]

While Salinas drastically cut regular expenditures on health, education and social programs after taking office, he greatly increased the expenditures of PRONASOL, a fund directly under his control. During visits to local communities, the president awarded funds to local public works projects. Over three years, $220 million (or 12 percent of all these funds) were spent in Michoacán alone.

The PRI also spent lavishly to win the election. The Mexican Institute of Public Opinion (IMOP) reported that in the ten state elections in 1992, the PRI spent $200 million, the PAN $5 million, and the PRD $2 million. In Michoacán, the PRI spent $32 million, or around $80 for every vote it recorded. The PRD spent $650,000.

Television and radio are controlled by the PRI, and this is reflected in their news coverage, which largely ignores the opposition. The daily newspapers in Michoacán are all controlled by the PRI, and during the election they stepped up their coverage of the PRI and cut back their coverage of the opposition parties. IMOP reported that the PRI accounted for 92 percent of the advertising space in Michoacán newspapers during the 1992 campaign.

Three important national observer organizations monitored the Michoacán campaign and election: the Citizens' Movement for Democracy (MCD), the Convergence of Civil Organizations for Democracy (COCIDE) and the Democratic Assembly for Effective Suffrage (ADESE). All three were extremely critical of the process. Another organization, the National Commission of Electoral Observation (CONOCE), declared that, based on their sampling, around 400,000 persons had been excluded from the official electoral list.

Cuauhtémoc Rivera, a Mexican expert on the electoral process, concluded that 329,000 names on the voters' list did not exist, another 325,000 voters had been excluded, and 106,000 people did not get their credentials and could not vote. In his own survey in Morelia he discovered that 112,000 people had been excluded from the voters' list, representing 36 percent of the potential voters.

The PRI candidate for governor was Eduardo Villaseñor-Peña, who had been personally selected by Carlos Salinas. He is a wealthy businessman, a member of the Grupo Michoacán conglomerate, and sits on the board of the two biggest Mexican banks. In Michoacán, he is best known as the king of the pork ranchers.

The candidate for the PRD, Cristobal Arias Solis, was former secretary general of the state government under Cuauhtémoc Cárdenas. He was also a former senator and federal deputy while a member of the PRI. As a member of the Democratic Current, he left the PRI to back Cárdenas in the 1988 presidential election.

When the official results were announced, the state electoral commission gave 418,080 votes to Villaseñor and only 289,000 to Arias. No one believed that the anti-PRI vote had fallen from 75 percent in 1988 to only 35 percent in 1992.

PRD supporters responded with angry demonstrations and marches. A large group of them camped out in front of the Government Palace and the legislative building in Morelia. On July 27 over 20,000 supporters began to march to the capital. Beginning on August 7, thousands of PRD supporters shut down the central part of Morelia and surrounded the Government Palace and legislative building. They stayed.

On September 16, Mexico's Independence Day, the new governor was to be sworn into office at the Government Palace. But for weeks the protestors had prevented Villaseñor from entering the Government Palace. Instead, the PRD candidate Arias was "sworn in" as governor by the protestors.

President Salinas arrived in Morelia, but was forced to swear in the new governor in Morelos Theatre, near the edge of the city, which had been blocked off from the protestors by police. Villaseñor never was able to enter the Government Palace. He gave the traditional "independence cry" in Charo, a small town fifteen miles from Morelia. Salinas joined him there and then flew off in a helicopter for a tour promoting Solidarity. It was a humiliating experience for the president and his hand-picked governor.

The PRD supporters did not disappear. They blocked the government buildings for fifty days. On October 6, 1992, Villaseñor announced that he was stepping down for a year. President Salinas allowed the state legislature to pick a replacement for him.

But political conflict in Michoacán is not limited to non-violent civil disobedience. As local governments changed hands on January 1, 1993, there were armed conflicts between PRI and PRD supporters in a number of towns. Six people were killed.

Nor is the violence limited to these two parties. In Uruapan, seven PAN supporters were injured when attacked by members of Peasant Torch (*Antorcha Campesina*). The PAN supporters had been surrounding the city hall, protesting the last election where they were officially ousted by the PRI.

Peasant Torch is a right-wing paramilitary organization based in rural Mexico. It has a long history of violent physical attacks on peasants trying to break away from the PRI-affiliated National Peasant Confederation (CNC). It has been responsible for the murder of a number of peasant activists. Significantly, during the Salinas period it was invited to formally affiliate with the PRI.

While there is a long tradition of electoral fraud in Mexico, Salinas introduced a more sophisticated system of fraud by computer. The end result was to greatly increase public cynicism about electoral politics. In the three February 1993 state elections, voter participation dropped to around 25 percent.[31]

Testing Salinas

In his fourth state of the Nation address on November 1, 1992, President Salinas promised three reforms: "first, to make transparent the source of party funding; second, to place ceilings on the cost of electoral campaigns; and third, to work on the communications media and the procedures which will guarantee advances in the impartiality of electoral processes."

A test came one week later in the elections in the state of Tamaulipas, which borders Texas and the Gulf of Mexico. It is one of the northern states which has benefitted from the maquiladora export processing zones. While the PRI has dominated the state, opposition had been growing through the 1980s.[32]

In Mexico, the dominant political issue is the popular demand for free elections, and an end to corrupt rule by the PRI. In this election, the PRD formed an electoral alliance with the PAN in an attempt to get the PRI out of office. Following the election, all the ballots were brought to Matamoros, across the border from Brownsville, Texas, for the official counting by the state electoral commission. The only observers permitted in the offices for the official count were from the PRI and their small affiliated parties. Representatives from the opposition PAN and PRD were locked out. The PRI assembled riot police and dogs to defend the building.

A large crowd of people assembled in the streets protesting the process. They expected the usual fraud. A riot broke out, police attacked with truncheons, fire bombs were thrown, the building went up in flames, and the ballots were burned. The police arrested thirty people and issued warrants for sixty others, charging them with terrorism, arson, and inciting a riot. Several people fled to the United States and asked for political asylum, including Jorge Cárdenas Gutiérrez, son of the PAN/PRD candidate for governor, and Rolando Martínez Calderoni, the opposition candidate for the mayoralty of Matamoros. Two other PAN members of the state legislature also requested political asylum in the United States.

Cárdenas Gutiérrez, a wealthy owner of a local radio station in Matamoros, had station employees videotaping the events. The films show that the people who started the riot and threw the fire bombs were not those arrested. The opposition parties insist the four who started the riot and repeatedly threw the fire bombs were agents of the PRI. Why would the opposition want to burn the ballots? Two days later, the PRI-dominated state electoral commission announced that the PRI had won the Tamaulipas elections, even though the ballots had never been counted! In Mexico, this was just seen as business as usual.

On January 4, 1993, President Salinas announced a cabinet shake-up. He made José Patrocino Gonzáles Garrido the new Minister of the Interior, the most powerful position in the cabinet. The Minister of the Interior was responsible for elections and sat as chairman of the Federal Electoral Institute. He would be in charge of the 1994 Presidential elections. While governor of Chiapas, Gonzáles Garrido was notorious for electoral fraud and persecution of the political opposition. President Salinas was sending out a clear message to Mexicans, the U.S. government, and international investors.

Notes

1. For background on the Mexican political system see Martin C. Needler, *Mexican Politics: The Containment of Conflict*. New York: Praeger, 1990; John J. Bailey, *Governing Mexico*. New York: St. Martin's Press, 1988; and Judith Hellman, *Mexico in Crisis*. New York: Holmes and Meier, 1988.

2. Joseph L. Klesner, "Changing Patterns of Electoral Participation and Official Party Support in Mexico," in Judith Gentleman, ed., *Mexican Politics in Transition*. Boulder: Westview Press, 1987, pp. 95-127.

3. Wayne A. Cornelius, "Political Liberalization in an Authoritarian Regime: Mexico, 1976-1986," in Gentleman, *op. cit.*, pp. 25-39.

4. Stephen D. Morris, "Political Reformism in Mexico: Salinas at the Brink," *Journal of Interamerican Studies and World Affairs*, Vol. 34, Spring 1992, pp. 27-57.

5. Soledad Loaeza, "Political Liberalization and Uncertainty in Mexico," in Maria Lorena Cook et al, *The Politics of Economic Restructuring*. Center for U.S.-Mexican Studies, University of California, San Diego, 1994, pp. 105-122; Cornelius, *op. cit.*

6. Cornelius, *op. cit.*

7. For PRI electoral tactics, see Edgar Sanchez, "Electoral Fraud and Free Trade," *International Viewpoint*, No. 213, September 30, 1990, pp. 17-20; Paco Ignacio Taibo II, "A New Politics with Deep Roots," *The Nation*, December 17, 1990, pp. 764-768; Asa Cristina Laurell, "Democracy in Mexico: Will the First Be the Last?" *New Left Review*, No. 194, July-August 1992, pp. 33-53; and Denise Dresser, "Analysis of Elections in the State of Mexico," unpublished paper, December 1990.

8. Cornelius, *op. cit.*, p. 31.

9. Andrew Reding, "Mexico at a Crossroads: The 1988 Election and Beyond," *World Policy Journal*, Vol. 5, Fall-Winter 1988, pp. 615-649.

10. John Womack Jr., "The Meaning of the Mexican Elections," *Socialist Review*, Vol. 18, October-December 1988, pp. 157-162; Mike Tangeman, "Mexico: Prospects for Change," *Democratic Left*, Vol. 17, March-April 1989, pp. 19-20; and Andrew Reding, "Favourite Son," *Mother Jones*, November 1988, pp. 35-37.

11. "Detecto el PAN 'Fraude Cibernetico,'" *El Financiero*, July 11 and July 12, 1988; Darió Celis Estrada, "Persiste el Misterio Sobre la Causa que Calló al Sistema de Cómputo del RNE en 1988," *El Financiero*, August 16, 1994, pp. 34-35; and "Who Really Won the Mexican Election?" *Dollars & Sense*, No. 142, December 1988, p. 11.

12. Reding, "Favourite Son," *op. cit.*

13. Franz A. von Sauer, "Measuring the Legitimacy in Mexico: An Analysis of Public Opinion during the 1988 Presidential Campaign," *Mexican Studies/Estudios Mexicanos*, Vol. 8, Summer 1992, pp. 259-280.

14. Mariclaire Acosta, "En la modernización, motor del sexenio, ha cabido hasta el ajuste de cuentas," *Proceso*, No. 678, October 30, 1989, pp. 6-13.

15. Andrew Reding, "Mexico under Salinas," *World Policy Journal*, Vol. 6, Fall 1989, pp. 685-729.

16. Susan Eckstein, "Popular Movements and Political Change in Mexico," *Mexican Studies/Estudios Mexicanos*, Vol. 6, Spring 1990, pp. 213-239; and Jorge Alcocer, "Party System

and Political Transition in Mexico: A Pragmatic Approach," in Cook, *op. cit.*, pp. 149-157.

17. See "PAN Victory Marks Breakthrough," *Latin American Weekly Report*, July 20, 1989, pp. 10-11; *New York Times*, July 1, 1989, A-24, and July 12, 1989, A-5; *Wall Street Journal*, July 6, 1989, A-9; July 7, 1989, A-9.

18. Andrew Reding, "Mexico: The Crumbling of the 'Perfect Dictatorship,'" *World Policy Journal*, Vol. 8, Spring 1991, pp. 255-284.

19. Silvia Gómez Tagle, "Electoral Reform and the Party System, 1977-90," in Neil Harvey, ed., *Mexico: Dilemmas of Transition*. London: Institute of Latin American Studies, 1993, pp. 64-90.

20. Adolfo Aguilar Zinser, "Mexico: The Authoritarian Friend and Partner," *Peace and Democracy News*, Vol. 6, Winter 1992, pp. 1, 40-45; Elaine Burns, "Back in the Game in Mexico," *Guardian*, September 18, 1991, p. 14; Leon S. Lazaroff, "Countless Irregularities Mar Mexican Election," *In These Times*, Vol. 15, August 18, 1991, p. 11; and Reding, "Mexico: The Crumbling of the 'Perfect Dictatorship,'" *op. cit.*

21. Alcocer, *op. cit.*

22. Jonathan Fox, "Political Change in Mexico's New Peasant Economy," in Cook et al, *op. cit.*, pp. 251-252.

23. John Gledhill, "Michoacán is Different," in Harvey, *op. cit.*, pp. 91-117.

24. Guadalupe Pacheco Méndez, "Voter Abstentionism," in George W. Grayson, ed., *Prospects for Democracy in Mexico*. London: Transaction Publishers, 1990, pp. 63-74.

25. Cited by Stephen D. Morris, "Political Reformism in Mexico: Salinas At the Brink," *Journal of Interamerican Studies and World Affairs*, Vol. 34, Spring 1992, p. 43.

26. Reding, "The Crumbling of the 'Perfect Dictatorship,'" *op. cit.*, p. 269.

27. Quoted in Dresser, "Analysis of Elections in the State of Mexico," *op. cit.*, p. 10.

28. *Ibid.*

29. See Reding, "The Crumbing of the 'Perfect Dictatorship,'" *op. cit.*, pp. 261-264. I interviewed numerous political activists in Michoacán during visits in 1992 and 1994, and they all gave similar accounts of recent elections there.

30. The July 1992 election and its aftermath was covered in detail by *Proceso*, June 15, 1992, pp. 19-21; June 29, 1992, pp. 16-19; July 6, 1992, pp. 12-15; July 13, 1992, pp. 14-20; July 20, 1992, pp. 34-37; August 3, 1992, pp. 6-9; August 31, 1992, pp. 29-31; and September 14, 1992, pp. 6-9.

    See also "Ruler of Michoacán Opts to Step Down," *LAWR*, October 22, 1992, p. 8; "Governor Locked out in Michoacán," *LAWR*, October 1, 1992, pp. 8-9; "PRD Will not Get Benefit of Doubt," *LAWR*, August 6, 1992, p. 10; "PAN Starts Looking Like an Alternative," *LAWR*, July 30, 1992, p. 6; and "How to Win When You Lose," *Economist*, Vol. 324, July 18, 1992, pp. 40-41.

31. Margarita García Colín and César Romero Jacobo, "Ganar Credibilidad o Perder las Elecciones," *Epoca*, No. 91, March 1, 1993, pp. 8-13.

32. For coverage of the election in Tamaulipas, see Linda Diebel, "Mexico's Futuristic Nightmare," *Toronto Star*, March 13, 1993, D-1; "Violence Mars New Year Changeovers," *LAWR*, January 14, 1993, pp. 16-17; "U.S. Embroiled in Tamaulipas Dispute," *LAWR*, December 3, 1992, p. 4; "Bad Start for New 'Political Reform,'" *LAWR*, November 26, 1992, pp. 10-11; and "Fair or Fraud," *Economist*, Vol. 325, November 21, 1992, pp. 56-57.

Chapter 8

THE MEANING OF **NAFTA**

From the end of World War II through to 1973-74, the Western industrialized world experienced a long period of steady economic growth. Since then there has been a gradual decline in the average rate of growth and a corresponding increase in unemployment. Because the industrialized countries account for about 80 percent of the world's production, trade and investment, the decline has impacted on many Third World countries.

Latin America was hit hard by the economic crisis in the industrialized West. Under the direction of the International Monetary Fund (IMF), the World Bank (IBRD) and the large private banks Latin American countries changed the direction of economic development. They abandoned policies which put first priority on the development of the internal economy and shifted to production of exports for the industrialized countries.

The United States has seen its world economic hegemony decline over the years. In 1950, U.S. per capita income was about fifteen times that of Japan. By the early 1990s, it was roughly equal. From the rubble of World War II most European countries recovered to living standards which are the equivalent of those in the United States. U.S. domination of trade, foreign investment, and banking has disappeared.

In the face of the economic crisis, the Western European countries began to expand the European Common Market. Many hoped that a strong free trade zone, behind common tariffs, would help protect the high standard of living from the onslaught of the economic crisis.

The United States also saw its presence in Asia decline. Japan continued to dominate the area, but there was also growing competition from the newly industrializing states and China. The United States faced increased competition from these countries in their domestic market.

Fearing that it would be shut out of a world economy characterized by large trading blocs, the U.S. government has sought to create a Western hemisphere trading bloc which it can dominate. This can be seen as a revival of the old nationalism behind the Monroe Doctrine and the ideology of Manifest Destiny. The Canada-U.S. Free Trade Agreement (CUSFTA) and the North American Free Trade Agreement (NAFTA), which includes Mexico, are part of that strategy.

148

At the same time, the U.S. government has sought to protect foreign trade and investment rights of its nationals through the Uruguay round of negotiations on the General Agreement on Tariffs and Trade (GATT). In this effort it has had the strong support of the large transnational corporations and their organizations.

But the U.S. government did not come up with this strategy on its own. The new policy reflected the views of the organizations which represented big business. Not only was economic growth declining, so was the rate of profit; business organizations everywhere began to push for an end to the Keynesian policies of the welfare state and full employment. They wanted an end to government controls and regulations, like those for protecting the environment and the health and safety of workers.

The trend everywhere was towards a more "flexible" workforce, the greater use of part-time and temporary workers, and contracting out. This was designed to defeat trade unions and higher labour costs.

In order to increase profits, big capital demanded the right to invest anywhere in the world, to produce anywhere, and to sell their goods in any country without hindrance from tariffs and other regulations. It was thought that profitable state-owned corporations should be sold to private capitalists, so that they could accumulate the profits. Finally, taxes on the rich and corporations should be lowered to help increase "competitiveness," and state spending should be curtailed. Cheap food is necessary for cheap labour, so farm supports should be eliminated. Free trade was essential to this strategy for change.[1]

Canada-U.S. Free Trade

During the 1980 campaign for the presidency, Ronald Reagan called for the creation of a "North American Accord," a new economic agreement between the United States, Canada, and Mexico.

In May of that year, Prime Minister Pierre Trudeau and President López Portillo issued a joint statement rejecting the proposal.[2] In 1982, the U.S. government failed to get the General Agreement on Tariffs and Trade (GATT) to agree to include the service sector, and they began to push for bilateral agreements. Special talks were held with a number of countries, including Canada. The Trudeau government agreed to discuss special managed trade arrangements similar to the Canada-U.S. Auto Pact.

The impetus for the first comprehensive free trade agreement came from the Reagan administration, via their ambassador in Ottawa, Paul H.

Robinson Jr. In January 1983, Robinson began private talks with Canadian business leaders. As he told Peter C. Newman, the initiative had to come from Canada or else "it would look as if we were trying to gobble up our neighbour."[3]

Robinson met regularly with Jake Warren of the Bank of Montréal, Thomas d'Aquino, then in the prime minister's office, Ed Lumley, then Minister of Trade, and Gerry Regan, the Minister for International Trade.

At the same time, Robinson held special meetings with Sam Hughes, president of the Canadian Chamber of Commerce. These meetings were expanded to include d'Aquino, now president of the Business Council on National Issues, and Roy Phillips, executive director of the Canadian Manufacturers Association. All three of these key Canadian business organizations supported a general free trade agreement with the United States.

At the public hearings held by the Macdonald Royal Commission on the Canadian economy in 1983, business groups strongly supported free trade. The commission became a supporter. Their chance came when Brian Mulroney and the Progressive Conservatives were elected in 1984. At the "Shamrock Summit" in Québec City, March 1985, Mulroney and Reagan agreed to promote trade liberalization through GATT and the negotiation of a bilateral free trade agreement. President Reagan formally announced this to Congress on December 10, 1985.

In her study of the links between big business and the Mulroney government, Linda McQuaig emphasizes the role played by James D. Robinson III, then chairman of American Express corporation in the United States. In the 1980s, James Robinson was promoting the expansion of trade agreements to include services, investment and intellectual property rights. He helped campaign for the new U.S. trade bill of October 1984, which included services as a trade good. Ronald Reagan appointed James Robinson to the Advisory Committee for Trade Negotiations, and he became chairman in 1987.[4]

In 1986, James Robinson spearheaded the formation of the American Coalition for Trade Expansion with Canada, which was a who's who in American transnational corporations. Other big business support came from the Business Roundtable, the Chamber of Commerce, the National Foreign Trade Council, and the U.S. Council for International Business.

In Canada, the propaganda campaign for free trade with the United States was led by the Canadian Alliance for Trade and Job Opportunities. Like its American counterpart, it was a coalition of the largest corporations and financial institutions in the country. One of the key people in putting together this organization was David Culver, Chairman of Alcan, member of the board of American Express and friend of James Robinson.

The key Canadian organization in the promotion of free trade was the Business Council on National Issues, representing 150 chief executive officers of the largest Canadian businesses. They provided the finances for the Canadian Alliance.

In May 1986 negotiation began between the two governments, and the Canada-U.S. Free Trade Agreement (CUSFTA) was signed in October 1987. Big business and the American government were ecstatic. They got far more than they ever hoped for from Canada's Tory government. First, services were included in the agreement. Agriculture was also included. The U.S. government had been pushing to have GATT expanded to include these two areas, and the CUSFTA set an important precedent. While American control of the Canadian economy had always been a major Canadian concern in the past, U.S. negotiators obtained "national treatment" for U.S. investments in Canada. All U.S. companies in Canada were to be treated the same as Canadian companies. The Mulroney government unilaterally eliminated the Foreign Investment Review Agency and the National Energy Program. These two nationalist programs, introduced by the government of Pierre Trudeau, had been strongly opposed by U.S. corporations and the U.S. government. The Canada-U.S. Auto Pact was changed significantly. No longer would the U.S. Big Three be required to produce in Canada. The CUSFA required a 50 percent North American content, but all of this could be provided by American content.

Most shocking to Canadians were the energy provisions. For years the U.S. government had been pushing for a continental energy deal which would give the United States preferred access to Canada's energy resources. Public opinion in Canada was strongly opposed to such a policy, and previous Canadian governments refused American requests. But the new Tory government was different. When the text of CUSFTA was released, Canadians learned for the first time that the United States had been guaranteed access to Canadian oil and gas. Canadian governments could not reduce exports to the United States to below the average of the previous three years.

But Canada had to share more than energy with the United States. Other provisions of CUSFTA imposed proportional sharing of all natural resources, including water, even during periods of domestic shortages. Tariffs were to be phased out, but they hardly existed. The most important objective of the Canadian government had been to secure exemption from arbitrary U.S. trade actions on Canadian exports. The U.S. government had greatly expanded the use of nontariff barriers (NTBs) in recent years, and this had produced many problems for Canadian exporters. The U.S. government made no concessions here.

The main complaint of American corporations, economic groups, and the U.S. government itself was that Canada was subsidizing exports, and in turn they imposed countervailing duties. But CUSFTA did not define government subsidies. Trade dispute panels were established, but they could only consider whether U.S. trade protection actions complied with existing U.S. legislation. There were no impartial standards. Enforcement of any decisions would be based on the power of the two governments to impose penalties. Canada could not win such contests.

Big business in Canada was pleased with CUSFTA. They obtained their key goal, the right to invest in the United States without discrimination, and to export back to Canada without facing tariffs. They now had the option of transferring production to lower-cost sites in U.S. states.

The Canadian business alliance played a key role in the Canadian federal election in the fall of 1988, called the "free trade election." The Liberal Party took a strong stand against the free trade deal with the United States. The New Democratic Party also opposed the deal, although they downplayed the issue in their campaign. Public opinion polls revealed that a majority of Canadians were sceptical of the treaty. Near the end of the campaign, the business alliance flooded Canada with propaganda which predicted economic collapse and joblessness if Canadians voted for the Liberal or New Democratic parties.

The Tories won a majority of seats in the House of Commons, although the Liberals and the NDP received 56 percent of the popular vote. CUSFTA was ratified. Ronald Reagan called it the "new economic constitution for North America."

Negotiating NAFTA

During the 1988 Canadian federal election, Brian Mulroney and other Tory cabinet ministers insisted that they had no intention of expanding the CUSFTA to include Mexico. But in March 1990 Mulroney went to Mexico, accompanied by representatives from the Business Council on National Issues. While there they signed the Canada-Mexico Framework Agreement on trade and economic relations. When asked by reporters if Mexico was to be admitted as part of the free trade agreement, as originally projected by Ronald Reagan, Mulroney replied that he "wouldn't be scandalized" if that happened. Two weeks later, the *Wall Street Journal* reported that the American and Mexican governments were about to begin negotiations.[5]

In early 1990, Carlos Salinas went to Europe to seek freer trading relations and foreign investment. When that initiative was rebuffed, he turned to the United States. On June 11, 1990, President George Bush and Salinas announced that they were beginning negotiations to create a United States-Mexico free trade agreement. In September 1990, the Mulroney government announced it was going to join the negotiations to create a North American free trade agreement.

Two weeks later, George Bush announced his Enterprise for the Americas Initiative (EAI) at a meeting of the seven most industrialized capitalist countries, the Group 7, in Houston. The goal was to create a free trade bloc which would include the entire Western hemisphere. This would be the culmination of Ronald Reagan's dream — a free trade bloc which would offset the European Economic Community and the Japanese-dominated Asian trading bloc. But as Xabier Gorostiaga has pointed out, unlike the Alliance for Progress which was announced by President John F. Kennedy in 1961, the EAI is not the plan of a great power on the offensive, it is "the initiative of a declining power on the defensive."[6]

The EAI held out access to the U.S. market for all countries in Latin America and the Caribbean. The Bush administration promised some relief from large foreign debts. U.S. financial aid was to be made available for government programs for privatization of state-owned enterprises. But, in return, the U.S. government demanded that the Latin American countries pursue neoliberal structural adjustment programs.

Since the announcement of the EAI, most of the countries of Latin America and the Caribbean have signed Framework Agreements on Trade and Investment with the United States. These preliminary agreements have been designed to push structural adjustment further and to open these countries to U.S. foreign investment. The U.S. government is also insisting that the agreements include guarantees that the less developed partners protect the patent rights of U.S. corporations.

The EAI is a bipartisan foreign policy strategy. Following the approval of NAFTA by the U.S. Congress, President Bill Clinton immediately revealed a plan to admit other countries to create a Western Hemisphere free trade zone. U.S. officials revealed that they would require these countries to carry out "market reforms" which would include deregulation of their economies, harmonization, and "adopting similar product standards, investment and intellectual property rules."

The goals of the U.S. government are geopolitical. They want the Western hemisphere to once again be the captive sphere of influence of the

United States, and they want neoliberalism entrenched as the Western hemisphere's only political economy.

This objective was clearly stated in the leaked memorandum by John Negroponte, the U.S. Ambassador to Mexico during the NAFTA negotiations: "The free trade agreement can be seen as an instrument to promote, consolidate and guarantee continued policies of economic reform in Mexico beyond the Salinas administration." The ambassador also argued that a free trade agreement would institutionalize the foreign policy direction of the Salinas government, away from Latin America and toward closer ties with the United States.[7]

In 1979, the administration of José López Portillo signed agreements to join the General Agreement on Tariffs and Trade (GATT). However, the final decision was abandoned because of strong opposition within the PRI and throughout the country. But under the structural adjustment policy implemented by President Miguel de la Madrid, Mexico began moving towards the neoliberal model of economic development. In 1986, the decision was made to join GATT.

As a member of GATT, Mexico participated in the Uruguay round negotiations. The Salinas government won praise from the U.S. government for supporting them on the issue of expanding the GATT to include services, intellectual property rights and rights for foreign investors. At the same time, the Salinas government was making unilateral concessions by changing its own rules on trade and investment.

President Salinas promoted freer trade in general, signing agreements with other Latin American governments and free trade organizations and joining the Pacific Basin Agreement. But there can be no doubt that the central focus of his policy was a bilateral agreement with the United States.[8]

Nora Lustig points out that there were three reasons for advancing this radical policy change. First, it would insure that Mexico would continue to have open access to the U.S. market, which took over 75 percent of Mexico's exports. Secondly, it would encourage new foreign investment and the repatriation of Mexican capital that had been taken abroad. Thirdly, it was "to ensure the durability of Mexico's open economy strategy."[9]

President Salinas stated on many occasions that NAFTA is an attempt to constitutionalize the neoliberal reforms, to guarantee to foreign and domestic capital that there will never be a return to state-directed development policies. On foreign policy issues, Salinas stood with the U.S. government and distanced himself from the other countries in Latin America. For example, he refused to condemn the U.S. government for the invasion of Panama.

Big business in Mexico has strongly supported free trade with the United States. They want access to U.S. finance capital and the right to invest in the United States without discrimination. They also want a guarantee that no future Mexican government can impose restrictions on the export of capital. They see the free trade agreement as a way of "constitutionalizing" the free market policy changes made by the administration of Miguel de la Madrid and Carlos Salinas.

The exclusive and powerful Mexican Council of Businessmen (CMHN), the chief economic advisers to the Salinas government, have strongly supported the free trade agreements. The Business Co-ordinating Council (CCE), which represents big business in general, also strongly supports free trade with the United States. The CCE organized the Coordinator of Businesses for a U.S.-Mexican FTA (COECE), the main lobbying group for NAFTA. It was headed by Juan Gallardo of Industria Minera Mexíco and Guillermo Guemes, a senior executive with Banamex, Mexico's largest bank. It hired American professional lobbying organizations to convince U.S. legislators to support NAFTA.[10]

In the United States, large corporations created the Coalition for Trade Expansion to push NAFTA through the U.S. Congress. This organization included the Business Roundtable, the National Association of Manufacturers, and the largest American transnational corporations. Most of them are major investors in Mexico. In early 1993, USA-NAFTA was created by over 1,000 large corporations and trade associations to push the final agreement through the Congress. They spent $6 million on television advertising in November alone.[11]

In Canada, the big business organizations also pushed hard for NAFTA, including the Business Council on National Issues, the Canadian Manufacturers Association, the Canadian Chamber of Commerce and the Canadian Bankers Association. The Trilateral Commission also strongly supported NAFTA.[12]

Business executives in all three countries were strong supporters of NAFTA. Caldwell Partners/Amrop International surveyed 278 top executives of medium-sized to large firms and found that 95 percent backed NAFTA. A survey by Arthur Anderson & Co. of small and medium-sized companies in all three countries, found majority approval. However, business spokesmen were sceptical of the claims by the three governments that NAFTA would create more jobs. A survey of 1,600 small and medium-sized firms in Canada by the International Development Research Centre found 71.4 percent expected job losses as a result of NAFTA. The Caldwell/Amrop survey found similar sentiments. Douglas Caldwell reported that "they are trying to duck the question of jobs because they do not want to jeopardize NAFTA being passed." One respondent argued that "unemployment is a regrettable byproduct of the deal."[13]

In Canada the Mulroney government rammed the NAFTA implementing legislation through the Parliament without any public participation, with only a few token committee hearings in Ottawa, and drastically limited debate in the legislature. The Tory government was determined to avoid the public debate that was held in 1987-88 over the CUSFTA. Public opinion polls consistently showed a strong majority of Canadians opposed to NAFTA.

In Mexico NAFTA was approved without any public discussion of the issue. There were lectures, round tables, and meetings of the representatives of businesses and their organizations, and some discussion in the Senate. But the public was left out of the process. Business organizations worked with the government on the negotiation process.[14]

Ratification in the Senate was done in one day, with no debate or public involvement. Of the sixty-four seats in the Senate, the opposition held only three. In the one-party state, the opposition was simply stonewalled. The organizations affiliated to the PRI, including the trade union federations, all spoke out in favour of the treaty. President Salinas repeatedly promised Mexicans that NAFTA would provide many new jobs and an increase in their standard of living. A public opinion poll by *Esta Pais* in March 1991 found that of those who knew anything about NAFTA, 80 percent approved.[15]

This is not to say that there was no opposition to NAFTA in Mexico. Academics and intellectuals expressed opposition. A group of independent organizations formed the Mexican Action Network on Free Trade (RMALC).

Small business had major doubts, and their main organization, CANACINTRA, hosted a conference on free trade and invited opponents from Canada and the United States as major speakers. In October 1993, one of the oldest business organizations in Mexico, the Confederation of Industrial Chambers (CONCAMIN), came out against NAFTA. They argued that it would not solve unemployment or other domestic economic problems. They pointed out that over the past few years profits had increased but the number of jobs had decreased.[16]

The fear of many small and medium-sized businesses was that they would face greater competition from U.S. corporations in their own market while being unable to export to the United States. The National Council on Foreign Trade pointed out that the majority of national companies had no experience outside the Mexican market. Mexico's industrial model concentrated exports in the hands of a small number of very large corporations.[17]

Many Mexicans expressed concern over the proposed treaty itself. There was a widespread belief that the issues of Mexican emigration to the United States, the rights of migrant workers, and human rights for illegal Mexican immigrants in the United States should be covered by the treaty. But President Salinas dropped these issues, fearing that they would result in further opposition to NAFTA in the U.S. Congress.

The whole question of the manufacture and trade in illicit drugs and their control was consciously ignored by all three governments. It was deemed "too hot" for discussion.

There were demands for a Social Charter and a Human Rights Commission, as in the European Common Market. However, because big business was adamantly opposed, all three governments decided that these conditions should be left out.

Intellectuals were concerned about the asymmetry in power between the three countries. The United States and Canada were much more highly developed than Mexico. With these countries' more advanced level of education, and greater commitment to research and development, Mexico could not hope to compete except in the area of lower production costs.

Comparisons were often made with Spain joining the European Common Market. Spain had been given large sums of capital from the richer countries to help ease her entry. Nevertheless, the introduction of the free market had been very hard on Spain, with pronounced de-industrialization and unemployment rising to 24 percent, by far the highest in the industrialized world. The American and Canadian governments rejected any financial grants to Mexico, and President Salinas decided not to push the issue.

The only possible roadblock to NAFTA was the U.S. House of Representatives. President Bill Clinton came out strongly in support of NAFTA, but he had to undermine the strong opposition of the Democratic Party.

The Clinton administration had a great deal of difficulty in getting the U.S. House of Representatives to accept NAFTA. At the beginning of November 1993, Clinton determined that he lacked about fifty votes for approval. The general public was split on the issue, as revealed in public opinion polls taken during the second week of November: *Washington Post*/ABC News, 42 percent for, 42 percent against; *New York Times* Poll, 37 percent for, 42 percent against; and the *USA Today*/CNN Polls, 38 percent for and 41 percent against — this, in spite of a massive public relations campaign promoting NAFTA by the Clinton Administration and U.S. big business. The Mexican government hired Burson-Marsteller and paid them $30 million for a public relations and lobbying job.[18]

Over the next two weeks, President Clinton went on a vote-buying binge to line up approval for NAFTA. Numerous special deals were signed with individual Congressmen, the worst kind of pork barrel politics for which the United States is famous.

But other deals were made to protect special business interests who felt threatened by the terms of NAFTA as it was negotiated. The U.S. sugar industry was bought off when President Clinton agreed to limit Mexican exports to the United States to only 150,000 tons during the first seven years of NAFTA. The U.S. citrus industry got the administration to agree to automatically impose tariffs on Mexican frozen orange juice if prices fell below a prescribed level. These deals bought the votes of eighteen Congressmen.

Wheat growers were promised that the administration would step up its efforts to restrict the imports of durum wheat from Canada; this won five votes. On November 17, President Clinton wrote a letter to Florida tomato and vegetable growers promising to protect them from cheap Mexican imports during the winter season; this won an additional twenty-three votes.

Other special provisions were written into the U.S. implementing legislation, which are not in the text of NAFTA. For example, provisions to make it easier for Maytag Corporation to get protection against lower-cost Mexican imports. The U.S. Customs Service is required to monitor colour television imports for North American content, a requirement demanded by Zenith Electric Corporation. William Daley, hired by President Clinton to negotiate the agreement through the House of Representatives, argued that "without these recent agreements, we wouldn't be in a position to win much new support at all."[19]

In contrast, Jean Chrétien, who had promised to renegotiate NAFTA during the 1993, Canadian federal election, asked the Clinton Administration for a clear definition of what the U.S. government meant by "unfair dumping" of goods by Canadians and "unfair government subsidies." He got nothing. Mickey Kantor, the U.S. Trade Representative, said that NAFTA would not be reopened for any further negotiation.

On November 17, 1993 the U.S. House of Representatives approved NAFTA by a vote of 234 to 200. Analysis by *USA Today* showed that those representatives with the safest seats tended to support NAFTA. Those who had won in tight electoral races, and were more concerned with public opinion, voted more heavily against NAFTA.[20]

This whole process was very embarrassing to the Mexican and Canadian governments, but since they were committed to NAFTA they felt they had to accept the unilateral changes made by President Clinton. The U.S. ratification process dramatized the basic inequality in power and influence between the United States and its junior trade partners. NAFTA was to come into effect on January 1, 1994.

The Erosion of National Sovereignty

The U.S. government and big business in general were pleased with the NAFTA agreement. It included many of the goals that they had been pushing for during the Uruguay round of the GATT.

As Sylvia Saborio has correctly pointed out, "The main allure of the FTA has to do more with investment than with trade."[21] The key provision is the right to national treatment for foreign investment. Future governments may not require foreign investors planning takeover of national companies to maintain any standards, such as buying locally, requiring the participation of national capital, or maintaining exports. There can be no restrictions on the repatriation of dividends, interest, royalties, or management fees. If a government wishes to nationalize a company, they must immediately reimburse the owners at market value in the currency of the owner's country. There can be no restrictions on the movement of business personnel between countries, and no requirements to employ local people. NAFTA is a Bill of Rights for capitalists.

NAFTA bans any government restrictions on foreign investment which could pertain to trade balance, domestic content rules, and the transfer of technology. Jim Sanford points out that these provisions are an attempt to block the creation of sectoral trade agreements like the Canada-U.S. Auto Pact which was designed to ensure local production.[22]

There are controls on the creation of new state-owned enterprises. NAFTA specifies that these corporations must operate as commercial enterprises. Their goal cannot be to perform as a public service or at a loss to serve some other political objective. For example, public transportation cannot be provided by public enterprises on a subsidized basis. Power utilities cannot pursue energy conservation strategies unless they are on a commercial basis, i.e., the programs make a profit.

All new government-operated services must be open to competition from private companies from the other NAFTA members. For example, governments may not limit support of child care to public or nonprofit institutions. Foreign private companies have the right to compete. Ontario may not create a state program for automobile insurance without compensating U.S. companies which might want to get into the business. No level of government may give preference to local businesses when deciding which company will receive a contract. This is to create a "level playing field" for foreign corporations.

NAFTA stresses the neoliberal objective of deregulation. No regulations are to be imposed that make a corporation uncompetitive, and the onus of proof is on the regulator. As Maude Barlow and Bruce Campbell point out, "Written all through the NAFTA text, sometimes subtly, sometimes not, is the clear implication that regulations, from food safety to consumer protection, are a burden impediment to business."[23]

The service sector of the economy is included in NAFTA on an equal level with goods. For example, trucking and rail transportation can no longer be subject to national content requirements. Telecommunications and data processing are now open to foreign corporations. No preferential treatment can be given to state-owned enterprises. All corporations which provide services are granted national treatment, the right to set up shop and do business, the right to commercial presence, and the right to cross-border sales.

A key service sector is the financial area. Foreign financial corporations are to be granted "equal competitive opportunities" in the markets of the three countries. Canada and Mexico are to phase out their regulations which protect the domestic banking industry.

The U.S. government was successful in including intellectual property rights in NAFTA. The property rights of corporations are protected, including patents, trademarks, and copyrights. Drug corporations were given twenty-year monopoly rights against generic drugs, widely supported in Third World countries as part of public health policy. Computer programs were defined as literary works and guaranteed fifty-year patent rights. Corporations were guaranteed the right to patent life forms created through genetic engineering. Pharmaceutical and agribusiness corporations obtained the right to patent seeds and plants, almost always derived from gene pools in Third World countries.

These provisions have been strongly opposed by Third World countries. Intellectual property rights provisions benefit countries like the United States with large research and development expenditures. But even countries like Canada will be adversely affected. Ninety-five percent of all patents in Canada are held by foreigners. Pressure by the pharmaceutical giants to extend drug patents to twenty years undermined the Canadian generic drug industry and has cost Canadians an additional $500 million a year through higher drug prices.[24]

The automotive industry is the fastest growing industry in Mexico.

The provisions in NAFTA require that the North American content level of vehicles be raised from the 50 percent-level of CUSFTA to 62.5 percent. But there is no guarantee of production in any single country. In theory, all 62.5 percent could be manufactured in Mexico and then exported duty free to Canada. Mexico had to give up its foreign ownership restrictions. While Mexico will attract much of the future investment in this industry, it is a capital intensive industry which hires relatively few people.[25]

On the level of trade itself, the most serious problem has been the use of U.S. trade law to limit imports. The North American Trade Commission, with representatives from each country, can assign disputes to panels of experts. The U.S. government was successful in expanding CUSFTA to include the right of private parties (e.g., the corporate sector) to make claims against a state.

Nevertheless, NAFTA has no provisions that define an export subsidy or what constitutes dumping of goods and services in a country at prices below cost. When a panel makes a decision, there are no enforcement provisions. Each country can only rely on its retaliatory power, and obviously Canada and Mexico have very little vis-a-vis the United States.

A key objective sought by the large corporations and the Bush administration was the harmonization of standards. The free trade program sees high standards in food, health and safety and the environment as nontariff barriers to trade, which also raise costs to corporations. The supporters of NAFTA and GATT want to use trade agreements to override high local standards.

Already trade law is being used to undermine policies set by democratic governments. A few of those challenged include Dutch and American recycling programs, the U.S. Delaney clause prohibiting carcinogenic additives in food, reforestation programs in Canada, taxes on gas-guzzling cars, the European ban on using growth hormones in cattle, the U.S. Marine Mammal Protection Act, bans on the export of raw logs, the U.S. food labelling act, limits on pesticide residues in foods, and the Canadian ban on the use of bovine somatotropin (BST) in milk production. The goal of the push towards harmonization is to establish a low common denominator which then becomes the highest standard that parties to the trade agreements can adopt.[26]

Finally, NAFTA creates a North American Free Trade Commission which has extensive powers to interpret the agreement. It is a nonelected body which operates behind closed doors and is not accountable to the public. International bureaucratic structures are being created by the trade agreements, and they have sovereign powers to override decisions made by elected governments. The imposition of neoliberalism has greatly compromised the principles of democratic government.[27]

GATT: A New Imperialism

The free trade and free market provisions of NAFTA were strengthened in the final text of the Uruguay round of GATT negotiations, which culminated on December 15, 1993. Throughout the negotiations, the agenda was set by the "Quad Group," the United States, the twelve-nation European Economic Community, Japan and Canada. In the last-minute bargaining on the tough issues, decisions were made behind closed doors by the delegates from the United States and the EEC.

The Group of 15, representing the fifteen largest less developed countries, lobbied hard but had virtually no impact on the final agreement. Many see the GATT agreement as a return to a new form of colonialism, but no alternative seems to exist at this time.

The new agreement was welcomed by spokesmen for transnational corporations. In April 1992, when it appeared that the Uruguay round of negotiations was about to collapse, representatives from 120 of the largest corporations in the world issued an open letter calling on the world's political leaders to implement the draft prepared by Arthur Dunkel, the Director General of GATT. They argued that to fail was to "face a worsening world economy."[28]

The U.S. government succeeded in getting most of what it wanted in the agreement, including services. As Martin Khor Kok Peng points out, "in most Third World countries, the service sectors are the last remaining areas still under local control, since the import of manufactured products has increasingly taken over the market of locally-made goods." Foreign investors now have the right of establishment and the right to national treatment, and governments can aid their transnational corporations through the right to retaliate.[29]

GATT now prohibits the imposition of "trade-related investment measures," generally referred to as TRIMs. As under NAFTA, these GATT provisions prohibit countries from imposing any conditions on foreign investment.

The new GATT agreement also protects "trade-related intellectual property rights," commonly referred to as TRIPs. The industrialized countries have insisted on uniform rights for private owners, mainly corporations, imposed free of obligations on Third World countries. Protection periods are for much longer periods than has been the practice in Third World countries. In 1991, the United States earned $22 billion from patents and copyrights, and they want to boost that figure. In the United States, this section of the agreement was pushed for by the Intellectual Property Committee (IPC) which represents giant U.S. corporations.[30]

GATT now includes the demand of the U.S. government that there should be no restrictions on the export of raw materials and other natural resources. All of the industrialized countries are becoming more dependent on importing key resources from Third World countries. The goal of the new GATT agreement is to prevent countries from reserving natural resources for the use of their own people.

This provision applies to agricultural products as well. Stephen Shrybman points out that around 80 percent of the world's land is cultivated for export-oriented crops. Furthermore, 80 to 90 percent of the trade in tea, coffee, cocoa, cotton, forest products, tobacco, and jute are controlled by a small number of transnational corporations which want free trade.[31]

The U.S. government also succeeded in getting agriculture included in GATT. Much of the discussion centred on government subsidies for agricultural products by the most industrialized countries. Kevin Watkins points out that the share of agricultural trade controlled by the OECD countries has risen steadily since the early 1970s. The Third World countries have been unable to compete with the subsidized prices offered by the industrialized countries.[32]

The Uruguay agreement calls for the industrialized countries to reduce their agricultural export subsidy dollars by 36 percent and volume by 21 percent over seven years, starting in July 1995. Farm supply management programs, which are a traditional policy in Canada and which balance production with demand in the domestic market, are now prohibited.

At the same time, heavy government subsidies for the production of cereals in the industrialized countries have led to an increase in Third World imports. This has undermined food security in these countries and undercut the household incomes of the vast majority of their farmers. The U.S. and EEC proposals for GATT called for the prohibition of government assistance to agriculture in Third World states, which would act to "maintain domestic prices at higher than free-at-frontier prices."

The position of the U.S. government was stated by John Block: "The idea that developing countries should feed themselves is an anachronism from a bygone era. They could better ensure their food security by relying on U.S. agricultural products, which are available, in most cases, at lower cost." This also reflects the thinking of Carlos Salinas and the Mexican government.[33]

A concern of most Third World governments at the GATT negotiations was the use of nontariff barriers by the industrialized countries to restrict imports. "Voluntary" export restraints were supposedly abolished in the new GATT agreement, but in January 1994, the U.S. government signed a major agreement with China limiting textile exports to the United States.[34]

The United States, the European Economic Community, Canada and Australia are by far the major users of antidumping provisions in domestic trade law to provide nontariff protection for domestic industries. National authorities determine that dumping has taken place (i.e., goods are exported at a cost below production). They then impose duties to offset the effect. These authorities can also determine if there are export subsidies provided by the governments of the exporting countries. In these cases, countervailing duties equal to the value of the subsidy may be imposed. This form of protection is most suited to the industrialized countries as it permits the targeting of goods and countries and it is effective because of the high degree of vulnerability of Third World countries.

On November 26, 1993 the U.S. government presented the GATT negotiations with a list of eleven demands for the protection of existing U.S. trade law. In the final agreement, they won seven of these. The U.S. supposedly agreed to abolish dumping duties after five years. But leading U.S. congressmen made it clear that they were not going to give up U.S. trade actions permitted under U.S. trade law. They insisted that these trade actions would be protected by the U.S. implementing legislation for the new GATT agreement.[35]

The Uruguay round of negotiations changed GATT into the new World Trade Organization (WTO). The new institution will have power and authority similar to that of the International Monetary Fund and the World Bank. Like the two older organizations, the WTO will be dominated by the rich industrialized countries. The WTO is another nonelected bureaucratic organization cut off from popular control. Enforcement of decisions will be left to the countries themselves. This, of course, means that the industrialized countries have far more power than those of the Third World.

The WTO compliments the CUSFTA and NAFTA. It is another attempt to institutionalize and make permanent the neoliberal economic model.

Countries like Mexico will be disciplined through the conditions imposed on them and the threat of retaliation by the industrialized countries.

The institutions created by the WTO will significantly erode national sovereignty. They are an attempt to block actions by governments elected with a mandate to undertake national development.

The trend toward neoliberalism seems destined to accelerate the rate of environmental destruction and economic inequality. As it promotes the expansion of services provided by transnational corporations from industrialized countries, it also promises to further erode the cultural identity of Third World countries, including Mexico.

The WTO is not part of the United Nations system and this further erodes the influence of Third World countries. Like the IMF and the World Bank, it will be dominated and controlled by the governments of the most industrialized capitalist countries.

Notes

1. See Edward J. McCaughan, "Mexico's Long Crisis," *Latin American Perspectives*, Vol 20, Summer 1993, pp. 6-31; Joyce Kolko, *Restructuring the World Economy*. New York: Pantheon Books, 1988; Bennett Harrison and Barry Bluestone, *The Great U-Turn*. New York: Basic Books, 1988; Daniel Drache and Meric S. Gertler, eds., *The New Era of Global Competition*. Montréal: McGill-Queen's University Press, 1991; Richard Peet, ed., *International Capitalism and Industrial Restructuring*. Boston: Allen & Unwin, 1987, and John W. Warnock, *Free Trade and the New Right Agenda*. Vancouver: New Star Books, 1988.

2. For background to the Canada-U.S. Free Trade Agreement see Linda McQuaig, *The Quick and the Dead*. Toronto: Viking Books, 1991; G. Bruce Doern and Brian W. Tomlin, *Faith and Fear*. Toronto: Stoddard, 1991; Duncan Cameron, ed., *The Free Trade Deal*. Toronto: James Lorimer & Co., 1988; Maude Barlow, *Parcel of Rogues*. Toronto: Key Porter Books, 1990; Lawrence Martin, *Pledge of Allegiance*. Toronto: McClelland and Stewart, 1993; and Warnock, *op. cit.*

3. Peter C. Newman, "Free Trade's Real Godfather," *Maclean's Magazine*, April 18, 1988, p. 49.

4. McQuaig, *op. cit.*

5. On NAFTA see Sylvia Saborio, *The Premise and the Promise: Free Trade in the Americas*. New Brunswick: Transaction Publishers, 1992; Nora Lustig et al, *North American Free Trade*. Washington: The Brookings Institute, 1992; Fen Osler Hampson and Christopher J. Maule, eds., *A New World Order?* Ottawa: Carleton University Press, 1992; Duncan Cameron and Mel Watkins, eds., *Canada Under Free Trade*. Toronto: James Lorimer & Co., 1993; and Maude Barlow and Bruce Campbell, *Take Back the Nation*. Toronto: Key Porter Books, 1993.

6. Xabier Gorostiaga, "Enterprise for the Americas Initiative," *Latin American and Caribbean Trade Alert*, No. 1, July 1992, pp. 1-3; see also Yasmine Shamsie, "The Enterprise for the

Americas Initiative and NAFTA: Consequences for the Caribbean Basin." Toronto: Canada-Caribbean-Central America Policy Alternatives, February 1993.

7. Quoted in *Which Way for the Americas? Analysis of NAFTA Proposals and the Impact on Canada.* Ottawa: Canadian Centre on Policy Alternatives, November 1992.

8. James M. Cypher, "The Ideology of Economic Science in the Selling of NAFTA: The Political Economy of Elite Decision-Making," *Review of Radical Political Economics,* Vol. 25, No. 4, 1993, pp. 146-164.

9. Nora Lustig, "Mexico's Integration Strategy with North America," in Colin I. Bradford, Jr., *Strategic Options for Latin America in the 1990s.* Washington: Development Center of the Organization for Economic Cooperation and Development and Inter-American Development Bank, 1992, pp. 155-177.

10. See Juan Gallardo, "La Coordinadora de Organismos Empresariales para el Comercio Exterior," in Carlos Arriola, ed., *Testimonios sobre el TLC.* Mexico, D.F.: Miguel Ángel Porrúa, 1994; and Joyce Nelson, "The Zapatistas vs. the Spin-Doctors," *The Canadian Forum,* Vol. 74, March 1994, pp. 18-25.

11. William M. Welch, "Parade of Lobbyists Never Ends," *USA Today,* November 17 , 1993, pp. A1-2.

12. Joyce Nelson, "The Trilateral Connection," *The Canadian Forum,* Vol. 72, December 1993, pp. 5-9.

13. Joanne Chianello, "Managers Support Pact but Expect Job Losses," *Financial Post,* November 13, 1993, p. 8.

14. Gallardo, *op.cit.*

15. Damian Fraser, "Mexicans Hail Trade Talks," *Financial Post,* March 21, 1991, p. 11.

16. *Trade News,* Vol. 2, No. 193, October 23, 1993.

17. Equipo Pueblo, *Mexican News Summary,* December 1, 1993.

18. Nelson 1993, *op. cit.*

19. For an account of the political bargaining, see *USA Today* and *Globe and Mail* for the first two weeks in November 1993 and *Trade Week in Review,* Vol. 2, No. 204, November 12, 1993.

20. "How NAFTA Vote Was Split," *USA Today,* November 18, 1993, A-4.

21. Saborio, *op. cit., p. 22.*

22. Jim Sanford, "Investment," in Cameron and Watkins, *op. cit.,* pp. 151-172.

23. Barlow and Campbell, *op. cit.,* pp. 98-99.

24. See Linda Diebel, "How Trade Deals Work for U.S. Corporations: The Case of Patents and Pharmaceutical Drugs," in Cameron and Watkins, *op. cit.,* pp. 92-98.

25. Sam Gindin, "Auto Sector," in Cameron and Watkins, *op. cit.,* pp. 140-142.

26. See Lori Wallach, "Hidden Dangers of GATT and NAFTA," in Ralph Nader et al, *The Case Against Free Trade.* San Francisco: Earth Island Press, 1993; and Mark Ritchie, "Agricultural Trade Liberalization," in Nader et al, *op. cit.,* pp. 163-194.

27. For other comment on NAFTA see Thea Lee, "Happily Ever NAFTA," *Dollars & Sense,* January-February 1993, pp. 12-15; Sheldon Friedman, "NAFTA as Social Dumping," *Challenge,* September-October 1992, pp. 27-32; "NAFTA Pact Agreed at Last," *Latin American Weekly Report,* August 27, 1992, pp. 2-3; Fernando Ortega Pizarro and Carlos Puig, "Al descubierto, algunos de los cientos de corchetes que entorpecen al TLC," *Proceso,* No. 802, March 16, 1992, pp. 12-15; "Details of the Parallel Agreements," *Latin*

American Weekly Report, September 2, 1992, pp. 400-403; Steve Hellinger et al, "The New World Order and the Peoples of the Americas," *Why Magazine*, Fall-Winter 1992, pp. 30-34; Refik Erzan and Alexander Yeates, *Free Trade Agreements with the U.S.: What's in It for Latin America?* Washington: World Bank, 1992; Michael J. Twomey, *Multinational Corporations and the North American Free Trade Agreement.* Westport: Praeger, 1993; and "Free Trade and Common Markets," *Latin American Weekly Report.* Special Report SR-92-03, June 1992.

28. Madelaine Drohan, "Business Leaders Press for GATT Deal," *Globe and Mail*, April 16, 1992, B-5.
29. Martin Khor Kok Peng, "A New Global Giant to Rule the South," *Third World Resurgence*, Nos. 29/30, January-February 1993, pp. 20-23.
30. See Chakravarthl Raghavan, "MTO vs. GATT II: Behind a Giant's Creation," *Third World Resurgence*, Nos. 29/30, January-February 1993, pp. 24-30; Muchkund Dubey, "MTO and Uruguay Round: A Political Economy Critique," *Third World Resurgence*, Nos. 29/30, January-February 1993, pp. 31-35; and Frederick F. Clairmonte, "GATT: Countdown to Oblivion?" *Economic and Political Weekly*, Vol. 27, March 7, 1992, pp. 512-514.
31. Stephen Shrybman, "International Trade and the Environment," *The Ecologist*, Vol. 20, January-February 1990, pp. 30-34.
32. Mark Ritchie, "GATT, Agriculture and the Environment," *The Ecologist*, Vol. 20, November-December 1990. pp. 214-220.
33. Kevin Watkins, "GATT and the Third World: Fixing the Rules," *Race & Class*, Vol. 34, No. 1, 1992, pp. 23-40.
34. "China, U.S. Reach Deal to Avoid Textile War," *Globe and Mail*, January 18, 1994, B-24.
35. Eric Geguly, "High Noon Haggling in Geneva," *Financial Post*, December 11, 1993, p. 5; Madelaine Drohan, "Tradeoffs Lead to GATT Pact," *Globe and Mail*, December 16, 1993, A-1; and John Stackhouse, "Third World Countries fear GATT Sellout," *Globe and Mail*, December 20, 1993, B-2.

Chapter 9

THE IMPACT OF NEOLIBERALISM

The U.N. Economic Commission for Latin America and the Caribbean (CEPAL) has described the 1980s as the "lost decade." Gert Rosenthal, executive secretary of CEPAL, points out that the most general and conventional criterion used for measuring economic success is gross domestic product per capita. Between 1981 and 1992 the gross domestic product per capita for the region fell by 7.3 percent. In 1992 it stood at a level which was below that achieved in 1976. This decline was common throughout the region. Only Cuba, Colombia, Chile, Barbados and the Dominican Republic saw an increase over this period.[1]

The report of the United Nations Development Program for 1992 documented the decline over the decade. Between 1965 and 1980, the per capita gross domestic product for Latin America and the Caribbean grew at an average annual rate of 3.8 percent. Between 1980 and 1989, it declined on average 0.4 percent per annum.[2]

Gert Rosenthal argues that during the 1980s, 75 percent of the population in the region experienced a major reduction in their standard of living. For example, in 1992, the average wage of most workers in the region, when adjusted for inflation, was less than it was in 1980.[3]

The 1980s also saw an increase in the number of people living in poverty and indigence. The poverty line used in Latin America is absolute poverty, not the relative poverty line used in the industrialized capitalist countries. A person is said to live in poverty if their income cannot provide a basic minimum standard of food, clothing and shelter. Poverty lines are established by studies of household income and define a subsistence level.

In April 1992, the World Bank concluded that 46 percent of the population in Latin America and the Caribbean, a total of 207 million people, lived below the poverty line. This was an increase from 35 percent in 1980.

The previous month, CEPAL had estimated that thirty-five million people could be classified as indigent; those whose income could provide only 60 percent of basic food, housing and clothing. At a conference in Rome in March 1992, the World Health Organization (WHO) and the Food and Agricultural Organization (FAO) concluded that there were fifty-nine million people in Latin America living in "extreme poverty" which included malnutrition.[4]

The FAO has reported that poverty and indigence among Latin America's rural population increased during the 1980s. This was attributed to the rise in the number of people living on small production units, the growth in the number of landless peasants, the persistence of high illiteracy rates, and the lack of alternative employment. Poverty was found to be particularly high among the indigenous populations. The growing informal sector, characterized by low labour productivity and low income, had developed as a survival strategy. The result was an "enormous labour reserve" in the rural areas.[5]

Part of the reason for the rise in rural poverty was the stagnation in agricultural development. In the 1980s, agricultural production grew at an annual rate of less than 2 percent, well below the rate of rural population growth. The FAO concluded that the economic situation was hurt by the adjustment policies of the governments, which included loss of government support programs, reduction of agricultural credit, and reductions in subsidies and price supports.

The standard of living of the population as a whole was also adversely affected by the drastic cuts in government spending dictated by the structural adjustment programs (SAPs). Between 1982 and 1990 only a handful of countries experienced an increase in government expenditures as a percentage of gross domestic product. Many experienced a drop in spending on health and education.[6]

The major problem in all the countries of Latin America and the Caribbean has been the rise of unemployment and underemployment. Official government statistics for Latin American countries are very different from those in the advanced industrialized countries. Firstly, they only survey the large urban centres. Secondly, they generally classify a person as employed if s/he works even one hour a week at any kind of income generating activity. In countries with no unemployment insurance, and no social assistance programs, those without a formal job must work in the informal economy to survive.

Thus CEPAL's figures for urban unemployment in the area for 1991 reveal the official rates; they range between 6 and 8 percent of the labour force. Panama, more influenced by U.S. practices, listed their unemployment rate at 20 percent. The Caribbean countries measure unemployment more like the First World, and their figures give a more accurate portrayal of real unemployment in the region as a whole:[7] (See Table 9.1)

Much more significant has been the rise of what is commonly called the "informal economy." The International Labour Organization (ILO) and its Latin American Program (PREALC), define the informal economy

Table 9.1
Unemployment Rates, 1986-1987

Barbados	17.8
Belize	15.0
Dominican Republic	28.7
Guyana	30.0
Haiti	14.0
Jamaica	23.6
Netherlands Antilles	26.0
St. Kitts-Nevis	20.0
St. Lucia	18.6
St. Vincent-Grenadines	40.0
Trinidad-Tobago	22.3

Source: Deere et al, Table 2.3.

as those individuals and families who engage in household production and services outside the wage economy.

Edgar Feige attempted to create a more precise description. His classification is based on the form of the economy: (1) the illegal economy, which would include drugs, smuggled goods, stealing, and sometimes prostitution; (2) the unreported economy, those economic activities which avoid tax collection; (3) the unrecorded economy, which would include household production, and (4) the informal economy, those economic activities which avoid many or all business laws and regulations.[8]

Most of these activities are done for survival reasons. They involve long hours of work, and the returns are relatively low. Significantly, the informal economy expands when formal or regular jobs are not available, suggesting that it is not the preferred way of earning a living. In Latin America and the Caribbean, the existence of the informal sector permits the government to reduce state expenditures for unemployment insurance and social assistance.

The ILO World Labour Report for 1992 concludes that over the decade of the 1980s the informal sector in Latin America rose from 25 percent to 31 percent of the labour force. Combined with the official unemployment rate, this resulted in an underemployment level of 42 percent of the region's labour force in 1989.

As poverty increased during the 1980s in most countries in the region, so did inequality in income and wealth. The rich benefitted from reductions in the levels of taxation on higher-income groups and corporations and the privatization of state-owned enterprises. As governments reduced tariffs and other barriers to imports, small companies went out of business and large corporations grew larger.[9] Finally, there has been a significant degradation of natural resources and the environment over the 1980s. CEPAL notes that the economic crisis intensified over-exploitation of natural resources. Desperate farmers were pushed onto fragile agricultural frontiers. Deforestation has emerged as a very serious problem. The fisheries have been grossly overexploited. Rosenthal notes that "the cutback in public spending reduced the possibility of adopting measures to conserve natural resources and bring environmental degradation under control." All urban areas faced increased pollution problems due to the influx of the rural poor seeking jobs.[10]

The Recovery

The proponents of structural adjustment policies have always conceded that the change from import substitution industrialization could not be made without significant costs. It was the old argument that we have to make sacrifices now for a better future. How have the Latin American economies performed during the neoliberal revolution?

For the region as a whole, real rates of economic growth (adjusted for inflation) have continued to decline. Between 1960 and 1969, the average growth rate was 5.5 percent per year; between 1970 and 1979, it increased to 5.9 percent. However, during the "lost decade" between 1980 and 1989 it fell to only 1.1 percent.[11]

In October 1992, the Inter-American Development Bank (IDB) announced that the recovery was beginning, as the average real economic growth rate for 1991 had risen to 3.5 percent. For the first time in a decade it was above the annual rate of population growth. But this did not last for long. The rate of growth fell to 2.4 percent in 1992. For the region as a whole, economic growth rates remain well below the levels regularly achieved during the period of import substitution industrialization.[12]

One of the main goals of the structural adjustment program has been to reduce the rate of inflation. At the end of 1992, CEPAL could express satisfaction that there was a "pronounced downward trend" in the region. Leaving out Brazil, the average rate of inflation for the region in 1992 was 22 percent.[13]

Reducing the foreign and national debt has been a top priority goal of all the neoliberal regimes. However, the total external debt for Latin America has continued to grow, from around $250 billion in 1980 to $450 billion in 1992. The ability of governments to handle the debt has been aided by the fall in U.S. interest rates. CEPAL measures the annual interest due on these debts as a percentage of the export of goods and services. This percentage dropped from a high of 42.5 percent in 1982 to 19.2 percent in 1992.

The economies of Latin America and the Caribbean have been depressed by the large annual interest payments on the foreign debts. In addition, between 1983 and 1990 the region experienced a net loss of $204 billion as the outflow of capital exceeded new investment.

This changed in 1991 when the net inflow of capital reached $36 billion. In 1992, it rose to $57 billion. The IDB reported that about one half of this was foreign investment in state-owned enterprises which were being privatized, and thus did not represent investment in new production. The second most important source of capital was foreign investment in stocks and bonds. The IDB noted that most of this investment was "hot money" seeking to capture short-term profit opportunities. Of concern was the relative decline of direct foreign investment in productive enterprise.[14]

The advocates of the neoliberal model actively promote production for export. Exports earn foreign exchange which can be used to pay off foreign debtors. But the results so far have been disappointing.

First, the terms of trade for the region's main exports have continued to decline. CEPAL reports that over the period from 1981 to 1992, the value of exports dropped 28 percent in relation to the value of imports.

The volume of exports also slowed in the early 1990s, reflecting the economic recession in the industrialized world. In contrast, with the move towards free trade, imports rose much faster, reaching annual rates of 16.6 percent in 1991 and 17.2 percent in 1992. CEPAL notes that this "vigorous expansion of imports" was "stimulated by tariff liberalization and appreciation of local currencies." By 1992, the results had produced a negative trade balance in goods of $6 billion, and the current account balance of payments deficit had risen to $32 billion.

The structure of trade was also changing. Over the 1980s there was a decline in importance of intra-regional trade. As Rosenthal notes, "The slogan of the decade was integration with the rest of the world." The neoliberal model advocated a return to greater dependence on trade with the advanced industrial countries.

Another objective of the neoliberal model is balancing the national budget. Every structural adjustment program called for drastic cuts in public spending to achieve this goal. Tax systems were also changed, cutting taxes on corporations and increasing value-added sales taxes. The IDB reports that most countries in Latin America are making considerable progress in moving to balanced budgets. Between 1982 and 1991, the majority of governments managed to increase their revenues as a percentage of gross domestic product. They have been much more successful in reducing total government expenditures as a percentage of GDP.

In general, the economies of Latin America performed very poorly during the 1980s, when they were undergoing the change from import substitution industrialization to the neoliberal model of the free market and free trade. In the early 1990s, there was a recovery, however, the levels of economic growth, per capita income, trade, and job creation remained well below the achievements of the period between 1945 and 1980.

Salinas's Record

There has been a loud chorus of support for President Carlos Salinas and his neoliberal economic policies. Business leaders, international financial organizations, politicians, and the mass media have been unanimous in their praise for the changes introduced by the Mexican government over the past ten years.

But how did the Mexican economy performed under this new policy direction? There is widespread agreement that the most notable success of the Salinas government was to control inflation. In 1982, the year of the debt crisis, the annual rate of inflation rose to 98.8 percent. After a drop to 59.2 percent, it rose to 159.2 percent in 1987. By 1994 it had fallen to only 7 percent.[15]

The other major success regularly cited was the management of the external debt. In 1986, the total stood at $100.5 billion, and in 1992 it was at $106 billion. In his final State of the Nation address on November 1, 1994, Carlos Salinas claimed that the foreign public debt was $85 billion, only 11 percent higher than when he took office in 1988. Total foreign debt was estimated at $129 billion. However, the International Finance Corporation put Mexico's total foreign debt, public and private, at $165 billion at the end of 1994.[16]

Still, the impact of the debt on the overall economy had declined. In 1986, it was the equivalent of 459 percent of the exports of goods and services. By 1992, it had fallen to 252 percent of total exports. As Salinas stressed, the administration had been able to "reduce the real value of the debt and its relationship as a percentage of GDP."

Thanks mainly to the drop in U.S. interest rates, the total interest due on the external debt as a percentage of the exports of goods and services dropped from 42.5 percent in 1982-3 to 19.2 percent in 1992. The World Bank reports that in 1992 Mexico made payments totalling $9.979 billion. By the end of 1994, the debt was no longer the dominant policy issue.

The Salinas administration was relatively successful in stabilizing the value of the Mexican peso and the official exchange rate. There had been major devaluations of the currency in 1982, 1987, and 1988. In 1989, the Salinas administration introduced a "crawling peg" system to try to hold the peso close to the value of the U.S. dollar. As the rate of inflation was higher in Mexico than in the United States, the peso became overvalued. After 1989 there was a small but steady fall in the value of the peso compared to the U.S. dollar.

Foreign exchange reserves rose to $18 billion in 1991 and were reported to be $25 billion at the end of 1993. Despite all the political turmoil in 1994, in his *informe* of November 1, President Salinas claimed that the reserves stood at $17.2 billion. He argued that "this level of reserves allows us to strengthen the solvency of our currency." One month later Mexicans learned that this was false.[17]

The Mexican government has been quite successful in eliminating the federal budget deficit. In 1987, the budget deficit was the equivalent of 16 percent of the GDP; in 1992, President Salinas produced a budget surplus. Government spending as a percentage of GDP fell from a high of 45 percent in 1981 to only 17 percent in 1994.

Under the Salinas administration there was a major change in the taxation system. The tax rate on dividends was reduced from 50 percent to nothing. The fixed tax rate on interest income was maintained at 21 percent. The capital gains tax was cut from 42 percent to 35 percent, and exemption was granted for capital gains made on the stock market. The highest bracket of the income tax was cut from 60 percent to 35 percent. The value-added tax was increased to 15 percent, and then reduced to 10 percent.[18]

The corporate tax rate was cut from 42 percent to 35 percent and deductions were expanded. Furthermore, in order to encourage the repatriation of capital, the government introduced a "fiscal stamp," whereby repatriated capital would pay a much smaller tax rate.

A new 2 percent tax on assets was introduced in 1989, aimed at the 70 percent of businesses which did not report any profits and paid no taxes. Large corporations were not affected, as they already paid income taxes, and the asset tax could be deducted from taxes already paid.

The tax reform also eliminated special provisions for small businesses and self-employed people. Around 17 percent of the population, mainly in the middle class, lost their tax exempt status. Finally, the tax reform closed a number of loopholes and increased government auditing. A more vigorous tax collection increased revenues. As in all tax reforms under structural adjustment, the increases fell on the lower and middle classes.

Interest rates also declined under Salinas. The rates for government short term lending bonds were maintained at a high rate in order to try to entice capital to stay in the country. The interest paid on 30-day Treasury Bills (CETES) peaked in 1987 at 96 percent. The average interest rate on CETES fell to 30 percent in 1990 and to just above 21 percent in 1991. Just before the election in 1994, the rates were reduced to 13.4 percent.[19]

The structural adjustment policies were designed to attract foreign investment to Mexico. The World Development Report for 1993 shows that between 1970 and 1980 gross domestic investment rose, on average, 8.3 percent per annum. Between 1980 and 1991, it declined an average of 1.9 percent. Annual foreign investment went from $2.9 billion in 1989, to a peak of $15.6 billion in 1993, before falling off to $9 billion in 1994. The total of new foreign investment for the Salinas sexenio was around $50 billion.

However, the World Bank reports that in 1981 total investment in Mexico was 26.4 percent of gross domestic product. This fell to 17.6 percent in 1983 and had recovered to only 18.9 percent in 1990. The domestic rate of savings and investment fell. Furthermore, the World Bank pointed out that the new capital which entered Mexico between 1991 and 1993 was mainly "hot money" invested in the stock market and government bonds. Foreign direct investment in productive enterprises was declining.[20]

The restructuring of the economy has accelerated the polarization of the industrial sector. Edur Velasco Arregui notes that exports are concentrated in around 2,000 large companies. The National Institute of Statistics, Geography and Information (INEGI) reports that the productivity of this sector is only 40 percent that of the United States; this is offset by significantly lower wages. However, the larger corporations are adopting new foreign technologies and creating very few jobs.[21]

The other industrial sector includes about 135,000 small and medium-sized companies which employ one-third of the industrial labour force. They do not have the ability to change their production and adapt to free trade and American competition. Technological change will make it difficult for them to survive.

A survey by *Expansion* magazine for 1993 found that the 500 largest corporations in Mexico account for 74 percent of total exports and 22 percent of imports. Their sales were the equivalent of 32 percent of the GDP. Within this group, there is even greater concentration of economic power — the top ten companies account for 48.6 percent of the sales of the 500.[22]

Economic growth stagnated during the 1980s and only recovered slowly during the administration of Carlos Salinas. Between 1989 and 1994, the average real economic rate of growth was only three percent. This was better than the depressed period of the 1980s, but it was only half the rate of growth during the period of import substitution industrialization. The Bank of Mexico argues that a six percent growth rate is necessary to provide jobs for the 1.1 million new entrants into the labour force each year.

CEPAL reports that between 1981 and 1991, Mexico's per capita gross domestic product declined by 5.4 percent. There is a dispute over the birth rate in Mexico, but the figure most often cited in the early 1990s was 2.2 percent. That would mean that per capita growth was less than one percent over the six years of the Salinas administration. In contrast, between 1960 and 1980, the average annual per capita increase was 3.0 percent.[23]

The figures for trade have not been good. The terms of trade for Mexico's exports fell by 37.5 percent between 1981 and 1992. Between 1970 and 1980 the annual growth rate of exports was 13.5 percent. Between 1980 and 1991, it was only 3.5 percent. With the unilateral reduction of tariffs, imports rose steadily, so that in 1992 Mexico recorded a trade deficit of $18.8 billion. The crisis came in 1994, the first year of NAFTA. While exports rose, imports rose at a much faster rate, and by the end of the year the current account deficit had risen to $28 billion.[24]

NAFTA posed a major problem for micro, small, and medium-sized businesses in Mexico. The National Confederation of Chambers of Commerce reported in 1994 that 60 percent of their members were in dire need of financial assistance in order to adjust to U.S. competition, but loans were not available and interest rates were far too high.[25]

Individual industries reported the adverse effects of the new competition. The number of companies manufacturing sporting goods fell from 150 to thirty-eight. Of the 114 drug manufacturing firms that existed in 1989, only forty were left in 1994, and ten of these were going bankrupt. In 1994, they experienced a 30 percent drop in sales. Textile, clothing and shoe manufacturers were pushing the government to stop the flood of cheap Chinese imports headed for the new U.S. warehouse retailers. Over 1993-94, 40 percent of the Mexican clothes manufacturers went out of business.[26]

The food processing industry was in "desperate shape" after having to sell at below cost for two years. Hardest hit were eggs, chicken and pork.

The leather and footwear industries reported that shoe production fell from 210 million pairs in 1980 to 140 million in 1994, and the number of employees in the industry dropped by 50 percent. The Mexican toy industry reported that 78 percent of its companies had gone out of business since the mid-1980s, and the remaining 85 firms had only 20 percent of the market.[27]

Commenting on the first year of NAFTA, the Mexican Action Network on Free Trade (RMALC) concluded: "The trend towards deindustrialization and an increasingly lower capacity to generate employment, along with the process of denationalization, is without a doubt the most serious flaw of the model of growth."[28]

Thus even in the areas of particular interest to investors, the Mexican economy has not performed well under the policies of structural adjustment and neoliberalism.

The Social Impact

The most serious problem facing Mexico is the lack of jobs. As we have seen, the low rate of economic growth has not provided enough jobs for young people entering the labour force or for those who are underemployed.

Sergio Zermeño, an economist at the National Autonomous University of Mexico, reports that between 1982 and 1990 the Mexican economy created only 1.3 million jobs. But during that period of time ten million young people entered the labour force.[29]

In addition, a great many jobs have disappeared during structural adjustment. Hundreds of thousands of jobs have been lost as businesses have closed, unable to compete with imported goods after protections were eliminated, state-owned enterprises were privatized, and budget cuts curtailed services.

Alejandro Alvarez and Gabriel Mendoza note that 50 percent of the textile industries and 28 percent of the leather industries were shut down. Domestic production of household appliances has been hard hit. Around 25,000 jobs were lost in the steel industry. In addition, around 400,000 jobs were eliminated when state-owned industries were privatized. The majority of the 940 businesses privatized were just shut down. PEMEX cut its payroll by 100,000. When government budgets were cut, thousands of government employees were laid off, including 35,000 primary school teachers and 20,000 nurses.[30]

The move to the free market has forced manufacturing firms to stress labour productivity. While employment grew in manufacturing in the maquiladora border zone during the 1980s, economic stagnation and the reduction of protection resulted in a net loss of jobs in the metalworking, machinery and equipment, textile, and wood products industries. As Edur Velasco Arregui points out, the areas where industry expanded in Mexico during the past twelve years include chemicals and petrochemicals, metal, machinery and transportation equipment. These industries are highly capital-intensive and employ relatively few Mexicans.[31]

Citing figures from INEGI, *El Economista* reported that between 1980 and 1992, productivity had increased by 31 percent in the manufacturing industry but employment fell by 9.2 percent. In 1992, there were 96,000 fewer jobs in manufacturing than there were in 1980. INEGI reports employment in the manufacturing sector fell by 15 percent in 1993.[32]

Official government unemployment figures mean very little in Mexico. The government considers a person to be employed who works at anything for one hour a week, even if s/he is not getting paid. Thus "open unemployment" normally is listed at around 3 percent. When there is no unemployment insurance or social assistance, people without employment have no alternative but to work in the informal economy. The official survey also only covers 37 urban areas. Rural Mexico, which has high levels of poverty and seasonal work, is entirely excluded.[33]

A separate study by the National Solidarity Program (PRONOSOL), which covered rural areas as well, concluded that 40 percent of the economically active population were underemployed and 12 percent were in the category of open unemployment.[34] A 1994 study by the conservative Monterrey Technological Institute estimated that real unemployment was closer to 25 percent of the economically active population.[35]

The INEGI also records the number of people who work less than thirty-five hours a week. This part of the labour force is often described as the "underemployed." In 1992, they reported that 22 percent of the labour force fell into this category. In early February 1995, a study by *La Jornada* estimated that only 11.6 million Mexicans were formally employed, leaving about thirteen million either unemployed or underemployed.[36]

Mexican economists differ on the question of the significance of high unemployment and underemployment. Alejandro Hernández of the Autonomous Technological Institute of Mexico (ITAM) argues that "This is the logical result of Salinas's reforms to stimulate productivity. What is now needed is changes to the labour law to increase flexibility in contracting temporary workers and decreasing employers' health care and social security contributions."

Table 9.2
Employment in Mexico

Sector	1980	1990
Public sector	22%	25%
Large firms	29%	20%
Small firms	25%	20%
Informal economy	24%	36%

Source: PREALC, 1992.

In contrast, Julio Boltvinik of El Colegio de Mexico says the government "must pay attention to poverty. We need emergency measures including a huge increase in the minimum wage to recoup lost purchasing power, coupled with a promise from business not to raise prices. The problems won't be resolved with jobs only."[37]

As in the rest of Latin America, the 1980s have seen a dramatic increase in the number of people working in the informal economy. The 1990 census reported that 7.8 million Mexicans were working in the informal economy, which represented 30 percent of the labour force. In contrast, the 1970 census reported that only 747,000 Mexicans were in the informal economy, representing only 5 percent of the labour force. Economists believe that more than 30 percent of the labour force is working in the informal economy. It is widely agreed that the number of women and children working in the informal economy is significantly under-reported.[38] A study by the International Labour Organization's Latin American operation (PREALC) illustrates the change in the type of employment. (See Table 9.2.)

Throughout Latin America, working in the informal economy is seen as a survival strategy, and the vast majority of those working there put in long hours for low wages. In Mexico, those in the drug industry make relatively high incomes. Those in the *fayuca* sector also do well. They buy consumer goods in the United States at wholesale prices and smuggle them across the border, getting a good markup yet still underselling the retail stores. But most people do not do this well. A 1989 survey by INEGI found that the average monthly income for a worker in the informal economy was $171.[39]

Major cutbacks in government spending have made life more difficult for the majority of Mexicans. Between 1982 and 1991, government expenditures as a percentage of gross domestic product declined from 27.5 percent to 17.4 percent. Public expenditures on education, health and welfare declined from 8.4 percent to 7.4 percent of gross domestic product.[40]

In her study of the impact of the government's stabilization policies, María Balboa Reyna found that in 1992 the total budget for all social programs, including PRONASOL, was 20 percent less than similar expenditures in 1981.[41]

In 1993, when Mexico was admitted to the OECD, government spending was 26 percent of gross domestic product. The average for the OECD was 46.6 percent. Mexico ranked last.[42]

Official government figures show that social spending bottomed out in 1987 and then rose steadily up through 1994. But government figures are often greeted with suspicion in Mexico. Social services figures include spending on infrastructure, drinking water, ecology and urban development.[43]

Peter M. Ward points out that after 1987, "debt repayments were no longer included within the total expenditure. Calculations for sectoral expenditure, therefore, appeared to rise dramatically." He calculates that between 1972 and 1988 spending on social development dropped from 23 percent to 10 percent of total government expenditures.[44]

Between 1982 and 1990 the education budget was cut by 21 percent. In 1990, annual spending per student was only $180, compared to $2,000 in Canada. In the primary schools, the number of students per teacher was 40, compared to 17 in Canada.[45]

In 1990 CEPAL reported that Mexico was only average in Latin America in terms of literacy and percentage of children who finish primary education. Mexico ranked quite low compared to other Latin American countries in rate of enrolment in higher education (15.18 percent of 20-25 age group). Per capita expenditure on education in 1988 was only $73, compared to $158 in Brazil.[46]

The OECD's first report on Mexico concluded: "The six million people over 15 years of age who are illiterate, the eleven million who have started but not completed elementary schooling, the drop-outs from elementary school (880,000) and the 10 to 14 year-olds who are not enroled (1.7 million) constitute an important education backlog confronting Mexican authorities, in addition to the growing cohorts of new students."[47]

Over the 1980s, the budget for health was cut by around 50 percent. Asa Cristina Laurell points out that the health policies promoted by the IMF and the IDB in Latin American promote four principles: reduction of public expenditures, targeting the extremely poor, decentralization of services, and privatization.[48]

In 1990, CEPAL reported that only 53 percent of Mexicans were covered by a health program and only 42 percent of the labour force had some form of pension program. In these areas Mexico was well below the average for Latin America. Social security expenditures were only three percent of GDP, near the bottom in Latin America. The Salinas government was shifting the total cost of social security to employers and employees.

The World Bank reported in 1991 that per capita spending on health in Mexico in 1990 was only $89, well below the Latin American average of $105. Health expenditures were 3.2 percent of GDP, below the Latin American average of 4 percent. In numbers of doctors and hospital beds per capita, Mexico had about 50 percent of the average for the region.[49]

Laurell argues that the social policy that underlies the neoliberal approach to health is closer to that of charity than social welfare. "It does not recognize that citizens have social rights, nor does it propose to universalize social benefits to the whole population."[50]

One of the key objectives of structural adjustment programs has been the reduction in the cost of labour. The policies of Presidents Miguel de la Madrid and Carlos Salinas have been very successful in this area. The World Bank reports that labour productivity increased by 38 percent between 1980 and 1990. The share of wages in the cost of value-added production in Mexico has steadily dropped, from 44 percent in 1970 to 20 percent in 1990. The share of wages as a percentage of GDP fell from 37 percent in 1980 to 24 percent in 1991.[51]

There are different reports on the extent of the drop in real wages under structural adjustment. PREALC reports that in the 1980s the industrial wage in Mexico declined by 40.2 percent. In July 1993, the Mexican National Commission on the Minimum Wage (CNSM) reported that between 1970 and 1993 the average wage earned in Mexico declined by 56 percent in real terms. In the post-war period, real wages peaked in 1977 and then steadily dropped until 1990. Average wages have increased since that time.[52]

The biggest decline has been in the average minimum wage. CNSM reported in March 1993 that the average minimum wage peaked at $7.49 per day in 1981 and had fallen in real terms to only $2.65 per day in 1993. PREALC figures show that the minimum wage fell by 58 percent in the 1980s, the largest drop in Latin America outside Bolivia and Peru.[53]

There was no attempt by the Salinas administration to tie the minimum

Table 9.3
Distribution of Income

Income Category	1984	1990
Less than the minimum wage	18.7%	25.5%
Between 1 and 2 minimum wages	28.7%	38.7%
Between 2 and 3 minimum wages	20.4%	15.1%
More than 3 minimum wages	32.3%	21.7%

Source: 1990 Census; OECD, 1992

wage to the rate of inflation. Lowering the real minimum wage was a firm policy. Following neoliberal principles, the government saw this as a way of attracting foreign capital to the maquiladora industries and agriculture.

The inability of a worker to earn enough money to support a family was revealed in the 1990 census. The distribution of income was reported in relation to the official minimum wage, which averaged around $4 per day at the time. The labour force (referred to as the economically active population) was reported at 23.4 million. (See Table 9.3)

The figures above show the decline in incomes. In 1990, 64 percent of those working earned less than two minimum wages, or eight dollars a day. Two minimum wages at that time was the equivalent of 24 new pesos. But the cost of the basic food basket for Mexico City, as determined by the Faculty of Economics at the National Autonomous University of Mexico (UNAM), amounted to 26.9 new pesos.[54]

What is the real cost of living in urban Mexico? In March 1992, Walter Krohne of the German news agency DPA conducted a survey of the minimum wages in Latin American countries and compared it to the basic costs of a lower middle-class standard of living in major urban areas.[55] The findings for Mexico City are indicated in Table 9.4.

The middle class has been hard hit by higher unemployment and the decline in real wages. A study released by INEGI in July 1993 concluded that over the previous twelve years, the middle class had experienced on average a 50 percent decline in real wages. Public service workers had faced wage freezes imposed by the Salinas government; between 1989 and 1993, their wages had fallen by 33.6 percent.

The middle class was defined by INEGI as those people who earn between three and eight times the minimum wage ($12 to $32 per day in

Table 9.4
Cost of Living in Mexico City (per month)

Housing	$200
Food	150
Clothing	50
Transportation	35
Health	50
Education	00
Entertainment	75
Total	$560

1992). By this definition the middle class represented only 6.5 percent of the total Mexican population.[56]

But not everyone has experienced a decline in their income and standard of living. In March 1993, *Epoca* reported a survey done by GL Editorial Consultants, an organization which monitors the salaries and remuneration in the business community. Between 1989 and 1992, executives in private businesses experienced significant increases in annual net income: directors of operations, 241 percent; directors of human resources, 282 percent; management supervisors, 220 percent; and systems managers, 213 percent.[57]

Mexico has always been known as one of the countries with the most unequal distribution of wealth and income. There have been three surveys of household income in recent years. The results are summarized in Table 9.5.

Between 1984 and 1992, the top 10 percent of households increased their share of total income from 32.7 percent to 38.2 percent. Every income class below the top 10 percent experienced a decline in share of national income. The bottom 60 percent of households saw their share fall from 28.6 percent to 25.5 percent. The top 20 percent of households accounted for 54.2 percent of total income. As elsewhere, neoliberal policies in Mexico have increased income inequality.

To no-one's surprise, the level of poverty has remained high in Mexico during the period of structural adjustment. CEPAL reports that in 1990, 48.8 percent of Mexicans were living below the official poverty line. Of these, 13.4 percent were classified as "indigent" or living in "extreme poverty." Of the Mexican rural population, 50.5 percent were judged to be liv-

Table 9.5
Distribution of Household Income

Decile of Families	1984	1989	1992
10	1.72	1.58	1.56
20	4.83	4.39	4.28
30	9.04	8.13	7.96
40	14.36	12.86	12.68
50	20.76	18.76	18.42
60	28.62	26.06	25.53
70	36.34	35.03	34.45
80	50.50	46.45	45.82
90	67.23	62.07	61.84
100	100.00	100.00	100.00

Source: Sergio Díaz López and Bertha Alanis, "La Politica Economía y la Distribucion del Ingreso," *El Financiero*, August 17 and 18, 1994.

ing below the official poverty line. This places Mexico among the ten worst cases in Latin America.[58]

In Mexico there are twelve million people who are defined as Indigenous. In 1992 a report by the federal Chamber of Deputies concluded that 56 percent live in extreme poverty or indigence. PRONASOL reports that the highest rates of undernutrition are in the states of Quintana Roo, Oaxaca, Chiapas, Hidalgo, and Guerrero, where the percentage of the Indigenous population is well above the national average.[59]

Official Mexican government statistics on levels of inequality and poverty are difficult to find. Many believe that they are manipulated for political purposes. For example, the Salinas government reported that the infant mortality rate continued to fall during the period of structural adjustment. Data provided to UNICEF reported that between 1960 and 1990 the infant mortality rate in Mexico declined from 92 to 40 per 100,000 births. But the independent Mexican National Institute on Nutrition (INN) reported in 1992 that over the previous ten years the infant mortality rate in Mexico had increased from 40.04 to 118.5.[60]

A rise in the infant mortality rate could be expected because the government drastically cut back the subsidies on basic foods for the poor. Because of the decline in real income, over the 1980s there was a reduction in per capita consumption of meat, milk, beans, cheese, and even tortillas.

In his fifth State of the Nation address on November 1, 1993, President Carlos Salinas claimed that poverty had declined during his administration. Three weeks later the Catholic church issued a statement on Human Rights and NAFTA. They denounced policies which abandoned the people for "the whims of the free market." The government was criticized for ignoring the problem of steadily increasing unemployment, which had become a "moral disorder." Furthermore, the church argued that the government "could not eradicate poverty by using false numbers."[61]

Coping with the Crisis

How did Mexican families cope with the economic crisis? Mercedes González de la Rocha, a sociologist from Guadalajara, summarizes the strategies: they increased the number of salaries in the household; they stopped buying certain goods and services; they cut back on spending on health and education to maintain levels of food consumption; and they increased the size of the household to add workers with income. Despite these adjustments, Gonzáles de la Rocha concludes that "The diet of the working class can in no way be considered adequate ... It does not even fulfill the minimum food intake required for light work."[62]

Flor de María Balboa Reyna of the Faculty of Economics at UNAM concludes that men sought extra jobs, more children were put to work, and women were forced to enter the labour force in even greater numbers. Women took on the triple day: work at a formal job, working in off-hours in the informal economy and raising children and running the household.[63]

In 1990, official government figures reported that 26 percent of women were working outside the home. But most believe that this figure significantly understates the situation. Economist Alicia Giron believes that the figure for working women is at least 45 percent.[64] Many young women migrated from rural areas to cities where they were independent workers, primarily peddlers and artisans, or provided domestic services for the middle and upper classes. They also found employment in the service sectors: health, education, public administration and commerce. Some worked in factories.[65] Lourdes Benería reports that families increased the number of family members with jobs. Teenagers were forced to drop out of school to work and women with children at home worked in the informal economy.[66]

In the rural areas, women reacted to the economic crisis by cutting personal consumption, entering the labour force, and increasing the labour on the family subsistence plot. Peasant women normally worked from 5 a.m. to 10 p.m. They were responsible for all the unpaid labour of raising children, keeping the home, and producing artisan goods. Rural families commonly migrated to do farm labour.[67]

In 1991, Mexico had thirty million children under the age of fourteen, the legal age for work. The Salinas government estimated that 1.2 million children were working illegally, and only around 100,000 were working in the streets. But the Mexican Centre for Child Rights argued that only 30 percent of the children entering primary school at that time were finishing. Most quit school to work. In rural areas, children regularly do farm work with their fathers and mothers.[68]

Many Mexicans migrated to the United States, either as permanent immigrants, repeating seasonal workers, or as illegal immigrants. In 1993, it was reported that 13.5 million Mexicans were living in the United States. The U.S. government reported that in 1992 it returned 1.2 million Mexicans who had illegally entered. For individual Mexicans, the ability to migrate to the United States is very important. For the government, the ability to export the unemployed is an important safety valve needed for social control. Repatriated earnings are also very important to the Mexican economy.

Wayne Cornelius found that during the economic crisis there was a definite shift from short-term migration to permanent settlement. While Mexicans originally migrated to the United States to do farm work, by the late 1980s only 15 percent were employed in agriculture. A high percentage of immigrants are now women and families.[69]

The changing structure of work in the United States has encouraged Mexican immigration. Saskia Sassen notes the increase in low-wage jobs, subcontracting, the expansion of sweatshop factories, the rapid growth of the service sector, and the demand for domestic workers for the expanding well-paid upper middle class. "Immigrants are more likely than U.S. citizens to gravitate to these jobs," Sassen concludes.[70]

The other major factor is the political and economic integration of the two countries. Linkages promote immigration. Free trade promotes labour migration.[71]

The import substitution model was unsuccessful in solving Latin America's major problems of unemployment, poverty, inequality, environmental degradation, and the lack of democracy and respect for human rights. But it is evident that the neoliberal alternative has also failed to solve these problems.

Notes

1. CEPAL, *Preliminary Overview of the Latin American and Caribbean Economy.* Santiago: CEPAL, 1992.

2. United Nations Development Program, *Human Development Report.* New York: UNDP, 1992.

3. Gert Rosenthal, "Latin American and Caribbean Development in the 1980s," *CEPAL Review,* No. 39, December 1989, pp. 7-17.

4. International Labour Organization, *World Labour Report.* Geneva: ILO, 1992.

5. U.N. Food and Agriculture Organization, *Recession, Structural Adjustment and Rural Poverty in Latin America and the Caribbean.* Guatemala City: FAO, 1989.

6. Juan Carlos Feres and Arturo Léon, "The Magnitude of Poverty in Latin America," *CEPAL Review,* No. 41, August 1990, pp. 133-151.

7. Carmen Diana Deere et al, *In the Shadows of the Sun.* Boulder: Westview Press, 1990.

8. Edgar L. Feige, "Defining and Estimating Underground and Informal Economies," *World Development,* Vol. 18, July 1990, pp. 989-1002.

9. Nora Lustig, "América Latina: Desigualdad y pobreza," *Cuaderno de Nexos,* Vol. 24, May 1992, p. 173; Eliana Cardosa and Ann Helwege, "Below the Poverty Line: Poverty in Latin America," *World Development,* Vol. 20, January 1992, pp. 19-37.

10. Rosenthal, *op. cit.*

11. CEPAL, *Social Equity and Changing Production Patterns.* Chile: CEPAL, 1992.

12. Interamerican Development Bank, *Economic and Social Progress in Latin America.* Washington: IDB, October 1992.

13. CEPAL, *Preliminary Overview, op. cit.*

14. *CEPAL News,* various issues, 1992 and 1993.

15. "Salinas' Economic Tally," *El Financiero International,* November 7, 1994, p. 15.

16. World Bank, *World Debt Tables.* Washington: IBRD, 1993; Christopher Whalen, "The New Debt Crisis," unpublished paper, January 2, 1995, 5 pp.

17. Oscar Martínez Nicolas, "Economía de Salinismo," *El Economista,* August 22, 1994, pp. 35-36; James M. Cypher, "NAFTA Shock," *Dollars and Sense,* March-April 1995, pp. 22-25, 39.

18. Organization of Economic Co-operation and Development, *Mexico, 1991-2.* Paris: OECD Economic Surveys, 1992; Carlos Elizondo, "In Search of Revenue: Tax Reform in Mexico under the Administrations of Echeverria and Salinas," *Journal of Latin American Studies,* Vol. 26, February 1994, pp. 159-190.

19. Georgina Howard, "Caida Generalizada en Cetes," *El Financiero,* August 18, 1994, p. 5.

20. World Bank, *World Development Report.* Washington: IBRD, 1993.

21. Edur Velasco Arregui, "Industrial Restructuring in Mexico during the 1980s," in Ricardo Grinspun and Maxwell A. Cameron, eds., *The Political Economy of North American Free Trade.* Montréal: McGill-Queen's University Press, 1993, pp. 163-175.

22. Juan Antonio Zúñiga, "Concentran 500 empresas el 74% de las exportaciones: *Expansion,*" *La Jornada,* August 24, 1994, p. 42.

23. CEPAL, *Preliminary Overview, op. cit.*

24. Rick Wills, "Nation's Growing Trade Deficit Unlikely to Become Smaller Soon," *The*

News, August 25, 1994, p. 30; Guillermo Ortiz, "How We're Handling the Peso Crisis," *Wall Street Journal*, January 5, 1995.

25. Leticia Rodríguez López, "Siguen los Problemas Estructurales en la Pequeña Empresa," *El Financiero*, August 24, 1994, p. 26.

26. See *El Financiero*, August 24, 1994; *El Financiero International*, September 12, 1994; December 12, 1994; February 6, 1995; and February 13, 1995.

27. See *El Financiero International*, January 30, 1995; February 6, 1995; and February 13, 1995.

28. Mexican Action Network on Free Trade, "NAFTA"'s First Year: What does the Free Trade Agreement Mean for Mexico?" *The Other Side of Mexico*, No. 37, November-December 1994, p. 11.

29. Sergio Zermeño, "Globalización authoritaria con transito a la democracia?" *Nueva Sociedad*, No. 121, September-October 1992, pp. 90-103.

30. Alejandro Alvarez and Gabriel Mendoza, "Mexico: Neo-Liberal Disaster Zone," in Jim Sinclair, ed., *Crossing the Line*. Vancouver: New Star Books, 1992, pp. 26-37.

31. Velasco, *op. cit.*

32. Felipe Gazcon, "A costa del empleo los aumentos en la productividad," *El Economista*, March 9, 1993, pp. 1, 29; and "Hardly Encouraging: Horrible Employment Figures," *Mexico and Nafta Report*, March 31, 1994, p. 7.

33. Noé Cruz Serrano, "Habrá Problemas Económicos; Antonía y Desempleo," *Epoca*, No. 83, January 4, 1993, pp. 12-15; Ricardo Palacios Durán, "El Salario Quedará Vinculado a la Productividad," *Epoca*, No. 92, March 8, 1993, pp. 18-21; and OECD, *op. cit.*

34. Cited in Mario B. Monroy, *Socios? a Sociados? en Sociedad? Asimetrias entre Canada-EEUU-Mexico*. Mexico, D.F.:Servicios Informativos Procesados, November 1993, p. 58.

35. Rick Wills, "Analysts Question Unemployment Data," *The News*, August 20, 1994, p. 31, 39.

36. Equipo Pueblo, *Mexico Update*, Vol. 2, No. 17, February 8, 1995.

37. Sallie Hughes, "A Delicate Balancing Act," *El Financiero International*, September 19, 1994, p. 14.

38. *Report of the Director General*. 13th Conference of the American States, International Labour Organization, Caracas, September-October 1992.

39. INEGI, *Encuesta nacional de economía informal*. Mexico, D.F., 1990.

40. OECD, *op. cit.*

41. Flor de María Balboa Reyna, "La faz oculta de la Luna," *La Jornada Laboral*, February 27, 1992, pp. 4-5.

42. "Mexico," *New Internationalist*, January 1994, p. 18.

43. Georgina Howard, "Aumentó 8.8% el Gasto en Desarrollo Social en el Primer Semestre: SHCP," *El Financiero*, August 25, 1994, p. 27.

44. Peter Ward, "Social Welfare Policy and Political Opening in Mexico," *Journal of Latin American Studies*, Vol 25, October 1993, pp. 613-628.

45. Monroy, *op. cit.*

46. "Social Equity and Changing Production Patterns," *CEPAL News*, Vol. 12, May 1992.

47. OECD, *op. cit.*, p. 104.

48. Asa Cristina Laurell, "Crisis, Neoliberal Health Policy, and Political Processes in Mexico," *International Journal of Health Services*, Vol. 21, No. 3, 1991, pp. 457-470.

49. World Bank, *op. cit.*

50. Laurell, *op. cit.*, p. 463.

51. World Bank, *op. cit.*; OECD, *op. cit.*, pp. 53-57.

52. *La Jornada Laboral*, August 25, 1994, Graph 2, p. 2.

53. Alberta Oliver, "De Salarios y Sucesiones," *Excelsior*, March 3, 1993, pp. 1-F et seq.

54. Luis Lozano Arredondo, "La pobreza en al ultimo decenio," *La Jornada Laboral*, March 26, 1992, p. 5.

55. Walter Krohne, "Para une Vida Digna," *Excelsior*, March 16, 1992, pp. 3-4.

56. Equipo Pueblo, *Mexico News Summary*, No. 8, July 22, 1993.

57. Durán, *op. cit.*

58. Juan Dannell Sánchez, "En Extrema Pobreza, 17 Millones de Mexicanos," *Epoca*, No. 83, January 4, 1993, pp. 40-45.

59. "Poverty: An Issue Making a Comeback," *Latin American Weekly Report*, Special Report, October 1992; "Debating Social Cost of Adjustment," *Latin America Weekly Report*, October 29, 1992, pp. 4-5.

60. United Nations Children's Fund, *The State of the World's Children*. New York: UNICEF, 1992; Raúl Monge, "Expansiva, la desnutricion en México; más de la mitad de la población, de segunda," *Proceso*, No. 822, August 3, 1992, pp. 24-27.

61. Gerardo Albarrán de Alba, "Indebido abandonar la vida de la gente a los caprichos del libre mercado, dice la jerarquía catolica," *Proceso*, No. 891, November 29, 1993, pp. 26-28.

62. Mercedes Gonzáles de la Rocha, "Family Well-Being, Food Consumption, and Survival Strategies during Mexico's Economic Crisis," in Mercedes Gonzáles de la Rocha and Augustín Escobar Latapí, eds., *Social Responses to Mexico's Economic Crisis of the 1980s*. Center for U.S.-Mexican Studies, University of California, San Diego, 1991, pp. 115-128.

63. Balboa, *op. cit.*

64. Alicia Giron, "La Mujer en la Economía," *El Financiero*, February 2, 1992, p. 48.

65. Orlandina de Oliveira, "Migration of Women, Family Organization and Labour Markets in Mexico," in Elizabeth Jelin, ed., *Family, Household and Gender Relations in Latin America*. Paris: UNESCO, 1991, pp. 101-111.

66. Lourdes Benería, "The Mexican Debt Crisis: Restructuring the Economy and the Household," in Lourdes Benería and Shelly Feldman, eds., *Unequal Burden: Economic Crisis, Persistent Poverty and Women's Work*. Boulder: Westview Press, 1992, pp. 83-104.

67. Lynn Stephen, "Women in Mexico's Popular Movements," *Latin American Perspectives*, Winter 1992, pp. 73-96.

68. Matt Moffett, "Underage Laborers Fill Mexican Factories," *Wall Street Journal*, April 8, 1991, A-1.

69. Wayne A. Cornelius, "Los Migrantes de la Crisis: The Changing Profile of Mexican Migration to the United States,: in González and Latapí, *op. cit.*, pp. 155-193.

70. Saskia Sassen, "Why Immigration?" *Report on the Americas*, Vol. 26, July 1992, pp. 14-19.

71. Richard C. Jones, "U.S. Migration: An Alternative Economic Mobility Ladder for Rural Mexico," *Social Science Quarterly*, Vol. 73, September 1992, pp. 496-509.

Chapter 10

AGRICULTURE AND RURAL POVERTY

Just into the morning on New Year's Day 1994 in Chiapas, a rag-tag group of men and women entered the small cities of Altamirano, Chanal, Huistan, Las Margaritas, Oxchuc, Ocosingo, and San Cristóbal de las Casas and took over the town halls. Later, they attacked the federal army base at Rancho Nuevo. They wore rubber boots, had home-made military uniforms, carried a wide variety of weapons from carved wooden "rifles" to Uzi machine guns, and covered their faces with ski masks and bandannas.

Their leaflets and messages broadcast from the Ocosingo radio station declared war on the "illegal dictatorship" of President Carlos Salinas de Gortari, who had seized office through the greatest electoral fraud in Mexican history. They demanded democracy and the end of the one-party state, with its repression and injustice. They were the Zapatista National Liberation Army (EZLN), soon to be known as the Zapatistas.

The Declaration of the Lacandon Jungle called for a complete revision of the North American Free Trade Agreement (NAFTA), the repeal of the changes to Article 27 of the constitution which affected communal *ejido* lands, free and democratic elections, and a list of supports and rights for indigenous peoples and peasants. Following Emiliano Zapata, they insisted that "the land belongs to those who work it."

According to reports in *El Financiero,* Carlos Salinas and his family were celebrating New Year's in the plush presidential guesthouse on Tangalunda Bay, at the high-priced beach resort at Huatulco, Oaxaca. Their invited house guests were Luis Donaldo Colosio and his family. Colosio was Salinas's hand-picked successor, a staunch neoliberal, dubbed by the press as "Salinas with hair."

The two events were symbolic of the Mexico so beloved by the people who matter. On the one hand, political leaders consorted with the very rich, while just outside the enclave, was Oaxaca, one of the poorest states in Mexico, where 44 percent of the population is indigenous, second in number only to Quintana Roo.

Just before 2 a.m. on New Years Day, Carlos Salinas received a report from the military that there was an armed rebellion underway in Chiapas. For Salinas and the technocratic elite, it marked the beginning of a dramatic turn of events for the neoliberal experiment.[1]

The poor of Chiapas had been hard hit by the implementation of Salinas's policies. Chiapas is Mexico's main source of coffee, produced primarily by small farmers. In 1988, there were 73,742 growers, of whom 91 percent had less than five hectares of land. In contrast, there were 116 large private farmers, tied closely to the PRI, whose farms averaged 235 hectares in size.

Coffee growers had been aided by the Mexican National Institute of Coffee (INMECAFE), a marketing board which not only sold the crop but provided growers with technical assistance, subsidized credit and guaranteed purchase prices. Its effectiveness was undermined by the economic crisis of the 1980s and its domination by PRI loyalists. Under the privatization push, it was stripped of all its powers by President Salinas.

In June 1989, the International Coffee Organization failed to agree on production quotas, and the world price fell by 50 percent. Without the support of the marketing board and price subsidies, the income of the small producers fell by 70 percent between 1989-93.[2]

Then there was NAFTA. Every peasant organization in Mexico demanded that the government exclude maize and beans from the negotiations. Salinas refused. Almost all small farmers and subsistence peasants in Mexico grow these two crops. Maize is by far the most important crop grown in Mexico. The Salinas administration agreed to phase out all price supports for maize over a fifteen-year period, to bring it down to the world market price. This will mean a 58 percent drop in returns to the producer. It appeared to be a death sentence.

Roger Burbach and Peter Rosset describe NAFTA's threat to Mexican peasants. Mexican producers average 1.7 tons of maize per hectare. Corn producers in the United States average seven tons per hectare. U.S. growers have enormous technological and financial advantages over Mexican growers. In Mexico, 17.8 labour days are required to produce one tonne of maize. In the United States only 1.2 hours of labour is required to produce a tonne of corn. It takes 50.6 labour hours to produce a tonne of beans in Mexico; it takes only 4.8 hours of labour in the United States. Mexican peasants could not possibly compete with U.S. imports.[3]

Agrarianism or Agriculture

The Mexican system of agricultural production has often been cited as one of the best examples of a "bi-modal structure." Solon L. Barraclough describes this as a system where "a few owners of large estates control nearly all good agricultural land." There are no real competitive markets for agricultural land or labour; they are "transferred among landowners." The majority of the rural population live on landholdings which are too small to support a family, or are landless rural labourers.

In such countries, Barraclough argues, "The state is either controlled by the large landlords or at least dependent on them. Owners of large estates, whether national or foreign investors, are dominant in local and national power structures."

What is common in these situations is that there is always pressure from the poor for land redistribution. He notes that this pattern of land ownership, a "quasi-feudal situation," has prevailed in Latin America since the European conquest.

The old *hacienda* system has largely disappeared, replaced by the "modern capital-intensive agroindustrial enterprise" run according to the capitalist business goal of profit maximization. Yet, as Barraclough notes, agrarian structures have remained bi-modal.

Barraclough concludes that land reforms that have taken place in Latin America have not led to greater food security for people in rural areas. Nor have they resulted in more democratic processes. "Upward mobility for the Latin American peasant has been most frequently through escape to the cities or abroad and not by climbing the agricultural ladder from worker to tenant to commercial farmer."[4]

Jonathan Fox agrees with this assessment, noting that Mexican agriculture remains highly polarized. "Most producers fall into one of two categories: either they are medium- and large-scale farmers, usually with irrigation, or they are nonirrigated smallholders with less land than needed to provide the equivalent of a full year's employment even at minimum wage." The complete polarization between large farmer and poor peasant is broken by "a significant intermediate segment of market-oriented surplus-producing family farmers." But, Fox argues, this does not negate the overall bi-modal production pattern.[5]

While a hierarchical class system existed in Mesoamerica under the Aztec and Mayan state societies, based on peasant and slave labour in agriculture, the bimodal system became universal under Spanish colonialism. The indigenous peoples were driven from all the good agricultural land which was given to the colonizers.

Gustavo Esteva concludes that the "first great holocaust" was due not only to diseases and murder, but also to famines, as the indigenous peoples of Mesoamerica had no land on which to grow food. In the second century of colonialism, the production of traditional export crops expanded under mercantile capitalism. These crops included cochineal dye, sugar, henequen, cotton, tobacco, cocoa, and vanilla. Cattle ranching expanded to export hides. The *hacienda* system became entrenched.

When the liberals under Benito Juárez took land from the church and the indigenous people, the result was even greater concentration of land in the hands of large private landholders, the *latifundia* system.

Porfirio Díaz (1876-1910) introduced foreign ownership of land on a large scale. By 1910, fifty landowners held 20 percent of Mexico's agricultural land. At the outbreak of the revolution, less than one percent of the rural population owned 90 percent of the land. Around 90 percent of the rural population did not own any land, private or communal.[6]

The course of the Mexican revolution may have been controlled by the millionaire generals and the new bourgeois class, but the footsoldiers were trying to get access to land. Article 27 of the Constitution of 1917 gave them hope. It set forth the principle that all land and water belong to the nation as a whole, and that the government has the right and the power to regulate these resources including the right of appropriation and equitable distribution.

Thus the redistribution of land became the primary political objective of the rural poor. Under the rule of the generals (1920-1934) there was little land reform, and much of the land that was given to the communal *ejidos* was poor. However, President Lázaro Cárdenas rapidly accelerated the process and intensified the demands of the *agraristas*.[7]

Given the commitment of the political and economic ruling elite to the continuation of the bimodal system in rural Mexico, the task of the state was primarily one of social control. In the early period after the revolution there was heavy reliance on political repression. Not only did politically active peasants face the military and the police, there were the private armies of the large landholders (*gardias blancas*).

The other technique was the "politics of promises." There was some redistribution of land undertaken, even if it was only tokenism. Various agricultural support programs were introduced, which benefitted some family farmers. The government tried to control peasant organizations through the National Peasant Confederation (CNC), tied to the ruling PRI, and the process of co-optation. In spite of the enormous polarization between the rich and the poor, these strategies produced relative peace in rural Mexico.

Agriculture and Import Substitution

Mexican economic expansion began during World War II, when the Allies called on Mexico to provide them with strategic raw materials. Exports of food and agricultural materials for industry greatly increased. Mexican farm workers were admitted to the United States to fill a labour shortage. The lack of exports of manufactured goods from Europe and North America almost forced Mexico and other Latin American countries to adopt import substitution industrialization (ISI) as a development model.

Mainstream economists have criticized the ISI model of development for its impact on agriculture. With stress on manufacturing, credit was taken from farmers. Financing of irrigation and equipment lagged. There was an urban bias in public spending towards roads, water, and electrical services. Land reform was abandoned. Overvalued exchange rates lowered the returns from exports. Price controls on basic food items kept returns to peasant farmers low. The result was a growing dependence on importing basic foods.[8]

The *ejidos* were dependent on the state for government support, particularly credit and funds for irrigation. The PRI rewarded those who were loyal and punished those who took a more independent path.

Marilyn Gates describes this as a "dual-track agricultural policy." It separated social justice considerations from productivity objectives and created two clearly defined farm sectors, commercial and subsistence. They were linked through the agricultural labour market, with the poor peasants providing labour for the commercial operations.[9]

Steven Sanderson argues that agricultural development under ISI in Mexico was different from the rest of Latin America. During the "economic miracle" from 1940-1970, increased food production was an important hedge against wage inflation. New crops were developed and exported, earning important foreign exchange, and agriculture provided raw materials for basic manufacturing industries.

Then came the Green Revolution brought about by the development of new hybrid seeds by the Rockefeller Foundation. Under irrigation, and with significant government subsidies, production of rice and wheat expanded significantly. Cheap food for the labour force in urban areas was subsidized by cheap labour on commercial farms and cheap maize and beans produced by subsistence peasants.

Furthermore, during this period, basic foods were subsidized by the public sector. There was government credit through the rural bank. Marketing was supported through the National Staple Products Company (CONASUPO). Price supports were introduced in 1953. Furthermore, the rural sector as a whole provided almost no taxes to the federal government. While capital did flee the rural areas for investment in industry, it returned through government credit.[10]

The PRI presidents made their first commitment to the development of capitalist agriculture. Esteva and Gates point out that between 1950 and 1970, around 70 percent of federal investments went into the construction of large irrigation projects. Very little irrigation was developed for *ejido* lands. Almost all of this development occurred in the North and Northwest and benefitted large private landowners. The Green Revolution concentrated on high-yielding rice and wheat varieties which required irrigation, fertilizer and pesticides to outperform the traditional varieties.

Merilee Grindle adds that the large private farms were the primary beneficiaries of "government subsidized credit, research, extension, mechanization, marketing facilities, and distribution of inputs. Public investment in areas dominated by *ejidos* and poor peasant private farms was virtually nonexistent in this period."[11]

While CONASUPO bought basic foods from farmers at fixed prices, these prices did not rise with inflation. Grindle argues that this is because the economic strategy of ISI was to subsidize industrialization through the cheap food policy.

The result was increased inequality in the rural areas. Capitalist farms expanded and were profitable while small farmers became more marginalized. The new industrial farms could not begin to absorb the unemployed and underemployed who still lived in the rural areas. Mexico became dependent on the importation of basic foods. In 1965, "hunger caravans" emerged, and rural guerrilla fighting became a constant event. By 1970, it was evident that the capitalist model for rural development had only reenforced the bimodal nature of rural Mexico.[12]

Populist Reforms

President Luis Echeverría (1970-1976) tried to introduce a program of social and economic reform, including food and agricultural policy. The role of CONASUPO was greatly expanded. Its budget over the 1970s grew tenfold, and it expanded its subsidies of basic foods. It diversified its agricultural processing and farm implement corporations. It continued to operate as a state trading agency for all basic foodstuffs, and it established around 10,000 retail outlets, designed to bring basic foods to the neediest of Mexicans.[13]

The Echeverría administration introduced a new program to help the traditional farmer: integrated rural development initiatives. Price supports, subsidized credit, discount prices for agricultural inputs, crop insurance, storage and marketing assistance, education and health services, and new technologies were to be given to peasants depending on rainfed agriculture.

A new Agrarian Code was proclaimed, designed to strengthen the hold of peasants over the *ejido* lands. Secret ballot elections were required for officers. Power was redirected from PRI state officials back to the *ejidos* themselves. In 1972, the Mexican government officially adopted the goal of national food self-sufficiency.

The investment in agriculture was financed by borrowing from abroad. This was all co-ordinated through the Public Investment Project for Rural Development (PIDER), which received substantial funds from the World Bank.

President Echeverría also stepped up redistribution of land to the *ejidos*. But he met strong resistance from large landowners, who were very successful in using the courts to obtain injunctions against the government — even when the object was to reclaim land which was illegally held. Most of the land added to communal ownership was poor quality. When Echeverría tried to take over and redistribute valuable irrigated land, he faced a strike by big farmers backed by Monterrey businessmen.

President José López Portillo (1976-1982) was also concerned about the growing dependence on the purchase of basic foods from the United States. A major study completed in 1979 revealed that around thirty-five million Mexicans (out of sixty-seven million) did not have adequate nutritional diets. Within this group, thirteen million rural and six million urban people were identified as suffering from "serious malnutrition." While Portillo came into office facing problems with the International Monetary Fund and the World Bank over accumulated debts, the expansion of the oil industry provided revenues for agricultural development.[14]

In March 1980, President Portillo introduced the *Systema Alimentario Mexicano* (SAM), the Mexican Food System. The program was to give support to dryland and tropical agriculture in an attempt to increase the production of basic foods, and to build on the types of food supplement programs that were advocated by the World Bank in the period before the world economic crisis of 1981-82.

The goal for SAM was to obtain self-sufficiency in the production of corn and beans by emphasizing assistance and investment in small farmers in rainfed districts. Production would be increased by the expanded use of needed farm inputs. Potential arable land, then in pasture, was to be converted to food production. Self-sufficiency in wheat, rice, sorghum and soybeans was to be achieved by 1985. Credit from the National Rural Credit Bank (BANRUAL) was increased, and the government agreed to share the risk of crop failure. Demand for basic foods was increased through the network of CONASUPO stores, which offered subsidized foods in low-income rural and urban areas. Between 1979 and 1982, around $4 billion was invested in the Co-ordinating Commission for Marginal Areas (COPLAMAR).

But despite the heavy investment in agriculture, rural landlessness continued to grow. When the debt crisis came in 1982, both the Mexican government and the World Bank abandoned their Keynesian social welfare approach to agriculture and food distribution. Following the demands of international capital, they moved steadily towards the free market, free trade model of development.

Agribusiness and Structural Adjustment

The debt crisis of 1982 forced President Miguel de la Madrid to abandon the SAM policy in 1982. State subsidies to agriculture were curtailed. High interest rates put enormous pressure on farmers, and was compounded by the fraud and corruption in BANRURAL. The budget for agriculture was drastically cut, and many research institutes and technical assistance programs were abolished. In 1988, the gross value of agricultural production fell by 3.2 percent, to the lowest level in the 1980s. The goal of food self-sufficiency was abandoned, and Mexico became increasingly dependent on imported basic foods.[15]

Government investment in agriculture dropped. In real terms, investment in rural development fell by 80 percent between 1981 and 1989. The budget for agriculture and food fell from $8 billion in 1981 to $3 billion in 1988.

Under the direction of the structural adjustment program, President de la Madrid directed government assistance to commercial agriculture, emphasized expanding exports, abandoned land redistribution, and cut back government programs for nutritional assistance to the poor. The role of government in agriculture was steadily reduced as the administration emphasized reliance on free market forces and the development of a free trade policy.[16]

One of the major achievements of the "economic miracle" over the period from 1940 through 1970 was the transformation of Mexico from a peasant society to an urban society. In 1980, 36 percent of the population lived in rural areas; by 1990, this had fallen to 28 percent. In addition, 13.5 million Mexicans lived in the United States, and those who migrated were primarily underemployed residents of rural Mexico. It can be argued that the relative decline of the political influence of peasants permitted the administrations of Miguel de la Madrid and Carlos Salinas to put a very low priority on the issue of rural underemployment and poverty.

The policies of structural adjustment emphasize agricultural production for export. By 1990, around 90 percent of Mexico's farm exports went to the United States. The products grown for the world market are those consumed primarily by people in the higher income brackets. Some of this production does go to the upper 20 to 30 percent of the Mexican population who have enough income to enjoy a First World diet, but the majority of Mexicans cannot afford to eat these export crops on a regular basis.

Traditional plantation crops are still grown in Mexico and exported to foreign markets. But with the notable exception of coffee, which is grown primarily by small farmers, these traditional crops are declining in importance. For example, over the 1980s the value of exports of cotton, cocoa, bananas, and tobacco declined substantially.

Modernization of agriculture in Mexico has also meant the arrival of the transnational food corporations. One good example would be the fruit and vegetable industry, which is heavily subsidized by the government. Beginning in World War II, irrigation was expanded to provide the United States with fresh vegetables and fruits in the winter. Mexico had the advantage of low wages, low land costs, and heavily subsidized energy supplies, very important in irrigation farming. The Mexican government also subsidized farm inputs, particularly fertilizer. The state-owned rural banks provided subsidized credit.[17]

The production of these crops was truly international. Fresh crops were produced under contract with U.S. wholesalers who determined what was grown and how. Prices were set by the U.S. buyers. Large transnational processors located in Mexico; they also contracted with local Mexican farmers. The names are familiar: Green Giant, Birdseye/General Foods, Del Monte, Gerber, Campbell's, Safeway.

This system of production is most often identified with the Mexican strawberry industry, but tomatoes soon emerged as the most important single crop. Today, melons, grapes, pineapples, cucumbers, onions, squashes, broccoli, and cauliflower are important exports. But control of production, sales and prices is in the hands of the large American agribusiness corporations.

The other major change in agricultural production was the expansion of the cattle and feed industry. The rich in rural Mexico have traditionally had large grazing lands with cattle and horses. This has not changed. Indeed, in 1985 the Secretary of Agrarian Reform, Luis Martínez Villicana, declared that Mexico "is not an agricultural country. We are a livestock-raising nation."[18]

Peasants who want to raise cattle must look for land that is not presently being used. In Chiapas and Tabasco, the forests are being cut down to provide additional grazing land for cattle. Peasants are being driven off their lands in Veracruz and Oaxaca in order to provide more land for grazing and growing of feed grains.

From 1950 to 1980, the production of beef, pork and chicken grew rapidly. It dropped off significantly during the Mexican depression of the 1980s, then rose again. By 1990, Mexico was the largest supplier of feeder cattle for the U.S. market. But production of milk steadily declined, as the government opted for the importation of powdered milk, heavily subsidized by the exporting countries.

With the development of the meat industry there was a corresponding expansion of the feed industry. Under the direction of Ralston-Purina, Anderson-Clayton, and the Mexican state-owned ALBA-MEX, production of alfalfa, forage oats, barley, and sorghum expanded. Sorghum became the most important feed, providing 75 percent of the basic grain used in animal feed. Much of the cattle and most of the pork and chicken is produced for the relatively small minority of Mexicans with high incomes. By 1985, close to 50 percent of all grain produced in Mexico was being fed to animals.[19]

The social impact of the meat industry was clear. Land was taken out of production of basic foods — maize, beans, and wheat — and used to produce animal feed. Furthermore, much highly productive irrigated land was given over to feed production. Sorghum was introduced as a major commercial crop because it grows relatively well on land with little rainfall. But given the realities of market prices, 35 percent of all sorghum was being grown on irrigated land as early as 1970.

Linda Wilcox Young has shown that the shift to industrial agriculture has had a negative effect on labour employment in the central plateau known as El Bajío. This is a prime agriculture area and has experienced the invasion of U.S. transnational corporations.[20]

Young argues that the shift from traditional crops to the export crops for the United States has resulted in "extremely low employment generation" and has promoted the use of temporary workers on a seasonal basis. The average agricultural labourer in the area worked only 110 days per year in 1983.

The worst effect on agricultural employment has been the shift from maize to the production of sorghum. Irrigated maize employs more workers than broccoli or cauliflower, and considerably more than sorghum, wheat, or alfalfa.

In contrast, the Mexican government continued its policy of cheap food for urban dwellers. Rather than improve production by traditional Mexican farmers, it chose to increase imports of basic grains: corn, dry beans and wheat. Between 1965 and 1987, land planted to maize fell by about 1 percent and beans by 1.2 percent. During that same period, land planted to sorghum rose by 11.8 percent. The Food and Agriculture Organization reports that food production per capita dropped from a peak in 1983, and, in 1990, was four percent lower than it was in 1980. Agricultural production in general dropped six percent over the same period of time.

While urbanization was taking place, and the percentage of the population living in the rural areas was dropping, the reality was that the absolute number of people living in rural Mexico continued to increase. In 1980, 24.5 million people were classified as rural residents; by 1993, that had risen to 25.3 million. Over that same period of time the number of people actively engaged in agricultural production rose from 7.9 million to 8.9 million.

These trends are common in less developed countries, but they stand in direct contrast to developed countries like Canada and the United States. Over the same period of time, both Canada and the United States experienced an absolute drop in the number of people classified as agricultural labourers. The number of people actively engaged in farming dropped by 37 percent in Canada and 31 percent in the United States.

Salinas's Revolution

Moving quickly on agricultural policy, President Carlos Salinas announced the National Program for Modernization of the Countryside, 1990-1994. It called for (1) the end to marketing by national boards like CONASUPO, (2) the privatization of state-owned enterprises in agribusiness, (3) promotion of private investment in infrastructure in rural areas, (4) reduction in price supports for basic food products, and (5) a tightening of government credit and insurance programs. An unstated part of this program was to allow real wages for farm workers to decline with the official minimum wage.

Government policy encouraged "alliances for production" between corporations and *ejidos*. Arrangements of this kind had existed for years and had been legalized in 1980. The new minister of agriculture, Carlos Hank González, a wealthy businessman and leading figure in the PRI, re-

flected the views of the technocrats: the communal system of land ownership was out of date in the era of commercial agriculture. The Undersecre-
tary of Agriculture, Luis Tellez, expressed the opinion that the policies
undertaken by the Salinas administration would reduce the rural population in Mexico by one-half within a decade or two.[21]

The Salinas administration continued to cut back government expenditures on agriculture. Price supports were eliminated for all basic foods except maize and beans. Farm credit was greatly reduced.[22]

Under the move towards free trade, tariffs and other protections for
agriculture and food products were also reduced. By 1992 only maize and
beans were protected. Import regulations were removed for all crops except maize.

The most daring change was the one made to Article 27 of the Mexican Constitution, which protected *ejido* land. The changes were announced
in November 1991 and quickly rammed through the Chamber of Deputies
and the Senate. The PRI-dominated state legislatures all ratified the
changes by January 1992. The enabling legislation was then pushed
through the federal legislature. The strategy of the Salinas administration
was to get this very controversial change approved quickly in order to prevent the mobilization of any significant opposition.

The President was smart enough not to completely abolish communal
landholding; he knew there was strong opposition to changes in Article 27,
considered one of the most important achievements of the Mexican revolution. The new legislation made it easier for *ejidos* or groups of their members to make commercial contracts with outside business and financial
organizations. Individuals and *ejidos* now have the ability to sell or mortgage
their land. Before, they had only usufruct rights of use and inheritance. In
addition, those with usufruct rights can now make long-term lease arrangements with outside interests. Such leasing arrangement requires only the
approval of one-third of the *ejido* members.

The Salinas administration was committed to bringing the *ejido* agricultural lands into the capitalist market. It was argued that the communal system of land ownership discouraged the investment and consolidation
necessary for large-scale operations. Privatization would permit financing
from private rather than government sources. The new regulations would
likely result in greater concentration of ownership, and the development of
fewer, but larger and more commercial, family farm operations.

The new Agrarian Law of January 1992 formally declared that the federal government would no longer redistribute land to peasants and landless farm labourers.[23]

The Salinas administration abandoned any attempt at self-sufficiency in food production. Mexico now imports around 35 percent of basic cereal needs and is the world's largest importer of powdered milk.

Most Mexican consumers don't like being dependent on food imports. The powdered milk is of poor quality and sometimes contaminated. The corn is primarily American feed corn, not maize. Yellow corn does not make acceptable tortillas, and it has a much lower nutritional rating. But the rich and powerful of Mexico eat like well-off North Americans.

NAFTA is the first free trade agreement between advanced industrialized countries and a Third World country, and a great many Mexicans wonder if they can possibly compete with U.S. and Canadian farmers who are, in general, more advanced technologically and have much better access to credit.

Mexican farmers fear that they will be driven out of business by the subsidies that the U.S. and Canadian governments give to their farmers. In 1994, U.S. subsidies to agriculture amounted to about $11 billion. It is impossible for Mexico to match those subsidies. Jorge Calderón points out that the U.S. budget for subsidies is almost twenty times the size of the entire annual budget of the Mexican Secretary of Agriculture and Hydraulic Resources (SARH).[24]

Because of widespread opposition to the neoliberal reforms, one of the central problems for the Salinas administration was social control. What actions could be taken to make sure that peasants and their supporters would not mobilize resistance to the radical changes in agriculture policy?

The universal programs of assistance were replaced by special programs of a more limited nature, tied to specific producing groups. As Jonathan Fox reports, this meant making concession to the better off peasant groups. Those who were marginal were expected to leave farming. This change reinforced the differentiation between the organized and the unorganized. Those who did not co-operate faced the prospect of losing their benefits. Fox concludes that rainfed peasant producers are now "treated as targets of welfare rather than production policy."[25]

The Solidarity program fit in well with the process of *concertación*. Aside from rural development programs, it provided credit to more marginal farmers. Indigenous peasants were aided through the Solidarity programs administered by the National Indigenous Institute, a PRI organization.

The Salinas administration also had to respond to the defections of members of the official National Peasant Confederation (CNC) to Cárdenas during the 1988 election, the formation of the new Cardenista Peasant Confederation (CCC), and the existence of a growing number of independent organizations. First, Luis Donaldo Colosio, chairman of the PRI, spoke to a general congress of the PRI-affiliated CNC and promised to promote democracy within the organization. Then they formed the Permanent Agrarian Congress (CAP), which was to include all peasant organizations, those affiliated to the PRI and those who were independent. Officials of the Ministry of Agriculture pressured peasant organizations to join. At first, the independent peasant organizations refused to join, fearing that it was just another co-optation strategy. Later, however, most of them joined, concluding that the organization would allow them to have some influence on agricultural policy.[26]

The opposition of many peasants and peasant organizations to the neoliberal revolution was neutralized by the state. Organizations which approved (or at least were not vigorous in their opposition) received benefits like land titles, payments for land involved in ownership disputes, and Solidarity programs. Those who opposed were cut off. This had the effect of causing divisions within the independent peasant organizations.

In August 1993, President Salinas addressed the National Congress of the CNC. He told the delegates that he would provide some assistance to peasants who were in serious debt. He had instructed BANRURAL and FIRA to review "case by case," overdue loans. He had asked the Secretary of Social Development (SEDESO) to provide more credit and called on the agricultural cabinet to speed up the certification of land rights. It was implied that those peasants not supporting the PRI would not have their cases reviewed. In return, the leadership of the CNC pledged that they would ensure "a clear, convincing, legitimate, and unobjectionable electoral victory" for the PRI in 1994.[27]

There was also the stick. Neil Harvey reports, "During the first three months of the Salinas administration, over 30 peasants belonging to independent organizations were murdered, reflecting a darker side of concertation and a continuation of previous harassment of autonomous political movements." Human rights organizations in Mexico reported fourteen peasant leaders killed between December 1988 and November 1990.[28]

Finally, there was the National Program of Direct Aid to the Country (PROCAMPO), announced in October 1993. Over 3.3 million producers of seven crops would be eligible for payments of around $100 per hectare. The first payments were to be made in March 1994, co-incidently the beginning of the presidential election campaign. The schedule was drawn up by Carlos Hank González, Secretary of Agriculture, and later, campaign manager for PRI candidate, Ernesto Zedillo. A total of $3 billion was to be paid out for the period June to August 1994; the cheques were to be handed out just before the election. The payments would end after fifteen years, to co-incide with the phasing out of price supports under the terms of NAFTA.[29]

Structural Problems

The structure of Mexican agriculture is very different from that of Canada and the United States. First, there are the 2.7 million peasant farmers and their families who live on one of the 29,951 *ejidos*. Two-thirds of these farmers have less than five hectares of land. They represent over 60 percent of all farmers, control about 43 percent of all cropland, but produce only about 10 percent of agricultural products. They lack capital for investment. Historically, most *ejido* land has been marginal cropland.[30]

The farmers on privately-owned land can basically be divided into two classes. Most have less than five hectares of land and are classified by the government as "sub-subsistence," meaning they cannot provide a bare living for themselves. According to government figures, 60 percent of all farmers in Mexico have less than five hectares of land. Small peasant farmers represent over 70 percent of all Mexican farmers. Eighty-five percent of these farmers depend on the growing of maize and beans. Most of them also raise hogs for market, which provides between 20 percent and 30 percent of household cash income. A few also have a few cattle. These peasant farmers fear greater imports of cereals and pork from North America.

In contrast, there are the large commercial farms. Some of these farms grow what are called "wage foods": maize, rice, wheat and dry beans. The high yielding varieties of wheat were developed in Mexico, and their yields are almost twice those on the Canadian prairies. But they are grown on irrigated land. However, most of the large farmers grow export crops on contract for large agribusiness firms. The large feed companies have financially supported farmers who shifted from food production to the growing of animal feeds, particularly sorghum. Finally, we should not forget the development of new crops. As prices for traditional crops fell, and the number of landless people increased in the rural areas, peasants turned to the cultivation of marijuana and poppies.

Because their farms are not large enough to support a family, the vast majority of Mexican peasants also work as farm labourers. Thousands migrate to the U.S. each year, legally and illegally, to do farmwork. In the U.S. the average Mexican farm worker earns $7,500 per year, far more than he could dream of making in Mexico.

Migratory farm work is also very common in Mexico. Families migrate to different regions to harvest fruits and vegetables, coffee, sugar and sisal.

The Ministry of Agriculture estimates that farm work in Mexico requires annually around 500 million person work days. Of these, 200 million are given to raising corn and beans for survival, 200 million for the labour-intensive crops like vegetables, fruit, coffee, cotton, and sugarcane, and 100 million for other cereals, oilseed crops and cattle raising.

The average farm labourer in Mexico works between sixty and ninety days a year. But there are officially around seven million farm workers, and chronic unemployment is a serious problem. Of these, 4.5 million are *jornaleros*, day workers, moving from farm to farm, with no regular employment. In 1991, their average annual cash income from farmwork was only $175.

Case studies in the fruit and vegetable areas of northern Mexico demonstrate that over 50 percent of farmworkers are women and children, and they are not counted in the agricultural census. They work for less than the official minimum wage of $4 per day.

The policy of "divide and conquer" pursued by the Salinas administration was relatively easy, given the heterogenous nature of the peasant population. There were numerous differences which could be exploited: private farmers, individual *ejidos,* collective *ejidos,* agrarian communities, Roman Catholic versus new evangelical Protestants, supporters of the PRI versus supporters of the PAN and the PRD. The agrarianism of the revolution, and the desire to own a productive farm remains deeply entrenched in rural ideology. The failure of trade union organizers and political leftists to build a farm workers' movement can be traced to this reality.[31]

Disputes over land, which is in short supply, have served to undermine peasant solidarity. There is intercommunity conflict. Before the Revolution of 1910, peasants and indigenous peoples fought a common enemy, the large landowner. With land redistribution on the agenda, communal holders of land fight other *communaros,* individual *ejitarios* fight other *ejitarios,* and they all resist the demands of the landless people who want land.[32]

As Marilyn Gates stresses, the rural poor utilize many different strategies for survival. They may own their own plot of land, engage in sharecropping, tenant farming, or have some form of subcontracting arrangement. They may participate in agricultural collectives, colonization programs, and government development projects like Solidarity. They may simply grow for their own consumption or participate in the market. It is common for the rural poor to have other work, particularly farm labour on nearby commercial farms, or to be migrant labourers. Many participate in the craft industry and the drug industry. Some may travel regularly to cities to sell in the markets and on the street.[33]

Social scientists have debated the extent to which proletarianization or depeasantization has taken place in Mexico. Family ties to land have prevented complete proletarianization. Gates argues that, "Even in regions where wage labour is the predominant activity, rural social consciousness tends to remain more peasant than proletarian because of the insecurity of wage-earning employment and the consequent imperative of retaining ties to the land where feasible."

This attachment of the peasant to the land leads to relatively high land costs. Arturo Warman noted in 1980 that the price of land varied from $560 per hectare for dry-land farming to $1200 per hectare of irrigated land. These prices were "noticeably higher" than strict commercial value. The price could not be justified by a commercial farmer, but for a peasant who saw the land as replacing cash expenditure with unpaid family labour, and with other resources exchanged on a noncash reciprocal basis, the "absurd prices" for land were not absurd in local terms.[34]

The political culture of rural Mexico can be seen in the way the peasants dealt with the economic crisis of the 1980s. They adopted the same strategies as the urban poor: they curtailed shopping, cut back on meat consumption, cut back on recreational and other excursions, and stopped buying clothes and shoes except where absolutely essential. Enrolment in secondary schools dropped because families could not afford uniforms, school supplies, and where necessary, transportation.

But the main strategy for coping was at the household level. Peasants worked longer hours on their plots, travelled more for wage work, and cut back on farm inputs which had to be bought.

Political protest was mainly limited to putting their case to the local PRI. Gates reports that in Campeche, the candidacy of Cárdenas in 1988 did not inspire many. Most peasants saw Cárdenas as "more of the same," despite his illustrious name. They "tend to regard any kind of organized politics as a waste of time."[35]

Fox makes a similar conclusion. NAFTA and the neoliberal program has put the peasant under "qualitatively new levels of strain." But he expects that the response will not be overtly political. A few may be able to become small farmers. But most of rural society will respond with the family-based survival strategy. One alternative is to "engage in sometimes risky and often fruitless collective action," but the most common alternative is to just leave farming.

However, Fox believes that the voice of the peasants is growing rather than shrinking. The objective of the government is to keep the peasant movement small and segmented, but peasants may become more committed to political protest and action as they see a competitive party system develop. Peasant organization may move toward "class-wide representation and demands."[36]

One notable development has been the rise of the El Barzón movement, begun by peasants in 1992. Peasants saw this new movement as a collective way of dealing with their debt problems. After the December 1994 devaluation, and the subsequent dramatic rise in interest rates, the organization experienced an explosion in membership.

By April 1993 El Barzón claimed 300,000 members, welcomed an influx of small business owners, and a new wave of individuals who could not pay credit card debts and interest. They mobilized and shut down banks, had demonstrations where credit cards were burned, and even tarred and feathered a few bank officers. They also began to form alliances with other civil organizations protesting the government's draconian economic policies.[37]

The neoliberal reforms brought in by the Salinas government are designed to remove many people from the rural economy. But Mexicans always ask: Where will they go? What will they do? How many people can live in urban shantytowns and work in the informal economy? A high percentage of the population remains in rural Mexico living at a poverty level because there is no paid work available in Mexico. While the technocrats have been hoping for increased migration to the United States, in 1994 a right-wing, racist movement to exclude Mexican immigrants emerged in California and is now spreading across the country.

Politicians, business leaders, and the mass media tell North American farmers that NAFTA will be good for them as they can expand their exports to Mexico. But the effect of this will be to drive more Mexican peasants and farmers off the land. Consumers are told that free trade will give us cheaper food. But this can only be at the expense of the gross exploitation of the poor Mexican men, women, and children who do the farm work and food processing. What is the acceptable death rate in Mexico so that relatively well-off North Americans can have fresh fruits and vegetables in winter at low prices?

Despite the devaluation of the peso in December 1994, the cash crops for export policy remains in question. The export of fruits and vegetables has stagnated in the 1990s. Farm production costs in the United States are often lower than in Mexico, and the result can be seen in the expansion of exports south of the Rio Grande. Mexico's agricultural exports to other areas face stiff competition from Chile and Brazil.

Mexico's traditional export crops include coffee, tobacco, cotton, bananas, cacao and sugar. There is a glut of these commodities on the world market. Mexico has a negative balance of trade in agricultural products. It is difficult to see how NAFTA is going to change that.

Notes

1. For an account of the Zapatista rebellion, see John Ross, *Rebellion from the Roots.* Monroe, Maine: Common Courage Press, 1995; George A. Collier, *Basta! Land and the Zapatista Rebellion in Chiapas.* Oakland: The Institute for Food and Development Policy, 1994; and *Shadows of Tender Fury.* New York: Monthly Review Press, 1995.

2. See Neil Harvey, *Rebellion in Chiapas: Rural Reforms, Campesino Radicalism, and the Limits to Salinismo.* Center for U.S.-Mexican Studies, University of California, San Diego, 1994.

3. Roger Burbach and Peter Rosset, "Chiapas and the Crisis of Mexican Agriculture." San Francisco: Institute for Food and Development Policy, unpublished paper, December 1944; José Luis Calva, *Probables Efectos de un Tratado de Libre Commercio en el Campo Mexicano.* Mexico, D.F.: Distribuciones Fontamara, 1991; and David Barkin, "Agrarian Counter-Reform in Mexico," *New Solutions,* Vol. 3, Summer 1993, pp. 70-78.

4. Solon L. Barraclough, *An End to Hunger?* London: Zed Press, 1991. pp. 101-106.

5. Jonathan Fox, "Political Change in Mexico's New Peasant Economy," in Maria Lorena Cook et al, *The Politics of Economic Restructuring.* Center for U.S.,-Mexican Studies, University of California, San Diego, 1994, pp. 243-276.

6. Gustavo Esteva, "Food Needs and Capacities: Four Centuries of Conflict," in James E. Austin and Gustavo Esteva, eds. *Food Policy in Mexico.* Ithaca: Cornell University Press, 1987, pp. 23-47; and Alain de Janvry, *The Agrarian Question and Reformism in Latin America.* Baltimore: The Johns Hopkins Press, 1981, pp. 202-223.

7. See Frank Tannenbaum, *Peace by Revolution: Mexico After 1910.* New York: Columbia University Press, 1966; and Thomas G. Sanders, "The Plight of Mexican Agriculture," in Barbara Huddleston and Jon McLin, eds., *Political Investment in Food Production.* Bloomington: Indiana University Press, 1989, pp. 19-38.

8. See Eliana Cardoso and Ann Helwege, *Latin America's Economy.* Boston: MIT Press, 1992, pp. 73-107.

9. Marilyn Gates, *In Default; Peasants, the Debt Crisis and the Agricultural Challenge in Mexico.* Boulder: Westview Press, 1993, pp. 31-35.

10. Steven Sanderson, "Mexican Public Sector Food Policy under Agricultural Trade Liberalization," *Policy Studies Journal,* Vol. 20, No. 3, 1992, pp. 431-446.

11. Marilee S. Grindle, "Agrarian Reform in Mexico: A Cautionary Tale," in Roy R. Prosterman et al, eds. *Agrarian Reform and Grassroots Development.* Boulder: Lynne Reinner Publishers, 1990, pp. 179-204.

12. See P. Lamartine Yates, *Mexico's Agricultural Dilemma.* Tucson: University of Arizona Press, 1981.

13. See Grindle, *op. cit.,* pp. 190-194; Esteva, *op. cit.* , pp. 35-39; and Gates, *op. cit.,* pp. 36-40.

14. See Armando Andrade and Nicole Blanc, "SAM's Cost and Impact on Production," in Austin and Esteva, *op. cit.,* pp. 215-248; James E. Austin and Jonathan Fox, "State-Owned

Enterprises: Food Policy Implementers," in Austin and Esteva, *op. cit.*, pp. 61-91; and Gates, *op. cit.*, pp. 40-46.

15. Gates, *op. cit.*, pp. 46-49.

16. Steven E. Sanderson, *The Transformation of Mexican Agriculture*. Princeton: Princeton University Press, 1986, pp. 14-63.

17. *Ibid.*, pp. 64-118.

18. *Ibid.*, pp. 119-181.

19. See David Barkin, *Distorted Development*. Boulder: Westview Press, 1990, pp. 11-40.

20. Linda Wilcox Young, "Labour Demand and Agroindustrial Development: The Evidence from Mexico," *Journal of Development Studies*, Vol. 30, October 1993, pp. 168-189.

21. Fox, *op. cit.*, pp. 244-245; David Barkin, "The Spector of Rural Development," *Report on the Americas*, Vol. 28, July/August 1994, pp. 29-34; Burbach and Rosset, *op. cit.*, pp. 18-19.

22. Kenneth Shwedel, "Will the Countryside Modernize?" *Business Mexico*, July 1991, pp. 24-26, 50; and Calva, *op. cit.*

23. See Billie R. DeWalt and Martha W. Rees, *The End of Agrarian Reform in Mexico*. Center for U.S.-Mexican Studies, University of California, San Diego, 1994; Steven Sanderson, "Mexican Public Sector Food Policy under Agricultural Trade Liberalization," *Policy Studies Journal*, Vol. 20, No. 3, 1992, pp. 431-446.

24. Jorge Calderón, "Rural Development and Transnationalization of the Agro-Food Industry in Mexico." Mexico, D.F.: unpublished paper, 1991.

25. Fox, *op. cit.*, pp. 258-259.

26. Neil Harvey, "The Limits of Concertation in Rural Mexico," in Neil Harvey, ed., *Mexico: Dilemmas of Transition*. London: Institute of Latin American Studies, 1993, pp. 199-217.

27. Equipo Pueblo, *Mexico News Summary*, September 1, 1993.

28. Harvey, "The Limits of Concertation in Rural Mexico," *op. cit.*, p. 206.

29. See Harvey, *Rebellion in Chiapas, op. cit.*, pp. 14-17; Ross, *op. cit.*, p. 388.

30. Adriana Ló)pez Monjardin, "Organization and Struggle among Agricultural Workers in Mexico," in Kevin Middlebrook, ed., *Unions, Workers, and the State in Mexico*. Center for U.S.-Mexican Studies, University of California, San Diego, 1991, pp. 185-211; and Enrique Astorga Lira and Simon Commander, "Agricultural Commercialization and the Growth of a Migrant Labour Market in Mexico," *International Labour Review*, Vol. 128, No. 6, 1989, pp. 769-789.

31. The classic study, now in English, is Roger Bartra, *Agrarian Structure and Political Power in Mexico*. Baltimore: The Johns Hopkins Press, 1993.

32. Dewalt and Rees, *op. cit.*, pp. 22-23.

33. Gates, *op. cit.*, pp. 15-21.

34. Arturo Warman cited in DeWalt and Rees, *op. cit.*, p. 38.

35. Gates, *op. cit.*, pp. 232-234.

36. Fox, "Political Change in Mexico's New Peasant Economy," *op. cit.*, pp. 268-270.

37. Equipo Pueblo, *Mexico Update*, Vol. 2, No. 26, April 18, 1995.

Chapter II

TRADING THE ENVIRONMENT

In 1987, the World Commission on Environment and Development reported that the Earth's ecosphere was degrading at an alarming rate. The base for economic development and habitability was being undermined by deforestation, desertification, soil erosion, the degradation of irrigated land, urban and rural pollution, global warming, the destruction of the ozone layer, and the ongoing extinction of plant and animal species.

Latin America and Mexico are very much a part of this enormous problem. Governments have stressed industrialization and modernization over the past fifty years, and the growth strategy has been unregulated capitalism with scant attention paid to the ecological impact. Rapid growth during the period of import substitution industrialization was followed by the debt crisis and rising social problems. Under the direction of international lending organizations, the U.S. government, and the international banks, the governments of Latin American countries moved to export-orientated industrialization.

In the 1990s, the ability of Latin American countries to deal with the ecological crisis has been limited by the need to service the international debt, the deterioration of the terms of trade, and the reduced spending powers of government. At the same time, unemployment, underemployment, and poverty have increased. In such an atmosphere, governments have emphasized the need to attract foreign investment and assist private corporations. Environmental questions have received little attention.

Latin American governments, including Mexico, have been following development strategies which are clearly not sustainable. Nonrenewable natural resources are being exported as fast as possible to the overdeveloped First World. Forests and other renewable natural resources are being exhausted. Latin America is facing a serious problem of water shortage and pollution; agricultural resources are being degraded.

Much of this distorted development has been attributed to the policies of authoritarian and anti-democratic governments. However, there may be deeper, structural causes of the problem: the intervention of transnational corporations from the First World has heightened the expansion of imitative consumerism, political and economic dependency, the polarization of income, wealth and power, the increasing marginalization of a majority of the population, the overconcentration of population in large cities, the import of First World technology, and the ability of corporations to externalize the environmental costs of production.

Gilberto Gallopin has identified a few additional problems: the growing gap in standard of living between Latin America and the First World, the loss of autonomy for governments, their inability to define their own production goals, and the concentration of power within individual countries.[1]

With the increase in social tensions that result from this development process, Gallopin argues that governments are faced with "war economies." The economic and social crisis pushes governments to abandon environmental and social objectives in the drive to increase exports. It is not surprising that the ecological impacts associated with these trends are mostly negative.

Public recognition of the serious nature of Mexico's ecological problem developed during the administrations of Presidents Miguel de la Madrid and Carlos Salinas. There has been a proliferation of local and national environmental organizations. The Mexican Ecological Green Party (PVEM) emerged. However, this party has accepted support from the PRI and is now viewed as one of the "satellite parties."

Most of the environmental groups have chosen to stay independent of the ruling PRI. The most prominent organization is the Group of 100, a Mexico City group founded by prominent intellectuals. The Border Project for Environmental Education (PVEA) has worked closely with U.S. groups in the Border Ecology Project. The Mexican Forum of Civil Society/Rio 92 is a broad based association formed to participate in the U.N. nongovernmental conferences. The Pact of Environmental Groups (PGE) is an alliance of 70 member organizations. These last two organizations are affiliated with the Mexican Action Network on Free Trade (RMALC), and work with U.S. and Canadian organizations against the North American Free Trade Agreement (NAFTA).

During the negotiations leading to NAFTA, the environmental groups in Mexico spearheaded the opposition to the position of the Salinas government. Individually, and jointly, they produced study after study revealing the environmental costs of the Mexican government's export development policy, and the *maquiladora* program in particular.

President Salinas and his administration were firmly committed to neoliberalism. At the core of the free market and free trade policy is the belief that economic development works best when capitalists and large corporations are free to make their decisions without government or public interference.

As numerous Mexicans have pointed out, deregulation and anti-regulation are at the heart of the Mexican neoliberal reforms. But the ecological crisis that Mexico is facing demands increased regulation: therefore, the environmental movement is by necessity, pro-state. Given the well-known record, Mexican environmentalists distrust the motives of corporations, are sceptical of technological solutions, and oppose unregulated and unplanned economic growth. The ecological approach to development stresses the necessity of protecting and nourishing the life of the community.[2]

The ecological approach also stresses the need for decentralization of power and democratic control over governments and places of work. But in contrast, the free trade treaties supported by the Salinas government, NAFTA and the revised General Agreement on Tariffs and Trade (GATT), call for the creation of supranational bodies of nonelected bureaucrats who have power to make binding decisions on countries, regions and peoples. Democracy and accountability have no place in the international structures of free trade.

The Mexico City Disaster

Mexico City is known for its air pollution. When I was there in March 1992, the pollution levels reached record highs. The Metropolitan Index for Air Quality (IMECA) went over 400. A reading of over 200 is considered sufficiently dangerous for the government to order 30 percent of the industries to shut down. The Phase II level of contamination (over 400) required a 75 percent reduction in industry and schools were closed. Automobiles were ordered off the streets. I could only see about five blocks — beyond that there was just a brown cloud. It was much like Saskatchewan in the spring, when a dust storm rolls in.

A 1992 study by Integrated Program against Atmospheric Contamination in Mexico City, reported that transport vehicles were responsible for 42.4 percent of toxic emissions. With a metropolitan population of nearly twenty million, there are around three million private cars. They are the main problem. The government has been reluctant to crack down on pollution caused by private vehicles. It is a case of the better-off poisoning the poor.[3]

The Valley of Mexico has about 30,000 industries. Along with the oil-burning power plants, they produce around 28 percent of the toxic emissions. The Attorney for the Protection of the Environment (PPA) reports that only 10 percent of them comply with existing environmental regulations. The Secretariat of Urban Development and Ecology (SEDUE) has identified 4,000 of these plants as major contributors to air pollution. The many small businesses burn anything.[4]

Aside from pollution from industries and automobiles, there is the problem of faecal pollution in the air, as millions of people living in the poor *colonies perdidas* on the hillsides do not have any sewage disposal system. Lead poisoning from exhaust fumes is seriously affecting children. Ozone levels are three times the international average, and lead to respiratory problems. The water supply comes primarily from wells, and the water table is falling rapidly as the water is not being replenished. As a result, the valley bottom is sinking.

Industries dump tons of toxic wastes into the sewer system daily. Untreated sewage also gets into the water supply system, and the rivers and streams are among the most polluted in Mexico. The city has no capacity to deal with the amount of solid waste that is created. Garbage lies around uncollected. Meanwhile, the landfill sites on the edge of the city spread pollution with the wind.[5]

The PRI governments have not made pollution control a priority in Mexico City. In 1990, there were only nine pollution control inspectors working in the city. But in response to the criticisms of environmentalists, and the fear of losing the vote on NAFTA in the U.S. Congress, President Salinas decided to take action. In March 1991, he declared an air pollution emergency, shut eighty industries temporarily, shut down the oldest oil refinery, and increased the number of inspectors to fifty.

Juan Alvarez Barroso, president of the Ecological Commission of CANACINTRA, which represents middle and small businesses, denies that the companies are being negligent. His organization estimates that the cost of bringing these companies into compliance with existing regulations would be between five and seven billion dollars.

Under the Mexican Constitution, the administration of the Federal District is the president's responsibility. The mayor is appointed by the president, and is always a prominent PRI official, very often with no experience at running a city. Since 1929, the government of the Federal District has been completely in the hands of the ruling PRI. Over the ten years of the neoliberal regimes of Presidents de la Madrid and Salinas, hundreds of new polluting industries began operating in the valley of Mexico. When asked in March 1992 why these factories were allowed to set up operations, the response of the PRI was straightforward: these were factories that would not have been allowed to operate in First World countries. This kind of industrial production is one of Mexico's international comparative advantages.[6]

Environmental Regulation

In early 1982, newly elected President Miguel de la Madrid created SE-DUE. While the president talked about the need for protection of the environment, throughout the 1980s the budget for SEDUE was systematically reduced.

In 1988, President Carlos Salinas enacted the General Law of Ecological Equilibrium and Environmental Protectionism, which gave SEDUE greater enforcement powers. Its standards for air pollution, hazardous waste, and environmental impact requirements were patterned on existing U.S. legislation. But it is generally recognized that they are less specific and less comprehensive.

David Barkin has noted that, "By its own admission the SEDUE has been unable to meet most of its challenges." SEDUE's budget for 1990, for all of Mexico, was only about 6 percent of the pollution control budget of the state of Texas alone. The hazardous waste management budget was only $2.3 million. In 1991, SEDUE had a staff of only 140 who were charged with enforcing environmental laws throughout Mexico.[7]

Mexico's massive debt problem and other investment needs have meant that little has been spent on environmental protection. A 1990 study found that 77 percent of the country's river basins are polluted enough to pose health hazards to humans: beaches are polluted; forests have been ravaged; there have been major oil spills in the Gulf of Mexico; and soil erosion is a serious problem where cultivation has expanded onto fragile lands.[8]

Stephen Mumme, who has studied environmental problems in Mexico, has argued that the policy thrust of President Salinas was "containing public demands and managing dissent." The first priority was always economic conversion to neoliberalism.[9]

In the last half of his sexenio, the central focus of Salinas's administration was on passing the NAFTA accord. Many of the environmental initiatives taken by the president served to convince American congressmen that Mexico would not use its weak environmental standards to attract American investment.

Mumme argues that Salinas's actions on the environmental front were "largely formalist and symbolic," concentrating on a few demonstration projects. Paper reforms are very much a part of Mexican political culture, as is nonenforcement. Not surprisingly, it has been widely reported that offending companies escape such action by making payments to inspectors.[10]

Government co-optation was also somewhat effective. Like many of their North American counterparts, representatives of some of Mexico's more prominent environmental organization were co-opted by the government into sitting on panels and boards which did very little. Patronage and clientelism work in Mexico. Mumme notes that the Salinas administration was "partially effective in co-opting environmental activists directly into government service." Homero Aridjis, spokesman for the Group of 100, one of the most influential Mexican environmental organizations, has argued that the Salinas administration has also been far more coercive in its attempts to restrict the influence of the environmental movement.[11]

Domingo González, a representative for the Coalition for Justice in the Maquiladoras, argues that under Salinas the enforcement of environmental regulation was mostly for public relations: minimal, but highly visible.[12]

On March 14, 1991, President Salinas stated that, in accordance with the principles of NAFTA, Mexico would refuse entry to investments or manufacturing processes rejected by the United States and Canada as environmentally harmful. He proclaimed the General Ecological Balance and Environmental Protection Law. Government officials temporarily closed 1,500 companies, and permanently closed 100, due to pollution emissions.[13]

But Homero Aridjis was sceptical. "In general, Mexican laws are less strict and, what's more, they're not obeyed." This was confirmed by a study by the National Institute of Ecology (INE) in 1992. The government agency inspected 8,756 plants and found widespread violations. They closed 418 plants and temporarily closed another 1,909. Sergio Reyes, president of INE, estimated that "At least 95 percent of Mexico's 106,000 factories are releasing toxic wastes in violations of existing rules."[14]

The use of pesticides in Mexico is an example of how the government is promoting exports at almost any cost. Despite the protests from environmental and labour organizations in both the United States and Mexico, the Salinas administration continued to permit the use of pesticides banned in the United States and Canada for health reasons. Mexican farmworkers are regularly poisoned, and it is reported that hundreds die each year.

Fruits and vegetables, in particular, carry residues of banned pesticides. The U.S. Environmental Protection Agency (EPA) reports that residues on Mexican produce are generally twice as high as on domestically grown produce. The banned pesticides include the infamous "Dirty Dozen" as identified by Pesticide Action Network International. A number of these are organochlorines, as well as the highly toxic paraquat and pentachlorophenol. Mexican growers also use another thirty-six pesticides that are widely banned in other industrialized countries. The use of these chemicals gives Mexican growers a cost advantage over U.S. and Canadian farmers.[15]

In February 1992, SEDUE and the EPA announced the Integrated Environmental Plan for the Mexican-U.S. Border Area (IBEP). They pledged to strengthen enforcement of existing laws, reduce pollution through new initiatives, increase training and education, and publicize border environmental problems. The cost of the joint program was to be around $840 million. Mexican and American environmental groups described it as "a public relations game" designed to get NAFTA through the reluctant U.S. House of Representatives.[16]

Mary Kelly, director of the Texas Center for Policy Studies, argued that in their rush to sign NAFTA, the Mexican and U.S. governments were "relegating the border environmental issues to a high profile sideshow." The IBEP made no attempt to assess the impact of NAFTA on the border region.[17]

More significant were other actions taken by President Salinas in 1992; he closed SEDUE and incorporated its environmental programs in a newly created Secretariat of Social Development (SEDESOL). Many of SEDUE's responsibilities were in fact turned over to private consulting groups as part of the general privatization program.

Within SEDESOL the two major SEDUE programs — the National Ecological Institute (INE) and the Federal Attorney for Protection of the Environment — were clearly a low priority. Environmental groups dubbed the new office the "Department of Magic Realism" because its declarations were deemed to be fantasies. The Border Health and Environment Network (RFSA) pointed out that the two programs no longer co-operate or even share information.

Dick Camp of the Border Ecology Project, noted that "SEDESOL's total budget is between $66 and $78 million, and much of that is borrowed. Almost half of its environmental budget — about $31 million — has been dedicated to the border, leaving the rest for the remaining 98 percent of Mexico."[18]

The World Bank loan to Mexico to improve environmental regulations was directed by the Salinas administration to the building of transportation infrastructure. RFSA charged that "SEDESOL spreads concrete, but does nothing for ecology." The Salinas government responded by offering to give RFSA free office space, to publish its newsletter, and trying to hire one of its activists.

Environmentalists point out that the EPA and SEDESOL have shown little interest in water quality in the border zone. Neither has the joint International Boundary and Water Commission (IBWC), which was created in 1889. The studies of industrial pollution have been done by private groups like the Border Ecology Project or the U.S. National Toxic Waste Campaign. Tom Barry and Beth Sims point out that the IBWC has collected hydrological data on transborder ground water but "has been unwilling to stick its neck out on this issue by releasing the results of its studies." Despite pressure from environmentalists, the 1992 Integrated Border Environmental Plan was an inadequate response because of "its narrow scope, lack of funding guarantees, and vague promises."[19]

Environmentalists on both sides of the border argued that the position of the Salinas administration on the building of new electric power plants indicated where it really stood. One of these, Carbon II, is being built 32 kilometres south of Eagle pass, Texas, close to San Antonio. The plant will use low-grade high-ash coal from an adjacent strip mine, and then possibly dirty high-sulphur U.S. coal which is losing its American market.

Neither the new plant nor the existing one nearby will have scrubbers or other modern pollution-control equipment that is required in the United States. U.S. government officials claim that the two plants will significantly degrade the air quality in the nearby U.S. Southwest. The cost of the scrubbers alone would be an additional $300 million.

The Mexican government controls 51 percent of the project and the other 49 percent is controlled by SCE Corporation of Rosemead, California. Two other large coal-fired plants are planned for the border area. Mary Kelly of the Texas Center for Policy Studies points out that these projects "emphasize the serious weakness of existing binational agreements to crack down on pollution."[20]

The Border Zone

What can we expect from NAFTA? George Bush, Carlos Salinas and Brian Mulroney all insisted that the agreement will improve environmental standards in Mexico, and flatly denied the claim that more companies will move to Mexico to avoid environmental and health and safety standards. We can get an indication of what to expect by looking at the *maquiladora* export processing zones, which were the original core of the new Mexican free market and free trade policy.

The border zone with the United States has become highly populated since the development of the *maquiladora* program, but the area is largely arid and suffers from a lack of water. All the cities along the border are pumping ground water at a rate twenty times faster than the aquifers can be recharged. Surface waters are under intense pressure from overuse.[21]

Maquila companies do not pay taxes, and workers are paid such low wages that their property is worth little. There is no tax base to provide for infrastructure needs. For example, in 1992, there was not one municipal sewage treatment plant along the entire border. Nuevo Laredo alone dumped around twenty-five million gallons of raw sewage into the Rio Grande river every day.

In July 1993, a report for the British government concluded that "The influx of new workers and industry to the border area has completely overwhelmed the inadequate municipal water, wastewater and electricity services." All the communities on the border suffer from "contamination of transborder rivers, lack of sanitation and wastewater/sewage treatment facilities, illegal dumping of hazardous waste and poor air quality."[22]

The report found that "Rivers are awash with toxic substances." The New River, which crosses the border at Calexico, had "over 90 toxic chemicals, and a number of viruses, including polio, hepatitis, cholera and typhoid." Heavy metals like cyanide, copper, and mercury were found in many rivers. The Rio Grande, which is used for irrigation and drinking purposes, had "high levels of raw sewage."

The Council on Scientific Affairs of the American Medical Association called the border zone "a virtual cesspool and breeding ground for infectious disease." They documented the enormous amount of raw sewage that is dumped each day into the border rivers. This water is used to irrigate crops which are then exported to U.S. and Canadian markets. In the areas where farmers raise hogs, there is a major concern over the existence of cysticercus, which causes internal lesions in humans, including brain lesions which can cause death. This disease is spread through hog faeces which enter the water used for irrigation of fruits and vegetables.[23]

In September 1993, the Mexico-U.S. Business Council reported that the needs for developing border infrastructure over the next ten years would cost around $6.5 billion. Governments would have to pay for almost all of this, they argued, "since 60-70 percent of Mexican families on the border earn about $500 per month, and 25 percent of them earn $300 or less per month."[24]

Enforcement of environmental regulations is lax in the *maquiladora* zones. Gildardo Acosta of RFSA points out that in 1993, only 20 percent of SEDESOL's inspectors in the area were working full time. Government salaries are always late. "Many of them are good and honest people," Acosta notes, "but they are open to many inducements by the companies they inspect. The *maquilas* offer them as much as double the money they get from SEDESOL." In March of 1993, the ten inspectors responsible for monitoring Juárez were found to be getting company kickbacks.[25]

Ideal Equipment Co. of Montréal shifted its sewing machine parts company to Matamoros in 1978. Michel Folacci, the plant manager, told the *Montreal Gazette* in 1992 that "Cheap labour is the motive behind 100 percent of the companies that have set up down here. Anyone who says that's not the case is a liar."

Folacci insists that his company complies with Mexican environmental laws. He argues that when health inspectors come to his plant, "Their first intention is to see if I'll pay them to close their eyes." He says he refuses, but others do not.[26]

Luis Alberto Magalanes works in a *maquila* plant in Ciudad Juárez. There are 300 companies in the zone, including Ford, Chrysler, Panasonic, and Cummings. He says that the government officials have not regulated the toxics. "There've been occasions in which they've closed a factory, but with a bribe they have it opened right back up. A bribe of about $5,000 to $7,000 is what it takes." He notes that the 70 auto parts factories "throw acids and solvents into the city drainage, and it has been ending up in the Juárez water for 24 years."[27]

The U.S. National Toxic Campaign ran tests on plant discharges in Matamoros. They found zylene being flushed out of the General Motors plant at levels which were 6,300 times higher than the safe level. Levels being dumped by Stepan Chemicals were much higher. Other plants were discharging hydrofluoric acid, toluene, and other hazardous chemicals.[28]

Popular organizations in the Matamoros area documented the birth defects found among children of women who worked in the *maquiladora* factories. One of the most publicized was the pattern of retardation and birth deformities among children of women who worked at Mallory Capacitators, a U.S. electronic company operating in Matamoros. The mothers regularly handled toxic materials, including PCBs, with only rubber gloves for protection.[29]

In December 1992, the Center for Border Studies and Human Rights Protection released the results of a study of 253 employees working in *maquiladora* industries in Reynosa and Matamoros. Most of the employees interviewed reported that they regularly handled toxic material, often with inadequate protection. A majority said they suffered from ailments ranging from headaches and stomach upsets to vomiting, skin rashes and heart palpitations. The employees, mainly women, were regularly exposed to benzene, liquid nitrogen, chlorinated hydrocarbons, heavy metals and a variety of solvents.[30]

Can we expect tougher enforcement in the future? Paul Blanco, a Matamoros plant manager, told Bruce Selcraig that in 1990 foreign corporations brought $273 million to that city, mostly in wages. "You cannot kill the goose that lays the golden egg," he argued. "This is an issue for Mexico of 'do we eat or not?'"[31]

One of the most worrisome issues is the use and disposal of toxic wastes in the *mauiladora* zones. In 1991, the National Toxics Campaign, based in Boston, issued a report of the border rivers. They tested twenty-three industrial sites and found that one-third of them were regularly discharging serious toxic wastes like xylene, methylene chloride and pentachlorophenol, all suspected of being carcinogens. They described the border area as a "two-thousand-mile Love Canal."

The U.S. General Accounting Office estimated in 1992, that of the 2,449 *maquiladoras* in the border area, around 800 generated toxic wastes. But only 446 were registered as producing such wastes. Inspections revealed that offending plants illegally discharged wastes into the atmosphere and water, inappropriately managed their wastes, and failed to comply with the Mexican requirement to export toxic material to the country of origin.

Under a joint U.S.-Mexico agreement, U.S. companies producing hazardous wastes in the *maquiladoras* are required to ship them back to the United States. But SEDUE and EPA report that they cannot account for these wastes. Only ninety-one plants have returned hazardous wastes to the United States since 1987.[32]

In January 1992, Mexican officials admitted that only around 10 percent of the hazardous wastes created in the *maquiladoras* were being disposed of according to existing regulations. This is significant. In 1990 SEDUE reported that 1,035 of the 1,850 *maquila* plants produced toxic wastes. In 1991, it reported that only 35 percent of the U.S.-owned *maquila* plants were complying with Mexican laws in their use and disposal of toxic wastes.[33]

But hazardous wastes are also being dumped in Mexico. In 1993, the U.S. legally shipped 72,000 tons of hazardous wastes to Mexico for "recycling and confinement." U.S. companies face costs from $300 to $1,000 per barrel for toxic wastes in the United States. They can dispose of the same wastes for $40 a barrel in Mexico. Trucks carry the wastes cross the border easily. Inspection is limited, and often the waste is not recycled but just dumped or stored almost anywhere.[34]

Are companies being attracted to Mexico because of the lax enforcement of environmental legislation? For many companies, there is an incentive. In 1990, the EPA estimated that U.S. firms were spending $72.5 billion on controlling pollution. David J. Molina, of New Mexico State University, surveyed the growth of nine *maquiladora* industries between 1982 and 1990. He found that there was a strong correlation between moving to Mexico and pollution abatement costs in the United States.[35]

A study of *maquiladora* industries in Tijuana, by El Colegio de la Frontera Norte, found that 10 percent of *maquila* firms admitted that tougher environmental standards in the United States were the primary factor in their decision to move to Mexico. Another 17 percent said it was an important factor.[36]

The most widely cited example is the move of furniture manufacturers from southern California to Tijuana. They were escaping regulations restricting the use of solvents and paints and requiring spray chambers to control fumes. Mexico had no standards to cover paint and solvent emissions; furthermore, workers in Mexico did not have workers compensation for toxic poisoning.[37]

Health and safety standards for workers are limited in Mexico and rarely enforced. This can also be a factor in attracting investment. An example would be GTE Corporation. Factories were shut down in New York, California, and Ontario when workers complained about cobalt dust levels, which caused Hard Metals Disease. Backed by their union, they claimed compensation. GTE was found to have violated laws and regulations. They responded by moving these operations to the Mexicali border zone.

GTE Corporation also moved an electronics plant from San Carlos, California to Albuquerque, New Mexico to take advantage of nonunion labour. But the major issue was the company's disregard of health and safety regulations. When workers won a lawsuit for health problems associated with working conditions, GTE moved the most hazardous parts of its assembly operations to the Cuidad Juárez free trade zone.[38]

Tijuana is typical of the Mexican border zone cities. It has grown dramatically since the 1970s, and the metropolitan area is now home to around one million people. When I visited the area in January 1993, it had around 550 *maquila* plants, mostly American-owned. The infrastructure has not kept up with the population growth, and there is inadequate housing, sewers, water, roads, bridges, power, and social services. Squatter settlements had filled the watershed of the Tijuana River, so when the heavy rains came that month, the floods drowned people and left thousands homeless.

One of the overcrowded settler barrios is known as Ejido Chilpancingo, close to one of Tijuana's industrial parks. Toxic wastes are dumped all over this site. Residents of the area complain of illnesses which they are certain come from the wastes. Aside from the common acute sicknesses, a high level of birth defects has been reported. Tests done on the water in a creek that runs through the area revealed levels of lead and cadmium which were several thousand times higher than the U.S. legal limits.

Sewage and toxic waste disposal is a major concern in the Tijuana-San Diego area. Prior to 1991, when San Diego began treating Tijuana's sewage, the Tijuana River polluted the San Diego area. Toxic wastes are piled up behind *maquila* plants, put in the municipal dumps, or just dumped into the river.

Throughout Mexico, industrial wastes are commonly poured down the sewer system. Tijuana residents know about the gas flames coming out of the city's sewer system and fear an explosion like that in Guadalajara in April 1992. San Diego residents worry about the toxic chemicals that flow into the Tijuana River and out to the ocean, deposited on Imperial Beach.

In 1992, the U.S. government conducted a survey of U.S. plants operating in the Tijuana area. None of them had the proper environmental permits. San Diego residents complain that the Mexican government did nothing about this.[39]

A similar situation exists 100 miles east of Tijuana, at the twin cities of Calexico, California and Mexicali, Mexico. The primary concern in this area is the New River, said to be the most polluted river in North America, and the Colorado River, whose polluted waters are used extensively to irrigate crops in the Mexicali Valley. There is wide scepticism that the federal governments of either country can solve these problems.

Mexicans insist that American plants are moving to Mexicali to avoid stricter environmental laws and enforcement in the United States. There is a fear that NAFTA will mean even more polluting plants. Americans in the area wonder about the quality of produce grown with highly polluted irrigation water, and they are also concerned about Mexican farmers' use of many pesticides which are banned in the United States. Free trade and the free market have turned the border zone into an environmental nightmare.

NAFTA, GATT and Ecology

What impact will NAFTA have on environmental standards and enforcement? The supporters of NAFTA insist that the free trade, free investment treaty will improve the situation in Mexico.

William K. Reilly, director of the EPA under George Bush, put forth the position of the U.S. government in 1991: "A free trade agreement will spur economic growth to provide further resources for the environment.

The bottom line is that only through economic growth will Mexico ever be able to address critical issues of environmental protection adequately."[40]

The anti-free trade coalitions in the United States, Canada, and Mexico pushed for tough environmental controls to be included in the agreement. All three governments strongly resisted this. Their position changed, however, when it appeared that NAFTA might not be approved by the U.S. House of Representatives. To head off the criticisms of the anti-free trade coalitions, the three governments negotiated side agreements covering environmental and labour standards issues.

However, when the U.S. Congress passed the NAFTA implementing legislation in November 1993, the side agreements were left out of the process. Clinton administration officials told wavering congressmen that the side deals were meaningless. Just days before the vote in the House of Representatives, President Clinton himself was assuring his Republican supporters that the side agreements had no teeth and were voluntary codes at best.[41]

There is good reason to believe that the governments and corporations pushing for free trade through NAFTA and the revisions to the General Agreement on Tariffs and Trade (GATT) are really interested in the *reduction* of standards. The consistent position of the Reagan, Bush and Clinton administrations has been that government standards are used as unfair nontariff barriers to trade. A few examples will clarify the argument.[42]

In order to promote recycling of waste materials, the government of Denmark passed legislation that required all beer and soft drinks to be sold in returnable containers. Other members of the European Economic Community challenged this in the European Court, arguing that the legislation was designed as a nontariff support for the domestic industry. The Court agreed. In early 1992, the U.S. beer industry charged that the government of Ontario was protecting its beer industry by levying a 10-cent deposit charge on beer cans. They argued that since most Ontario beer was sold in bottles, this was an unfair subsidy. A GATT panel agreed.

Responding to consumer pressures, the European Economic Community banned all meat that had been fed growth hormones. The U.S. and Canadian governments protested vigorously that this was an unfair trade practice, discriminating against their cattlemen who widely use growth hormones. More than any other case, this convinced the U.S. government to push for global harmonization of health and safety standards, to be administered by GATT.

When the Danish government proposed to strictly decrease the levels of emissions from automotive vehicles, the other members of the European

Economic Community objected that the new high standards would be a technical barrier to trade.

In Canada, the Non-Ferrous Metals Producers Committee has objected to federal and provincial laws which are designed to reduce emissions and improve the workplace environment in lead, zinc and copper smelters. They claim these laws constitute unfair trade practices.

The government of British Columbia dropped a provincial reforestation program because U.S. corporations objected and the U.S. government had agreed to impose a countervailing duty. B.C. feared the loss of U.S. markets for lumber exports.

Consumer groups in Canada are demanding that irradiated foods be clearly labelled, but U.S. food corporations selling irradiated foods are threatening that this would constitute an unfair barrier to trade. In Canada, pesticides and food additives are registered by the federal government according to strictly scientific criteria. If they pose a hazard to human health, or are an environmental hazard, they are rejected. The U.S. risk/benefit analysis approach balances off health risks against economic benefits. This approach is strongly supported by business interests and strongly opposed by U.S. and Canadian environmental organizations. It is feared that under the pressure of NAFTA, the U.S. standard will be forced on Canada.

In 1989, U.S. tobacco giants R. J. Reynolds, Philip Morris, and Brown and Williams (a subsidiary of British American Tobacco) asked the U.S. government to begin a complaint under GATT against the government of Thailand. Thailand prohibited imports, controlled tobacco manufacturing by a state-owned monopoly, and prohibited advertising. The companies argued that a ban on advertising would be an unfair barrier to trade because of the current market advantage held by the Thai monopoly.

Under NAFTA, the three governments may introduce "generally agreed international environmental or conservation rules or standards." But such standards must be "the least trade-restrictive necessary for securing the protection required." Article 106 prohibits regulations that might be considered "a disguised restriction on trade" or that would "otherwise nullify or impair any benefit reasonably expected to accrue to one or more of the parties, directly or indirectly, under this Agreement."

The terms of NAFTA specify that a Committee on Standards-Related Measures is to be appointed to harmonize all "safety, health and sanitary measures." There is no public involvement in this process and no democratic controls, not even by national legislatures. The standard of risk assessment will be used, including potential economic benefits, with the objective being "minimizing trade effects."

A similar process took place during the negotiations leading to the new GATT. Clayton Yeutter, Secretary of Agriculture during the Bush Administration, stated that he wanted to see GATT standards used to overturn strict U.S. state and local food safety regulations. One example he cited was a citizens' referendum in California which passed a law prohibiting the use of any carcinogenic pesticide on foods. The objective of the Bush and Clinton administrations has been to try to block individual U.S. states from adopting new strict environmental standards.[43]

In the Uruguay Round of negotiations on revisions to the GATT, the European Economic Community and the United States proposed the creation of the World Trade Organization (WTO), a new organization designed to be as powerful as the World Bank and the International Monetary Fund. It will be dominated by the industrialized countries and will have the power to enforce GATT standards and rules. As with NAFTA, important decisions are to be made behind closed doors, by non-elected bureaucrats, with no public involvement.

In North America, the large food corporations have been pushing for changes in food safety and environmental standards. Under GATT, and eventually also under NAFTA, national standards will be limited to prevailing international standards. This is a clear move towards the lowest common denominator.

Firstly, "scientific evidence" will be the only criterion for national standards which might limit imports. No social, economic, religious or cultural concerns can be considered in making such decisions. For example, Canada will not be permitted to ban milk from cows given the growth hormone BST. The ban on BST by the European Economic Community is deemed to be based on political not scientific reasons and undoubtedly will be challenged.

Secondly, standards for contaminant residues in foods will be set by the U.N. Codex Alimentarius Commission. This commission is dominated by representatives from food corporations and the agricultural industry. Tolerance levels for pesticide residues in foods is many times higher than those in Canada and the United States and Codex does not ban a number of pesticides banned in Canada and the United States. GATT can now be used by corporations to oppose national bans on production and export of these chemicals, or bans on imported food with chemical residues.[44]

Walter Russell Mead argues that GATT and NAFTA are "about more than sending First World factories into the Third World; they are about importing Third World economic pressures and social conditions into the West." Ralph Nader adds that "the Bush Agenda is to degrade existing health and safety standards to the lowest common denominator — drive our standards down to the levels of less fortunate countries."

The Mexican Action Network on Free Trade argues that the environmental provisions of NAFTA and GATT are a form of neocolonialism. The new international bureaucracies, dominated by representatives from the First World, can impose their economic policies on less developed countries like Mexico. And this is done in the name of free trade and the free market.[45]

The bureaucracies which will enforce the provisions of GATT and NAFTA will be appointed, not elected. Only the executive branch of a government can bring a case before the organizations. All the processes remain secret, carried out behind closed doors. They are not even required to publish a final report or give reasons why a decision is made. The entire process is profoundly anti-democratic, following the wishes of the large corporations.

The purpose of NAFTA and GATT is to open up all countries to the free flow of trade and investment. In the world of global free market competition, where the emphasis is on deregulation, a country whose people choose to enact and enforce environmental standards is at a disadvantage.

As Herman E. Daly of the World Bank has pointed out, the failure to regulate can be considered the equivalent of providing a subsidy. Producers are encouraged to adopt processes which pass on the costs to workers and the public at large. In addition, free water and free air are enormous public subsidies.[46]

As we can see from the *maquiladora* program, the transnational corporations have benefitted from nonregulation and have grossly polluted the environment. The cleanup of the disaster is to be paid for by the public, through the U.S. and Mexican governments.

An alternative approach to the environment and trade was put forth in 1993 by the three national coalitions opposing NAFTA. Their position was originally drafted by the Mexican environmental organizations, and then adopted by the three coalitions.

The tri-national conferences called for sustainable development, striving for the highest possible environmental and health standards, making the polluters pay for the damage they do, sanctions against persistent polluters, prohibition of the production, use and importing of hazardous products banned in North America, and recognition of the gross differences in economic development between Canada, the United States, and Mexico. Mexico must have assistance from the two First World countries in order to catch up with them.

The coalitions called for the creation of a North American Commission on Health and the Environment which would be elected and include representatives of citizens' organizations, promoting a free flow of information. NAFTA and GATT, dominated by national elites and corporations, primarily concerned with trade issues, cannot be the vehicles for solving environmental issues. As the coalitions concluded, "The neoliberal economic model of unchecked consumption is a threat because it does not recognize social and ecological limits and because it encourages a lifestyle that is unjust and irresponsible."[47]

Notes

1. Gilberto Gallopin, "Science, Technology and the Ecological Future of Latin America," *World Development*, Vol. 20, October 1992, pp. 1391-1400.

2. For a discussion of this contradiction, see Adolfo Aguilar Zinser et al, "Neoliberalismo," *El Financiero: Zona Abierta*, Vol. 1, No. 4, March 5, 1993, pp. 1-13.

3. For a description of the ecological situation in Mexico City, see Stephen P. Mumme, "Clearing the Air: Environmental Reform in Mexico," *Environment*, Vol. 33, December 1991, pp. 26-30; Stephen P. Mumme, "System Maintenance and Environment Reform in Mexico," *Latin American Perspectives*, No. 72, Winter 1992, pp. 123-143; Stephen P. Mumme and Roberto A. Sanchez, "New Directions in Mexican Environmental Policy," *Environmental Management*, Vol. 16, July-August 1992, pp. 465-474; and Miriam Alfie, "Las transformaciones de la politica gubernamental en materia ecologica," *El Cotidiano*, No. 52, January-February 1993, pp. 51-56.

4. María Eugenia Calleja, "90% de las Fábricas Contamina," *Epoca*, March 1, 1993, p. 31; Rosalba Carrasco Licea and Francisco Hernández y Puente, "La Contaminación en Cifras," *La Jornada*, April 6, 1992, p. 33.

5. Herberto Castillo, "Colapso Ecológio," *Proceso*, No. 804, March 30, 1992, pp. 34-36; Héctor Gomez Vázquez, "Invasión de Ozono," *Motivos*, No. 35, March 23, 1992, pp. 46-48.

6. Castillo, *op. cit.*

7. David Barkin, "State Control of the Environment: Politics and Degradation in Mexico," *Capitalism, Nature, Socialism*, Vol. 2, February 1991, pp. 86-108.

8. Mary E. Kelly et al, "U.S.-Mexico Free Trade Negotiations and the Environment," *Columbia Journal of World Business*, Vol. 26, Summer 1991, pp. 42-58.

9. Mumme, "System Maintenance and Environmental Reform in Mexico," *op. cit.*

10. Mumme, "Clearing the Air: Environmental Reform in Mexico," *op. cit.*

11. Mumme, "System Maintenance and Environmental Reform in Mexico," *op. cit.*, pp. 136-137.

12. Bruce Selcraig, "Up Against the Wall in Mexico," International Wildlife, Vol. 22, March-April 1992, pp. 20-25.

13. Salvador Herrera Toledano, "The Ecological Factor in NAFTA," *Business Mexico*, Vol. 2, April 1992, pp. 28-31.

14. "Rules Breached by 95% of All Factories," *Latin American Weekly Report*, October 1, 1992, p. 8.

15. Barry and Sims, *op. cit.*, pp. 48-57; Lane Simonian, "Pesticide Use In Mexico: Decades of Abuse," *Ecologist*, Vol. 18, No. 2, 1988, pp. 82-87; and Angus Wright, *The Death of Ramón González*. Austin: University of Texas Press, 1990.

16. Anne Alonzo and Edward M. Ranger, "The U.S.-Mexico Border Plan," *Business Mexico*, Vol. 2, April 1992, pp. 35-36.

17. Cited in Tom Barry and Beth Sims, *The Challenge of Cross-Border Environmentalism*. Albuquerque: Resource Center Press, 1994, pp. 26-27.

18. Ricardo Hernández and Edith Sánchez, "Environmentalists Target Mexican and U.S. Agencies," *Borderlines*, Vol. 1, July 1993, pp. 6-9.

19. Barry and Sims, *op. cit.*, p. 32.

20. Andy Pasztor, "Mexican Plants Spark Heat in U.S.," *Globe and Mail*, September 14, 1993, B-9.

21. See Barry and Sims, *op. cit.*, pp. 7-23.

22. Chris Brogan, "U.S.-Mexican Border a 'Disaster area,' Says Report," InterPress Service, July 14, 1993.

23. Kelly, *op. cit.*, p. 51.

24. "Border Incomes Must Rise to Pay for Infrastructure," *Trade News Bulletin*, Vol. 2, No. 169, September 23, 1993.

25. Edith Sánchez, "Environmentalists Target Mexican and U.S. Agencies," *BorderLines*, Vol. 1, July 1993, pp. 1, 6-9.

26. Ingrid Peritz, "Montreal Firm found Cheap Labour, Lax Rules in Maquiladoras," *Montreal Gazette*, March 16, 1992, A-1, A-7.

27. "A View from the North — of Mexico," *Multinational Monitor*, Vol. 15, January-February 1994, p. 8.

28. Cited in Barry and Sims, *op. cit.*, pp. 44, 69-60; Charles McCoy, "Study Says Firms Dump Toxic Waste At Mexican Plants," *The Wall Street Journal*, May 10, 1991, B-5.

29. James E. Garcia, "Factory Blamed for Birth Defects," *The Gazette*, October 11, 1991, D-12.

30. Linda Hosse, "NAFTA Will Fuel Mexican Woes, Study Concludes," *Globe and Mail*, March 12, 1993, A-6.

31. Selcraig, *op. cit.*, p. 24.

32. Mary E. Kelly, "The Politics of Toxic Waste," *Report on the Americas*, Vol. 26, September 1992, pp. 4-7.

33. Lourdes Cárdenas, "Generan residuos altamente tóxicos 800 maquiladoras," *La Jornada*, February 7, 1992, pp. 1, 16; and Jan Gilbreath Rich, "Bordering on Trouble," *Environmental Forum*, Vol. 8, May-June 1991, pp. 25-33;

34. Barry and Sims, *op. cit.*, pp. 57-59; and "Hazardous Waste Moves Across Border," *NAFTA Monitor*, Vol. I, No. 4, January 20, 1994.

35. Cited in Harry Browne and Beth Sims, *Runaway America*. Albuquerque: Resource Center Press, 1993, p. 44.

36. *Ibid.*, pp. 44-45; Barry and Sims, *op. cit.*, pp. 64-65.

37. Barry and Sims, *op. cit.*, pp. 67-68; Browne and Sims, *op. cit.*, pp. 45-46.

38. Barry and Sims, *op. cit.*, p. 64; Browne and Sims, *op. cit.*, pp. 38-42.

39. Kathryn Balint, "Border Dwellers Fear Renewed Flow of Tijuana Sewage," *San Diego Union-Tribune*, January 6, 1993, B-3; Tim Golden, "Hope Washed Away in Border Town,"

Globe and Mail, February 2, 1993, A-7; Joel Simon, "Will Tijuana be a Free-trade Tinderbox?" *Globe and Mail*, December 19, 1992, D-3; Paul Ganster, "Community Forum on Border Environment," *Twin Plant News*, Vol. 8, January 1993, pp. 49-51; and Gerardo Albarrán de Alba, "Empresas estadunidenses y mexicanas intoxican sin freno toda la faja fronteriza," *Proceso*, No. 800, March 2, 1992, pp. 14-17.

40. See Walter Russell Mead, "Bushism, Found," *Harper's Magazine*, Vol. 285, September 1992, pp. 37-45.

41. Lauri Henderson, "Forging a Link; Two Approaches to Integrating Trade and Environment," *Alternatives*, Vol. 20, November/December 1993, pp. 30-36; Zen Makuch, "A Critic's View of NAFTA's Environmental Side Agreement," *Alternatives*, Vol. 20, November/December 1993, p. 34; Michelle Swenarchuk, "Environment," in Duncan Cameron and Mel Watkins, eds. *Canada Under Free Trade.* Toronto: James Lorimer, 1993, pp. 196-202; and Mel Watkins, "The NAFTA Side-Deals," in Cameron and Watkins, *op. cit.*, pp. 283-286.

42. The examples are taken from Lori Wallach, "Hidden Dangers of GATT and NAFTA," in Ralph Nader et al, *The Case Against Free Trade.* San Francisco: Earth Island Press, 1993, pp. 23-64; Mark Ritchie, "GATT, Agriculture and the Environment," *Ecologist*, Vol. 20, November-December 1990, pp. 214-220; Michelle Swenarchuk, "Putting Profit Ahead of the Planet," *Action Canada Dossier*, No. 38, December 1992, pp. 24-25; and Christopher J. B. Rolfe, "Effects of NAFTA on the Environment and the Regulation of the Environment in Canada." Vancouver: West Coast Environmental Law Association, February 15, 1993, 33 pp.

43. See Mead, *op. cit.*; and Ralph Nader, "Free Trade and the Decline of Democracy," in Nader et al, *op. cit.*, pp. 1-12.

44. See Chakravarthi Raghavan, "MTO vs. GATT II: Behind a Giant's Creation," *Third World Resurgence*, No. 29/30, January-February 1993, pp. 24-30; Martin Khor Kok Peng, "The Uruguay Round and the Third World," *Ecologist*, Vol. 20, November-December 1990, pp. 208-213; and Mark Ritchie, "Agricultural Trade Liberalization," in Nader et al, *op. cit.*, pp. 163-194;

45. Mexican Action Network on Free Trade, "Environmental Problems in Relation to the Free Trade Agreement." Mexico, D.F.: Unpublished paper, March 1993, 16 pp.

46. Herman E. Daly, "From Adjustment to Sustainable Development: The Obstacle of Free Trade," in Nader et al, *op. cit.*, pp. 121-132.

47. See Alliance for Responsible Trade, Citizens Trade Campaign, Mexican Action Network on Free Trade, and the Action Canada Network. "A Just and Sustainable Development Initiative for North America," Washington, D.C., March 27, 1993; and "General Declaration from the 'Alternatives to the NAFTA and to Continental Economic Integration' Meeting," Mexico, D.F., July 11, 1993.

Chapter 12

PROMOTING THE DRUG INDUSTRY

On May 24, 1993, Cardinal Juan Jesús Posadas Ocampo arrived at the Guadalajara airport in his chauffeur-driven white Gran Marquis sedan. There was a hail of bullets from a group of men carrying AK-47 assault rifles, and the Cardinal, his driver, and five other people lay dead.

Carlos Rivera Aceves, the PRI governor of Jalisco, told the press that the Cardinal was caught in a shootout between two rival drug organizations and had been killed by mistake.

This interpretation was endorsed by Jorge Carpizo, Attorney General in President Salinas's cabinet. The official story was that the Tijuana drug organization was there to assassinate Joaquin Guzmán Loera, the recognized leader of the Sinaloa cartel.[1]

But the Mexican public was sceptical. The gunmen put their AK-47 rifles into their hand luggage and escaped on an Aeroméxico scheduled flight to Tijuana that was delayed twenty minutes so that they could get aboard. They boarded the plane without passes, no arrests were made when they arrived in Tijuana, two hours later, and they escaped. Official collusion seemed likely.

In June, the Pastoral Commission of the Roman Catholic Church in Mexico issued a letter which complained about the power and influence of the "drug-trafficking mafias which have bought or have become associated with an important number of public officials and military men."

President Salinas responded in the well-known Mexican tradition. He announced the creation of a new National Institute for Combatting Narcotrafficking (INCN). By July his administration had dismissed sixty-seven agents from the Attorney General's Office, and they even took legal action against some. The number included fifteen commanders of the Federal Judicial Police (PJF). They arrested the head of the judicial police in Jalisco, who was accused of helping the Cardinal's murderers escape. Arrest warrants were issued for the Arellano Félix brothers, leaders of the Tijuana drug organization, but they remained at large.

Juan Sandoval, the new Archbishop of Guadalajara, stated that "High ranking Attorney General Officials informed me that 40 percent of the people who work in the Attorney General's Office are not trustworthy, that they themselves don't know who is who, that is, who is a dignified, reliable agent or who is engaged in narcotrafficking. That is the reason they have not gotten to the bottom of the investigation of the assassination."

Sandoval went on to express the concern of most Mexicans: "When an operation to arrest an important drug lord gets under way, there are other agents who warn and facilitate their escape. Drug dealers have a lot of money to impede any action against them."[2]

In October 1994, an interview with Sandoval appeared in the Italian Catholic magazine, *30 Giorni*. He reported that six people had come to him with eyewitness accounts of the shooting at the airport. They insisted that there was no crossfire; it was a direct hit. The testimony came from a group of Jehovah's Witnesses who proselytize in the airport.

Sandoval said that "The eyewitnesses claimed they saw a large group of plainclothes police arrive at the airport two hours before Cardinal Posadas — as if they were waiting for him." When the Cardinal arrived, "Heavily armed gunmen went directly to his car and opened fire." When this testimony was given to then-Deputy Attorney General Mario Ruiz Massieu it was dismissed as "insufficient evidence" because the witnesses wished to keep their anonymity.[3]

Supplying the Market

Over the past decade the drug industry in Mexico has grown more powerful and its links with the government have deepened. This was dramatized in the assassinations of Cardinal Juan Jesús Posadas Ocampo, presidential candidate Luis Donaldo Colosio, and Francisco Luiz Massieu, leader of the government in the federal Chamber of Deputies. All three cases demonstrated links with the drug industry, and the government covered up and blocked a complete investigation.

The most important single industry in Mexico is the production and export of illicit drugs. The United States is the most important market for these substances, consuming an estimated 60 percent of the world's total.

Mexico, sharing a long border with the United States, is the ideal location for the production, export and shipment of these products. The move towards free trade and the linking of Mexico to the United States through NAFTA will be a boon to the industry.

The U.S. National Narcotics Intelligence Consumers Committee estimates that around 75 percent of all the marijuana imported into the United States is grown in Mexico. In the 1970s, when the U.S. government put pressure on Turkey to shut down its heroin industry, poppy cultivation shifted to Mexico. It is now estimated that around 35 percent of all the heroin consumed in the United States comes from Mexico.

While coca plants for cocaine are not grown in Mexico, U.S. government officials argue that over half of the imports go through Mexico. The role of Mexico in the shipment of cocaine increased dramatically after 1981, when Ronald Reagan created the South Florida Task Force to attempt to cut off the Caribbean-Florida route.[4]

In 1986, Ronald Reagan proclaimed an intensified "war on drugs." Like previous U.S. attempts to deal with the issue of drug dependency, it focused on trying to cut off the supply at the source, rather than looking at why the demand had become so great. Inevitably, the campaign has failed, because when the market is there and enormous amounts of money can be made, the suppliers will find a way to deliver the goods.

While most of the profits from the illicit drug industry are made in distribution in the United States, large sums of money are still made at the level of production and transportation. The foreign exchange earned by Mexico through these activities is estimated to exceed that earned by oil exports. The U.S. government estimated that for 1988, drugs accounted for around 20 percent of all of Mexico's export earnings.[5]

In 1988, the U.S. Department of State estimated that the value of the illicit drugs to Mexico was between $2.2 and $6.8 billion. In 1990, the Mexican National Program for Drug Control (PNCD) reported that the revenues from the drug trade were $41 billion, the equivalent of 10.3 percent of the gross domestic product.[6]

It is hard to determine accurately the value and volume of the drug industry in Mexico. For example, in 1985, the U.S. Bureau of International Narcotics Monitoring estimated that Mexico was producing only 4,500 tonnes of marijuana per year.

Yet in early November 1984, Mexican enforcement officials raided marijuana plantations in the state of Chihuahua. They seized 10,000 tonnes of marijuana and forty-five trucks with 30-tonne capacity, some of them loaded and ready to head for the U.S. border. This was the largest seizure of illicit drugs this century. U.S. official, Jon R. Thomas, said that "The amount was staggering. We have been seriously underestimating drug production around the world, as well as our estimates of the number of people who use heroin, cocaine and other drugs, too."[7]

Mexicans have always been in the business of supplying illicit drugs for the U.S. market. There is only a very small market for these drugs in Mexico. The industry took off during the economic collapse of the 1980s; with growing unemployment and falling incomes, drug production and export became the most important industry in the "informal economy." Farmers who earned around $400 a year for growing a hectare of the staple crops of corn or beans could earn between $2,000 and $4,000 a year growing a hectare of marijuana.[8]

Rosa del Olmo, of the Central University of Venezuela, argues that the U.S. government's emphasis on terms like "narcotrafficking," "organized crime," the "Mafia," or the "Medellin Cartel" is a way of stereotyping the industry which identifies "the problem of domestic consumption with an 'external enemy' outside U.S. society."[9]

The U.S. government has provided the Mexican government with hundreds of millions of dollars worth of equipment and assistance in the war on drugs. In the 1970s, the Mexican government began Operation Condor, aerial chemical defoliation of marijuana and poppy plants. The amount of drugs seized by both governments has steadily increased over the years, but there has been no reduction in the amount which has entered the American market.

U.S. government aid to Mexico comes through the Bureau of International Narcotics Matters of the State Department, the Drug Enforcement Agency, the Central Intelligence Agency, the Federal Bureau of Investigation and the Agency for International Development. Recently, the emphasis has been on airborne surveillance and interdiction of drug shipments.

In response, producers have become more sophisticated. As in Canada and the United States, horticulturalists developed plants with higher potency and better techniques for hiding their operations.

The transporters introduced new techniques for smuggling: special compartments in containerized shipments, false bottoms in crates of fruits and vegetables, and compartments in boxcars and fuel tanks of trucks. With increased high-tech surveillance, there are fewer flights across the U.S. border. Instead, illicit drugs are smuggled across the border in vehicles and by individual "mules" in remote areas. With the increased trade between the two countries, under the NAFTA, smuggling will undoubtedly become easier.[10]

Profits from the drug trade are enormous. U.S. dollars are very important to the regional economies in Mexico, and it is not surprising to find that the growing of the crops takes place in the poorer areas of southern Mexico, among the people hit hardest by the structural adjustment programs and neoliberal economic policies.

Beth Sims of the Resource Center for Inter-Hemispheric Education in Albuquerque, New Mexico, notes that the drug trade is also important to particular areas of the United States. She states, "In some communities the drug trade occupies wide sectors of the population, leaving visible marks on the economy." Those at the top of the business are identified by their huge mansions, from Starr County, Texas to posh La Jolla near San Diego. A 1990 study of Douglas, Arizona concluded that 30 to 60 percent of the town's economy was based on the drug trade.[11]

Money laundering has also become a very important business. In Mexico, families in the drug industry invest heavily in land, tourist hotels, restaurants, movie theatres, and shopping centres. Mexican economists have pointed out that the privatization of state-owned enterprises by the administration of Carlos Salinas provided legitimate investment opportunities for hundreds of millions of dollars made in the drug trade. In May 1995, the U.S. Federal Bureau of Investigation provided the Mexican government with its own studies showing the links between drug money laundering and top Mexican businessmen.[12]

In Mexico, it is widely known that the drug barons have heavily invested in the tourist industry. This type of business operation has provided an easy method of laundering U.S. cash. All a business needs to do is inflate the number of customers.

The accumulation of large amounts of U.S. currency in relatively small notes has been a problem for the industry. Beginning around the mid-1980s, the U.S. government shifted its control effort to making it more difficult to launder cash. U.S. banking legislation and supervision was stiffened, and pressure was put on other countries.

David Andelman, Washington correspondent for CNBC, reports that this has paid off: "The cost of laundering money has risen from six percent to a maximum of 26 percent for full-service laundering." Nevertheless, he concludes that "Money launderers have been finding, more quickly than their pursuers can detect, new countries and a panoply of innovative, if often expensive, techniques." In addition, there are a number of countries "where bank secrecy is still marketed as a service."[13]

The importance of the drug money to poor countries is stressed by Peter Andreas of Cornell University. Despite pressure from the U.S. government, Latin American countries have chosen to pursue their own interests. The governments of Bolivia, Peru and Colombia have actually loosened their disclosure requirements for cash deposits; banks welcome cash with no questions asked. The Fujimori government in Peru "has given every incentive for drug dollars to flow into the country's financial institutions."[14]

Government policies aid the process: loose foreign exchange controls, strict bank-secrecy laws, and financial deregulation. Cash is moved around through manipulated accounting techniques. Andreas argues, "From Chile to Panama to many Caribbean islands, this basically translates into a legal-ized form of drug money laundering."

Stephen Flynn of the Brookings Institute agrees. NAFTA and other free market/free trade arrangements are making it easier to launder money. In 1993, a report prepared by the U.S. embassy in Mexico City con-cluded that drug traffickers were investing in factories, warehouses and trucking firms in Mexico, particularly in the *maquiladora* free trade zones near the border. NAFTA will make it easier for these operations to expand their exports to the United States.

A year after this report, the National Drug Intelligence Estimate pre-pared by the RCMP concluded that NAFTA would make it much harder for enforcement officials to track drug-laundered money. Inspector Tim Kil-lam, of the anti-drug profiteering squad, said that "Free trade would cut the paper trail needed to detect money laundering." Furthermore, an in-creased volume of goods going across the border would make detection much more difficult.[15]

The U.S. government's war on drugs has emphasized the countries in the Andean highlands. During the administrations of George Bush and Bill Clinton, the U.S. government and the mass media have generally played down the growth and importance of the industry in Mexico. As Rosa del Olmo argues, Mexico is treated differently, because of its "status as a strate-gic ally of the United States." The most important goal of U.S. policy is to maintain a stable pro-American government in Mexico. That inevitably means support for the one-party state and the governing Institutional Revo-lutionary Party (PRI).[16]

President Carlos Salinas (1988-1994) declared the illicit drug industry a threat to national security and over the years made a number of changes to how the control effort was organized. The U.S. government also increased its military aid to Mexico. But, as María Celia Toro of El Colegio de Mexico has pointed out, the campaign has demonstrated "the impossibility of signifi-cantly reducing the drug market through current enforcement policies."[17]

Washington consciously downplayed the role of Mexico in the supply-ing of illicit drugs during the administration of Carlos Salinas. The U.S. government and big business strongly supported his administration be-cause of its commitment to free market policies, free trade, and closer eco-nomic and political links to the United States.

Thus, during the negotiations over NAFTA, the issue all but disap-peared from the mass media, and it was deliberately left out of all aspects of the treaty. Gary Hufbauer, of the Institute for International Economics in Washington, argues that the issue was "too hot to handle."[18]

Rosa del Olmo concludes that in the free trade, free market model of development pushed by the U.S. government and recent Mexican governments, "An economy's driving force is consumption, so attacking production will not eliminate the drug phenomenon." The new economy stresses deregulation and the removal of government controls on business operations. In this general atmosphere of laissez faire, it is unlikely that the government will succeed in singling out one industry for special treatment.[19]

Drugs and Politics

The Mexican political system is ideally suited for the illicit drug industry. To begin with, enormous political power is concentrated in the office of the president. The legislature merely rubber stamps budgets and legislation put forward by the president. There is no such thing as an independent judiciary. Judicial appointments are made on a patronage basis. The Supreme Court has never declared any action by the president to be unconstitutional. The state and local governments receive most of their revenues from the central government.

Secondly, Mexico is a one-party state. The PRI has ruled in one form or another, since 1929, with virtually no opposition. While the country is governed by an oligarchy of well-off technocrats, they depend on the local political machine to provide majority votes in national, state, and local elections. Historically, the president, as the head of the PRI, names all PRI candidates for the Senate, the Chamber of Deputies, the state governors, and even important municipal officials.

Thirdly, almost all bureaucratic positions with the government are filled by patronage. Government jobs are even sold, and the price paid is determined by the ability to obtain "fees" while in office. While there is a law that requires competitive bidding for government contracts, companies with ties to the PRI seem to get most of the contracts.

As Alan Riding put it, in his widely-read book on Mexico, *Distant Neighbors*, patronage is "both the glue that holds the Mexican system together and the oil that makes it work." This ranges from *la mordida* (the bite), the bribe paid to local officials, to large scale kickbacks for contracts.[20]

In a country with very high unemployment and underemployment, where 50 percent of the population have incomes below the official poverty line, and where there are enormous disparities in income and wealth, allegiance to the ruling PRI has clear benefits. Mexico is still a less developed country when measured against the United States or Canada. People who work as government employees, police officers, or in the military receive very low salaries, which make them open to bribery.

Illicit drugs are a very important part of the Mexican economy precisely because they are illegal. In *Beyond the War on Drugs*, Steven Wisotsky argues that government prohibition produces "just enough pressure to inflate the price of cocaine from $2 to $100 per gram, but not enough to keep the product from the market." From the Mexican perspective, this is the ideal situation.[21]

The history of the illicit drug industry demonstrates that it is not possible to cut off production at the source. When one country cracks down, the industry just moves to another. Throughout the world, where poverty and unemployment are high, the illicit drug industry is important. Also, wherever the industry operates, there is the issue of "corruption."

Peter Andreas stresses that the drug industry must pay the "informal tax," a tax on doing business. The tax rate depends on the degree of government enforcement of anti-drug laws, and is collected by politicians and local drug enforcement officials. For example, the U.S. Government Accounting Office reports that since the military invasion of Panama removed Manuel Noriega as president, that country has become a preferred corridor to the United States because the informal tax has dropped significantly.[22]

The traditional Mexican system of drug production and marketing has been described by Peter Lupsha, professor of political science at the University of New Mexico. On the local level, there is La Plaza, a system for determining who controls the central plaza that characterizes all Mexican towns. The local powers are the police, the military, the political bosses or powerful businessmen or ranchers. In every area there is a recognized political power structure. Inevitably, they are linked to the PRI, which has until recently controlled all state and local governments.[23]

Those who are in the business of producing and exporting illicit drugs are required to get official approval from the local bosses and pay them the informal tax. Invariably, they will also have to pay an additional tax to the state and the federal police.

As Lupsha points out, buying permission to operate is not a guarantee against any problems. Every six years, the president changes in Mexico, and a new group of powerful office holders takes over. Then again, a rival producer may pay a higher tax and get official sanction.

But if a local producer happens to lose his permit, he does not expect to be jailed. With the payment of bribes, he can obtain an *amparo*, a writ from the courts which holds that his constitutional rights have been violated. This allows him freedom to move or change his operation.

A 1989 report to the U.S. Congress concluded that "Mexicans would rather destroy plants than catch people." It is the small fry who most commonly are arrested and jailed. When high-level officials are exposed, and there is pressure to remove them from office, the political tradition in Mexico is that the president moves them to another job, in another area. Often federal officials are moved to state-level jobs.[24]

While North Americans see this system as "corruption," in Mexico it is generally viewed as a natural part of the patronage system. While there are laws against the drug industry, the system of the informal business tax is deeply entrenched. When officials accept bribes, there is no victim. Producers and distributors are in no position to complain.

The U.S. war on drugs has been ideal for Mexico. This most important single industry could continue to grow and produce big profits and needed foreign exchange. Those outside the La Plaza loop are raided, arrested, and their crops seized. The PRI-controlled mass media runs stories on the success of the war on drugs, and the federal government produces photographs and tonnage figures of seized drugs to please the U.S. government.

In the 1970s and 1980s the illicit drug industry grew significantly, and important families headed organizations commonly referred to as "cartels." In some cases they were the most powerful political figures in large areas — even states. In their study of the Mexican-U.S. drug issue in the 1980s, Peter Reuter and David Ronfeldt of the Rand Corporation, conclude that there were "about 200 drug trafficking organizations in Mexico." But they argue that only around a half dozen or so were major operations. At this time federal enforcement authorities became deeply involved in the system of the informal tax.[25]

In the 1970s, the Federal Security Directorate (DFS) was primarily in charge of drug enforcement. It was headed by Javier García Paniagua and his sub-director, Miguel Nazar Haro. The DFS operated as the national political police, under the Secretary of Government, the most important position in the president's cabinet.

Nazar Haro gained fame in Mexico as the organizer of the White Brigade of the DFS, which in the 1970s killed, disappeared and tortured hundreds of Mexicans who were members of radical political organizations. Those in the top levels of the DFS became rich from payments from the large drug operators.

One example will illustrate the point. In the 1980s, the DFS owned 600 tanker trucks which were supposedly used to transport natural gas to the United States. The tanker trucks were usually filled with marijuana when they crossed the border. Jonathan Marshall reports that, in 1988, ten to twelve trucks a day would cross the border, headed for Los Angeles and Phoenix. The DFS bribed Mexican and U.S. officials $50,000 for every truck which crossed the border.[26]

At the other end of the scale, Reuter and Ronfeldt report that "Gangs of highway patrolmen have been caught smuggling marijuana into the United States over routes that they were patrolling." They argue that the "intractability" of drug trafficking has been compounded by a chain of lower-ranking officers who have created "a system of organized crime co-opted by, and loyal to, the very officials trusted to root out the smugglers."[27]

The Mexican military has been deeply involved in drug law enforcement. In the 1980s, around one-quarter of its personnel were involved in this activity, much of it in crop eradication. However, they have a reputation for profiting from the drug industry.

The other main organization concerned with enforcing drug laws is the Federal Judicial Police (PJF). While this organization has had the primary responsibility for enforcing drug laws, it has always been closely linked to the industry itself.

For example, in 1982, President Miguel de la Madrid appointed Manuel Ibarra Herrera to head the PJF. Ibarra's brother Antonio was involved in laundering drug money in Tijuana. In turn, Ibarra named his cousin, Miguel Aldana Ibarra, to be head of INTERPOL in Mexico and conduct Operacion Pacifico against the industry on the west coast. But, in 1984, these officials and Javier García Paniagua met with representatives of the Guadalajara organization to jointly work out plans on how to sidetrack the efforts of the U.S. Drug Enforcement Agency.[28]

In 1985, Enrique Camarena, a U.S. DEA agent operating in Mexico, was kidnapped, tortured and murdered by Guadalajara drug lords. The legislative hearings that followed revealed the degree to which they were supported by former DFS head José Antonio Zorilla Perez, Manuel Ibarra Herrera, and Miguel Albana Ibarra. Pressure from the U.S. government forced President de la Madrid to abolish the DFS.[29]

The U.S. government continued to press the case. In January 1993, evidence was presented at a federal trial implicating high-ranking PRI officials: Manuel Bartlett Díaz, a former Secretary of Government, Juan Arevalo Gardoqui, a former Secretary of Defence, and Enrique Alvarez del Castillo, former Attorney General and governor of Jalisco.

Javier García Paniagua, formerly head of the DFS, became wealthy by protecting leading drug traffickers. The DFS had close links to the Guadalajara cartel, and this was widely known in Mexico. Yet President Carlos Salinas appointed him chief of police to Mexico City in 1989.

Enrique Alvarez del Castillo was governor of Jalisco while the Guadala-jara organization was expanding. U.S. officials had accused him of refusing to round up those involved in the murder of DEA agent Camarena. Yet when Carlos Salinas named his first cabinet in 1989, Alvarez was appointed Attorney General, in charge of drug enforcement!

Despite the co-operation of President Salinas with the U.S. government in the war on drugs, the industry is as prosperous as ever. Salinas removed thousands of police from office, but others took their places. The problem is not corrupt individuals but the importance of the trade and the ability of of-fice holders at all levels to make large sums of money from the trade.

During the Salinas period (1988-94) the Mexican government concen-trated its anti-drug enforcement on those involved in the cocaine transpor-tation business. In most cases this involved people from Colombia. There was much less effort made to stop the production and transportation of Mexican-grown marijuana and heroin.[30]

In one highly publicized incident in November 1991, Colombian co-caine transporters were landing a load at Tlalixcoyan, near Veracruz. The aircraft, tracked by U.S. surveillance, was intercepted by agents from the PJF. However, the landing strip and the operation was being guarded by 100 soldiers from the Mexican Army. In the resulting shootout, which lasted three hours, seven PJF officers were killed. The local areas com-mander, General Alfredo Moran Acevedo, had been warned of the coming raid, but he did not restrain his soldiers. Those involved in this smuggling case escaped.[31]

Terry Poppa's book, *Drug Lord: the Life and Death of a Mexican Kingpin*, provides a good look at how the industry operates. Pablo Acosta was a local drug operator in the Big Bend area of Chihuahua, south of Texas. He paid the PJF $60,000 a month for protection. But following a series of articles in the *El Paso Herald*, both the Mexican and American governments felt it was necessary to hunt him down. He died in a shootout with the PJF. But by the summer of 1990, uniformed Mexican military personnel and police were seen loading illicit cargo into trucks and cars heading for the U.S. border at Ojinaga.[32]

The enforcement of drug laws in Mexico has been complicated by the U.S. government's war against left-wing political movements and govern-ments. The U.S. Central Intelligence Agency has had close ties with the U.S. DEA operating in Mexico, has used Mexican drug dealers in their op-erations, and has provided some support against prosecution.[33]

For example, Alberto Sicilia Falcon, an anti-Castro Cuban exile, was at the top of the drug organization in Tijuana in the 1970s. He had formed close ties with important PRI officials. When arrested he revealed that he had been recruited and trained by the CIA in the war against Castro. He helped the CIA move weapons to right-wing organizations in Latin America. Sicilia also was protected by Miguel Nazar Haro, head of the DFS.

Miguel Félix Gallardo, the head of the huge drug operation based in Guadalajara, provided financial and other support to the Contras in their war against the Sandinista government in Nicaragua. In return, his drug smuggling activities were overlooked.

The Zambada family were also kingpins in the Guadalajara drug operation. They were anti-Castro Cuban exiles. They supplied drugs to the Cuban Nationalist Movement, an organization linked to the Cuban National Liberation Front (CORU), which was responsible for the murder of Orlando Letelier, the Chilean ambassador to the United States.

Nazar Haro, head of the DFS between 1977 and 1982, was deeply involved in the war of subversion. He was the key link between the CIA, the anti-Castro Cuban organizations operating in Mexico, and the drug business.

The FBI revealed that Nazar was the central figure in a ring of DFS officers that had smuggled 4,000 stolen cars from California to Mexico. The FBI and the CIA in Mexico pressed Washington not to lay charges. Elaine Shannon reports that when U.S. Associate Attorney General Lowell Jensen blocked Nazar's indictment, U.S. Attorney William Kennedy went public on the role of the CIA in obstructing justice, and he was fired.[34]

Jonathan Marshall asks, "Why do some drug traffickers prosper and grow powerful while others languish behind bars?" And he provides the answer: "This depends less on the relative organizational skill, financial sophistication or ruthlessness than on the level of political protection."[35]

It is widely recognized that the Guadalajara drug operation is the biggest in Mexico. It has remained relatively immune to government harassment because of its close ties to the PRI, Mexican drug enforcement officials, and the CIA.

The connections between the drug industry, other business interests, enforcement officials, and politicians continued through the Salinas presidency. A few examples from 1994 will illustrate the point.

Guillermo González Calderoni formerly worked on drug enforcement with the PJF. Today, he is reported to be worth around $400 million and spends most of his time at his estate in Texas. He was the right-hand man to Javier Coello Trejo, who had been in charge of narcotics control in the Attorney General's Office (PGR). González made his money in association with Juan García Abrego, who heads the so-called Gulf Coast Drug cartel.

In 1988, González worked on the presidential campaign of Carlos Salinas, tapping the telephones of his major opponent, Cuauhtémoc Cárdenas. He was named by Eduardo Valle, former special assistant to the Attorney General, as one of the top police officials directly involved in the drug industry. Because of the publicity, an extradition request was made to the U.S. government. On December 2, 1994, González appeared in a Texas court, put up one million dollars in a cash bail bond, and disappeared.[36]

In 1994, Colombian cocaine producers began to fly Boeing 727s into Mexico. Each aircraft could carry six tons of cocaine. The wholesale value of one load would be about $120 million. They are much faster than the Cessnas used by Mexican drug enforcement officials and impossible to catch.

In May of that year, U.S. and Mexican enforcement officials tracked one aircraft which landed at an airfield near Lagos de Moreno, in the state of Jalisco. Tim Golden of *The New York Times* reported that suspicions were raised because of the links of "a rapidly expanding Mexican airline" to the airfield.

The airfield is the home of Taesa Airlines, founded by Carlos Hank Rohn, the eldest son and business manager of Carlos Hank González, powerful PRI politician, Minister of Agriculture under President Salinas, and manager of the presidential campaign of Ernesto Zedillo. Christopher Whalen, who publishes *Mexico Report*, insists that Hank González "is one of the biggest money launderers in the country." Businessmen are the main drug money launderers in Mexico. Hank González has "billions of dollars in visible net worth — airstrips, ranches, aircraft, real estate holdings, and bank accounts all over the world."[37]

Jorge Hank Rhon, another son, has major real estate holdings in the Tijuana area, and owns the Agua Caliente race track and 10 major betting operations throughout Mexico. Hank Rhon's personal bodyguard was one of the two people convicted of killing Hector Félix Miranda, reporter for the Tijuana daily *Zeta*, who had exposed illegal activities at the race track. Eduardo Valle has reported that Jorge Hank Rhon and Marceline Buerrero, an associate of Juan García Abrego, are involved in land purchases around the popular resort at Cancun.

Shortly after the August election, the Mexican government revealed that the financial empire of Grupo Financiero Cremi-Union, owned by Carlos Cabal Peniche, had collapsed. Cabal was originally based in banana and citrus plantations in the state of Tabasco but had developed wide-ranging business interests, including part of the Del Monte food conglomerate.

Cabal is a friend and associate of former President Carlos Salinas, assassinated PRI presidential candidate Luis Donaldo Colosio, as well as the new president, Ernesto Zedillo. In 1991, Cabal bought the state-owned Banco BCH bank. Press reports say his assets grew to over $2 billion by 1994. The bank collapsed and was taken over by the state after $700 million were lent to Cabal in "improper loans."

But the Tabasco entrepreneur was also involved in running drugs through his export businesses, and laundering money. Trucks carrying Cabal's bananas have been caught transporting cocaine. He had been named in several criminal investigations, including the Bank of Commerce & Credit International (BCII) scandal. He fled the country, disappeared, and remains at large.[39]

President Carlos Salinas declared his own war on drugs in early 1989. During his administration, co-operation with American enforcement agencies greatly improved. The U.S. government increased its financial assistance to Mexico to enhance drug enforcement activities. But the production and transport of illicit drugs to the United States continued to grow to meet the market demand, and ties between the industry, PRI politicians, and government officials continued as in the past.

Abusing Human Rights

Pressure by the U.S. government on the Mexican government to control illegal drug production and export has opened the door to extensive human rights abuses. In the war on drugs, Mexican enforcement police and the military have been given a free hand to do whatever they want. As the human rights organizations in Mexico stress, there is little hope for curtailing these abusive practices as long as there is almost total impunity extended to those in positions of power.

The abuse of human rights dramatically increased during the tenure of General Javier Coello Trejo as Deputy Attorney General, in charge of the anti-narcotics division of the Federal Judicial Police (PJF). As Amnesty International has pointed out, in the hundreds of reports of torture, the forces most frequently cited are the Federal Judicial Police and the various state judicial polices.

In September 1990, human rights organizations in Mexico intensified their criticism of violations of human rights by the federal narcotics officers under the command of Coello Trejo. He responded by asserting that "Drug wars had to be fought with an iron fist," and that when they were caught, the accused could not be "collared with caresses."[40]

As a result of the bad publicity, President Salinas removed Coello Trejo from office in October 1990. But he was not charged with any offenses. He was *promoted* to head the federal Department of Consumer Protection. This prompted Mexican businessmen to say, "Now we're going to get tortured if we raise prices!"[41]

The removal of Coello Trejo from his position as director of the War on Drugs program, was lamented by the U.S. government. They had repeatedly praised him for his efforts. One U.S. official was quoted as saying "I think the human rights policy is going to diminish effectiveness at the street level ... You have to treat suspects like you do in the United States now, which means they have all the leeway in the world to say nothing. Investigations will go more slowly."[42]

Yet the 1990 U.S. State Department *Country Reports on Human Rights Practices* noted that detainees in Mexico were often abused and tortured by authorities, and identified the PJF as the main offender.[43]

Amnesty International's 1991 report on Mexico concludes that the PJF, particularly, the anti-narcotics investigation branch, "most consistently have been held responsible for human rights abuses including illegal detention, ill-treatment, torture, arbitrary killings and extrajudicial executions as well as harassment and extortion directed at detainees." They add that "These abuses are widespread and well-documented yet their perpetrators appear to be largely immune from investigation or prosecution."[44]

One well publicized case was taken to President Salinas's National Commission on Human Rights (CNDH). In January 1990, in Ciudad Juárez, Chihuahua, the PJF arrested Hector Ignacio Quijano and Sergio Maximo Quijano in connection with a drug investigation. The next day their father was arrested in Mexico City in the bar he ran. Shortly thereafter another son, Francisco Flavio Quijano, a former police officer, was confronted by unidentified PJF officers when he went to visit his father. The officers, in plain clothes, stopped him at gunpoint. Fearing for his life, he snatched the pistol from one of the officers, and a gun battle resulted in which two PJF officers were killed. The son escaped.

The following day, fifty PJF officers with helicopters surrounded the Quijano house in Ojo de Agua, Mexico State. Francisco was not there, but two of his brothers were. Jaime Mauro Quijano and Erik Dante Quijano came out of the house unarmed with their hands up. They were both shot on the spot — after having been taken into custody by the PJF. The house was raided and everyone was arrested. The PJF then took Hector Ignacio Quijano into the house and shot him as well.

The father, Francisco Quijano, made formal complaints to the government and the CNDH over the murder of his three sons. In March 1991 he "disappeared" and his body was later found. The case was taken to the CNDH, which recommended that the Attorney General of the Republic conduct a full investigation and suspend the police officers involved. The Salinas administration took no action.[45]

In the Mexican war on drugs, the enforcers have commonly been linked to the drug business itself. For example, in September 1990, the PJF engaged in a shootout with state and municipal police in Culiacan, Sinaloa, a centre of drug production and trafficking. The commander of the State Judicial Police and four others were injured. The local authorities were trying to catch Luis Hector "el Güero" Palma, a big drug trafficker and a suspect in the murder of human rights lawyer, Norma Corona Sapien. Local authorities insisted that the PJF participated in the shootout in order to protect Palma.

Corona had been assassinated in Culiacan, in May 1990, while investigating the deaths of a Mexican lawyer and three Venezuelans, who had been tortured and murdered by the PJF. It is widely believed that Corona was killed because during her investigation she discovered the complicity of the PJF in drug trafficking.[46]

One drug story which made the American press broke in May 1991, when violence erupted in the Centro de Readaptacion Social (CERESO), a prison in Matamoros, Tamaulipas, across the border from Brownsville, Texas. A gun battle between two gangs in the jail resulted in eighteen deaths and eight wounded.

The conflict centred around Oliverio Chavez Araujo, an inmate with close ties to the Medellin Drug Cartel. He had been given an eight-year sentence. He had a lavish cell, ran his drug operation out of the prison, provided food and other necessities to inmates, and paid for the upkeep of the jail. He had used his money and influence to have the PRI governor name a friend director of the prison. Within the prison he had seventy fully-armed inmates as his bodyguards. The prison and local police also supported him, reportedly because of regular payoffs.

In this case, the anti-narcotics division of the PJF intervened and prevailed. Rather than storm the prison and risk getting shot, they chose another path of action. They abducted one of Chavez's close friends, Jesús Botero, his wife Judith, and their lawyer, Dolores Mendoza. Their dead, handcuffed bodies were found five days later. One week later Chavez's lawyer, Francisco Camacho Guzmán, was abducted by unknown armed men and later found dead. Chavez capitulated.[47]

Everyone in Mexico fears the Federal Judicial Police. They know that being picked up for questioning and taken to the police station means that they are likely to suffer verbal and physical abuse. This is a product of the war on drugs.

Jorge Carpizo, the first president of the National Human Rights Commission, acknowledged this problem. He remarked that police officers "know that in most cases, even when they exceed themselves to the point of homicide, they won't be punished because their chiefs will defend or cover up for them."[48]

Murder in the Official Family

Events in 1994 demonstrated how deeply the members of the ruling PRI were involved in the drug industry, including the laundering of money. The political fallout from the assassination of people in high places suggests that the total impunity given to high government officials may be coming to an end.

The Tijuana drug organization, headed by the four Arellano Félix brothers, has had strong links with the PRI on the state and municipal level. This cosy relationship was threatened, in 1989, when President Carlos Salinas removed Governor Xicoténcatl Leyva from office. In the 1988 presidential election, Leyva had allowed Cuauhtémoc Cárdenas to win the state of Baja California Norte. The task of removing the governor from office went to Luis Donaldo Colosio, then president of the PRI.

In the July 1989 election for governor of Baja California Norte, the PRI had appointed Margarita Ortega to be the PRI candidate, over the strong opposition of the Leyva organization. Furthermore, the Salinas administration decided to allow the PAN the electoral victory. This was announced by Luis Donaldo Colosio, President of the PRI; the state and local PRI in Baja California Norte angrily denounced Colosio.

Five years later, on March 23, 1994, Colosio flew into Tijuana as the PRI candidate for the presidency. It is widely recognized that for a long time the State Judicial Police and the police of Tijuana had been in the pay of the major drug organizations. In early March, just a few weeks before Colosio's visit, there was a shootout between the State Judicial Police and the PJF in downtown Tijuana, and five people had been killed.[49]

Colosio's campaign caravan moved to Lomas Taurinas, a shanty-town colony noted for its involvement in the trade in drugs and guns. Over 3,000 people turned out to hear the candidate's speech. Security for the event had been delegated to the local PRI organization. They chose people from the TUCAN group, a militant PRI organization formed to harass the PAN; other federal security police were also present. The Tijuana municipal police had been excluded from the event, because the Mayor and the Chief of Police were members of the PAN. However, they were at the rally, hanging back from the crowd.

As Colosio and his bodyguards moved up the hill, he was shot in the head from the right and in the body from the left. Mario Aburto Rinconada, a young man from Michoacán, was arrested for the shooting, after being attacked and beaten by the crowd. Vincent Mayoral, one of the TUCAN guards, was also taken. He was a former head of the State Judicial Police.

The third man seized was José Antonio Sánchez Ortega, a member of the Centre for Investigation and National Security (CISEN), a secret police organization. But he was captured by the Tijuana municipal police as he was running up the hill to escape. His shirt was covered with Colosio's blood, and he tested positive in a paraffin test, revealing that he had recently fired a gun. Late that night, the PJF appeared at the Tijuana police station, took Sánchez away, and he disappeared.

The Salinas administration proclaimed that there had been a lone gunman and that they had him in jail. A public opinion poll in *La Reforma* found that 70 percent of Mexicans had no confidence in any government investigation and that 71 percent believed that the PRI was behind the assassination.

President Salinas appointed Miguel Montes, a PRI loyalist, as a special prosecutor to investigate the assassination. In 1988, Montes had served as chairman of the electoral college that had ratified Salinas's "victory" in the great presidential election fraud. He had been rewarded with a seat on the Supreme Court.

Public suspicion of a conspiracy was validated when a home video revealed how the TUCAN security team had cut Colosio off from his bodyguards and opened a lane for the main assassin, Aburto. Seven members of the TUCAN team were arrested and charged with conspiracy in the murder.[50]

One of those arrested was José Rodolfo Rivapalacio, a former state judicial investigator known to human rights activists as a torturer. He was head of security for the PRI in Tijuana and was in charge of putting together the security team for the Colosio visit. A number of the people he hired had previously served as security for PRI governor, Leyva.

On April 4, 1994, Miguel Montes held a press conference in Mexico City to announce that he had concluded that at least seven people had been involved in a conspiracy to kill Colosio. Other government officials gave detailed descriptions of the movements of those who had been arrested.

The tune soon changed. One by one those arrested were released and on June 3, Montes released his report insisting that a lone gunman had done the killing. He presented his final report on July 12. No one believed Montes. Antonio Sánchez Díaz de Rivera, president of the Confederation of Business Owners, said "It would seem that the next time we see Special Investigator Montes on television, he's going to tell us that the death of Colosio was a suicide."

Federal authorities also released Sánchez Ortega. He claimed he had not fired a gun in two years and that the blood on his shirt was from having helped carry the wounded Colosio. However, videos and photos do not show him near Colosio. But photos do show him right next to Mario Aburto.

Aburto's family fled to the United States, fearing assassination. Once there, they told reporters they had seen Mario with four of the suspects arrested in the conspiracy, including Sánchez Ortega.

Meanwhile, outside the PRI there was another investigation underway, headed by Frederico Benítez, Chief of Police for Tijuana. His men had been the ones to grab Sánchez Ortega, having combed the field and found the only shell. But though the two bullets held by the PJF "disappeared," city police had seen the PJF find, and take, a second .38 pistol from the ground. There were two wounds on Colosio's body, one from each side. Benítez concluded that there had to be two gunmen involved.[51]

On April 28, Benítez was interviewed in his office by Tod Robberson of *The Washington Post*. When he unlocked his desk drawer to take out his files, he found that they had been stolen. The next evening, as Benítez and his bodyguard were returning from the airport, two men in separate vehicles blasted them with AK-47s.

One month later, government officials announced that drug traffickers had killed Benítez and closed the case. With the presidential campaign building over the summer, the murder cases dropped out of the news. But not for long.

Eduardo Valle was a senior aide to the Attorney General, working on the narcotics industry. Following the assassination of Colosio, he fled to the United States, taking with him important documents. On August 25, he met with Mexican congressmen and officials behind closed doors in the Mexican Embassy in Washington, D.C. In a formal statement made at the hearing, Valle released information linking high officials of the government to several drug organizations in Mexico. He also argued that these drug lords and PRI officials were involved in the assassination of Colosio.[52]

In a statement made to reporters, Valle said he would provide evidence linking officials in the pay of Juan García Abrego to the assassination of Colosio. García is recognized as the leader of the so-called Gulf Coast Cartel, which ships cocaine from Colombia through Mexico into the United States.

Valle also charged that two key officials in the Salinas government had ties to the important drug organizations: José Cordoba Montoya, former chief adviser to the president, who had been shipped off to Washington as ambassador to the Inter-American Bank, and Emilio Gamboa, former top aide to President Miguel de la Madrid, and now Secretary of Communications and Transportation in the Salinas administration. The Attorney General's office simply dismissed the evidence and the charges.

On July 18, 1994, the Salinas administration appointed Olga Islas de González Mariscal to continue the investigation into the assassination, but it was clear that nothing more was to be done. Mario Aburto was jailed as the lone assassin.

On September 28, Daniel Aguilar walked up to a car with a Tec 9 Uzi-style sub-machine gun under a newspaper, and fired one shot into the neck of José Francisco Ruiz Massieu, killing him. His gun jammed, and he was caught by an armed policeman one block away. Ruiz Massieu was secretary general of the PRI, and was to be the leader of the ruling party in the Chamber of Deputies. He was a close associate of Carlos Salinas.[53]

Aguilar talked, and many others were quickly identified as part of the conspiracy. The assassination was planned by Manuel Muñoz, a PRI member of the Chamber of Deputies from Río Bravo, Tamaulipas. Muñoz disappeared. Tamaulipas borders on Texas and the Gulf of Mexico and is the primary route for smuggling cocaine into the United States.

For the Mexico City operation, Munoz enlisted Fernando Rodríguez, a PRI office holder from Tamaulipas. Rodriguez hired four people for the assassination. The killers were to be his brother, Jorge Rodríguez, plus Daniel Aguilar and Carlos Cantu. They worked on Abraham Rubio's ranch in Tamaulipas. Jesús Sánchez, Muñoz's chauffeur, was to drive the getaway car. Aguilar was promised $15,000 for being the trigger man.

The investigation into the assassination was led by Deputy Attorney General Mario Ruiz Massieu, the brother of the victim. At the centre of the conspiracy was Abraham Rubio, an important businessman and PRI supporter from Tamaulipas. He had been a close associate of the PRI secretary general. But in 1992, Rubio was exposed as having defrauded the government of $7 million. He was denounced by his friend José Francisco, charged, convicted, and given a fourteen-year jail sentence. Their friendship ended bitterly.

Federal investigators have explained that Rubio, from his prison in Acapulco, used his connections with the Gulf Coast cartel to carry out the assassination. He has close family ties to important leaders of the drug organization. Rubio enlisted Manuel Muñoz to do the job.

The investigation probed deep into the ranks of the PRI. The Deputy Attorney General sought an end to the legislative immunity of Senator Enrique Cárdenas González, former governor of Tamaulipas. Other PRI officials in the state were arrested and interrogated, although in the Mexican tradition, there was an upper limit to those questioned and charged. Nevertheless, the assassination seemed to validate the revelations by Eduardo Valle about the connections between Juan García Abrego and the PRI.

In the past, all similar investigations had been held in check by top officials in the PRI. The "intellectual assassins" were never identified. The political crisis of early 1995 broke this tradition.

Notes

1. "Drugs and Diplomacy," *Latin American Weekly Report*, June 10, 1993, p. 254; "Anti-Drug Drive," *Mexico and NAFTA Report*, July 15, 1993, p. 3; and "Fighting Drugs," *The Economist*, Vol. 328, August 7, 1993, pp. 39-40

2. Equipo Pueblo, *Mexico Update*, No. 6, May 26, 1994.

3. "Cardinal Says Prelate's Murder No Accident," *El Financiero International*, December 12, 1994, p. 2.

4. See Peter H. Smith, ed. *Drug Policy in the Americas*. Boulder: Westview Press, 1992; and Alfred W. McCoy and Alan A. Block, eds., *War on Drugs; Studies in the Failure of U.S. Narcotics Policy*. Boulder: Westview Press, 1992.

5. "Drugs and Diplomacy," *op. cit.*

6. Peter Reuter and David Ronfeldt, "Quest for Integrity: The Mexican-U.S. Drug Issue in the 1980s," *Journal of Interamerican Studies and World Affairs*, Vol. 34, Fall 1992, pp. 89-153; and Hector A. González, "Los Ingresos de los Narcos en México," *El Financiero*, January 29, 1992, p. 41.

7. Joel Brinkley, "Vast, Undreamed-of Drug Use Feared," *New York Times*, November 23, 1984, A-3.

8. Tom Barry et al, *Crossing the Line*. Albuquerque: Resource Center Press, 1994, p. 59.

9. Rosa del Olmo, "The Geopolitics of Narcotrafficking in Latin America," *Social Justice*, Vol. 20, Fall-Winter 1993, pp. 1-23.

10. Barry et al, *op. cit.*, pp. 70-73.

11. Beth Sims, "The Mexican Connection," *Resource Center Bulletin*, No. 29, Fall 1992, pp. 1-6.

12. "Privatizations under Salinas Scrutinized," *El Financiero International*, May 15, 1995, p. 8.

13. David A. Andelman, "The Drug Money Maze," *Foreign Affairs*, Vol. 73, July/August 1994, pp. 94-108.

14. Peter Andreas, "Profits, Poverty and Illegality; The Logic of Drug Corruption," *NACLA Report*, Vol. 27, November/December 1993, pp. 22-28.

15. Stephen Flynn, "Worldwide Drug Scourge," *Brookings Review*, Vol. 11, Winter 1993, pp. 6-11; and "Drug Lords Seek to Exploit NAFTA, RCMP Reports," *Globe and Mail*, December 19, 1994, A-2.

16. del Olmo, *op. cit.*, p. 13.

17. María Celia Toro, "Unilateralism and Bilateralism," in Smith, *op. cit.*, pp. 314-328.

18. Kate Doyle, "The Militarization of the Drug War in Mexico," *Current History*, Vol. 92, February 1993, pp. 83-88.

19. Del Olmo, *op. cit.*, p. 17.

20. Alan Riding, *Distant Neighbors; A Portrait of the Mexicans*. New York: Vintage Books, 1984, pp. 164-165.

21. Steven Wisotsky, *Beyond the War on Drugs*. Buffalo: Prometheus Books, 1990, pp. 31, 36.

22. Andreas, *op. cit.*, p. 24.

23. Peter A. Lupsha, "Drug Lords and Narco-Corruption: The Players Change but the Game Continues," in McCoy and Block, *op. cit.*, pp. 177-195.

24. Reuter and Ronfeld, *op. cit.*, p. 109.

25. *Ibid.*, p. 103.

26. Jonathan Marshall, "CIA Assets and the Rise of the Guadalajara Connection," in McCoy and Block, *op. cit.*, pp. 197-208.

27. Reuter and Ronfeldt, *op. cit.*, pp. 98-99.

28. Lupsha, *op. cit.*, pp. 184-188.

29. Christina Jacqueline Johns, *Power, Ideology and the War on Drugs*. New York: Praeger, 1992; Barry et al, *op. cit.*, pp. 64-70; and "Former Cabinet Ministers Accused," *Latin American Weekly Report*, January 14, 1993, p. 4.

30. Reuter and Ronfeldt, *op. cit.*, p. 109.

31. Andreas, *op. cit.*, p. 25; Barry et al, *op. cit.*, pp. 63-64.

32. Cited in Lupsha, *op. cit.*, p. 183.

33. See Peter Dale Scott and Jonathan Marshall, *Cocaine Politics: Drugs, Armies and the CIA in Central America*. Berkeley: University of California Press, 1991; Jonathan Marshall, *Drug Wars: Corruption, Counterinsurgency, and Covert Operations in the Third World*. Forestville, Calif.: Cohen and Cohen Publishers, 1991; and Marshall, *op. cit.*

34. Elaine Shannon, *Desperados: Latin Drug Lords, U.S. Lawmen and the War America Can't Win*. New York: Viking, 1988.

35. Marshall, "CIA Assets and the Rise of the Guadalajara Connection," *op. cit.*, p. 197.

36. Sallie Hughes, "Justice for All," *El Financiero International*, December 12, 1994, p. 16.

37. Tim Golden, "Colombian Cartels Bringing in 727s Loaded with Cocaine," *New York Times*, January 11, 1995; Russell Mokhiber, "Interview with Christopher Whalen on the Peso Crisis." Washington, D.C., January 19, 1995.

38. Claudia Fernández, "Jorge Hank Rhon Busted on Smuggling Charges," *El Financiero International*, May 29, 1995, p. 3.

39. Sallie Hughes, "Politicians Duck for Cover as Cremi-Union Scandal Grows," *El Financiero International*, September 12, 1994, p. 3; and Ted Bardacke, "The Long Arm of the Law," *El Financiero International*, September 12, 1994, p. 13.

40. See Amnesty International, *Mexico: Torture with Impunity*. New York: Amnesty Interna-

tional, September 1991, pp. 16, 42; and Americas Watch, *Unceasing Abuses; Human Rights in Mexico.* New York: An Americas Watch Report, September 1991, p. 6.

41. Mariclaire Acosta, "The Democratization Process in Mexico: A Human Rights Issue," *Briarpatch Magazine, Vol. 20, September 1991, pp. 6-7.*

42. Americas Watch, *op. cit.,* p. 33.

43. *Ibid.,* pp. 32-33.

44. Amnesty International, *op. cit.,* p. 17.

45. Americas Watch, *op. cit.,* pp. 12-14; Amnesty International, *op. cit.,* pp. 33-36.

46. Americas Watch, *op. cit.,* pp. 7, 10-11.

47. *Ibid.,* pp. 18-21.

48. Quoted in Amnesty International, *op. cit.,* p. 42.

49. For an account of the assassination, see Paul B. Carroll and Craig Torres, "Candidate's Slaying in Mexico has Thrown Election into Turmoil, *Wall Street Journal,* March 25, 1994, A-1, A-4; Sergio Sarmiento, "Mexican Assassination at a Political Crossroads," *Wall Street Journal,* March 25, 1994, A-11; Jeff Shallot, "Killing Shakes Mexican Politics," *Globe and Mail,* March 25, 1994, A-1, A-8; and John Ross, *Rebellion from the Roots.* Monroe, Maine: Common Courage Press, 1995, pp. 303-329.

50. For details on the arrests, see *Weekly News Update on the Americas,* No. 218, April 7, 1994; Equipo Pueblo, *Mexico Update,* No. 2 & 3, April 22, and 29, 1994; Timothy Appleby, "Plot Thickens in Mexican Murder Mystery, *Globe and Mail,* May 24, 1994, A-8; and "Seven Implicated in Colosio Killing," *Globe and Mail,* April 5, 1994, A-10.

51. *Weekly News Update on the Americas,* No. 223, May 1, 1994; No. 222, May 5, 1994; Equipo Pueblo, *Mexico Update,* No. 4, May 13, 1994.

52. Carlos Marin, "Alerté a Colosio y comenzó a dar pasos para librarse de los narcopolíticos," *Proceso,* No. 928, August 15, 1994, pp. 18-23; and Equipo Pueblo, *Mexico Update,* Vol. 2, No. 3, September 22, 1994.

53. For an account of this assassination, see Sallie Hughes, "Politicians Among Leading Suspects in Assassination Probe," *El Financiero International,* October 3, 1994, p. 3; Sam Quinones, "Assassination Plot Reveals Bogeymen," Pacific News Services, October 4, 1994; Sallie Hughes, "Prosecutor Links Politicians, Drug Lords to Assassination," *El Financiero International,* October 10, 1994, p. 3; Carlos Ramírez, "Weak Links," *El Financiero International,* October 24, 1994, p. 6; Michael Tangeman, "Charges, Counter-Charges Fly in Ruiz Massieu Case," *El Financiero International,* November 21, 1994, p. 3.

Chapter 13

THE BUBBLE BURSTS

As 1993 began, Salinas's neoliberal project appeared to be right on track. Inflation was under control, and the economy was showing respectable levels of growth. Foreign investment was pouring into Mexico. The trade unions had accepted his wage control program, and the peasants had accepted his radical changes to agricultural policy. The president was receiving widespread international praise.

In the political area, Salinas's war on the opposition Party of the Democratic Revolution (PRD) had been quite successful. The carrot of the Solidarity program reminded the poor that the PRI could deliver programs that the PRD could not. Through its control of the electoral process, the PRI had successfully denied the PRD any major victories.

Then there was the stick. Salinas looked the other way as the state apparatus and local PRI functionaries repressed not only the PRD, but also leaders of those popular organizations that pushed for democratic changes.

The major task for 1994 was to choose the next president and get him elected. In January 1993, Salinas appointed José Patrocinio González Garrido the new Secretary of Government, the second most powerful person in the Mexican state. He came from a family which was very close to Salinas, and he was married to the daughter of Antonio Ortiz Mena, Salinas's uncle.[1]

González Garrido had been selected to be the PRI governor of Chiapas in 1988. In that position he had waged a relentless war of repression against the indigenous and peasant opposition. In the 1988 presidential election, he delivered 90 percent of the votes to Salinas.

Mexicans were shocked by the appointment. The Secretary of Government was president of the Federal Electoral Institute (IFE) and was in charge of running the presidential election. Mexicans saw this as a clear warning from Salinas that he was not going to permit another 1988, where the opposition had a chance to win.

At the same time, Salinas dropped Fernando Gutiérrez Barrios from the cabinet. He had been in charge of negotiations with the opposition PRD and National Action Party (PAN) after state and local elections. He was dropped just as he was leaving to negotiate with the PAN over the disputed election in Sinaloa.

González Garrido made it known that he was not going to engage in any "negotiations" after elections. He would insist on confirming the election of the PRI even if there was massive evidence of electoral fraud.

On February 23, 1993 there was the famous dinner at the home of Ortiz Mena, where Salinas got thirty of the richest men in Mexico to put up $750 million for the 1994 presidential election. The public revelation of the dinner caused some temporary embarrassment to Salinas. In his State of the Nation address on the previous November 1, Salinas had pledged that he would introduce "greater transparency" in the financing of elections. But the PRI controlled the damage, and under a revised system, wealthy businessmen came up with an even bigger campaign fund of around $1 billion.

The fact that both domestic and foreign big business strongly backed the PRI and its neoliberal program signalled the major change in the Mexican political system. Without support from big business, the PAN could not mount an effective challenge.

On February 25, local elections were held in Guerrero, a stronghold for the opposition PRD. The official results gave 63 percent to the PRI and only 27 percent to the PRD. The rate of abstention was 67 percent. In the March 21 plebiscite on political reform for the Federal District, 80 percent of the voters approved the PRI's proposals, but 90 percent of the eligible voters abstained. In the election in San Luis Potosí on April 20, around 60 percent of eligible voters abstained. If there was opposition to neoliberalism, the response of Mexicans was to opt out of the electoral process.[2]

The opposition parties continued to charge the PRI with extensive fraud in all state and local elections, but Salinas stood above the controversy. The administration's new tough line was revealed in the local elections in Puebla on November 8, 1992. In the election for mayor of Izucar de Matamoros, Miguel Cazares García received a majority of the votes cast. He was backed by both the PRD and the small Popular Socialist Party (PPS). Electoral authorities ruled that coalitions between parties were illegal under the new electoral laws, refused to combine their votes, and gave the election to the PRI candidate. Protests went on into May 1993, when González Garrido refused a proposal by the local PRI Mayor for a referendum to settle the dispute.[3]

Nevertheless, there was pressure on President Salinas to enact electoral reforms. There was the opposition in the U.S. Congress, and NAFTA still had to be approved. The U.S. press was pushing as well. In addition, Mexican business groups were insisting that reforms were necessary to reassure foreign investors. These sources could not be ignored.

In early August, the PRI's legislators presented proposals for amendments to the constitution. The first proposal was to increase the number of senators from each state from two to three, and to give the third Senate seat to the opposition. This was rejected. Instead, the PRI's second proposal was to give each state four seats in the Senate and allocate only one to the opposition. This would give the opposition parties greater representation but allow the PRI to easily keep a two-thirds majority needed to guarantee easy passage of constitutional amendments.[4]

The PRI agreed to drop the "governability clause" in the Electoral Law, which guaranteed a party with more than 35 percent of the vote an automatic 50 percent of the seats. To balance off this concession to the democrats, the distribution of the 200 seats in the Chamber of Deputies allocated by proportional representation would be changed. The distribution would not be based on the European system of balancing seats according to the proportion of the votes. The 200 seats would now be divided among all the parties according to their popular vote, giving the dominant PRI extra seats above those won on the constituency level. But the PRI did agree to a new provision that no party would be allowed to have more than 63 percent of the seats.

Political commentators agreed that while the new reforms would provide a greater voice for the opposition parties in the legislature, they were designed to preserve large majorities for the PRI.

Despite pledges for political reform, Salinas held fast to the long tradition of appointing PRI candidates for office. Also, despite pressures from within the PRI to democratize the party, he insisted on continuing the practice of the *destape*, the personal selection of the successor.

Who would succeed Salinas? The three front runners in the summer of 1993 were Manuel Camacho Solís, the mayor of Mexico City; Pedro Aspe, the Secretary of Finance; and Luis Donaldo Colosio, the Secretary of Social Development. Ernesto Zedillo Ponce de León, the Secretary of Education, was considered to have only an outside chance. Colosio, president of the PRI between 1988 and 1991, and head of the Solidarity program, was considered the front runner.

The most popular potential candidate was Camacho, who was identified with the left wing of the PRI and the faction that was pushing for democratic reforms. However, he was opposed by big business, which worried about his less than enthusiastic support for the neoliberal reforms.

The first choice of big business was Aspe, the author of NAFTA. His right-wing policies were not popular with the left in the party and the small satellite parties. However, the left had been marginalized within the PRI.

President Salinas's economic policy had put a high priority on cutting government expenditures, balancing the budget, and keeping interest rates high to attract foreign investment. During the first half of 1993, the rate of economic growth fell to only 1.3 percent. In the second quarter, it increased by only 0.3 percent. In early September President Salinas finally responded to pressures from business and labour and introduced an expansionary program of government spending.[5]

On October 4, Salinas announced a new program to aid small farmers. PROCAMPO would provide direct subsidies to around 3.3 million producers of maize, beans, sorghum, wheat, rice, soya, and cotton. The cash payments of around US $100 per hectare were to peak in 1994 and then be phased out over fifteen years. The program was widely seen as an attempt to buy votes for the 1994 election.[6]

The final piece in the neoliberal program was NAFTA. President Salinas was determined to get the treaty approved. In early November, six Mexicans critical of the PRI and neoliberalism testified before the U.S. Senate on NAFTA and the state of Mexico's political economy. Salinas refused to allow the testimony to be carried by Mexican television. Those who testified were denounced by PRI officials as "traitors to Mexico."[7]

Criticism also came from Bishop Samuel Ruis of Chiapas, a supporter of liberation theology. On August 6, Bishop Ruiz wrote a letter to Pope John Paul II criticizing Mexico's anti-democratic electoral processes and the neoliberal economic reforms, which had been particularly hard on the poor. On October 26, the Pope's ambassador in Mexico, Girolamo Prigione, acting on behalf of the Vatican, asked Ruis to resign as bishop. While the government denied that it had any role in the affair, Prigione was reported to have told priests in Ruis's diocese that the Mexican government had lobbied the Vatican.[8]

On November 17, 1993, the U.S. House of Representatives gave approval to NAFTA, but only after President Bill Clinton made many concessions to individual Congressmen. These unilateral changes to the agreement were a great embarrassment to Salinas and to the Mulroney government in Canada. Their capitulation reflected the gross imbalance in power between the United States and its treaty partners.[9]

On several occasions, President Salinas told journalists that he would not commit the same blunder that Mikhail Gorbachev had in the Soviet Union. Opening the country to real democratic reform would probably lead to the end of the PRI as the state party. Thus, on important issues like NAFTA, there was no civic participation. The negotiation of the treaty was an executive affair. The PRI-dominated legislature quickly gave it the rubber stamp, and the PRI's control of the mass media insured that there was no public debate.

On November 28 Salinas named Colosio to be his successor. On the same day there was an election for the governor of the state of Yucatan. It was one of the most fraudulent in recent years. In many voting stations there were more votes recorded for the PRI than there were eligible voters. The election made a joke of Salinas's many pledges to have "transparent" and democratic elections in 1994. The final outcome was a farce, as the elected PRI mayor of Meridia resigned and the defeated PAN candidate was named to replace him.[10]

The Yucatan calamity reminded Mexicans that the central focus of the Salinas administration had always been the neoliberal economic program and the implementation of NAFTA. One of the keys to this was the political alliance with the leadership of the PAN.

The Zapatista Uprising

On January 1, 1994, NAFTA came into effect. On that day members of the Ejercito Zapatista de Liberación Nacional (EZLN or Zapatistas) occupied San Cristóbal de las Casas and four towns in the state of Chiapas, and declared war against the Salinas government and NAFTA. They demanded land, food, freedom, justice, democracy, and recognition of rights for indigenous peoples.

The Mexican government had known that the guerrilla army was operating in the area at least since May 1993. They hid their existence, fearing that the news might threaten the passage of NAFTA and scare away foreign investors, but President Salinas moved an additional 15,000 soldiers into the area.

The president's immediate response to the uprising was to send in the military to crush the rebellion. Precedents for such a policy had been set in the 1970s. Fidel Velázquez, head of the Confederation of Mexican Workers (CTM), called for the "extermination" of all of the rebels.[11]

The military forces began an all-out assault. U.S. helicopter gunships bombed and strafed villages and poor barrios. Opponents of the PRI were rounded up, taken to prisons, beaten and tortured. In Ocosingo, five suspected Zapatista supporters were shot and dumped in the city square for all to see. Houses of political opponents of the PRI government were raided and ransacked. Human rights centres were attacked.

But 1994 was different from the 1970s. The NAFTA negotiations had opened up Mexico as never before. The national and foreign press descended on Chiapas. Mexican, Canadian, and American human rights organizations immediately sent observers to Chiapas and documented and publicized human rights abuses. The world witnessed the repression on international television. Capitalists began to take their money out of Mexico.

At first, Salinas tried to downplay the conflict. He accused the Zapatistas of not being an indigenous movement, not even peasants. They were foreign communists from Guatemala, Salinas insisted.

But the reality of the situation could not be denied. On January 12, around 150,000 people demonstrated in Mexico City in support of the rebels. Numerous national and international organizations declared their sympathy for the poor of Chiapas and support for their political and economic demands.

In southern Mexico, peasant and popular organizations took over municipal buildings, demanding the removal of corrupt officials and democratic elections. Indigenous people and peasants began to occupy land taken away from them by local landowners.

"Chiapas is Mexico" is the graffiti one sees on the walls throughout Mexico, and in many ways it is true. Chiapas has gross disparities between the small class of the rich and powerful and the large majority who are poor. The rich are closely tied to the PRI. The natural resources of the state are extracted by large corporations for export; little of that wealth stays in Chiapas and none goes to the poor majority.[12]

Bowing to national and international pressure, President Salinas shifted from repression to negotiation. He chose a close friend, Manuel Camacho Solís, for the job. Camacho, while mayor of Mexico City, had pursued a political strategy of negotiation with the political opposition; he declined to use repression as a state weapon. Public opinion polls showed that he was the general public's first choice to be the next PRI president.

As a condition for accepting the position, Camacho demanded the resignation of Patrocinio González as Secretary of Government. The notorious former governor of Chiapas strongly supported military repression. He also demanded the resignation of Elmar Setzer, the PRI governor of Chiapas. A large landowner, Setzer had supported the expulsion of indigenous peoples from their lands and had backed military repression.

Igacio Flores Montiel, the director of state security in Chiapas, was also removed from office. He was then arrested on charges of drug and arms trafficking and corruption. He was directly involved in the political kidnapping of twenty-six campesinos in land disputes.

Camacho also convinced Bishop Samuel Ruiz, hated by the PRI, to act as mediator between the EZLN and the government. He also convinced Salinas that the negotiation process would not work unless there was a cease fire and a withdrawal of the military to their permanent camps.

Amnesty for all participants in the brief war was granted by the Congress on January 21. On January 25, President Salinas met with the State Council of Campesino and Indian Organizations of Chiapas (CEOIC), which represents 280 organizations, in Tuxla Guitiérrez. They repeated to him the demands of the Zapatistas. Formal negotiations between Camacho and the EZLN began.

On January 27, President Salinas declared that he would not change his economic policies, he would not renegotiate NAFTA, and he would not reverse the decision to change Article 27 of the constitution. The Zapatistas would not be able to change the fundamental economic goals of his presidency.

But the demands of the EZLN for democratic changes were widely supported and put additional pressure on Salinas and the PRI. On January 27, all parties except the small Popular Socialist Party (PPS) signed the Agreement for Peace, Justice and Democracy. Among other things, the agreement called for a new lower ceiling on electoral expenses, free time for opposition parties in the media, a new externally-audited national voters registry, a new office to prosecute electoral crimes, a new system for selecting poll workers, numbering of all ballots, national and foreign election observers, and a new Federal Electoral Institute dominated by nonparty citizen counsellors. These were reforms that had been sought by democrats for years.[13]

On March 2, the EZLN and the Mexican government signed agreements ending the first stage of their negotiations. The federal government agreed to promote a new law guaranteeing the rights of indigenous communities. It also agreed to call a new general election for Chiapas and to create a new electoral law for the state, to work to promote solutions to the agrarian conflicts, and provide support to the victims of the war, to pass a general amnesty, create a new penal code for Chiapas, and to increase social spending in the state.

The first demand of the Zapatistas was for "free and democratic elections with equal rights and obligations for all political organizations contending for power." President Salinas agreed to a special session of the Congress to implement reforms that would "guarantee a fair electoral process with no advantages for any political forces." He named Jorge Carpizo McGregor as Minister of Government and chairman of the Federal Electoral Council (IFE). Carpizo was not a party man and had a good reputation when he was president of the National Autonomous University of Mexico (UNAM) and chairman of the National Commission on Human Rights (CNDH). The Zapatista rebellion had focused international attention on the inequities of the neoliberal economic program and the lack of democracy, and forced Salinas to change his electoral strategy.

The Presidential Campaign

The campaign was not going well for Luis Donaldo Colosio, the PRI candidate for president. A public opinion poll in mid-January conducted by MORI for *Este País,* found 27 percent support for Colosio, 21 percent support for Cuauhtémoc Cárdenas of the PRD, and 14 percent for Diego Fernández de Cevallos of the PAN, with 37 percent remaining undecided.

Ernesto Zedillo, the manager of the campaign, was blamed for the lacklustre effort. By early March, Colosio's supporters were demanding that he be replaced. President Salinas and his right hand man, José Cordoba Montoya, had chosen Zedillo for this job.

On February 16, Colosio spoke to a gathering of 800 of the richest men in Mexico at the Nikko hotel. On this occasion each guest paid only $500 to attend. He assured them that he would continue along the path set by Salinas, that what the country needed was stability, and that he would manage the finances in a responsible manner.[14]

Manuel Camacho remained a very popular figure. A poll, by *El Norte* of Monterrey, in mid-January revealed 50 percent believed that he would be a good presidential candidate. He had made it clear that he was very disappointed when Colosio had been named by Salinas to be the PRI candidate for president.

When Camacho assumed the role of negotiator for the government he resigned from the cabinet. He insisted that the role of commissioner not be a government position and that there be no government pay. This was widely seen as an attempt to get around Article 82 of the constitution, which stipulates that a presidential candidate shall resign any government job six months before the election.

As a result, there was widespread speculation that Camacho would run for the presidency for some other party. He met with President Salinas on March 11, but made no announcement. The March 15 deadline passed and there was still no statement. Finally, on March 22, he stated that he would not be a candidate in this election but that he wanted to be president in the future.

On March 4, Colosio officially became the candidate of the PRI. Two days later he gave a major speech at the sixty-fifth anniversary meeting of the PRI. The speech was seen by many as a repudiation of the Salinas presidency. He called for a change of direction in economic policy to protect the poor and to restructure Mexican agriculture to give more security to family farmers.

Colosio also called for major democratic reforms, including changes in the PRI and guarantees that future elections would be "impartial and open." He pledged to work to separate the ruling party from the state. He claimed that the "excessive concentration of power" in the hands of the president was the main barrier to democracy. Furthermore, he broke with Salinas and said that he would welcome foreign observers for the August 21 presidential election. These proposals worried big business and traditionalists in the PRI. Political observers pointed out that the "new king" always starts out by criticizing the "old king."

The Salinas administration was shaken on March 15, when Alfredo Harp Helú was kidnapped. Harp Helú was president of Grupo Financiero Banamex-Accival, the biggest financial organization in Mexico, and he was one of the famous billionaires. The Mexican stock market fell by 2.9 percent.[15]

Then on April 25, Ángel Losada Moreno was kidnapped. He was a top executive of Grupo Gigante, the largest supermarket chain in Mexico, and son of the owner. Ransom was paid for both, and no one was arrested.

Businessmen are regularly kidnapped in Mexico, and this problem had escalated during the economic crisis. There were around 1,200 kidnappings in 1993 and the average ransom paid was around $100,000. The *Wall Street Journal* reported that "Police officers, and former police officers, are reputed to be the kidnappers in many Mexican cases." They noted that, probably because of the involvement of the police, none of the kidnappers in a "big-money case" have ever been caught.

The PRI campaign was also hurt by the reality of the economic recession. In March, it was announced that there had been a negative growth rate in both the third and fourth quarters of 1993, and the economy was still stagnant in the first quarter of 1994. The overall growth rate for 1993 was a dismal 0.4 percent. The opposition demanded to know when there would be a payoff from the harsh neoliberal reforms.[16]

The economic recession contributed to the decline in support for President Salinas's key project, NAFTA. The *Chicago Tribune* reported in March that public opinion polls in Mexico showed that support for NAFTA had fallen from a high of 80 percent in 1990 to only 42 percent in 1994.[17]

The campaign was stumbling. Few felt that Colosio and the PRI would get a majority of the votes cast. Many Mexicans felt that Cuauhtémoc Cárdenas of the PRD had a chance to win.

The Assassination

Then there was the earthquake of March 23 — Colosio was assassinated while speaking at a political rally in Tijuana. The nation was stunned.

The assassination created another political crisis for President Salinas. Within the PRI, a grassroots movement demanded that the selection of the new candidate be made by the party, in a democratic manner.[18]

Many believed that the only candidate who could save the PRI was Camacho. He was the only potential candidate with popular support, and he had saved the reputation of the government by shifting the Zapatista conflict to the negotiating table. But he had also earned the intense animosity of Colosio supporters within the PRI.

Once again, Salinas resorted to the *destape*. There would be no democracy. Foreign investors and the U.S. government had to be reassured, and that would come through the appointment of Ernesto Zedillo: Yale-educated technocrat, right-wing economist, and strong supporter of Salinas's neoliberal reforms. But there was no formal announcement of Zedillo's appointment by the president, nor by the president of the PRI. The announcement was actually made by several radio and TV reporters.

The strongest support for Zedillo came from the "dinosaurs" of the PRI, the old-guard politicians who do not want to see the Mexican political system democratized. Most notable was the support from Carlos Hank González, Salinas's Secretary of Agriculture, who then became Zedillo's campaign manager. A group of fifty-seven of the old guard ran full-page advertisements in all the major newspapers supporting Zedillo. Among these was Xicoténactl Leyva, the former governor of Baja California Norte and protector of the drug organizations.[19]

How would Zedillo do as the second choice PRI candidate? A poll by *Este País* in mid-April, put Zedillo at 34 percent, Cárdenas at 24 percent and Fernández de Cevallos at 16 percent. The *New York Times* argued that a "truly independent poll" would show Cárdenas and Zedillo running neck and neck, each with around 38 percent of the vote.

The assassination of Colosio caused a great deal of concern in Mexico. Violence is not new to Mexico, of course. But as Sergio Sarmiento of *El Financiero* noted, "The bullets no longer reach only the marginalized, workers and opposition party activists." As of April 1994, 235 militants of the opposition PRD had been murdered.[20]

The public's distrust of the PRI was reflected in a poll taken in April for *Reforma*, an important national daily newspaper. Seventy percent responded that they had no confidence in the investigation process established by Salinas to find Colosio's "intellectual assassin." Seventy-one percent believed that the PRI was behind the assassination. Only 4 percent believed that the assassin was acting alone.

Violence seemed to be on the upswing in Mexico. Following the Zapatista uprising, bombs were set off in several places. In early March, Baja California police chief Alejandro Casteñeda was murdered by a drug gang. In early June a large car bomb was detonated in Guadalajara, by another drug gang. Attorney General Diego Valdes resigned in mid-May after an aide, Eduardo Valle, called Mexico a "narco-democracy." In this atmosphere, the PRI began its real campaign for reelection.

The Election

Sunday of August 21, 1994 was a very important day for Mexicans. They began lining up in front of voting stations early in the morning, believing that for the first time in history their vote would be worth something. Many hoped that they might see the end of the one-party state. The PRI had ruled Mexico for sixty-five years, and the people were tired of fraud, corruption and repression.

I was one of the "foreign visitors" invited by the Civic Alliance, the coalition of nongovernmental organizations created to provide independent observers on election day. I went to the state of Michoacán, where I had spent some time in 1992. It was one of the strongholds of the opposition PRD. The state had a long history of electoral fraud under the PRI, and in recent years, violence, demonstrations, and civil disobedience always followed elections.

I operated with a group of observers from California. The stations we visited in Morelia, the capital, were well-run. They had observers from the PRD and the PAN. Many also had national observers from Civic Alliance. The only significant problem we observed was "shaving" — voters unable to vote because their names were not on the national register. At a special voting station my U.S. partner and I were caught up in a crowd of about 1000 angry Mexicans who had been denied the right to vote. This was the case all across Mexico. The PRD argued that six million voters had been left off the voters list or did not have their identification cards.

But for the first time the opposition parties were guaranteed the right to monitor the counting of the votes and the transportation of the ballots to the regional districts of the Federal Electoral Institute. Everyone believed that rigging the vote would be much more difficult this time.

It was obvious that there was a heavy voter turnout. It had always been believed that abstention had aided the PRI. Given the electoral reforms adopted by the parties after the Zapatista uprising, it seemed unlikely that the PRI would be able to win by falsifying the actual count. Our supporters in Morelia from the Civic Alliance thought the PRI might lose the election.

Late that night, back in our headquarters, we exchanged election day stories. We heard from observers in the rural areas of Michoacán. They all cited many irregularities in the voting stations. Intimidation of voters by PRI militants was widespread. In many cases there were no observers from the opposition parties. Some observers claimed that the vote count was manipulated with many PRD-marked ballots annulled.

No returns were to be released until late Monday. But the radio station carried the results of the exit polls. They projected a slim majority victory for the PRI, a strong showing for the PAN, and a rather dismal showing for the PRD. Our Mexican friends were stunned. What had happened?

There was general agreement that while the actual vote on election day was the cleanest in Mexican history, that was not saying a great deal. In the rural areas, the PRI was still able to manipulate the vote. The PRD insisted that the election was stolen by the PRI as in 1988 and 1991.

However, most Mexican political observers agreed that while the traditional "prehistoric practices" were still widespread, they were not enough to affect the outcome. That was decided long before election day.

Government programs had been used to bolster the state party. There was PRONOSOL, the local public works program begun in 1989. PRO-CAMPO, begun in 1993, provided direct subsidies to farmers. Voters in rural areas were told that if the PRI wasn't reelected, they wouldn't get their cheques. In addition, Salinas had significantly increased general public spending in the 1994 election year. State funds were lavishly spent during the campaign period.

For example, trailer trucks filled with staples like beans, cooking oil and jalapenos went from the local PRI headquarters, distributing free food to people in the poor *colonias*. This was part of the Basics Program run by the state. The slogan "For the well-being of your family" was there on the side of the trucks, the official slogan of the PRI in the 1994 campaign.

The PRI still exerts strong influence over those Mexicans who are members of PRI-affiliated organizations. Most important is the control of the trade unions. The unions spent a great deal of money in the campaign and exerted the usual pressure on their members.

Then there was the usual intimidation. A few examples were cited by Lorenzo Meyer, the noted Mexican historian. A Mexico City worker explains, "Where I live, employees of the Power company told us that if the PRI lost, they would cut us off, since we have a makeshift connection to the power network." A maid tells her employer, "People are saying that if you do not vote for the PRI, you will not be given permission to bury the dead in the village." A woman says her health care worker at the Social Security

Institute told her that "those of us who would not vote for the PRI would have their service suspended." A plumber says that "People voted with fear, because on TV they were saying that if the PRI lost, there would be war."

Since the 1980s the PRI has provided funds to a group of small, phantom parties on the left. In this election the PRI channelled its financial support to the Workers Party (PT), which they helped create in 1990. The PT candidate for president was Cecilia Soto, who got her political start in the Labour Party, which was allied with Lyndon B. LaRouche's neofascist organization in the United States. In 1985, she shifted to the Party of the Authentic Mexican Revolution (PARM), another PRI satellite, and was given a seat in the legislature.[21]

Salinas's right-hand man for elections, Patrocinio González Garrido, arranged with the PT to have Soto join the party and become their presidential candidate. The PT, with funds from the PRI, out-spent the PRD in the campaign. Soto got special coverage in the PRI-dominated media, and her campaign took votes from the PRD and the PAN.

While the January 27, 1994 Agreement for Peace, Justice and Democracy limited party spending in the presidential campaign to $42 million, there is no way to enforce this. In 1993, the PRI had raised $1 billion from wealthy businessmen for the campaign.

The Civic Alliance monitored spot advertisements for the parties on the two main television channels over a three week period in July and August. At commercial rates, the PRI spent over $6 million on these advertisements, equivalent to 13 percent of their allotted spending. Given the full range of their electoral spending, down to free food baskets and breakfasts for voters, they could well have spent the one billion dollars.[22]

The Mexican Institute for Public Opinion (IMOP) monitored spending during the election. They estimate that the PRI spent $1.25 billion, the PAN $6 million and the PRD $3.5 million. This was for all campaigns: presidential, Senate, and Chamber of Deputies.

The PRI also has overwhelming support from radio, television and the daily newspapers. An extensive opinion poll conducted by the Civic Alliance found that 67 percent of Mexicans depend on television for their political information and that 65 percent believe that television news coverage favours the PRI.[23]

The Mexican Academy of Human Rights surveyed election campaign news coverage for the Civic Alliance. They found the two primary television news programs were consistently biased for the PRI over the opposition parties in time allotted, number of news reports, voice and image coverage, and placement on the news show.

Family and Society, another nongovernmental organization, surveyed nine daily newspapers for the Civic Alliance. The papers strongly favoured the PRI in number of articles, length of articles, headlines, front-page stories, and photographs.

A study by the Federal Electoral Institute (IFE) covering the period from June 22 to July 5 found that radio news programs were strongly biased towards the PRI, and that several actually gave more coverage to the minuscule PT than they did to the PRD.[24]

In his initial statement after the election, PAN presidential candidate Diego Fernández de Cevallos described the election process as "profoundly unequal and profoundly unjust." Rodolfo Peña, a deputy citizen counsellor in the General Council of IFE, proclaimed that "It is a fact that there was fraud in the August 21 elections, and it is also a fact that the political system as a whole is fraudulent, because, by keeping millions of Mexicans in misery and ignorance, it makes them an easy prey of manipulation and propaganda of the government." Most Mexicans would probably agree with this assessment.[25]

Marie Claire Acosta, well-known human rights activist, spoke to the Canadian visitors the week before the election. She argued that Mexico is deeply divided at this time. One half of the population wants to move towards a much more democratic society, and this can happen only when the PRI is removed from office. The other half does not want change, or fears that change might bring instability.

The official election results reflected this division. Ernesto Zedillo, the presidential candidate of the PRI, received 48.8 percent of the vote. Diego Fernández de Cevallos of the PAN received 25.9 percent. Cuauhtémoc Cárdenas of the PRD received 15.6 percent. Cecilia Soto of the PT received 2.7 percent, and the other five parties received less than 1 percent. In the newly expanded Senate, the PRI will have 74 percent of the seats and in the Chamber of Deputies 60 percent of the seats. Political commentators declared that the government of Mexico had moved from Harvard to Yale.

Denise Dresser has pointed out that during his campaign, Zedillo made important alliances with the most backward elements in the PRI. With an overwhelming majority in the legislature, and NAFTA approved, would he have any incentive to continue the political reform process?[26]

During the campaign, a broad-based citizens' group promoted a plan for change called "20 Agreements for Democracy." The proposal was accepted by Cárdenas and Fernández de Cevallos, and it was widely reported that Colosio, the original PRI candidate for president, was also about to accept it. Then he was assassinated.[27]

Representatives of this organization met with Zedillo near the end of May, and the PRI candidate refused to sign. Those present at the meeting reported that he did not really agree with any part of the declaration.

It should be remembered that Carlos Salinas never pushed for democratic reforms. Changes were forced on him by pressure from Mexican civic organizations, business interests, foreign investors, and the Zapatistas.

The mainstream media in Canada and the United States regularly argues that the PAN is a right-of-centre party. It is true that its leaders support the neoliberal economic reforms, and they are strong supporters of the orthodox Roman Catholic church.

But Mexicans who want to oust the PRI vote for either the PAN or the PRD, whichever is stronger in a particular region. The PRD and the PAN have also formed electoral alliances on the state or municipal level and run only one candidate, hoping that the PRI could be removed from office and reforms could be introduced.

The Mexican left was stunned by the election results. The PRD lost badly in the areas where Cárdenas was strongest in 1988: Mexico City, the State of Mexico and Michoacán. This dramatic reversal could not be explained by fraud.

The largest exit poll, conducted by Mitofsky International and BIMSA, revealed that of the majority of Mexicans who live below the poverty line, 54 percent voted for the PRI and only 16 percent for the PRD. Of those of university age, 41 percent voted for the PRI and only 13 percent for the PRD. The PRI did well among women, gaining 53 percent of their votes with only 13 percent going to the PRD.[28]

The PRI had a very extensive campaign supporting "family values" and "social peace." Mexican commentators concluded that the fear-of-violence campaign emphasized in television commercials convinced many people to vote for the PRI. They were successful in identifying the PRD with violence.[29]

The PRI campaign also claimed that if the PRD were elected there would be a return to economic chaos. A vote for the PRI was a vote for economic stability. The PRD had a difficult time defending itself against this charge. It has been beset by internal turmoil, with constant conflict between the ex-PRI members led by Cárdenas, who dominate the party, and the left and the popular organizations. The party has been criticized by the Zapatistas, and others, for lack of internal democracy.

Cárdenas did very poorly in the national TV debate of May 12. Fernández de Cevallos effectively attacked his record as the PRI governor of Michoacán. He argued that the economic policies advocated by the PRD would bring back high inflation and more debt problems. Cárdenas did not offer any credible alternatives. After the debate, Cárdenas fell to third place in all the polls.

During the campaign Cárdenas moved steadily to the right, even ending up supporting NAFTA and privatization. Many political activists who were looking for a clear alternative to neoliberalism and the PRI were discouraged.[30]

The Collapse of Legitimacy

On September 28, 1994, José Francisco Ruiz Massieu was assassinated. He was one of the most important PRI figures, and leader of the party in the Chamber of Deputies. The investigation quickly revealed that the assassins were acting on behalf of prominent people within the PRI. The investigation was headed by the victim's brother, Deputy Attorney General Mario Ruiz Massieu.

In mid-November, Mario Ruiz Massieu charged that his investigation was being obstructed by prominent officials in the PRI, and in particular General Secretary María de los Angeles Moreno and PRI President Ignacio Pichardo Pagaza. He resigned on November 23, charging that his investigation was being blocked by high PRI officials, including his boss, Attorney General Humberto Benítez Trevino.

Federal prosecutors were focusing on the "Grupo de Atlacomulco," a powerful PRI clique led by Carlos Hank González, PRI President Pagaza, and Attorney General Benítez Trevino.[31]

On December 1, 1994, Ernesto Zedillo was sworn in as president and named his new cabinet. The economic cabinet was dominated by neoliberal technocrats, most of whom had advanced degrees from U.S. universities. Ignacio Pichardo Pagaza, who had been a key member of Zedillo's campaign team, was appointed Secretary of Energy.

In his presidential address, Zedillo promised a future of peace and prosperity and a "profound transformation" of the justice system. He promised to expand democracy, to fight poverty, and to end peacefully the dispute with the Zapatistas.

Zedillo also pledged to pursue the investigation into the assassinations. As part of that strategy, he appointed Antonio Lozano Gracia of the opposition PAN to be the new Attorney General. However, a poll by *Reforma* found that only 33 percent of Mexicans believed that Zedillo would carry out his promises.[32]

When I was in Mexico in August 1994, there was wide speculation on the issue of the overvalued peso. From the beginning of 1989, the Bank of

Mexico had intervened in the currency market to keep the peso in a band close to the U.S. dollar. This was fundamental to President Salinas's strategy of attracting foreign capital and capital held abroad by Mexicans.

The problem was that interest rates were much higher in Mexico than in the United States. Between 1989 and the end of 1994, prices had doubled in Mexico while they rose by only 25 percent in the United States. The value of the peso did not reflect this change. Economists I talked to all estimated that the peso was overvalued by around 35 percent.[33]

The decision to keep the peso overvalued was also a political decision. Cheap imported goods bought the PRI the support of the middle class. Expanding exports to Mexico would help to undermine opposition to NAFTA in the U.S. Congress.

The previous three presidents had all devalued the peso before leaving office. Would Salinas follow suit? There was widespread agreement that it was unlikely, as it would be seen as a failure of economic policy and would undermine Salinas's campaign to be the new head of the World Trade Organization.

But the figures were worrisome. Around 70 percent of the new foreign capital was "hot money," invested in the stock exchange and short-term government bonds. Very little was direct foreign investment in productive assets. The fact that this money could be taken out of Mexico on short notice created a climate of uncertainty.[34]

Capital began to move out of Mexico following the Zapatista uprising. In addition, the U.S. Federal Reserve Bank began raising U.S. interest rates in February 1994, and this encouraged some U.S. capital to return home. The U.N. Conference on Trade and Development reported in mid-1994, "An outflow of about $11.5 billion from Mexico is estimated to have taken place during the early months of 1994 ... This figure is of a magnitude similar to estimates of flight capital repatriated to the country during 1989-1993."[35]

The vast majority of Mexicans did not know that they were on the brink of another economic crisis. In the final State of the Nation address on November 1, 1994, President Salinas painted a rosy picture of the Mexican economy. The trade deficit was nothing to worry about, he said, because the imports were mainly capital goods used to increase production. Salinas claimed that foreign reserves were at $17.2 billion as of November 1, but we now know that this was not true.[36]

The move toward free trade, culminating in the implementation of NAFTA, resulted in a dramatic increase in imports. The overvalued peso discouraged Mexican exports, and the deficit in the trade balance rose to $28 billion in 1994. The relative lack of exports meant that Mexico had to attract around $2.5 billion from abroad each month to balance the trade deficit in the current account.

The crisis came to a head when the new budget was revealed in early December 1994. It called for a deficit of $31 billion, or 7.8 percent of the gross domestic product. While President Zedillo claimed that the deficit could be financed by external credit, big business was sceptical. Capital began to flow out of the country at a rate of $1 billion per week. Foreign currency reserves fell from $28 billion in February to only $6 billion in December.[37]

The Salinas administration had financed much of its debt through the *tesobono*, a short-term bond in pesos which was tied to the value of the U.S. dollar. Throughout 1994 investors began converting their bonds into U.S. dollars and taking their capital out of the country. The Bank of Mexico was unable to sell enough new bonds in the money market to cover the capital flight. Foreign currency reserves steadily fell.

In retrospect, the editor of the *Wall Street Journal* argued that the devaluation could have been avoided if the Bank of Mexico had raised interest rates. But President Salinas could not do this in the middle of the crucial election for president, because the illusion of a robust economy had to be maintained. One of the major PRI campaign arguments was that the election of the PRD would bring an economic crisis. Defeating the PRD decisively was a major political goal of the neoliberal strategy. When Zedillo took office, there really was no choice but devaluation.[38]

On December 20, Finance Minister Jaime Serra Puche announced a 12.7 percent devaluation in the peso. The Mexican stock market plunged, and capital flight intensified. Interest rates on short-term government bonds (CETES) were raised to 30 percent, with no signficant effect. Two days later, the administration chose to let the peso float on the international market. With only $6 billion left in reserves, they could not defend the peso in the market. As the value of the peso continued to fall, the Finance Minister resigned.[39]

By the end of March the peso had stabilized, having lost 40 percent of its value since early December. Annual interest rates on twenty-eight-day government bonds (CETES) were around 40 percent. The rate of inflation was running at 60 percent on an annual basis. Interest on unpaid credit card balances rose to 80 percent. Bank interest rates on home mortgages and car loans rose to an annual rate of 90 percent.

The Mexican government had about $26 billion outstanding in *tesobonos*, and 82 percent were held by foreigners. The majority were held by twenty large U.S. investment groups. The biggest losers in the devaluation were Goldman Sachs ($5.17 billion), J.P. Morgan ($2.0 billion), and Bear Stearns ($1.81 billion).[40] Investor confidence in Mexico collapsed. However, the government had to refinance $59 billion in foreign debt in 1995. When the Bank of Mexico offered bonds on the international money market, there were few buyers. The government faced another crisis like 1982. In early January, President Zedillo announced a new austerity plan, promising to hold down wages while increasing privatization and deregulation. But it was not enough to stem capital flight, and at this point the U.S. government came to the rescue.

At first, President Bill Clinton offered a $40 billion loan guarantee. However, this had to be approved by the Congress. With public opinion polls showing over 80 percent of Americans against financing the bailout, support in Congress began to crumble. The bailout was being pushed by U.S. Secretary of the Treasury, Robert Rubin. Prior to joining the Clinton cabinet, he had been co-chair of Goldman, Sachs & Co., a bank which had invested heavily in Mexico. In this position he had handled the privatization of Teléfonos de Mexico and Grupo Televisa. Americans knew that it was wealthy U.S. investors who were really being bailed out.[41]

On January 31, Clinton announced a new package. The president took $20 billion from the Exchange Stabilization Fund; this did not require Congressional approval. He got the International Monetary Fund to agree to put up $17.5 billion, the largest credit line ever granted, and without Board approval. The Bank for International Settlements, representing the central banks of the industrialized countries, originally agreed to put up $10 billion, but later withdrew the offer. The private banks were to put up $3 billion, but they withdrew from the proposal in late March. Thus, the total bailout package of $37.5 billion was only slightly larger than the $34.5 billion due to be refinanced by the Mexican government in 1995.[42]

The U.S. loan would be covered by requirements that U.S. importers of crude oil, oil products, and petrochemicals deposit their payments in the U.S. Federal Reserve Bank in New York City. The U.S. government would have first access to this money if Mexico did not make their debt payments. Zedillo agreed to U.S. demands that Mexico follow an even tougher monetary policy. Short-term interest rates were raised another 10 percent.

In order to obtain support from the U.S. government and international investors, President Zedillo proposed to permit greater foreign ownership of Mexican banks and to privatize transportation and telecommunications. These were concessions that the Salinas government had refused to make during the NAFTA negotiations. Julius Katz, chief negotiator for the U.S.

government on NAFTA, gleefully noted that alternatives to further neoliberalism "were foreclosed by NAFTA."[43]

U.S. Secretary of the Treasury Robert Rubin revealed that the government of Mexico would be required to make weekly, monthly, and trimester financial reports to the U.S. government. U.S. financial aid would be limited to short-term restructuring and exchange stabilization, and would require the Mexican government to give the U.S. government confidential information on future economic trends.[44]

On March 9, the Mexican government announced a new economic austerity plan for the year. It included a 10-percent cut in government spending, designed to create a fiscal surplus equivalent to 4.4 percent of the GDP. There would be a 35-percent increase in the price of gasoline and a 20-percent increase in the price of electricity. The value added tax would be increased to 15 percent. Wage increases were limited to 7 percent, but the minimum wage would be increased by 10 percent. Finance Secretary Guillermo Ortiz estimated that the annual inflation rate for 1995 would be 42 percent. While the government projected a 2-percent decline in the economy, other analysts predicted the economy would contract by at least 4 percent.[45]

But there was little support for the bailout or the austerity program in Mexico. Public opinion polls showed that 80 percent were opposed to the bailout. Mexicans did not want to compensate U.S. investors, increase the foreign debt, or surrender so much sovereignty.

It was not only the popular sector that opposed the bailout and the austerity program. The Mexican Roman Catholic bishops, meeting in April 1995, denounced the policies of neoliberalism that "had left 40 million Mexicans in poverty while concentrating the nation's wealth in the hands of the privileged few."[46]

Cracks appeared in the ranks of the business organizations which had strongly supported the neoliberal program. Fernando Cortina Legarreta of the Confederation of Industrial Chambers of Commerce (CONCAMIN) said, "The government should scrap its absurd anti-inflation policy and replace it with a medium term plan that emphasizes the defence of our productive capacity and employment — we need to grow."

Luis German Carcoba, president of the Business Co-ordinating Council (CCE), warned that the economy was paralysed because of high interest rates and uncertainty about the peso and the future. Hundreds of thousands of people were being thrown out of work. All Mexican banks were in danger of defaulting because of high interest rates and the inability of debtors to make their payments.[47]

The National Chamber of Consumer Goods Industries (CANACIN-

TRA) charged that Mexico had "undergone a ten-year period of de-industrialization." The liberalization of Mexico's foreign trade was "at the root of such problems as unemployment, a rampant external debt, as well as the inability to generate jobs."[48]

The economic crisis was closely linked to the political crisis in Mexico. Foreign investors were concerned over the stalemate in the conflict with the Zapatistas. In a widely cited presentation on January 11, 1995, Riordan Roett, a Mexican expert at Johns Hopkins University working for Chase Manhattan Bank, stated: "The government will need to eliminate the Zapatistas to demonstrate their effective control of the national territory and security policy."[49]

On February 9, 1995, President Zedillo ordered the military to move in on the Zapatistas and arrest the leaders. The Zapatistas and thousands of peasants fled into the jungles. Towns and villages occupied by the military were looted and desecrated as a way to punish Zapatista supporters. But popular opposition to a military solution was extensive, and Zedillo went back to the negotiation strategy within a week.

The economic crisis also provoked a conflict between Salinas and the new president. Zedillo, apparently in an effort to boost his sagging popular support, decided to push ahead with the investigations into the assassinations. On December 16, 1994, Pablo Chapa Benzanilla had been named special prosecutor for this purpose. He briefed the Senate commission on February 7 on the Colosio case, revealing that they had evidence of a conspiracy and a major cover-up. They argued that the cover-up was done for political reasons, to protect the PRI until after the August 1994 election.

On February 24, Attorney General Antonio Lozano announced that they had arrested Othon Cortez Vázquez, who had been part of the security team guarding Colosio. The government now admitted that there had been at least two gunmen, and that physical evidence had been tampered with. Senator José Guadarrama announced that the Senate commission planned to call as witnesses both José Cordoba Montoya, Salinas's chief adviser, and the ex-president himself.[50]

That was just the beginning. Two days later Chapa arrested Raúl Salinas de Gortari and charged him with having ordered and paid for the assassination of José Francisco Ruiz Massieu. Raúl Salinas, the brother of the former president, was a close friend of Manuel Muñoz Rocha, who had been charged with arranging the assassination.[51]

The announcement stunned Mexico. The leaders of the "revolutionary family" were always exempt from attacks after leaving office. But this had been changed because of the high-level assassinations. Salinas had broken another rule by going to the press to defend his position on the peso and devaluation. Before the arrest was announced, Zedillo met with the leaders of the Old Guard in the PRI, and the leaders of the armed forces.

Carlos Salinas vehemently denied that his brother had anything to do with the assassination, denied that he had participated in the cover-up of the assassinations, and staged a one-day hunger strike on March 3. President Zedillo responded by issuing a formal statement absolving the ex-president. Salinas went into exile in the United States, moving into a house owned by Carlos Hank González in Boston.

On March 3, Mario Ruiz Massieu was arrested at an airport in New Jersey for carrying $18,000 in undeclared cash. It was revealed that during the previous year, while deputy Attorney General, he had deposited $6.9 million in a Houston, Texas bank. The Mexican government asked for his extradition. He was charged with obstruction in the investigation of the murder of his brother. He was accused of altering legal depositions, in an effort to divert attention away from Raúl Salinas.[52]

One month later, federal agents charged two top federal police officials with the murder of José Frederico Benítez, the Tijuana chief of police. However, they continued to deny that the assassination had anything to do with his investigation of the assassination of Luis Donaldo Colosio.[53]

In the six months that followed the August 1994 election, Mexico has been profoundly shaken. The devaluation of the peso and the austerity program have meant that the vast majority of Mexicans have seen their standard of living fall back to the level of the mid-1980s. By May 1995 open unemployment was at a record high. The cost of basic food products had risen by between 40 and 130 percent. The government was bailing out banks and a number of the state governments faced bankruptcy. The Ministry of Agriculture estimated that there would be a 41 percent drop in the production of the 10 basic grains in 1995. Real wages were projected to fall by 25 percent. Businesses were estimating that the sale of nonessential goods would fall by 50 to 70 percent. Illegal emigration to the United States was up 30 percent. The economy was in shambles.

The legitimacy of the PRI has been destroyed by the assassinations and the conspiracies, the connection with the powerful drug industry, and the intense infighting. A public opinion poll carried out by *Reforma* on April 17, 1995, found that only 1 percent of those polled felt Carlos Salinas was the best among the last five presidents. But the economic and political crisis also highlighted the failure of the neoliberal economic program. Far too many people in Mexico are living in poverty. Far too many people cannot find a real job. The inequalities in income and wealth are grotesque, and military repression can no longer be an answer.

Notes

1. "Cronies Abound," *Mexico and NAFTA Report*, February 18, 1993, pp. 2-3.

2. Margarita García Colin and Cesar Romero Jacobo, "Ganar Credibilidad o Perder las Elecciones," *Epoca*, No. 91, March 1, 1993, pp. 8-13.

3. "Bartlett Does It Again," *Mexico and NAFTA Report*, June 10, 1993, p. 2.

4. Andrew Reding, "Chiapas is Mexico," *World Policy Journal*, Vol. 11, Spring 1994, pp. 11-25; "President Salinas's Strange Notion of Electoral Transparency," *Mexico and NAFTA Report*, March 25, 1993, pp. 1-3; and "President Salinas Adjusts Policies," *Mexico and NAFTA Report*, September 23, 1993, pp. 1-5.

5. "Salinas Shifts Economic Gears," *Mexico and NAFTA Report*, October 28, 1993, pp. 1-5.

6. "What PROCAMPO Means," *Mexico and NAFTA Report*, October 28, 1993, pp. 6-7.

7. Carlos Marin, "Una insercion pagada convierte in 'traidores' a México a los criticos del TLC," *Proceso*, No. 887, November 1, 1993, pp. 20-24.

8. "Government Gets Vatican to Drop a Bishop," *Mexico and NAFTA Report*, November 18, 1993, p. 8.

9. Carlos Acosta Cordova, "En el TLC, el gobierno mexicano convirtio el arte de negociar en arte de ceder," *Proceso*, No. 890, November 22, 1993, pp. 12-17; and "NAFTA through but at a Heavy Cost to Both Clinton and Mexico," *Mexico and NAFTA Report*, December 2, 1993, pp. 1-4.

10. "What a Way to Run a Country: Yucatan," *Mexico and NAFTA Report*, January 20, 1994, p. 8.

11. For an account of the uprising, see Olivia Gall, "Mexico's Difficult Futures," *Against the Current*, Vol. 9, May/June 1994, pp. 31-38; Elizabeth Kadetsky, "Rounding Up the Usual Suspects," *The Nation*, February 14, 1994, pp. 201-202; Alex Taylor de Cid, "Race Hatred and Class Warfare in Mexico's South," *Canadian Dimension*, Vol. 28, March/April 1994, pp. 8-10; Neil Harvey and Luis Hernández Navarro, "Rebellion in Chiapas." Center for U.S.-Mexican Studies, University of California San Diego, 1994; and John Ross, *Rebellion from the Roots*. Monroe, Maine: Common Courage Press, 1994.

12. For a background on the Chiapas situation, see Peter Rosset and Shea Cunningham, "Understanding Chiapas." San Francisco: Institute for Food and Development Policy, March 19, 1994, unpublished paper, 12 pp.; June Nash and Kathleen Sullivan, "Return to Porfirismo," *Cultural Survival Quarterly*, No. 16, Spring 1992, pp. 13-16; and Salvador Peniche, "The Mayas and the Global Market." Unpublished paper, National Autonomous University of Mexico, January 25, 1994, 10 pp.

13. José Luis Tejeda, "Elección clave," *Cemos Memoria*, No. 69, August 1994, pp. 7-12; and Carolina Ballesteros Niño, "Perfil de los Estrategas del PRI, Pan, PRD y sus Tácticas de Campaña," *Epoca*, No. 167, August 15, 1994, pp. 32-33.

14. Pascual Beltran del Rio, "Los supermillonarios (el 0.2% de los mexicanos), con Colosio," *Proceso*, No. 903, February 21, 1994, pp. 32-37; "Colosio Tries to Dismiss Camacho," *Mexico and NAFTA Report*, March 31, 1994, pp. 2-3; and "Colosio Calls for International Observers," *Mexico and NAFTA Report*, March 31, 1994, p. 5.

15. Paul B. Carroll, "Mexico Becomes Hunting Ground for Kidnappers," *Globe and Mail*, March 21, 1994, B-6.

16. "Dismal Investment Brings Recession," *Mexico and NAFTA Report*, March 31, 1994, pp. 6-

7; and Salvador Corro and Guillermo Correa, "Desempleo y cierre de empresas, desastres que despiden a Salinas y reciben al TLC," *Proceso*, No. 896, January 3, 1994, pp. 20-22.

17. Ken Marshall and Stephen Ravencraft, "Mexicans Grow Increasingly Leery of NAFTA," *Chicago Tribune*, March 28, 1994, p. 5.

18. Elías Chavez, "Cambios con Zedillo: nobramientos por dedazo, vigilancia agresiva y el regreso de 'dinosaurios'," *Proceso*, No. 910, April 11, 1994, pp. 12-13; and Gerardo Albarran de Alba, "El PRI acaba la era Salinas derrotado, dividido, y empantanado en los vicios que se propuso superar," *Proceso*, No. 910, April 11, 1994, pp. 11-17.

19. "The Aftermath: President Salinas Asserts Himself," *Mexico and NAFTA Report*, April 21, 1994, pp. 1-3; "The Assassination," *Mexico and NAFTA Report*, April 21, 1994, p. 6; "Zedillo: Another Technocrat," *Mexico and NAFTA Report*, April 21, 1994, p. 8.

20. Sergio Sarmiento, "Regarding the Violence," *El Financiero International*, October 3, 1994, p. 7.

21. Oscar Camacho Guzmán, "Cecilia Soto González," *La Jornada*, August 21, 1994, Perfil, p. 5.

22. "Las Elecciones Presidenciales de Agosto de 1994," Alianza Civica, August 19, 1994, unpublished paper.

23. Sergio Aguayo et al. "Las Elecciones Federales en México segun los noticieros." Unpublished paper, August 1994; and Alianza Civica, "Los cuidadanos ante los medios y las campañas politicas." Unpublished paper, July 1994.

24. Delfos Communicación. "Report to the Federal Electoral Institute." July 1994.

25. Alonso Urrutia and Ismael Romero, "Un proceso profundamente injusto e inequitativo: Diego Fernández," *La Jornada*, August 22, 1994, p. 13.

26. Denise Dresser, "The Impending Elections: The Only Certainty is Uncertainty," *Report on the Americas*, Vol. 28, July/August 1994, pp. 22-28.

27. "Zedillo Postpones Signing '20 Agreements for Democracy'," *Mexico Update*, No. 7, June 1, 1994.

28. "Portrait of the Electorate," *The News*, August 25, 1994, p. 5.

29. Marisa Taylor, "Votes for PRI Couched in Fear, Analysts Say," *The News*, August 24, 1994, p. 4.

30. Alberta Carrillo Armenta, "Autocrítica y refundación de la izquierda," *El Economista*, August 25, 1994, p. 49; Mauricio Merina, "Las tragadias del día 21," *La Jornada*, August 25, 1994, p. 13; Francisco Gil Vellegas, "Por qué perdió el PRD?" *El Economista*, August 26, 1994, p. 9; and "Dos Grandes Ganadores: Zedillo y Diego; un Gran Perdedor: Cuauhtémoc," *Epoca*, No. 168, August 22, 1994, pp. 5-20.

31. Sallie Hughes, "Politicians among Leading Suspects in Assassination Probe," *El Financiero International*, October 3, 1994, p. 3; Michael Tangeman, "Charges, Counter-Charges Fly in Ruiz Massieu Case," *El Financiero International*, November 21, 1994, p. 3; and "Ruiz Massieu Gives Nod to PAN Prosecutor," *El Financiero International*, December 5, 1994, p. 2.

32. Scott Morrison, "All the President's Men," *El Financiero International*, December 5, 1994, pp. 14-15; and Sallie Hughes, "A New President Takes Office," *El Financiero International*, December 5, 1994, p. 14.

33. See "The Wobbly Peso," *Forbes*, July 4, 1994, p. 161.

34. See James M. Cypher, "NAFTA Shock," *Dollars and Sense*, No. 198, March/April 1995, pp. 22-25, 39; "Heritage of a Thief," *Counter Punch*, Vol. 1, December 1, 1994; and Christopher Whalen, "The New Debt Crisis," unpublished paper, January 1, 1995.

35. *Trade and Development Report, 1994*. New York: United Nations Conference on Trade and Development, July 1994.

36. Sallie Hughes, "Salinas' Economic Tally," *El Financiero International*, November 7, 1994, pp. 14-15.

37. Equipo Pueblo, *Mexico Update*, Vol. 2, No. 12, December 14, 1994.

38. Robert L. Bartley, "Mexico: Suffering the Conventional Wisdom," *Wall Street Journal*, February 8, 1995, A-18.

39. Craig Torres, "Mexico's Devaluation Stuns Latin America — And U.S. Investors," *Wall Street Journal*, December 22, 1994, A-1; and "Mexico Drops Efforts to Prop Up Peso," *Wall Street Journal*, December 23, 1994, A-3; A-4.

40. Thomas T. Vogel, Jr., "'Brady Bonds' Seen Slumping Still Further," *Wall Street Journal*, January 3, 1995, A-21; Thomas T. Vogel, Jr., "Mexico Official to Seek Debt Rollover From Investors," *Wall Street Journal*, January 5, 1995, C-1.

41. Andrew Wheat, "Rubin's Moral Hazard," *Multinational Monitor*, Vol. 16, April 1995, p. 10.

42. *NAFTA and Inter-American Trade Monitor*, Vol. 2, no. 15, May 12, 1995.

43. Bob. Davis, "NAFTA is Key to Mexico's Rescue of Peso," *Wall Street Journal*, January 4, 1995, A-8; Drew Fagan, "Clinton Orders New Bailout for Mexico," *Globe and Mail*, February 1, 1995, A-1; and Tim Carrington and Craig Torres, "U.S. Unveils Rescue Plan for Mexico," *Wall Street Journal*, February 22, 1995, A-3.

44. Equipo Pueblo, *Mexico Update*, Vol. 2, No. 18, February 15, 1995.

45. Daniel Dombey, "Welcome to the Plan," *El Financiero International*, March 13, 1995, p. 1.

46. *NAFTA and Inter-American Trade Monitor*, Vol. 2, No. 16, May 19, 1995.

47. Institute for Agriculture and Trade Policy, *NAFTA and Inter-American Monitor*, Vol. 2, No. 5, March 3, 1995.

48. Equipo Pueblo, *Mexico Update*, Vol. 2, No. 31, May 25, 1995.

49. Harry Cleaver, "Chase Calls for Crushing Zapatistas." Department of Economics, University of Texas at Austin, February 10, 1995.

50. Michael Tangeman, "Cover-Up Alleged," *El Financiero International*, February 13, 1995, p. 4; Michael Tangeman, "Salinas Rejects Colosio Charges," *El Financiero International*," March 6, 1995, p. 15; and Paul B. Carroll and Dianne Solís, "Arrest of Suspected Second Gunman in Colosio Killing Rocks Mexico Anew," *Wall Street Journal*, February 27, 1995, A-9.

51. Tim Golden, "Salinas' Brother Held in Assassination Plot," *Globe and Mail*, March 1, 1995, A-1; and Michael Tangeman, "In the Halls of Moctezuma," *El Financiero International*, March 6, 1995, p. 14.

52. Equipo Pueblo, *Mexico Update*, Vol. 2, No. 22, March 15, 1995; and Dianne Solís, "Many Mexicans See Big Fall from Grace for Former Leader," *Wall Street Journal*, March 6, 1995, A-10.

53. Tim Golden, "Federal Officers in Mexico Tied to Killing of Police Chief," *New York Times*, April 8, 1995, p. 1.

Chapter 14

ALTERNATIVES TO NEOLIBERALISM

In March 1964, the military in Brazil overthrew the elected civilian government. The justification for the coup was to defend the country against the rise of totalitarian communism. Later that year, the military seized power in Bolivia. At the time, Paraguay was the only South American country ruled by a military dictatorship.

The U.S. government had historically supported repressive right-wing dictatorships in Central America and the Caribbean. Now it moved to give strong support to the new dictatorships in the south. It intervened directly to support the military coups in Chile and Uruguay in 1973. It also gave extensive support to the military regime in Argentina after 1976.

The military seized power in Peru in 1968, but in the initial phase, undertook progressive reforms. The shift towards implementing a neoliberal agenda came after Morales Bermudez took power within the military ruling group in 1975; U.S. government support followed.

As Tómas Vasconi has stressed, these military regimes did not come into power simply to repress the political left. They had a much broader project which included economic, social, and political reorganization of these societies. They built strong ties with U.S. and other foreign capital, and began the process of dismantling import substitution industrialization. Neoliberalism became the order of the day. The old "populist" governments and political parties with their links to organized labour were to be liquidated.[1]

As the economic crisis of the 1980s worsened, these military regimes stepped down in favour of elected governments. They negotiated their way out of office, protecting themselves against punishment for their horrendous human rights abuses and guaranteeing that the military would remain powerful.

The "restricted democracies" that took over these countries continued the policies set by the military regimes. The common characteristics of these limited democracies are described by Vasconi: (1) the insertion of the national economies into the circuit of transnational capital, which restricts the ability of the new governments to develop national economic policies; (2) the disarticulation of the internal productive process, a result of liberalization of investment and trade; (3) the continuation of domination by the U.S. government and finance capital; (4) the intensive concentration of property and wealth; (5) the pauperization of broad sections of the population, and the lowering of the standard of living of the middle class; (6) the disorganization of the corporative and political institutions of the popular classes; (7) the continued authoritarianism of the government and major institutions of society; and (8) the military's continued presence, which limits the power of the government and remains a permanent threat.[2]

In Mexico, a military coup wasn't necessary. The one-party state remained in control, and, after 1982, it began to implement the same policies that the military dictatorships had introduced in Latin America. The administrations of Miguel de la Madrid and Carlos Salinas became more authoritarian, electoral fraud became more pronounced, and human rights abuses increased. The two presidents moved to strengthen links to both international capital and the U.S. government. Thus the characteristics that Vasconi attributes to the "restricted democracies" of Latin America apply to Mexico as well.

The authoritarian regimes repressed the political parties of the left and the trade union movement. Throughout the hemisphere the leadership was murdered, disappeared, tortured, imprisoned, exiled and threatened. The impact was to weaken seriously the political opposition to right-wing politics and economics.

Over the 1980s, the social democratic parties came to embrace neoliberal economic policies. In some cases they even joined in right-wing governments. Thus the traditional parties of the popular left ceased to function as the representatives of the working class and the poor majority. When there was a move back to electoral democracy, the alternative to the politics of neoliberalism was very weak.

The result was the proliferation of new social movements throughout the 1980s. Lacking a national political movement, and facing the economic depression and the disappearance of the welfare state, Latin Americans responded by developing local community organizations. Disillusioned by the politics of the social democrats and the bankruptcy of the old communist parties, there was a dynamic expansion of new groups representing the interests of oppressed groups. At the same time there was an expansion of the Christian base communities, inspired by liberation theology.[3]

Jorge G. Castañeda notes that the new grass roots organizations were not class organizations. They reached far beyond the organized labour movement and the intellectual left. They were church groups, human rights organizations, urban dwellers, women, students, environmentalists, gay rights activists, and others organized along lines of issue, not class. But at the same time, in many cases they reproduced the rich/poor cleavage of Latin American society.[4]

Everyone, including political leaders in the United States, praises the return to democracy in Latin America. But what does this really mean? José Alvaro Moises stresses that there is a great deal of difference between democratic governments and democratic regimes; it is necessary to distinguish between processes of liberalization and democratization.[5]

The fact is that in all the countries of the Western hemisphere where elected governments have replaced dictatorships, immense inequalities are the norm. A democratic government "will not inevitably be a regime of social justice; in and of itself, it will not eradicate social inequality."

Alvaro sets out his criteria for a democratic regime as follows: (1) the contest for political power has clear rules, accepted by the majority; (2) the practices and procedures foreseen under these rules enjoy continuity and regularity; (3) the democratic rules must guarantee that fundamental changes can be made in economic and social organization, based on the principle of majority rule; and (4) norms of conduct must guarantee that the government will be accountable to its citizenry. As he comments, "The mere listing of these characteristics is enough to show how far Latin America still has to go in democratic consolidation." Very few people in Mexico would argue that the Mexican political system conforms to these principles in any way.

Furthermore, in the 1990s, the democratic neoliberal regimes in Latin America have been characterized by widespread corruption, which have forced several presidents from office. In that respect, they mirror the record of the Bush Administration in the United States. One of George Bush's last acts as president was to pardon his close friends who were involved in the Iran-Contra scandal.[6]

Throughout Latin America, the left has adopted the expansion of democracy as a central principle. The experience with military dictatorships, and the failures of the Soviet model, have convinced nearly everyone on the left of the importance of formal, political democracy. Aside from fair elections, there is a demand for limitations on terms of office plus a mechanism for the recall of governments and elected officials.[7] The present neoliberal governments are not interested in reforms or deepening democracy. As Castañeda points out, the business, landed, and political elite's "conditions for the democratic opening entailed the maintenance of the prevailing social and economic order."[8]

There is also the demand for democracy in the social area. Neoliberalism has resulted in mass underemployment and greater inequality than ever before. Democracy means a recognition that all people have basic fundamental human rights and needs.

Finally, there is the question of participatory democracy. This final demand reflects the experience of the new social and neighbourhood organizations in all Latin American countries.

But as Jaime Osorio reminds us, "Liberals will accept democracy so long as universal suffrage does not call into question the social organization of the economy or development projects." For liberals, the key freedom is located in the economy. They are only interested in a "minimal democracy," where people "vote and elect, and vote and elect again, yet never achieve any influence over substantive questions that would improve the conditions of their lives."[9]

Marta Harnecker, a Chilean political theorist, notes the changes in the radical left in Latin America. "Marxism is now seen as a tool of analysis and there is the acceptance of ideological pluralism." There is greater recognition that the social movements cannot be "mere transmission belts" but must have an autonomous role. The left can no longer just proclaim themselves the vanguard — they can win this role only by proving it in practice. Furthermore, there is as obvious shift "from the only vanguard and from single party to multiparty politics." Finally, there is the shift from seeing armed struggle for democracy as the only road to socialism, to viewing it as "one means which is imposed by the enemy."[10]

Three examples will serve to illustrate the new democratic and socialist politics in Latin America: the Partido dos Trabalhadores in Brazil, the Causa R in Venezuela and the Frente Amplio in Uruguay.

The New Politics

After the military seized power in Brazil in 1964, they instituted an extremely repressive regime. However, the onset of the economic recession in 1978 eliminated any legitimacy that the military had. Unable to cope with the crisis, they decided to turn the government over to civilians, hoping to control its direction from the barracks.

The push for democratization came from a revitalized trade union movement which began to organize mass strikes in April 1978. Leigh Payne points out that the new trade union movement was committed to three principles which distinguished it from the old movement. "Union democracy, which meant participation of the rank and file in union decisions and responsiveness of leaders to rank and fiie demands; combative strategies, a new willingness to risk losing your job, being imprisoned and facing government repression; and autonomy from the government."[11]

To a large degree this change was due to the leadership of Luis Inacio "Lula" da Silva, president of the Metalworkers' Union of São Bernardo do Campo and Diadema. The more militant and democratic trade unions formed a new federation, the Central Workers Union (CUT). But half of the trade unions remained attached to the old federation, the General Confederation of Workers (CGT), which supports social democracy, business unionism and has close links to the U.S. government.

However, Lula and the leaders of the new trade union movement believed that it was also necessary to build a new socialist party. In 1979, activists in the new trade union movement and the mass popular organizations founded the Partido dos Trabalhadores (the PT or Workers' Party). Ideologically, the party is committed to replacing capitalism with a socialist society.[12]

Margaret Keck notes, "Lula defended a definition of 'workers' that included wage earners in general, as well as others with a low standard of living — a definition, in other words, based on a person's social condition rather than on his or her position in production."

From the beginning, the party included a heterogeneous set of actors. These included middle class intellectuals; 'new' working-class sectors (bank workers, teachers, university professors); social movement activists from more traditional neighbourhood movements; members of Catholic base communities; and activists from 'new' social movements (concerned with the rights of women, blacks, gays and lesbians, as well as with environmental issues). It also included members of clandestine organized left parties, including Trotskyists and various offshoots of the Brazilian Communist Party.[13]

The PT puts a great deal of emphasis on extra-parliamentary activities: building new social movements, expanding the trade unions, and supporting urban and rural land occupations. They believe that social empowerment through grass roots activity builds political empowerment.

The party did quite well in the 1985 municipal elections, electing more than 1,000 city council members across the country. Maria Luiza Fontalelle was elected mayor of Fortaleza, the fifth largest city in Brazil. In the November 1988 municipal elections, the PT were elected in many cities. Luiza Erundina was elected mayor of São Paulo, the third largest industrial centre in the world, with thirteen million people.

The presidential election was held in November and December 1989. In the first round of voting, the PT candidate, Lula, finished second with 11.6 million votes. In the run off election, right-wing candidate Fernando

Collor de Mello won, but Lula received thirty-one million votes, 47 percent of the total.

The requirement for PT party membership is active participation in a grass roots social movement, a neighbourhood organization, or a *nucleos* at their place of work. Within the party there are various open factions or tendencies. The majority tendency is identified with trade unionists, Roman Catholic and Protestant activists, and independent socialists. Party decisions are made according to proportional voting, and once a majority decision is made, party members and factions are required to accept the decision.

Maria Helena Moreira Alves, a political scientist and a founder of the PT, argues that "Members of these movements have a double militancy, permeating all levels of the PT and exerting considerable influence to determine party program and draft government policy. The presence of these movements, interconnected to the PT, has enabled the party to make some innovative proposals and pass progressive legislation and also affected the new Constitution of 1987. The movements *shape* the policies of the PT but maintain a position of independence and autonomy vis-a-vis governments."[14]

There were high expectations for the PT for the November 1994 presidential election. In June 1994, Lula was at 41 percent in the public opinion polls, compared to only 19 percent for Fernando Henrique Cardoso of the Social Democratic Party/right-wing coalition. But this support collapsed when the PT failed to deal with the issue of inflation and Lula moved his policy steadily to the right, trying to appease the business class. In the end, he lost because his supporters among the poor revolted: eighteen percent abstained, though voting is mandatory, and an incredible 23 percent cast spoiled ballots. The right voted and Cordoso won.[15]

Nevertheless, the experience of the PT in Brazil is seen as a very important development in Latin America. A new political movement has been launched, committed to participatory democracy and socialist transformation. Many Latin American political activists see it as the new alternative model, now that bureaucratic state socialism is dead and social democracy has embraced neoliberalism.

In Venezuela, the most important political development has been the rise of Radical Cause (Causa R). It began as a small group of Marxists who broke with the Movement Towards Socialism (MAS). One branch began political work in the Catia district of Caracas, and the other in the steel industry (SIDOR) in Ciudad Guyana, in the state of Bolivar. Today it calls itself a movement and does not have the formalized structure common to parliamentary parties.[16]

The movement won the control of the steel workers union at SIDOR by emphasizing democracy, worker safety, and breaking with the social democratic union structures, with their authoritarianism, corruption and ties to the U.S. government. They also won control of the unions in the iron ore and aluminum industries. Today, forty trade unions and co-operatives have formed a new, separate federation.

In December 1989, Andreas Velázquez and Radical Cause were elected to form the government of Bolivar, Venezuela's largest state. Three years later they were reelected with 63 percent of the vote. At the same time, Aristobulo Isturiz was elected mayor of Caracas.

Radical Cause is winning support by stressing popular democracy, honesty in government, and expansion of the social service sector. They have also rejected megaproject development for social development and secondary industry.

The new party is a workers' party. Its leaders insist that workers can govern, and its candidates dress and act like the ordinary people that they are. During the 1993 presidential campaign, Andres Velázquez never once put on a suit and tie. This was a deliberate strategy to stress that they were not social democrats. They see their base in the poor majority.

The new left is also on the rise in Uruguay. The Broad Front (Frente Amplio or FA) is a coalition of political parties, popular movements, and left-wing individuals. Its open democratic system of operation has been praised by political activists looking for a new road to socialism and democracy.[17]

Encouraged by the success of the Chilean left in the 1970 election, the Uruguayan left formed the FA in 1971. The founding parties included the Communist Party (PC), the Socialist Party (PS), then a Marxist-Leninist party, and a number of independent left-wing parties. It also included two parties from the centre: the Party for the Government of the People (PGP), a social democratic party which came out of the Colorados, and the Christian Democratic Party (PDC).

But the FA is more than a coalition of formal political parties. It is also a movement, which includes community groups and individuals. Its organization is not structured as a federation of interests. The FA is built on Base Committees, geographical in nature, which bring together all of the active supporters, regardless of party or group. The structure is described by Luis Stolovich:

> The FA operates as a great familial 'cloak' that covers and protects all who operate within it, beyond the disputes and conflicts. There are many internal problems, but they take place within the 'family' and, in principle, do not question its perma-

nence. The FA has become a political space that allows for the maintenance of basic loyalties ('to be left'), without being tied to party formulas. One can cease to be a communist, socialist, or Tupamaro, or change one's party, or have no party, yet retain a lasting identity of belonging to the Frente. The FA is the basic common framework for a diversity of ideological expressions and political sensibilities.[18]

In the 1971, election the FA won 18 percent of the national vote for president and 30 percent of the vote in Montevideo, the capital, where half the people live.

But the U.S. government grew fearful of the left. They backed the military in Uruguay, which in 1972 launched an all-out attack on the Tupamaros, who were waging an urban guerrilla war. By September they were crushed and 2,000 supporters were in jail. With the support of the right wing of the Colorado and Blanco Parties, the military seized power in 1973 and began a sustained program of repression of the political left and the trade unions. However, the military could not solve the economic crisis. In 1984, they negotiated a withdrawal from political office. In return, they received amnesty from prosecution for their murders and violations of human rights.

Many did not expect the FA to do well in the 1984 election. But their vote rose to 21 percent. Between 1985 and 1989 there was a major debate within the FA on its policy direction and system of operation. The social democrats wanted the FA to become a coalition rather than a movement and to adopt a more reformist policy orientation. When the majority refused to move in this direction, the PGP and the PDC withdrew and formed the Nuevo Espacio (New Space).

In the 1989 election, the FA won 21 percent of the national vote and came first in Montevideo with 35 percent. In March 1990 the FA won the municipal election for Montevideo and elected Socialist Party candidate Tabaré Vázquez as mayor.

The FA is committed to increased democratization both within the organization and in society at large. As Stolovich argues, "The Frente as such has developed a unique action, differentiated from its own component parts, that makes it one of the most democratic forces in the country." He adds that while the traditional parties are still based on the dominant leader, "The FA has been constructing a culture of internal debate that is one of its more precious attributes."

As the government of Montevideo, the FA has implemented open, democratic decision-making, involvement of the people in the decision making process, and decentralization and democratization of the government. As Harnecker argues, the lesson of Chile is understood. It is impossible to carry out a socialist program without large democratic support. Democratization reduces the ability of the right to undermine the popular will.[19]

In the November 1994 presidential election, the FA increased its vote to 29.8 percent, and was only 28,000 votes behind the winning Colorado Party. It elected one-third of the members of the Congress. Not only did the FA win the municipal election in Montevideo, they broadened their support throughout the country.[20]

The question is whether the new political developments that are found in South America have any relevance for Mexico. The culture of Mexico is still Latin American, but its growing economic integration with the United States may be transforming the country.

The U.S. government has demonstrated over many years that it is not at all interested in promoting democracy or human rights in Latin America. It has used its political, economic, and military force to overthrow elected democracies. Its guiding policy has been to support regimes that are favourable to U.S. investment and trade. This has been particularly true of the Caribbean area, usually described as "the backyard" of the United States, where there are "special interests." Presumably that includes Mexico.

Through the six years of the Carlos Salinas administration, Presidents Ronald Reagan, George Bush, and Bill Clinton all demonstrated that all they wanted from Mexico was NAFTA and a neoliberal government.

"Poor Mexico, so far from God and so close to the United States." One hears that popular saying often in Mexico, and Canadians know well what it means. Sharing a long border with an imperial giant has a major impact on political development. Can Mexico move towards a more democratic politics? Can they adopt a different economic policy?

The Mexican Left

The political left has never been strong in Mexico. It has a long tradition of sectarianism and division, with factions and leaders splitting and forming new parties. They have been accused of being elitist, following the pattern of the state party, the PRI. They have imported models and ideologies from other countries.[21]

The left has had to deal with co-optation by the PRI and significant political repression. Around the world, the base for most social democratic, socialist, and communist parties has been the trade union movement. In Mexico, however, the vast majority of trade unions are under the control of the PRI. Over the years the independent left and trade union militants have been unable to break the authoritarian control of the trade unions and their dependent relationship with the PRI.

The PRI has also supported a number of smaller leftist parties over the years in order to give the impression that Mexico has a competitive, multi-party political system. This strategy was also designed to divide the left and to prevent the development of a significant left-wing party. These "satellite" or "loyal" parties of the left have received financing from the PRI and the state, and have been given votes and seats in the legislature when the official election results have been released.

The "loyal opposition" on the left has included the Socialist Workers Party (PST), the Popular Socialist Party (PPS), the Party of the Cárdenas Front for National Reconstruction (PFCRN), the Party of the Authentic Mexican Revolution (PARM), and most recently, the Party of Labour (PT). These parties have often used the rhetoric of socialism and nationalism, but in the crunch, the PRI knew it could count on them.

The independent left has concluded that the PRI cannot be changed or transformed. They have refused state subsidies. But they have remained quite small and their influence has been limited.

The most important formation on the left has been the Mexican Communist Party (PCM), which was founded in 1919. It joined the Third International and followed the party line from Moscow, which greatly limited its effectiveness. At the beginning of the Cold War in 1946, the party was banned. Under the electoral reforms introduced by President Luis Echeverría, the PCM was registered again in 1978. In the 1979 elections, the PCM emerged as the third largest party in Mexico, behind the PRI and the National Action Party (PAN).

The PCM, declining in members and financial support, called for a united front for the left for the 1982 presidential election. In the end, they were able to get only four small Marxist-Leninist parties to merge with them. Nevertheless, the new formation, the Socialist Unification Party of Mexico (PSUM), remained the third most important political formation.

Another attempt to form a broader socialist party was made in the spring of 1987. PSUM merged with the Mexican Workers Party (PMT), led by Heberto Castillo, which grew out of the 1968 student uprising. It was joined by three other smaller left-wing parties to form the Mexican Socialist Party (PMS). The new party chose Castillo to be its candidate for president in the 1988 election.

In 1988, Cuauhtémoc Cárdenas and the Democratic Current (CD) withdrew from the PRI and formed the National Democratic Front (FDN) to challenge the PRI in the presidential election. Seeing the groundswell of support for Cárdenas, the major "satellite" parties (the PPS, PFCRN and PARM) abandoned the PRI and joined the FDN. In 1988, the PMS and Castillo withdrew from the presidential race and joined the FDN. Following the presidential election, the "satellite left" returned to the fold of the PRI. But in 1989 the PMS joined the CD to form the first major party of the left, the Party of the Democratic Revolution (PRD).

The New Social Movements

The authoritarian one-party state, the absence of a major party on the left, and the worsening economic situation for the majority all contributed to the growth of popular social movements in Mexico. Many identify 1968 as the turning point, with the massacre of the students ending what legitimacy the PRI had.

After 1982, the PRI elites who ran the government embraced the policies of neoliberalism advocated by Mexican big business. No longer could the PRI claim to represent the interests of workers and peasants. The failure of the government to respond effectively to the earthquake of 1985 also spurred the growth of popular groups.[22]

There is a long tradition of popular mobilization in Mexico. Within the trade union movement there has been a continuous struggle to end domination by the authoritarian PRI leaders and to make unions democratic. Organized groups were formed within the unions, and a major effort was made in this direction in the 1970s. In the end they were crushed by the state apparatus, but Mexican workers do not give up. Major battles and confrontations occur every year.

The goal of the National Peasant Confederation (CNC) was to prevent the development of new peasant organizations independent of the PRI. But in the 1940s poor peasants formed the General Union of Workers and Peasants of Mexico (UGOCM) and the Independent Peasant Confederation (CCI). In the 1970s, there were land invasions mobilized by independent regional peasant groups. In 1975 the Independent Confederation of Agricultural Workers and Peasants (CIOAC) began organizing landless rural labourers.[23]

The National Coordinator/Plan of Ayala (CNPA) was formed in 1979. This was a confederation of local and regional peasant organizations whose primary demand was to gain land for peasants. In the early 1980s it was responsible for organizing many mass demonstrations. It has been replaced today by the National Union of Regional Peasant Organizations (UN-CORA) as the most important independent peasant organization.

Organizations representing the poor in urban centres expanded significantly after 1968. In 1981, they formed the National Coordinator of Urban Political Movements (MUP), which included groups representing shantytown *colonias*, tenants' associations, groups representing street merchants and self-employed workers, and barrio organizations demanding urban renewal and services.

Laura Carlsen points out that these organizations are different, in that people join as consumers rather than producers, they lack any legal or formal status, and that they are organized according to territory. She argues that they have had three goals: to resolve their basic demands, to maintain their independence from the PRI state, and to "construct grassroots democracy through daily life experiences."[24]

On September 19, 1985, Mexico City was struck by an earthquake. The PRI government took days to respond. Spontaneous popular organizations were formed to deal with the emergency. The city was run effectively by the people. The influential Neighbourhood Assembly (AB) was formed to promote housing demands for the victims. It has continued as an "assembly of democracy," holding mass meetings in barrios to make decisions and to pressure the PRI civic administration.

There is a long history of student movements in Mexico, but they were shattered by the massacres of 1968 and 1971. The movement revived in 1987 when the PRI government proposed major changes in the structure of universities which would have changed the open admission policy and increased fees. The University Student Council (CEU) mobilized students to oppose PRI control of the schools and demanded participatory education.

Women have always played important roles in popular organizations in Mexico. They have been the primary organizers of the urban organizations. Women in the Communist Party formed the United Front for Women's Rights in 1935, and they were denounced as traitors from Russia. Women were also active within the PRI.

In 1979, the National Front for Women's Rights and Liberation (FNALIDM) was formed by activists to push women's issues. They were denounced by the PRI and the organization collapsed in two years. The Benita Galeana Women's Coalition was formed in 1988 to promote marches on International Women's Day. Other, smaller, feminist, gay, and AIDS support groups also exist and are growing in numbers.

Liberation theology also has had some impact on Mexico. Christian base communities exist in many areas and claim 150,000 members. They have helped organize popular groups and non-governmental organizations, and they have worked particularly closely with peasant and aboriginal organizations.

Today, there are many environmental groups, including the networks, the Pact of Ecological Groups (PGE), and the Mexican Conservation Federation (CCM). Few environmental organizations existed even ten years ago. The first popular human rights organization was founded in 1978. Today there are over sixty in a national organization. A number of other broad-based organizations have been formed to monitor electoral fraud.

The proliferation of these groups has led to the expansion of civil society. There are now many organizations, involving the participation of many people, which are formally independent of the state and PRI apparatus. In South America, these organizations have formed the basis for the new political parties and are usually seen as a key development in the transformation to a more democratic society. But is this true in Mexico? There is a difference of opinion on this question.

First, there is the ability of the PRI and the one-party state to co-opt these organizations. Paul Lawrence Haber has recounted how effectively President Salinas used PRONASOL to buy off the urban popular organizations. The funds were targeted to independent groups which leaned towards the PRD. If they were to deliver the goods to their members, they had to participate in the *concertación* process, signing agreements, and inevitably toning down their criticism of the government. The offer of state funds inevitably led to splits in all these organizations.[25]

Jonathan Fox catalogues the proliferation of peasant groups in Mexico, including militant movements opposed to the PRI. But he adds that "By the 1980s most had succumbed to internal divisions and pressures from the state."

Again, many of these organizations were co-opted, or at least split, by the offer of funds from PRONOSOL. They could not form a united front to combat President Salinas's changes to Article 27 of the constitution. Even the CIOAC, the national peasant organization most opposed to the change in *ejido* ownership, split on the issue. Fox concludes that the gap between the peasant groups and the different political parties is growing.[26]

Popular groups in Mexico have struggled to maintain their independence from PRI organizations, which conditioned most of them to reject electoral politics. This began to change in the mid-1980s when a coalition of popular groups and three socialist parties was formed for the 1985 federal election, but the results were not significant.

The change came in 1988 when the Democratic Current broke from the PRI and Cuauhtémoc Cárdenas ran for president under the National Democratic Front. Many popular organizations joined the coalition and participated in the election, but not many chose to join the PRD when it was formed in 1989.[27]

Judith Hellman argues that Mexico is different from South America, and this effects the role of the popular organizations. "Mexico is not democratizing as rapidly as the slowest South American case, if, indeed, it is even limping along in that direction." Coercion, repression and electoral manipulation increased under President Salinas. Hellman asks, "Under these largely unfavourable circumstances, what, conceivably, could be the democratizing impact of the popular movements?"[28]

Clientelism is central to the Mexican political system. Hellman argues that under this system, the real agenda for popular groups was to extract results from the PRI. No one expected these groups to promote democratization. Thus, PRONOSOL and the *concertación* process have worked well. Hellman points out that encouraging the proliferation of groups outside the official party is another long-standing technique of social control.

Finally, Hellman argues that the organizations themselves do not have a history of participatory democracy. She points to the study by Lynn Stephen on the role of women in the urban popular movements. While they have been the majority of participants, leadership positions are monopolized by men. Hellman cites Carbajal Rios to show that the situation for women is even worse in peasant organizations.

Nevertheless, this does not mean that the rise of popular movements is not a good thing in itself. They result in the expansion of civil society. They should not be faulted for failing to create democracy when the political parties have been unable to do so.

The Party of the Democratic Revolution

In 1989, Cuauhtémoc Cárdenas and his supporters formed the Party of the Democratic Revolution (PRD) in an attempt to transform the 1988 electoral coalition into a permanent force in opposition to the ruling PRI. Only one of the parties of the FDN coalition joined, the Mexican Socialist Party.

Adolfo Gilly has described the four major ideological streams in the new party: (1) *cardenismo* and the tradition of Mexican nationalism; (2) state nationalism, of the PRI tradition, ousted by the move towards neoliberalism; (3) independent socialism; and (4) the Mexican Communist Party, with its strong defence of Cuba.[29] From the beginning the PRD had at least two major factions, the left and the social democrats from the Democratic

Current of the PRI. The latter included Cárdenas and Porfirio Muñoz Ledo, president of the PRI in 1975-76. The main polarization that developed within the PRD was between the former *priistas* who dominated the leadership and the more left-wing and militant rank and file.

The ideology of Cuauhtémoc Cárdenas has dominated the PRD's official policy. It was fundamentally a continuation of the Mexican tradition of populist state-directed economic and social development. It was clearly not socialism but mild social democracy.

Under the leadership of Cárdenas and Muñoz Ledo, the PRD concentrated on trying to win elections. Many believe that the electoral route was a bad choice, given the PRI's control of the electoral practice, their complete domination of the mass media, and their enormous financial resources. Jorge Castañeda says that the PRD was "doomed to failure."

The leadership of the PRD has been criticized for being elitist and anti-democratic — for making the PRD too much like the PRI. At the July 1993 party convention, Muñoz Ledo was chosen chairman of the party, replacing Cárdenas who was nominated as their presidential candidate. The national council of the party rejected Heberto Castillo's presidential candidacy, and instead chose Pablo Gómez, a former communist. Castillo had publicly criticized the leadership for importing "*priista* tactics" into the PRD. He announced that he was going to form a "critical current" within the PRD to push for democratization and more radical policies.[30]

As the PRD entered the 1994 presidential campaign, Cárdenas took a moderate social democratic position. He stressed the need for a regulated, mixed economy, with more emphasis on job creation and social equity. He rejected a return to the old import substitution policy which he said "was hallmarked by the creation of one of the most unjust patterns of income distribution in the world."

While Cárdenas rejected renationalization of privatized state enterprises, he called for a reversal of much of the neoliberal policies of Carlos Salinas. He promised to restore the principles behind Article 27 of the constitution, guaranteeing *ejidos* their land, and to bring the oil industry again under national control.[31]

But the central focus of the PRD remained to introduce a democratic political system, end human rights abuses, and guarantee labour rights. They promised to end state control over trade union and peasant organizations.

The official policy of the PRD argues that an alternative North America trade agreement must be based on the principle of raising the standards of living in Mexico up to the levels in Canada and the United States. This requires an agreement to greatly reduce Mexico's foreign debt.[32]

Such an agreement must be based on a recognition of the gross economic differences between Mexico and Canada and the United States. As in the European Economic Community, the rich states should provide compensatory financing to help Mexico close the gap and to adjust to more open trade with her two much more highly-developed partners. Mexico's labour force should also have broad legal access to jobs in the American labour market, with human and social rights.

The PRD rejects giving foreign corporations "national status" in Mexico. Elected governments must have the right to impose standards on foreign investment. Rules of origin requirements, under a trade agreement, should be used to punish those who exploit low wages. The PRD demands that all environmental standards be harmonized upward to the higher levels in Canada and the United States.

The PRD is opposed to free trade in agricultural products because of the vast difference in the levels of development and government support between the three countries. Mexican governments must be able to implement policies of food security as well as rural development policies which involve government subsidies.

The PRD was astonished to learn that the Mulroney Government gave the United States guaranteed access to natural resources in the free trade agreements. They regard control of resources as a fundamental requirement of national sovereignty. Elected governments must have the ability to plan for the general public good.

The PRD has been widely criticized in Mexico by those who support it. It is too much the party of one man. The leadership of the party is from the PRI, and the party is run like the PRI; it is too centralized and too authoritarian.

By concentrating on the electoral strategy, the PRD has allowed the movement of 1988 to dissipate. Popular groups have withdrawn from the party because they feel they have no influence. The continual emphasis on electoral fraud provides a convenient scapegoat so that the party does not have to look at its shortcomings. The intellectual leadership of the party is arrogant with its local supporters. The party policy is too vague, and became even more so during the 1994 campaign.

Many on the left are sceptical of what the PRD could actually do if it were to obtain office. It is, at best, a mild social democratic party. The other social democratic parties in office in Latin America and elsewhere have embraced neoliberal economics. Would the PRD be any different? How much freedom of movement would it have in a country so closely tied to the United States?

Coalitions and NGOs

The other new development in Canada, the United States, and Mexico is the formation of broad coalitions of organizations opposed to free trade and advocating progressive social and economic policies. In 1990, while the governments of the three countries worked with big business to create NAFTA, the coalitions in the three countries began building trinational alliances.

The Action Canada Network was formed in 1987 to oppose the Canada-U.S. Free Trade Agreement. It is an alliance between organized labour and popular organizations representing women, anti-poverty groups, senior citizens, teachers and students, farm organizations, church groups, environmentalists, aboriginal Canadians, and artists. It also has representation from provincial social justice coalitions.

The coalitions were formed in Canada largely because of the failure of the New Democratic Party, Canada's social democratic party, to oppose the neoliberal agenda. On the provincial level, the NDP governments in Ontario, Saskatchewan, and British Columbia implemented policies that were no different from those of the traditional right-wing parties, the Conservatives and the Liberals. In their economic, financial, and taxation policies, they were often more right-wing.

In Australia and New Zealand, people disillusioned with social democratic governments have been turning to new red-green parties. In Europe in 1993 and 1994, there has been a popular swing to the reformed former communist parties and the new greens. That has not yet happened in Canada. Many believe that Canadian politics is becoming more like that of the United States, where the only choice is among right-wing parties, and the majority choose to opt out of electoral politics.

In the United States, there is even less of a political choice than in Canada. There is very little difference between the Republican and Democratic parties. On the key issue of NAFTA, President Bill Clinton used all the power at his command to coerce Democrats in the House of Representatives to support passage.

Coalitions of popular organizations were created to oppose NAFTA. They included the Citizen Trade Watch Campaign, the Coalition for Fair Trade and Social Justice, the Fair Trade Campaign, Mobilization on Development, Trade, Labour and the Environment, the Alliance for Responsible Trade, the Coalition for Justice in the Maquiladoras, and the Minnesota Fair Trade Coalition.

In Mexico, the fight against NAFTA and for a progressive alternative was led by the Mexican Action Network on Free Trade (RMALC). It is a coalition representing non-governmental organizations and organizations representing independent labour, peasant, and environmental groups.

RMALC worked on an alternative trade and development strategy to NAFTA. Their proposals were very close to those presented by the Canadian and American coalitions at the trinational meetings. In March 1993, the three coalitions adopted a common position paper at the trinational meeting in Washington, D.C.

Their alternative approach is similar to that proposed by the PRD but goes farther in some respects. It starts with the inequalities between the three countries and the need to provide a funding system similar to that in the European Economic Community. The rich countries must contribute funds to help raise Mexico's living standards up to those of Canada and the United States.

If fairness is to be achieved, there has to be reform in multinational organizations like the World Bank, the International Monetary Fund, the GATT, and the Inter-American Development Bank. These organizations must be democratized. Mexico's debt must be reduced, and structural adjustment programs forced on Mexico by international lenders must be removed.

The trilateral conference agreed that there is a need for comprehensive and enforceable protection of worker rights, and workplace health and safety standards, as well as rights for migrant workers. International human rights must be enforceable in all three countries. Environmental standards must be raised to the highest level, and the "polluter pays" principle must be enforced.

The three countries must provide democratic structures to enable the enforcement of the U.N. Code of Conduct on Transnational Corporations and the Maquiladora Standards of Conduct.

In contrast to the approach of CUSFTA, NAFTA, and GATT, the trilateral agreements stress the need for open decision making, full access to information, and democratic participation in all aspects of policy formation and implementation.

In Mexico, and throughout the Western hemisphere, people are mobilizing for change. They are demanding an expansion of democratic and human rights, and they are beginning to construct a new alternative to the hegemonic neoliberal agenda.

The success of the São Paulo Forum is one indication of this development. In 1990, the Workers Party in Brazil called a conference of political parties and movements to meet to discuss the possibility of a "left convergence" for the hemisphere. Annual conferences are being held. At the

1993 Havana meeting there were 112 members groups representing nearly every country in the hemisphere. There were also forty-three observer groups from the Rainbow Coalition in the United States to the Green Left in Australia.

The Forum includes a wide variety of parties, from social democrat to Marxist, from major political parties like the PT and the PRD to small revolutionary parties. The Forum is a place to exchange views and experience, but it has also set up commissions to develop alternative policies and political strategies. Since 1992 it has been working closely with the Lima group of economists, who are designing alternative economic models to neoliberalism

The end of history has not arrived. The authoritarian state and the economics of inequality are not the best that we can hope for. The popular tide is swinging back to democracy in Mexico and around the world. Where does this leave Mexico?

Alternative Roads to Change

On January 1, 1994, the Zapatista Army of National Liberation entered San Cristóbal in Chiapas and read the Declaration of the Lacandon Jungle from the balcony of the government palace. Their demands called for free and democratic elections, an end to centralized government, revisions of NAFTA, decent jobs with reasonable wages for all workers, an end to the plunder of Mexico's national wealth, cancellation of debts, an end to hunger and malnutrition, and freedom for political prisoners.[33]

The first round of negotiations between the government and the EZLN ended in early June 1994. Manuel Camacho Solís presented a thirty-two point program for ratification by the Zapatistas. The government's proposal was closely examined by the people living in the areas under the Zapatista's control. They voted 98 percent against acceptance. The Salinas administration was humiliated.

On June 11, 1994, the Zapatistas issued the Second Declaration of the Lacandon Jungle. It shifted the push for change away from armed rebellion and towards civil society. It called for a National Democratic Convention to be held in early August at "Aguascalientes," in the Zapatista-held territory in the Lacandon Jungle. The goal of the convention was to organize the people in defence of the democratic and social justice principles set forth by the Zapatistas.

In early August, 6,000 Mexican leftists gathered at a cleared area in the jungle of Chiapas for the first convention of the National Democratic Convention (CND). There were representatives from peasant groups, trade unionists, journalists, intellectuals, PRD political activists, and indigenous peoples. It was the *coyuntura*, the "coming together" of the people oppressed by the one-party state and its neoliberal policies.

They resolved to monitor the August presidential election, prepare resistance to the expected fraud, and defend the goals and existence of the EZLN. An executive and a national committee were chosen. The names were familiar to Mexicans, and even North Americans would probably recognize a few, like Rosario Ibarra de Piedra, Mariclaire Acosta, Elena Poniatowska, Rodolfo Stavenhagen, and Pablo González Casanova.

Following the election, the CND called for a second national convention for San Cristóbal de las Casas, October 10-13, 1994. There was an even bigger turnout this time. On the National Day for Democracy and Peace in Chiapas, an estimated 35,000 indigenous people from across the state came to demonstrate, to say no to the PRI, and to oppose NAFTA and the sellout of the country.

In January 1995, the third convention of the CND met in Queretaro, north of Mexico City. It followed the collapse of the economy and President Zedillo's sell-out of sovereignty to gain cash from the U.S. government. The convention called for the creation of the Movement for National Liberation (MLN), an alliance between the EZLN, the CND, and the PRD. Supporters believe that this is the only road to democracy and economic justice.[34]

A second political current is represented by the Group of San Ángel, an elite but small club of prominent intellectuals, writers, businessmen, social leaders, and politicians, most commonly identified with Jorge Castañeda. On June 9, 1994, they called a meeting to talk about their concerns over the climate of instability that would result if there were another major electoral fraud. They proposed a democratic accord to be approved by all parties and agreed to pressure the elected government to implement changes that would guarantee a democratic transition and a political accord between all national forces and sectors.

This alternative was a "pluralistic" coalition among the progressive and democratic forces, including those in the three major political parties. Ideologically, they represent moderate social democracy.[35]

In his book, *Utopia Unarmed; The Latin American Left After the Cold War*, Jorge Castañeda argues that the only democratic option for Mexico is a moderate social democracy. Many in Mexico believe that this is all that can be achieved, given the conservatism of Mexicans and the presence of the United States.

But Castañeda recognizes the problems of following this path to change. The "large, organized, homogeneous working class" that formed the base of the successful social democratic parties in Europe does not exist in Latin America or Mexico. The traditional Latin American social democratic parties are "the most traditional and conservative today." They have embraced neoliberalism.[36]

Castañeda describes the present social democratic parties in Latin America as "exclusively electoralist." They work within a system where there are gross differences in campaign spending, the mass media is totally controlled by the rich, and the state parties use "fiscal intimidation, harassment or overt repression."

Social democratic parties in the first world prefer the British Parliamentary system and its first-through-the-post electoral system, which allows them to win elections with less than 40 percent of the votes and guarantees them five years of rule by "executive dictatorship." Social democratic parties in the First World strongly oppose proportional representation. Given the experience of these parties when in government in recent years, it is hard to see how a social democratic government would make much difference in Mexico.

The vast majority in Mexico today are angry and bitter over the devaluation of the peso and the economic austerity program implemented by President Ernesto Zedillo. The anger towards Carlos Salinas is widely recorded everywhere.

But how have most Mexicans responded to all this? They are voting against the PRI — and for the PAN. In the state election in Jalisco on February 12, 1995, the PAN received 55 percent of the vote, the PRI 36 percent, and the PRD only 4 percent. In the election for governor in Guanajuato on May 28, the voters chose the PAN by two to one over the PRI. But the leadership of the PAN completely supported Salinas's economic policies, and they strongly supported NAFTA. Would a PAN government offer any alternative?

Despite gross poverty and inequality, most Mexicans are generally conservative in their political views. That is my own subjective conclusion. Many attribute this to the indoctrination by the Roman Catholic church. In my opinion, the conservatism of most Mexican people is rooted in the strong cultural commitment to the patriarchal family.

Jonathan Fox points out that under economic strain, "Most of rural society will respond with family-based survival strategies most of the time, including out-migration and illicit crop cultivation, rather than engage in sometimes risky and often fruitless action." But this could change if a viable option becomes available.[37]

Many studies of how people dealt with the economic crisis of the 1980s demonstrated that they adopted a household survival strategy. This strategy intensified gender conflicts. Sylvia Chant argues that "The key question for the future is at what point a line may be drawn where poor households shift efforts away from exploiting their own resources to demanding that the state provide them with more satisfactory and dignified means of survival."[38]

It seems almost trite to conclude that Mexico is at a turning point in history. But I think that this is true. The neoliberal revolution was very good for a small minority of the Mexican population. They did very well. But for the vast majority, in economic terms they are no better off today than they were in 1981. They managed to cope for years by working longer and harder. The devaluation of the peso in December 1994 hit them hard. There is no way they can compensate for this new setback by additional work. They have no option but to cut back.

The legitimacy of the PRI has been shattered. They can no longer rule by electoral fraud. The assassinations and the revelations have destroyed their right to rule. Everyone always knew that officials of the government and the PRI were deeply involved in the illicit drug industry, but now it is all out in the open. The mass media can no longer be completely controlled.

Many well-informed Mexicans believe that the economy will continue to decline throughout 1995. The United States reached the peak of its business cycle in late 1994, and another recession is near at hand. This would make the Mexican situation even worse. At this point, the widespread, uncoordinated resistance that we see today may develop into a new political movement for change.

Notes

1. Tómas A. Vasconi, "Democracy and Socialism in South America," *Latin American Perspectives*, Vol. 17, Spring 1990, pp. 25-38.

2. Tómas A. Vasconi and Elina Peraza Martell, "La social democracia y la America Latina," *Casa de Las Americas*, No. 181, July-August 1990, pp. 14-26; James Petras and Morris Lozano, "Adjustment and Democracy in Latin America," *Economic and Political Weekly*, Vol. 26, July 17, 1991, PE103-PE111; and Carlos M. Vilas, "Latin America: Socialist Perspectives in Times of Cholera," *Social Justice*, Vol. 19, Winter 1992, pp. 74-83.

3. See Arturo Escobar and Sonia E. Alvarez, eds. *The Making of Social Movements in Latin America*. Boulder: Westview Press, 1992; Susan Eckstein and Manuel A. Garreton Merino, *Power and Popular Protest*. Berkeley: University of California Press, 1989; Elizabeth Jelin and J. Ann Zammit, eds. *Women and Social Change in Latin America*. Geneva: U.N. Re-

search Institute for Social Development, 1990; and David Slater, *New Social Movements and the State in Latin America*. Amsterdam: CEDLA, 1985.

4. Jorge G. Castañeda, *Utopia Unarmed*. New York: Alfred A. Knopf, 1993, p. 205.

5. José Alvaro Moises, "Democracy Threatened: The Latin American Paradox," *Alternatives*, Vol. 16, Spring, 1991, pp. 141-160.

6. See "The Politics of Corruption and the Corruption of Politics," *Report on the Americas*, special issue, Vol. 27, November/December 1993.

7. Lucrecia Lozano, "Adjustment and Democracy in Latin America," *Social Justice*, Vol. 19, Winter 1992, pp. 48-59; and David Lehmann, *Democracy and Development in Latin America*. Cambridge: Polity Press, 1990.

8. Castañeda, *op. cit.*, pp. 339-340.

9. Jaime Osorio, "Liberalism, Democracy and Socialism," *Social Justice*, Vol. 19, Winter 1992, pp. 25-33.

10. Marta Harnecker, "Democracy and Revolutionary Movements," *Social Justice*, Vol. 19, Winter 1992, pp. 60-73.

11. Leigh A. Payne, "Working Class Strategies in the Transition to Democracy in Brazil," *Comparative Politics*, Vol. 23, January 1991, pp. 221-238.

12. See Emir Sader and Ken Silverstein, *Without Fear of Being Happy*. London: Verso Books, 1991.

13. Margaret E. Keck, *The Workers Party and Democratization in Brazil*, New Haven: Yale University Press, 1992.

14. Maria Helena Moreira Alves, "Building Democratic Socialism: The Partido dos Trabalhadores in Brazil," *Monthly Review*, Vol. 42, September 1990, pp. 1-16.

15. James Petras and Steve Vieux, "The Brazilian Presidential Elections," *Z Magazine*, Vol. 7, December 1994, pp. 48-49.

16. See Fred Rosen, "The Temperature Rises in the Crucible of Reform," *Report on the Americas*, Vol. 27, March/April 1994, pp. 23-28; Margarita López Maya, "The Rise of Causa R," *Report on the Americas*, Vol. 27, March/April 1994, pp. 29-34; and Federico Alvarez, "Deciphering the National Elections," *Report on the Americas*, Vol. 27, March/April 1994, pp. 16-22.

17. See Luis E. González, *Political Structures and Democracy in Uruguay*. Indiana: University of Notre Dame Press, 1991; and Charles E. Gillespie, *Negotiating Democracy: Politicians and Generals in Uruguay*. Cambridge: Cambridge University Press, 1992.

18. Luis Stolovich, "Uruguay: The Paradoxes and Perplexities of an Uncommon Left," *Social Justice*, Vol. 19, Winter 1992, pp. 138-152.

19. Harnecker, *op. cit.*, p. 72.

20. Calvin Sims, "Moderate Leftist Elected in Close Uruguayan Presidential Race," *New York Times*, November 29, 1994, A-8.

21. See Barry Carr, "Mexico: The Perils of Unity and the Challenge of Modernization," in Barry Carr and Steve Ellner, eds. *The Latin American Left*. Boulder: Westview Press, 1993, pp. 83-100; Barry Carr, "Labor and the Political Left in Mexico," in Kevin Middlebrook, ed. *Unions, Workers and the State in Mexico*. Center for U.S.-Mexican Studies, University of California, San Diego, 1991, pp. 121-152; and Joseph L. Klesner, "Changing Patterns of Electoral Participation and Official Party Support in Mexico," in Judith Gentleman, ed. *Mexican Politics in Transition*. Boulder: Westview Press, 1987, pp. 95-127.

22. See Joe Foweraker and Ann L. Craig, eds. *Popular Movements and Political Change in Mexico*. Boulder: Lynne Rienner Publishers, 1990; and Arturo Escobar and Sonia E. Alvarez, eds. *The Making of Social Movements in Latin America*. Boulder: Westview Press, 1992.

23. See Jonathan Fox and Luis Hernández, "Mexico's Difficult Democracy: Grassroots Movements, NGOs, and Local Government," *Alternatives*, Vol. 17, Spring 1992, pp. 165-208.

24. Laura Carlsen, "Mexican Grassroots Social Movements," *Radical America*, Vol. 22, July-August 1988, pp. 35-51.

25. Paul Lawrence Haber, "The Art and Implications of Political Restructuring in Mexico: The Case of Urban Popular Movements," in Maria Lorena Cook et al, *The Politics of Economic Restructuring*. Center for U.S.-Mexican Studies, University of California, San Diego, 1994, pp. 277-303.

26. Jonathan Fox, "Political Change in Mexico's New Peasant Economy," in *Ibid*, pp. 243-276.

27. Jaime Tamayo, "Neoliberalism Encounters Neocardenismo," in Foweraker and Craig, *op. cit.*, pp. 121-136.

28. Judith Adler Hellman, "Mexican Popular Movements, Clientelism, and the Process of Democratization," *Latin American Perspectives*, Vol. 21, Spring 1994, pp. 124-142.

29. Cited in Castañeda, *op. cit.*, p. 157.

30. "The PRD Elections," *Mexico and NAFTA Report*, August 19, 1993, p. 3.

31. "New 'Moderate' Cárdenas Emerges," *Latin American Weekly Report*, November 4, 1993, pp. 514-515; and "Cárdenas's Break for the Middle Ground," *Mexico and NAFTA Report*, December 2, 1993, pp. 2-3.

32. Cuauhtémoc Cárdenas, "Misunderstanding Mexico," *Foreign Policy*, No. 78, Spring 1990, pp. 113-130; Cuauhtémoc Cárdenas, "The Continental Development and Trade Initiative," *Social Justice*, Vol. 19, Winter 1992, pp. 84-91; and "The Partido de la Revolución Democratica is in favour of a Continental Trade and Development Agreement." Policy position paper, Mexico City, 1991.

33. The communiques of the Zapatistas can be found in Frank Bardacke and Leslie López, eds. *Shadows of Tender Fury*. New York: Monthly Review Books, 1995.

34. See John Ross, *op. cit.*, pp. 363-376 for an account of the Aguascalientes convention; "La Convención Nacional Democratica," *La Jornada Perfil*, August 20, 1994; Olivia Gall, "The Left vs. The Party-State," *Against the Current*, Vol. 9, January-February 1995, pp. 39-45; and Reports from the CND carried on the WEB (Canada) and Peacenet (U.S.A.).

35. Equipo Pueblo, *Mexico Update*, No. 9, June 17, 1994; No. 10, June 23, 1994.

36. Castañeda, *op. cit.*, chapters four and twelve.

37. Jonathan Fox in Cook et al, *op. cit.*, pp. 268-269.

38. Sylvia Chant, "Women's Work and Household Change in the 1980s," in Neil Harvey, ed. *Mexico: Dilemmas of Transition*. London: Institute of Latin American Studies, 1993, pp. 318-354. See also Lourdes Benería, "The Mexican Debt Crisis: Restructuring the Economy and the Household," in Lourdes Benería and Shelley Feldman, eds. *Unequal Burden; Economic Crisis, Persistent Poverty and Women's Work*. Boulder: Westview Press, 1992, pp. 83-104.

News Vendor, Mexico City

Cactus Leaves, Food Stall, Mexico City

Blind Beggar, Mexico City

Guatemalan Refugees, Chiapas

Coffee Trail, Oaxaca, Mexico

308

Mountain Trail, Oaxaca, Mexico

Coffee Growers, Oaxaca, Mexico

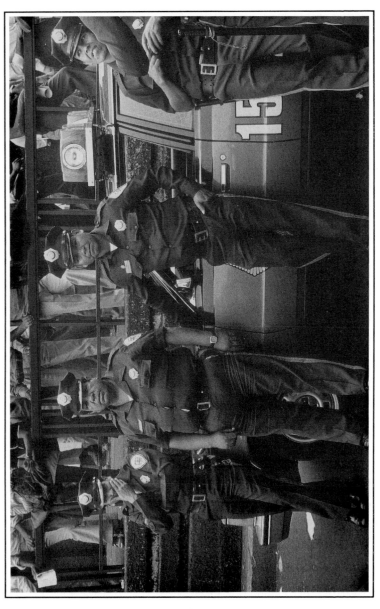

Police, May 1st Labour Day Parade, Mexico City

May 1st Labour Day Parade, Mexico City

May 1st Labour Day Parade, Mexico City

May 1st Labour Day Parade, Mexico City

Committee for the Disappeared, May 1st Labour Day Parade,
Mexico City

Committee Against Nuclear Power, May 1st Labour Day Parade,
Mexico City

"Death, Misery, and Hunger," May 1st Labour Day Parade,
Mexico City

Transportation, Mexico City

Coffee Growers, Oaxaca

Index

Also published by

MASK OF DEMOCRACY
Labour Rights in Mexico Today

Dan LaBotz

an ILRERF Book

Following scores of interviews with Mexican rank and file workers, labour union officials, women's organizations, lawyers, and human rights activists, Dan LaBotz presents this study of the suppression of workers' rights in Mexico.

... an important offering... it puts the cheerful advocates of open markets and their desire for "economic unity" into moral question... Anybody who has the interest, time or energy to devote to understanding the future of Canadian labour had better read the Mask of Democracy.
Montréal Mirror

223 pages, index
Paperback ISBN: 1-895431-58-1 $19.99
Hardcover ISBN: 1-895431-59-X $38.99

THE CUBAN REVOLUTION
A Critical Perspective

Sam Dolgoff

A historical perspective on Cuba that arrives at new insights into social and political change.

199 pages, index, appendices
Paperback ISBN: 0-919618-35-9 $9.99
Hardcover ISBN: 0-919618-36-7 $19.99

MEXICO
Land and Liberty

Ricardo Flores Magón

As background to the events in Chiapas, here is a seminal collection of essays by the famous theorist and activist Ricardo Flores Magón who influenced the Mexican revolution, particularly the movements of Villa and Zapata.

156 pages, illustrated
Paperback ISBN: 0-919618-30-8 $12.99
Hardcover ISBN: 0-919618-29-4 $29.99

HOT MONEY AND THE POLITICS OF DEBT

R.T. Naylor

2nd edition

As conspiracy theories go, here is one that is truly elegant. It involves everybody.
Washington Post

... a fascinating survey of international finance scams.
Globe and Mail

532 pages, index
Paperback ISBN: 1-895431-94-8 $19.99
Hardcover ISBN: 1-895431-95-6 $48.99

MANUFACTURING CONSENT: NOAM CHOMSKY AND THE MEDIA

Mark Achbar, ed.

"... challenging... controversial... the unravelling of ideas."
Globe and Mail

"... invaluable as a record of a thinker's progress towards basic truth and basic decency, and it hints that the two might be inseparable."
The Guardian

Manufacturing Consent is the companion book to the celebrated film. A complete transcript of the film is complemented by key excerpts from the writings, interviews and correspondence of Chomsky and others. Also included are further exchanges between Chomsky and his critics, additional historical and biographical material, filmmakers' notes, a resource guide, and more than 270 stills from the film.

264 pages
270 illustrations, bibliography, index
Paperback ISBN: 1-551640-02-3 $19.99
Hardcover ISBN: 1-551640-03-1 $48.99

THE POLITICAL ECONOMY OF INTERNATIONAL LABOUR MIGRATION

Hassan N. Gardezi

While former studies on labour migration have concentrated on its effect on GNP, foreign exchange earnings, and labour exporting countries' rates of investment, Gardezi's work refocusses attention on the migrant workers themselves, their hopes and aspirations, family and community life, and working conditions both at home and abroad.

210 pages
Paperback ISBN: 1-551640-16-3 $19.99
Hardcover ISBN: 1-551640-17-1 $48.99